Corporate Strategies
in Recession and Recovery

Corporate Strategies in Recession and Recovery

Social Structure and Strategic Choice

RICHARD WHITTINGTON

London
UNWIN HYMAN
Boston   Sydney   Wellington

Published by the Academic Division of
Unwin Hyman Ltd
15/17 Broadwick Street, London W1V 1FP, UK

Unwin Hyman Inc.,
8 Winchester Place, Winchester, Mass. 01890, USA

Allen & Unwin (Australia) Ltd,
8 Napier Street, North Sydney, NSW 2060, Australia

Allen & Unwin (New Zealand) Ltd
in association with the Port Nicholson Press Ltd,
Compusales Building, 75 Ghuznee Street, Wellington 1, New Zealand

First published in 1989

British Library Cataloguing in Publication Data
Whittington, Richard C.
  Corporate strategies in recession and
  recovery.
  1. Corporate planning
  I. Title
  658.4'012
ISBN 0–04–445122–9

Library of Congress Cataloging in Publication Data

(applied for)

Typeset in 10/11pt Times
Disc conversion by Columns of Reading
and printed in Great Britain at the University Press, Cambridge

Contents

List of figures

List of tables

Acknowledgements

A lot of people have helped me over the six years – too long! – this book has taken and I need to thank them all. First of all, of course, are the 60 or so managers who were so generous with their time and knowledge during my field research. I suspect that few of them will agree entirely with my interpretation of their experiences, but I hope that they will recognize here at least a few things about their work that before have usually been left unsaid. The Economic and Social Research Council funded the beginnings of this study while I was at the Manchester Business School, and since then Imperial College and Warwick University have allowed me enough space finally to complete it. Being paid to think and write is wonderful. Then there are family, friends and colleagues. All have been more tolerant than I deserved, and many have made direct and important contributions to the work itself.

Here I would like to thank specifically Daniel Benjamin, Richard Butler, David Edgerton, Karen Legge, Roderick Martin and Anne Witz, who have all helped me shape my ideas; and Cathi Maryon, Brian Price and Marianne Slattery who helped me get them down on paper. I should mention specially Gerry Johnson and Andrew Pettigrew, whose searching examination of my thesis in many ways provoked the final book. I hope they will take the distance I have travelled from their positions since then as some sort of back-handed compliment. Lastly – and perhaps most of all – I must thank Richard Whitley, who supervised the original thesis and continued to comment on later versions. Both as stimulus and critic, his role has been vital. While the usual disclaimer applies to all the above, I most emphatically absolve Richard; it was certainly not for want of trying on his part that any faults remain.

Richard Whittington
University of Warwick
July 1988

ix

To my parents

Chapter One

Strategic choice and recession

THE PROBLEM OF STRATEGIC CHOICE

'Exemplar' and 'Rose' are the pseudonyms of two rival British domestic appliance manufacturers. At the onset of the 1980s, both companies were industry leaders and household names; both were subsidiaries of large general engineering companies; both were dependent on the home market; and both were direct competitors in key market segments. Though superficially so similar, these two companies adopted almost opposite strategies in response to the 1979–81 recession. This is how two of their senior directors summed up their different recession strategies.

The director from Exemplar

When we come out of a recession in England, what happens? You begin to import like fury because everybody has abandoned their production capacity and run down. This cycle has destroyed British industry – this up and down – because no one can afford, due to the tax system et cetera, to develop during the recession. But that's what you've got to do, and that's why we hung on and that's what we did! (*Bangs table*)

The director from Rose

It is important to preserve things for the future and one would like to do that, and to drive one's way through the recession by investment. But on the one hand the theory is good; but if you are faced with a factory loss this month one has to decide what to do . . . We cut back heavily.

Thus Rose responded to the recession by disinvesting, while Exemplar hung on and developed. As we shall see later, these different strategies had widely different consequences for the companies' performances, both during the recession and, in the longer term, during the recovery

1

of 1982–5. Despite these divergences in strategies and performances, the two companies survived all seven challenging years of recession and recovery.

This contrast between the strategies of Rose and Exemplar takes us at once to the central issue of this book: how was it that two firms, outwardly so similar, could adopt such radically opposed strategies in response to the same recession yet each survive the most hostile economic conditions of the post-war period? Here we plunge into a fundamental debate within organization studies, and wider – between those who grimly adhere to the belief that human conduct is determined, and those who have faith in our capacity for strategic choice.

The divergent strategies of Rose and Exemplar are particularly awkward for the deterministic traditions that still dominate organizational and strategic studies. As these deterministic traditions will constitute my chief antagonists in this book, let me introduce them briefly now. I shall argue in Chapter 2 that these theorists take broadly two approaches to explaining corporate strategic conduct. For some – the environmental determinists – determinate conduct is guaranteed by external disciplines. Firms failing to conform to environmental contingencies are remorselessly eliminated by (usually) market selection mechanisms. If they are to survive, all must converge on the optimal solution. This environmental determinist approach constitutes a powerful stream of thought that, in recent times, stretches from Friedman (1953) in economics to Donaldson (1987) in organizational studies. But there exists another set of determinists who, rather than relying on external disciplines, prefer to trust in people's own readiness to conform. For these theorists – the action determinists – environments do not so much execute the deviant as feed simple human types with the stimuli that prompt them to programmed response. The same type will always respond to the same stimulus in the same way. This too is a substantial tradition. Within economics, action determinism remains fundamental both to managerial theories of the firm (for instance, Baumol, 1959) and to those concerned with the 'principal-agent' problem (Raviv, 1985). Action determinism takes a different form in sociology, but there too it has proved strangely influential upon both functionalist (Parsons, 1951) and Marxian (for instance, Nichols, 1969) approaches. Unfortunately, its influence does not end even here. It will be my contention that action determinism continues to corrupt many contemporary claims for strategic choice.

These are no more than caricatures of the two basic deterministic positions – finer distinctions will be drawn in the next chapter. However, the main thesis of this book is that neither form of determinism – action or environmental – provides an adequate grasp on explaining the divergent strategies of Rose, Exemplar, or indeed any of the six other companies that make up the empirical material to follow. The three UK domestic appliance manufacturers and the five office furniture manufacturers whose strategies I examine failed to conform to the dictates of determinism. Strategic decision-makers at these companies, far from corresponding to the simple, reactive stereotypes of action determinism, proved to possess both the active wills and the internal complexities necessary for generating strategies personal to themselves. Most, moreover, successfully called the bluff of the environmental determinists by pursuing their idiosyncratic strategies right in the midst of the hostile market conditions of deep recession. I will argue, therefore, that the strategies adopted by these eight firms were, in general, not determined but chosen.

This claim for strategic choice is made in the strongest sense. Loasby (1976, p. 5) has declared: 'To be worth studying, choice must be meaningful, and this implies, first, that choice is genuine and second, that choice matters.' For choice to matter, there must be a range of alternative actions available, each associated with different outcomes yet each compatible with survival. For choice to be genuine, decision-makers should have the internal capacity to choose independently between these alternatives. Contrary to action determinism, decisions should be free of all prior programming; contrary to environmental determinism, decisions should make a difference to subsequent events. Within contemporary organizational studies, this strong claim for strategic choice represents an extreme position. By comparison with recent moderate accounts, however, it does have the merits of significance and consistency.

More moderate organizational theorists have attempted two forms of accommodation between choice and deterministic approaches. The first seeks to resolve the conflict by confining the extent of choice to means towards the same end. Decision is merely between 'functional equivalents' (Child, 1981, p. 318) or 'equifinal' strategies (Hrebiniak and Joyce, 1985; Ford and Baucus, 1987, p. 375). This resolution does not entirely satisfy. The point can be quickly made that the existence of absolutely equifinal strategies is somewhat implausible. The possibility that firms have widely available to them strategic alternatives that possess exactly equal value for significant stakeholders at every moment during their implementation is empirically unlikely. More relevant here is that this form of choice effectively surrenders to determinism. Choice confined to equifinal outcomes presumes there is either no scope or no desire to pursue diverse objectives. Whether by civilized consensus, natural inclination or external disciplines, decision-makers are fated all to work towards some single unifying objective – more often than not, assumed to be the maximization of shareholder wealth. This is rather dull. In Loasby's (1976) stringent terms, choice between equifinal strategies is not worth studying, for it makes no difference to the predetermined unrolling of events. Just as in environmental determinism, it allows only one outcome to be feasible.

Moderate organizational theorists propose a second form of accommodation. Regretting the dichotimization of organizational studies, they urge a 'dialectical' synthesis in which both strategic choice and determinism are admitted to influence organizational action (Astley and Van de Ven, 1983, p. 267; Bourgeois, 1984; Hrebiniak and Joyce, 1985; Zammuto, 1988). Thus Hrebiniak and Joyce (1985, p. 337) assert: '1) choice and determinism are not at opposite ends of a singular continuum, but in reality represent two independent variables and 2) the interaction and interdependence of the two must be studied to explain organizational behaviour.' This respect for both choice and deterministic approaches displays an attractive tolerance; it is not, unfortunately, tenable.

The problem with the moderates' second attempt at reconciliation is that the two perspectives are irreducible to equivalent variables operating within the same sphere. As I shall be arguing in the following chapters, deterministic and strategic choice approaches possess accounts of human actors and their environments that are fundamentally opposed. Determinism either demeans humanity so far or exhalts the environment so high that, in one way or another, actors are denied all control over both themselves and their surroundings. The strong form of strategic choice differs radically in being based on a vigorous assertion of human actors' potential for *agency* (Giddens, 1984; Reed, 1988). As agents, people do have control: internally they enjoy the capacity for constructing strategic objectives for themselves, externally they hold the power to realize these objectives in ways that alter their social and material environments. There exists between these views of actors and environments no ontological compatability. The human beings of determinism are not the same as the human beings of strategic choice theory, and they exist in different worlds. Analysts cannot, therefore, casually transport explanatory mechanisms from one world to the other according to their own convenience. Instead, analysts are confronted by a strategic choice of their own: in their research, they must decide which perspective best describes the world they experience and then stick rigorously within its distinct ontological and epistemological assumptions.

Seeking a complete repudiatiation of determinism, this book refuses to accept either of the moderates' attempts at compromise. Choice between equifinal outcomes is too trivial; mixing of determinist and agentive perspectives too indiscriminate. However, commitment to the strong form of strategic choice proposed by Loasby (1976) imposes a twofold task, empirical and theoretical. This book will have to demonstrate that the world really does afford corporate decision-makers significantly different strategic options between which genuine choice is possible; and it will have also to provide a coherent account of the world and its actors in which the exercise of strategic choice is plausible. Necessary is a theoretical perspective that, independent of determinism, establishes human beings as potential agents, with sufficient control over themselves and their environments both to select their own personal objectives and then to act upon them in a manner which significantly alters the course of events.

It will be my charge in Chapter 3 that existing approaches to strategic choice fail quite to establish an adequate account of human agency. This failure, I shall argue, is rooted in a neglect of social structures that is common to both the major traditions upon which these approaches rely. On the one hand, there are the Action Theorists (Weick, 1969; Smircich and Stubbart, 1985; Berg, 1985), who, in their repudiation of environmental determinism, insist too much on the subjectivity of social structure. On the other hand are the individualists of the Carnegie School (Cyert and March, 1963; Quinn, 1980): they abstract their actors so purely from society that they finally risk condemning them to the same passive, internal simplicity as that typical of action determinism. While these two traditions, Action Theory and the Carnegie School, have inspired and informed a number of important accounts of strategic choice (e.g Child, 1972; Miles and Snow, 1978; Pettigrew, 1985; and Johnson, 1987), my contention in Chapter 3 will be that the subordination of social structure by the first and its neglect by the second ultimately prove fatal to an adequate notion of human agency. Deprived of social structural context, actors are stripped of both the intrinsic capacity to choose between courses of action and the extrinsic powers they need to carry them out.

I shall prefer, therefore, to base my claim for strategic choice upon the Realist social theory developed particularly by Rom Harré and Roy Bhaskar. The distinctive quality of this Realist perspective is its grounding of human activity in social complexity and its insistence on real social structures as preconditional for the agency upon which strategic choice depends. Indeed, it is precisely in their necessity for human action that social structures reveal themselves as 'real'. Let me preview the central Realist argument of Chapters 4 and 5.

To become agents, ordinary human beings require two things. They need tools for action – not just one tool, but a whole box full allowing them to do all sorts of things. And they must be able to use these tools in different ways, with the self-confidence to choose positively between all the various courses they can take. According to Realism, it is society that provides people with the necessary tools, skills and confidence. Social hierarchies offer us a range of material and authoritative resources with which to act; social norms teach us the various codes of conduct by which we may act; and social interaction cultivates the confidence to choose how we actually do act. Thus people are agents because they operate in a complex society and have access to diverse social identities: they can choose to act as capitalists, as parents or as Christians, and employ the resources and interpret the practices that go with each identity according to their own wills. Moreover, as people synthesize from existing social structures novel and idiosyncratic ways of acting, they gradually alter the social and material foundations of their activities, making new forms of action possible and old ones redundant. In short, genuine strategic choice depends not on a denial of social structure, as in Action Theory, but rather on recognition of its luxuriant plurality.

As Alvesson (1987) and Willmott (1987) have recently observed, such a recognition of the social remains wholly alien to the traditions of contemporary organizational studies. Yet organizations – economic enterprises as much as any other – are deeply 'embedded' in society (Granovetter, 1985). Their members are always toing and froing between the various organizations that make up our world – firms, churches, households, communities – and in their organizational activities they constantly draw on and work on society as a whole. We cannot expect people, participants in a complex society, to act in one sphere purely in their capacity as members of the particular relevant organization; neither can we expect their actions in this sphere to be isolated in their effects. Except in the most artificial circumstances, economic activities are also social activities. Polanyi (1944, p. 46) insists:

> Man's economy, as a rule, is submerged in his social relationships. He does not act so as to safeguard his individual interest in the possession of material goods; he acts so as to safeguard his social standing, his social claims, his social assets. He values material goods only in so far as they serve this end.

Thus even at work the capitalist does not act simply as capitalist; and his or her powers are not confined exclusively to some discrete capitalist economic sphere. Within limits, the capitalist can choose how and where to deploy his or her powers.

Converse to agency's dependence on social structure are the implications of strategic choice for society. Society exists in whatever form it takes only because of the activities of its members. If these members have the capacity to choose their actions, then they have also the power to change their society. In a society as large and established as ours, however, the effects of any single individual's actions must be infinitesimally small, cancelled out by those of everyone else. Only collective efforts can achieve the transformation of society as a whole. Certainly organized labour, in the form of either trade unions or political parties, possesses this capacity for collective, transformation-ary action. But, as Giddens (1987, p. 223) has recently remarked in ironic understatement, to assume that the labour movement alone enjoys this capacity for collective agency is 'faintly absurd'.

Through its control over the labour of its employees, the capitalist enterprise too constitutes a powerful instrument for collective agency. This power is, moreover, highly concentrated. In 1985 (the latest year for which data is available), the largest 100 UK private manufacturing companies made total sales of £82,000 million and directly employed more than one-and-a-half million people, besides indirectly influencing the employment of many more (*Business Monitor* PA 1002, 1985). In 1987, just one company, the General Electric Company, gained external sales of £5,250 million and employed 122,000 people in the UK alone (General Electric Company Annual Report, 1987). This concentration of economic activity endows these privately controlled companies with a decisive influence over the wealth and welfare of the nation. The decisions these companies take can have devastating effects upon employment: between 1979 and 1982, Courtaulds, TI and GKN alone shed 104,000 jobs (Bryer and Brignall, 1986). These companies can combine to undermine government policies – as with the organized resistance to the British Labour government's incomes policy in 1978 (Grant with Sargent, 1987, p. 121). They can work to deny a whole nation technological autonomy – as French and American electronics companies did in their collusion against the French government's Plan Calcul (Cohen and Bauer, 1985). Indeed, private companies can even adopt deliberate strategies for the infiltration of the democratic political process itself – as (most openly) in the case of corporate controlled Political Action Committees in the United States (Ryan, Swanson and Bucholz, 1987).

In short, these large corporations constitute major actors within our society, whose strategies have vast repercussions. But deterministic theories absolve them from any real responsibility for their actions. Protected from internal query by rank and from external challenge by commercial secrecy, the small elites controlling these companies protest that they are merely servants of the abstract economic rationality of the markets. They are captains of industry, not generals. However, the notion of strategic choice, by subverting the old dogma that firms can do no other than what they do, fundamentally challenges this dissimulating servility. It declares that corporate conduct, instead of having a subsidiary significance as merely one of several transmission mechanisms for social development, exercises in fact a primary role, either in generating change or entrenching stasis. Far from being dependent upon the macro environment, these firms are active forces in determining it. For good or ill, corporate strategies are not dictated by abstract market forces or monomaniacal pursuit of profit, but are the outcome of deliberate choices by small groups of socially privileged people. Of course, recognition of the role of strategic choice does more than just pin down responsibility. It is the first step towards shifting responsibility out of the unaccountable elites who currently monopolize it. The fact of strategic choice inescapably raises the issue of whether and how society should intervene to control the actions of the few relatively autonomous but hugely influential decision-makers who manage the dominant corporations of our society (cf. Salaman, 1981, p. 162).

The basic task of this book, then, is to deny determinism and assert strategic choice. The 1979–85 recession and recovery offers a particularly apt opportunity for testing both environmental and action determinism. For the environmental determinists, the 1979–81 recession, as the worst in the post-war period, provides an instance when market selection mechanisms should be especially merciless towards companies neglectful of their duty of profit maximization. Only the conformists should survive. For the action determinists, the crisis of recession constitutes as near as can be the sort of common and unequivocal stimulus to which they expect their simple types to respond with obedient unanimity. This book will compare the actual conduct of eight UK domestic appliance and office furniture companies against the sort of expectations these determinists might have. Confusing action and environmental determinists alike, it will show that, in fact, these companies behaved with a near impervious eccentricity.

But strategic choice is not the only issue that these companies' conduct can illuminate. The divergent strategies of Exemplar and Rose with which I began raise a number of subsidiary issues. Firstly, how *should* strategic decision-makers ideally respond to recession: should firms 'drive through the recession by investment', as Rose would have liked; should they 'cut back heavily', as Rose actually did; or is there perhaps some sort of balance to be struck between the two? Secondly, what are the kind of pressures that led Rose to abandon its preferred strategy, and what, by contrast, accounts for Exemplar's ability to hang on, strategy intact? Thirdly, how do the various strategies adopted during recession actually contribute to the alleged 'destruction' of British industry, and which strategies are most successful in resisting the rush of imports that seems to attend every cyclical recovery in Britain? These are complex issues, not to be resolved by eight case studies, but they are important enough to demand consideration.

However, the main issues of the book remain the following. Were the recession strategies of the eight firms determined or were they rather the product of deliberate choices? If they were chosen, how should we explain these choices? Does the Carnegie School provide an adequate account of the human agency essential to strategic choice; does Action Theory provide a sustainable one? Arguing against both these approaches to strategic choice, I shall prefer instead a Realist position that firmly establishes the agency of the choosers upon the basis of social structure. Finally, broadening out the perspective beyond the strategic choices of just these eight firms, we need to consider the implications of this Realist position for our conception of the firm within society and for the possibility of bringing it under democratic control.

THE 1979–85 RECESSION AND RECOVERY

The 1979–81 recession was the worst of the post-war period. In the space of two years, unemployment in the UK practically doubled, from 1.3 million to 2.5 million; company liquidations rose by the same proportion, from 4,500 in 1979 to 8,600 in 1981; and manufacturing output collapsed in real terms by 14 per cent (*Economic Trends* and *Employment Gazette*, December 1983). Thus the recession presented British manufacturing companies with an acute challenge to their very survival. This section will outline the course of the 1979–81 recession and subsequent recovery, highlighting aspects particularly relevant to the two industries – domestic appliances, a consumer goods industry, and office furniture, an investment goods industry – from which the cases are taken. In order to provide some context for any general conclusions that might be drawn from the experience of 1979–85, this overview will also stress certain differences between this and other business cycles.

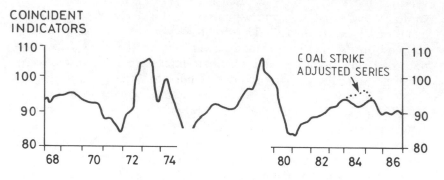

Figure 1.1   Coincident Cyclical Indicators, 1968–86
Source: *Economic Trends* and *Employment Gazette*, March 1988.

According to the coincident cyclical indicators (see Figure 1.1), the recession began in May 1979, reaching its trough in May 1981, and then commencing a prolonged recovery which, relative to the trend, petered out during 1985. The recession and recovery were not experienced evenly however. Gross Domestic Product (GDP) was affected far less severely and recovered more strongly than manufacturing alone – indeed, by 1985, manufacturing output had still not recovered to its previous peak of 1979 (see Figure 1.2). This weak recovery on the part of manufacturing highlights a second process underlying the cycle: a period of long-run manufacturing decline or de-industrialization which may have begun in absolute terms as early as 1966 (Smith, 1984; Coates, 1985).

The 1979–85 recession and recovery was only one of seven complete business cycles Britain had experienced since 1951 (Meyer, 1985). However, it differed from most of these in that during the 1950s and 1960s cycles took the form of fairly mild fluctuations around a trend of continuous growth (Mathews, 1969). This pattern was decisively broken in the mid–1970s. The 1974–5 and 1979–81 recessions stand apart from the earlier 'growth cycles', both in their unprecedented severity – the only other occasion this century when industrial production declined for two or more years in succession was during the 1930–32 Great Depression – and in taking place against background trends of near stagnation (Mullineux, 1984, p. 3; London and Cambridge Economic Services, undated). Writing in early 1988, it is not yet clear whether the British economy has been restored to those happy days of the 'growth cycle' or, rather, whether it faces another collapse on the same scale as the two preceding ones. What is more

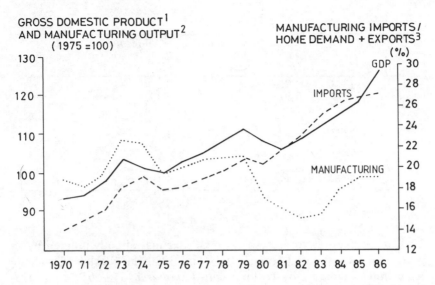

Figure 1.2 GDP, Manufacturing Output and Import Penetration, 1970–86.

Sources: *Economic Trends* and *Employment Gazette*, August, 1977; October, 1979; May, 1982; March, 1988; *Monthly Digest of Statistics*, August, 1983; *British Business*, 11 April 1986.

certain is that, within capitalist economic systems, business cycles of some sort will always be with us.

The 1974–9 and 1979–85 cycles have more in common than their unusual severity. Both were preceded by 'oil shocks': oil prices quadrupled during the winter of 1973–4, while between 1978 and 1979 the oil price rose by 45 per cent, with a further 68 per cent rise in 1979–80 (Glyn and Harrison, 1980; Smith, 1984). Both recessions took place against backgrounds of rapidly increasing inflation: the general price index records increases in 1974 of 16.1 per cent and in 1975 of 24.2 per cent, to be compared with increases in 1979 of 13.4 per cent and in 1980 of 18.0 per cent (*Economic Trends*, December 1983; April 1986). However, the Thatcher government's policies towards exchange and interest rates provides a significant source of contrast between the two cycles, besides contributing to a recession in manufacturing industry that was markedly more severe than in other countries (Smith, 1984; Pratten, 1985).

During the early 1980s, the government's peculiar interpretation of monetarist economics led it to maintain unprecedentedly high interest rates (Keegan, 1984). The base rate rose to 17 per cent at the end of 1979, and was still at 14.5 per cent at the end of 1981, before it finally sank to 9 per cent by the end of 1983 (*Economic Trends*, April 1986).

Table 1.1   UK Investment, 1978–86

	Gross domestic fixed capital formation (£m 1980 prices)	Manufacturing fixed investment (£m 1980 prices)
1978	42,726	7,220
1979	43,913	7,496
1980	41,561	6,478
1981	37,571	4,870
1982	39,593	4,709
1983	41,623	4,784
1984	44,968	5,756
1985	45,965	6,430
1986	46,180	6,331

Source: *Economic Trends* April 1986; March 1988.

This, of course, reinforced the value of Sterling, already inflated by its petro-currency status; between 1978 and 1980 the Sterling Exchange Rate Index increased by 17.9 per cent (*Economic Trends*, April 1986) while import price competitiveness increased by 13.1 per cent between 1978 and 1981 (*Economic Trends*, December 1982). During the mid–1970s, on the other hand, interest rates fell slightly, even as inflation rose; and import price competitiveness only increased by 4.9 per cent between 1973–4, before beginning a steady reversal (*Economic Trends*, January 1977; January 1980).

The Thatcher government's high interest and exchange rate policies, combined with the absence of an explicit incomes policy, help account for the rather surprising concentration of the recession's worst affects on business rather than consumers: 'The primary impact of the 1978–81 recession was on the financial position of companies. As earnings – for those in work – continued to rise, profits fell sharply' (Smith, 1984, p. 24). High interest rates had an especially acute affect on manufacturing companies, as they inhibited capital investment (Table 1.1), inflated the value of the pound, and put pressure on stocks. Of course, manufacturers' cutbacks in investments and stocks only aggravated the overall recession. Pratten (1985) estimates that the self-reinforcing effects of destocking accounted for 50 per cent of the decline in manufacturing output during the second half of 1981. Distributive and service sectors did better, however. As the National Institute noted: 'Investment by the distributive and service industries has been relatively buoyant. It has risen throughout the current recession, in marked contrast to behaviour during the 1974–75 recession when it fell very sharply' (*National Institute Economic Review*, February 1983, p. 11).

The *National Institute Economic Review* (February 1983, p. 10) drew

Table 1.2   *Income and Consumption, 1978–86*

	Real personal disposable income (1980 = 100)	*Real consumer expenditure on durable goods (£m: 1980 Prices)*
1978	93.1	12,109
1979	98.6	13,930
1980	100.0	13,019
1981	98.9	13,415
1982	97.9	14,475
1983	100.2	16,629
1984	103.1	16,700
1985	105.5	17,878
1986	109.5	20,959

Source: *Economic Trends*, April 1986; March 1988.

attention to another 'sharp contrast' between patterns of consumption in 1974–5 and in 1979–81: 'during the earlier period, real income and consumption both fell by about 2.5 per cent. Since 1979, real income has fallen by a similar amount, but consumption by about 1 per cent.' As Table 1.2 demonstrates, real consumer expenditure on durable goods in particular fell by over £900m. (6.5 per cent) between 1979 and 1980, but thereafter recovered rapidly, easily surpassing its former peak by 1982.

It was this upturn in consumer spending that provided the first nudge to economic recovery during 1981 (Britton, 1986, p. 77). Initially stimulated by improved confidence following the fall in inflation, consumer spending began to boom during 1982 as interest rates came down and as hire purchase restrictions were abolished in July. Analysing the 1983 recovery in output, the *National Institute Economic Review* (February, 1984, p. 9) observed that the 'chief feature has been the strength of consumer spending, particularly on durables'. By 1985, real consumer expenditure on durable goods had exceeded the 1980 low by 33.5 per cent (see Table 1.2). However, the benefits of this consumer boom only percolated down to manufacturing industry in a slow and uncertain fashion.

Although by 1984 gross domestic fixed capital formation had climbed past its 1979 level, manufacturing investment lagged severely behind (Table 1.1 on p. 12). British manufacturing industry, ever sluggish and prone to bottlenecks, appeared yet again to be vulnerable to the inrush of imports that had attended previous recoveries (cf. Cairncross, Henderson and Silberston 1982; Smith, 1984, pp. 26–7). Not only had manufacturing companies responded to the recession by a 37 per cent reduction in investment, they had also cut their stocks (down by 11 per cent between 1979 and the third quarter of 1981:

Table 1.3   Output constraints in manufacturing, 1978–86

	Factors likely to limit output over next four months: % of firms ticking:		
October:	Skilled labour	Plant capacity	Materials/ component shortage
1978	27	13	6
1979	23	11	10
1980	4	3	1
1981	3	7	3
1982	3	5	2
1983	9	13	6
1984	8	15	6
1985	15	17	4
1986	12	13	6

Source: Confederation of British Industry's *Industrial Trends* Surveys.

British Business, 28 February 1986); they had curtailed previous growth in research and development (all intramural research and development expenditure fell by 3 per cent between 1978 and 1983 – *British Business*, 18 January 1985); and they had severely reduced employment (down by 13.3 per cent between 1979 and 1981 – *Employment Gazette*, April 1986). The anxiety once more was that the recession had impelled such a sharp cut-back in manufacturing resources and capacity that companies would be unable to react quickly and fully enough to meet the rapid increase in demand. As the recovery gained in strength, the Confederation of British Industry reported a steadily increasing proportion of its members as experiencing capacity constraints: in terms of plant capacity, 13 per cent were complaining of constraints by 1983, as much already as at the previous peak of 1978 (see Table 1.3). And worst fears were indeed confirmed: while by 1985 manufacturing output was only marginally above its 1980 level, manufacturing import penetration was up by more than 30 per cent in the same period (see Figure 1.2 on p. 11). Amputated in recession, British manufacturing could only limp along in recovery.

So far this part of the chapter has surveyed the course of the 1979–85 business cycle in general terms, stressing its uniqueness relative to other business cycles but only hinting at the possible variability of sectoral experiences within it. The experiences of the domestic appliance and office furniture industries will be examined in more detail in Chapter 6, but we can note here the differential impact of some of the general cyclical factors. The domestic appliance manufacturers suffered particularly from the high interest rates of the early 1980s, as they forced retailers into radical destocking and pushed up Sterling to the advantage of the importers. The resilience of consumer spending during the recession was, of course, a help, but the surge in consumer spending following the cut in interest rates and abolition of hire purchase restrictions in 1982 was only a mitigated bonus. This sudden surge risked opening a gap between domestic demand and British capacity to supply which importers would be only too happy to exploit. The office furniture industry was, for its traditional bulky low value-added products at least, slightly less vulnerable to imports. However, as an investment goods industry, office furniture suffered particularly from the collapse of manufacturing investment. Opportunities remained in the distribution and services industries where investment spending was buoyant, but this involved a regional shift away from established customers in the old industrial heartlands to new and growing companies in the south east of England. Thus, though the two industries endured the same general recession, they did not experience it in exactly the same way.

Just as industries varied within the general course of the cycle, so might the experiences of individual firms. As the British economy was entering its recovery phase, Silberston (1983, p. 39) observed: 'At the time of writing, many British firms were doing badly because of the recession, while many others have gone out of existence. At the same time, many firms were doing well.' It is time now to descend from the macroeconomic level in order to consider how the various strategies of individual firms may contribute to these performance differentials. Accordingly, the following section will examine the existing literature on recession strategies in order to tease out the main strategic dilemmas and options. My contention shall be that the business cycle presents the strategic decision-maker with a particularly intriguing, even paradoxical set of problems, which the strategy and economics literature has so far lamentably neglected.

STRATEGIES IN RECESSION AND RECOVERY

The shocks of recession are often held to have salutary effects upon managers supposedly grown too lax in years of prosperity. So concluded Kennedy and Payne (1976, p. 251) from their review of the business history literature: 'There is little question that booms promote growth, yet in a number of case studies, it is apparent that a crisis provoked by a sharp national recession led to very far reaching beneficial changes in business strategy.' Similarly, Pettigrew (1985, p. 429), in his study of ICI, observed how cyclical recessions

constituted important stimuli to radical organizational change: 'The
periods of high levels of change activity [at ICI] have tended to occur
every decade, and are associated with the second low point of the 4.5
year business cycle.'

This argument, that recession prompts reform, was seized upon with
some eagerness by government apologists during 1980 and 1981. John
Biffen, Treasury Chief Secretary, declared that it was time for British
industry to 'have a bomb put under it' (Keegan, 1984, p. 158).
Reporting the recent actions of several large British manufacturers –
improving work practices, cutting overheads, diversifying abroad and
pruning inefficient operations – the *Economist* (4 July, 1981 pp. 73–6)
epitomized the rhetoric of the day by hoping that industry would
emerge from the recession 'leaner and fitter'. Another commentator,
writing later, contended that the firms which did finally emerge into
the recovery would '. . . enjoy good prospects. It is not unreasonable
to suppose that it is those firms with the strongest management which
have come through relatively unscathed. Indeed, economic adversity
may well have forced them to eliminate sources of inefficiency
(organizational slack) and hence to have become more cost competitive' (Coates, 1985, p. 134).

Some were more sceptical. Bowers, Deaton and Turk (1982, pp.
144–5) wondered whether the 1979–81 'shake-out' was selecting for
survival simply those firms which, by a fortuitous failure to invest in
the preceding period of growth, entered the recession with low debt
and low technological inflexibility. It would be these low investors who
would best withstand high interest rates and the sudden reduction in
demand. Bowers and his colleagues feared the recession was forcing
change upon those firms which had been most innovative and
expansive before, rather than on those which were basically inefficient.
They speculated, therefore, that the long-run effect of the recession, in
so far as it penalized innovation and expansion, might actually be
destructive. Thus opinion on the 1979–81 recession was sharply
divided: on the one hand there were the purgative optimists; on the
other the punitive pessimists. Clearly there is a need for some critical
examination of the sort of changes stimulated by recession and the sort
of strategies favoured by it.

However, as Andrews (1949, p. 252) long ago noted, economists
have generally failed to link individual firms' strategies with the
macroeconomic processes of business cycles. Loyal to neo-classical
conceptions of the firm, economists have either ignored the possibility
of divergent strategies or preferred to subsume them within the
comfortable embrace of large numbers. So far as they are concerned,
all firms can be supposed to respond to falling demand by reducing

output, employment, stocks and investment equally, each exactly in line with the type of aggregate cyclical statistics introduced in the last section. One or two economists have made a few finer distinctions. For instance, Penrose (1980, Chapter 7) argues that firms for whom recession has exposed large surpluses in resources will seek new uses for them by attempting counter-cyclical diversification. Similarly, Eichner (1976, pp. 25–6) suggests that powerful 'megacorps' may take advantage of recessions to gain greater market shares by squeezing out weaker competitors. Kay (1979, pp. 43–5) observes the different responses of firms to periods of 'distress' (such as recession), with some, rather than cutting their research and development budgets, deliberately protecting them to enhance their long-term positions. In short, beneath the economic aggregates it does seem that some firms may try to buck the trend by responding to recession not with rationalization, but with long-term investment, diversification or innovation.

As yet, the corporate strategy pundits have provided little more guidance on recession strategy than the economists. The focus of the corporate strategy literature has always tended to be on more epochal shifts of environments – for instance, the implications of new railway systems (Chandler, 1977) or the secular decline of whole industries (Harrigan, 1980). The leading contemporary theorist of the 'Industrial Organization' school, Porter (1980, p. 6) dismisses the business cycle as being of merely 'tactical' significance, and then only for markets in which penetration is nearly complete. The Product Life Cycle school has produced the somewhat banal warning against launching new products during downturns (Standt, Taylor and Bowersox, 1976, p. 229), but otherwise it has generally ignored general economic cycles (Rink and Swan, 1979, p. 232).

Thus the issue of business cycle strategy has been addressed directly in only two articles – and these are largely anecdotal and hortatory. Clifford (1977), examining the mid-1970s period, highlighted the widely different performances achieved by US companies. Without providing systematic evidence, he suggested the best performers were those characterized by: disciplined pricing policies and the avoidance of discounts; product discipline, in terms of discarding ailing products and revamping others; cost discipline; and focus on niches rather than diversification. Norburn (1983) reviewed the UK experience between 1979 and 1982 in general terms, and concluded by urging companies to combine 'revenue boosting' strategies (more research and development, better segmentation, and so on) with the 'cost reducing' strategies of cuts and rationalization. He also recommended management and organizational change.

A more substantial but rather oblique approach has been made in the recent 'corporate turnaround' literature (Bibeault, 1982; Slatter, 1984; Kharbanda and Stallworthy, 1987), which includes the business cycle as just one of several possible triggers of decline. Unfortunately, Slatter's (1984) UK study of 437 turnaround efforts largely defines out recessions by focusing only on those recoveries following three or more years of falling profits (recessions are generally shorter). None the less, out of eighteen posited causal factors of decline, he still found recessions to be the fifth most common. Despite this relative frequency, Slatter (1984) does not pick from his ten generic turnaround strategies any that might be particularly relevant to companies suffering in recession. Bibeault's (1982) US study found that only 10 per cent of turnaround companies attributed their original decline to 'external' factors such as changes in the economic environment; however, this may partly be an artifact of his reliance on the reports of new senior managers, who had everything to gain by fastening blame internally on their ousted predecessors. Anyway, the general conclusions for strategy from the turnaround literature are largely unremarkable: the turnaround manager should reduce costs and assets, drop bad businesses while protecting core ones, improve and focus marketing and, the most emphatic lesson, change top management.

This neglect of business cycle strategy is surprising, especially with the apparent demise of the old growth cycle since the 1960s. The strategic threat posed by business cycles has increased since then, not simply because recessions have become deeper but also, particularly in the United Kingdom, because they have taken place against a background of industrial stagnation. During the years of rapid growth of the 1950s and 1960s, strategic decision-makers could more or less count on the eventual utilization of long-term capacity investments made under recessionary conditions; now they risk being stuck with permanent capacity surpluses for which demand will never catch up (Fildes, Jalland and Wood, 1978). Profitability and liquidation data certainly suggest that recent recessions have been taking their toll. Figure 1.3 presents the gross returns on capital employed of manufacturing companies and the annual number of company liquidations since 1970. If compared with Figures 1.1 and 1.2 on pp. 10 and 11, the figures for return on capital employed demonstrate a particularly strong cyclical pattern, with low points in profitability coming in the troughs of 1975 and 1981. The picture for liquidations is slightly less clear, the data showing roughly a year's lag on the business cycle and confused by what appears to be an upward secular trend, especially in the 1980s. However, liquidations more than doubled between 1973 and 1975, and

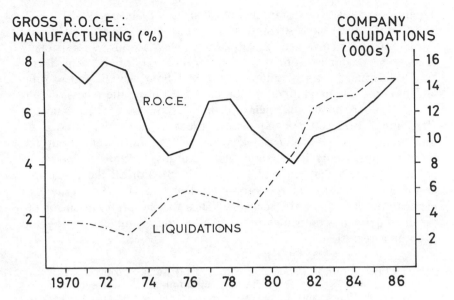

Figure 1.3   Company Profitability and Liquidations, 1970–86.

Sources: *Trade and Industry*, 5 November 1976; *British Business*, 25 April 1986; 9 October 1987.

leapt ahead again in the early 1980s. In short, recessions threaten not just profits, but the very survival of many companies. Moreover, in Britain at least, the pattern of increased import penetration (see Figure 1.2 on p. 11) demonstrates that subsequent recoveries endanger market shares as well. Thus, with regard to profitability, share and very survival, business cycles are to be ignored only at great peril – and probably more so in recent years than at any time in the post-war period.

But the fascination of the business cycle for corporate strategy lies in more than its contemporary intensification. The problem for the strategist lies in coping – at a time of heightened economic constraint – with a phenomenom that is inherently contradictory and ambiguous.

The contradiction at the level of the firm is how to balance short-term survival during the recession with the need to preserve long-term competitiveness for the recovery. As the recession bites, profits can only be safeguarded by reducing capacity, investment, research and development, labour and other costs in line with falling revenues. Upon the recovery, however, it is exactly the resources represented by these costs that the firm will need if it is to be able to take prompt and full advantage. The difficulties arise because neither contraction nor expansion are easy or instantaneous. Penrose (1980, pp. 47–8; 128–9) and Slater (1980) have stressed how expansion is constrained by the costs and time involved in absorbing new resources, especially managerial resources, into the existing operations of the firm. Firms face 'adjustment costs' – redundancy pay, labour search, and so on – which on the one hand might inhibit cutbacks during the recession, but on the other hand will delay firms' responses to the recovery (Brechling, 1975, pp. 38–48). These problems are compounded by uncertainty: a firm facing delivery delays and uncertain about the duration of a spurt in demand will naturally hesitate to invest in capacity to meet that demand (Nickell, 1978). For all these reasons, severe rationalization in recession may leave the firm vulnerable to capacity bottlenecks in the recovery. This was the predicament of the paper and board companies in 1973 after their cutbacks during the preceding recession:

> The brief upturn in the economy in 1973 saw some improvements in the sector's fortunes. Yet the rationalisation had itself set some constraints on expansion. There was now a *shortage* of capacity. The question was now which firm(s) could expand fast enough to benefit form the expected market increase (Massey and Meegan, 1982, p. 118).

This cruel irony is, of course, no more than a micro instance of the type of recovery capacity constraint that is typical of British manufacturing as a whole.

Hence the business cycle ruthlessly exposes the strategic decision-maker to the enduring conflict between 'proximate' and 'long run' profitabilities (Ansoff, 1969, p. 52) or what Silberston (1983, pp. 31–7) terms 'static' and 'dynamic' efficiencies. Contrasting the 'dynamically efficient' firm (capable of surviving changing circumstances) with the 'statically efficient' firm (which makes most efficient uses of resources in given circumstances), Silberston (1983) arrives at two almost paradoxical conclusions for strategy in recession. Silberston suggests that the firm at a peak of static efficiency immediately before the recession will actually be disadvantaged during its course; the firm would be so lean that it lacked the surplus resources, especially liquid financial reserves, necessary to buffer it against hard times. Thus static efficiency before recession translates into dynamic inefficiency during recession. Silberston goes on to argue that at the trough of the recession the statically most efficient firm – retaining no capacity or developments beyond what is immediately required – will again prove to be dynamically inefficient; this time static efficiency impedes the firm from responding quickly enough to the opportunities of the recovery. In other words, to be lean in recession does not necessarily help fitness for recovery.

This contradiction between the proximate and the long-run, the static and the dynamic, is aggravated by the ambiguous nature of the business cycle. Secular decline, as opposed to cyclical recession, poses a set of fairly unambiguous questions: how fast in demand declining; how far will it go will there be room for a particular firm; if not, when should it exit; (Kotler, 1978; Harrigan, 1980; Siamkos and Shrivastava, 1987). The business cycle is more perplexing. The firm must distinguish recessionary declines from the secular trend – especially difficult in many British manufacturing sectors, where long experience of de-industrialization might lead the decision-maker to misinterpret a temporary downturn as simply the acceleration of long-run decline. Undue pessimism may allow competitors a head start that will give them permanent advantage in a fast recovering market; ill-judged optimism about the trend may tie the company to a doomed industry, preventing it from achieving prompt exit. It was exactly this confusion between secular and cyclical decline that inhibited the Greek fur industry's response to its crisis at the beginning of the 1980s (Siamkos and Shrivastava, 1987).

Faced with the contradictory exigencies of short-run survival and long-run prosperity, and perplexed by the ambiguous nature of downturns in demand, selection of appropriate cyclical strategies is harder than ever. Neither the economists nor the business strategists offer the strategic decision-maker much help. The literature offers plenty of rhetorical praise for the changes supposedly stimulated by recession, but few cogent recommendations as to what these changes should be. The cost and product disciplines variously urged would presumably yield benefits at any time. Some recommendations actually conflict. Clifford's (1977) warning against discounts would inhibit Eichner's (1976) megacorps intent on squeezing out the small fry. Again, Clifford's (1977) advice to focus on niches does not fit well with Penroses's (1980) suggestion that surplus resources be redeployed in diversification. However, one clear distinction in attitudes to recession can be distinguished. At one extreme are the long-run optimists who, anticipating full recovery, conserve and even invest in their existing positions. At the other extreme are the short-run pessimists who, either to maximize immediate static efficiency or in the expectation of secular decline, respond to recession by cutting back as far as possible. I do not pretend that my eight case studies will allow confident conclusions on which is the most effective recession strategy – all recessions differ and strategists will themselves disagree on the criteria for effectiveness anyway. These cases may, however, provide sufficient material to explore and perhaps even clarify these complex issues. And we can certainly see from this discussion that recessions present decision-makers with intriguing problems of strategic choice.

I conclude with one last point. The cyclical strategies of individual firms and Britain's macroeconomic problems in recoveries are not entirely separate issues. As Hannah (1976, p. 1) has argued, examining the conduct of particular firms should illuminate the nature of general economic processes. If the British economy as a whole is to get 'fitter', we need to know something about how individual firms achieve fitness themselves. Recently a number of authors have sought more than mere illumination of these processes, going on to contend that strong performing or 'excellent' companies can teach lessons whose generalization may improve the performance of the macroeconomy as a whole (for example Peters and Waterman, 1982; Williams, Williams and Thomas, 1983; Pettigrew, 1985; Grinyer, Mayes and McKiernan, 1987). No simple general formulae exist for achieving 'excellence' in any sphere of managerial action, and this book will certainly not propound any for cyclical strategies in particular. None the less, focusing on the cyclical strategies of individual firms does achieve a disaggregation that undermines any conception of the business cycle as a detached and homogeneous phenomenon imposing itself ineluctably upon hapless managers who must bow uniformly to its progress. The argument that these managers may exercise strategic choice does entail the possibility that they can act otherwise. If they can choose, then they can also learn to act in new and better ways. Fuller understanding of cyclical strategies may help to mitigate the self-reinforcing effects of business cycles and, in Britain, counter the waves of imports which have hitherto accompanied successive recoveries.

SUMMARY AND PROGRAMME

The last two sections have introduced the 1979–85 recession and recovery and the strategic challenges it posed. However, I do not want to lose sight of the main issue of this book and the one I began with, that of strategic choice versus determinism. Indeed, the nature of the 1979–81 recession is closely connected with this issue – in its unequivocal severity it provides a particularly rigorous test for the possibility of strategic choice.

Thus, Chapter 2 enters straight into a discussion of the various deterministic approaches to explaining strategic conduct. Investigating their fundamental assumptions about human nature and society, I shall conclude that both major strands of determinism are fundamentally implausible and unhelpful. Either humanity is rendered too simple or social life too monolithic. This investigation of determinism provides an apt introduction to the recent accounts of strategic choice discussed in Chapter 3. I shall argue that in their continued debt to the Carnegie School these accounts fail to defend the actor's intrinsic potential for agency; in their too eager embrace of Action Theory, they neglect the social structural conditions for this agency. An adequate account of strategic choice requires an affirmation of human agency that breaks both with the implicit determinism of the Carnegie tradition and the disabling voluntarism of Action Theory. Chapters 4 and 5, therefore, develop an alternative Realist approach to strategic choice, one which grounds our capacity for agency on the complexity of the society in which we live and work. We are potentially agents because society is structured at once by capitalist, patriarchal and ethnic principles; even within the single sphere of the firm, we have available a plurality of structural rules and resources according to which we can choose how to act.

The next chapter, Chapter 6, serves as methodological introduction to the empirical material, and will besides describe the two industries, domestic appliances and office furniture, that provide the context for my case studies. Chapter 7 introduces the products, markets, histories and ideologies of the three companies that will make up my domestic appliance industry cases. Chapter 8 goes on to examine the domestic appliance companies' actual strategies during the 1979–85 recession and recovery, the processes by which they chose them and the repercussions of their choices on organization and financial performance. Chapters 9 and 10 follow a similar structure, this time examining the strategies of five office furniture companies in the same period. These four empirical chapters will be largely narratives, so Chapter 11 provides a chance to re-examine the material in the light of the various opposed theoretical perspectives. Arguing that none of the determinist approaches are capable of accounting for the strategic conduct of the eight case study firms, I will prefer to reinterpret this material according to the Realist model advanced in Chapters 4 and 5. I shall emphasize how, in most of these companies, strategic choices emerged from the agency of a structurally empowered but socially complex elite of dominant actors. In making and implementing their choices, these dominant actors drew not only upon capitalist social structural rules and resources but also upon the intersecting and conflicting structures of patriarchy and ethnicity. Finally, Chapter 12 will begin by considering the case studies' implications for managerial strategy and organization in recession. However, its main task will be to suggest some of the implications of the Realist approach to strategic choice for our conception of the capitalist enterprise, not just within organization studies but also within society more widely.

If I wanted to be glib, I might summarize the aims of this book thus: they are to put the sociology into corporate strategy, and the social structure into strategic choice.

Chapter Two

Determinist accounts of corporate strategy

INTRODUCTION

The last chapter introduced the central debate of this book: between those who hold that corporate conduct is determined and those for whom it is the outcome of processes of strategic choice. The following four chapters will examine the diverse implications of these competing theoretical approaches for the analysis of strategy in recession. Each approach focuses on different sorts of issues, offers different modes of explanation and entails different empirical methodologies. Some deterministic accounts, indeed, would dismiss the strategic decisions of individual firms as altogether irrelevant. Clearly, therefore, any empirical analysis of strategic decisions in recession presupposes a choice between the alternative perspectives offered by deterministic and more voluntaristic positions.

The grounds for preferring one or other of these positions can be analysed in terms of Elster's (1984, p. 113) 'two-step' model of human action. Elster proposes that any piece of human action may be seen as the end product of two successive filtering processes. The first is a set of exogenous structural constraints which cuts down the range of feasible actions – conceivably as far as permitting only one. The second filter is the mechanism that selects from this range the option actually to be acted upon. Again, it is possible that this mechanism will permit only one sort of action.

Two forms of determinacy can be derived from this model, each relying on one or other of the two filters. The first, environmental determinism, posits a set of exogenous constraints so tight that, though the individual actor may well select any from a range of available courses of action, in fact only one is compatible with survival – all others lead to extinction. Choice is not meaningful because, in order to survive, the decision-maker *can* follow but one course of action.

Outcomes are determinate because survivors have necessarily followed this one course and no other. The second, action determinism, turns away from the nature of external constraint to the action selection mechanisms internal to the actor him or herself. Action determinism holds that, given certain drives, the actor *will* take only one type of action. Outcomes are determined by something intrinsic to the actors themselves. Thus the two determinisms stand in neat opposition to each other. Environmental determinists have no need for a theory of human propensities to action; they can rely wholly on the environment to ensure that, whatever the actions, only one outcome is attainable. Conversely, for the action determinists it is the environment that is of secondary importance; for them, outcomes can be traced immediately to the constitutions of the actors themselves.

Elster's model also provides the basis for defining the requirements for an adequate theory of strategic choice. A deterministic theory could combine both action and environmental determinism, but this would be unnecessary – either model would suffice to provide determinate outcomes. The problem for a theory of strategic choice, however, is that it must provide non-determinate accounts of *both* human action and environmental constraint. The theory should provide actors with at least some autonomous control over both their action-selection mechanisms and their environments. It will be the task of the following chapters to establish a theory of strategic choice that does satisfy these dual criteria.

Meanwhile, this chapter examines the fundamental elements first of the action determinist positions and then of the environmental determinist positions, considering in each case their methodological implications, their adequacy for the explanation of firms' strategies in recession and the type of predictions they make. The chapter will conclude that the assumptions upon which the determinist approaches rest, and hence the predictions that they provide, are either implausible or, at best, unhelpful to the problem of explaining firms' strategic conduct in recession.

ACTION DETERMINISM

For action determinists, the explanation of behaviour proceeds outwards from the action selection mechanisms of the actors themselves. These mechanisms exhaust their possessors' identities in the sense that they are beyond the scope of autonomous self-alteration

– they are treated as given. Actions are selected according to in-built preference and information-processing systems. These selection mechanisms are often conceived of as universal, or at least as defining very broad types of actor. Despite their generality, these actors all possess a wonderful internal simplicity that, securing them from the possibility of any ambiguity in character, guarantees the reliability of their conduct. Understand their action-selection mechanisms, and actors' responses to environmental stimuli will be entirely predictable.

However, action determinists do differ in how they account for the formation of the action-selection mechanisms. I will distinguish between 'psychologistic' and 'over-socializing' accounts. Psychologistic accounts tend to derive action-selection mechanisms from certain drives or capacities presumed innate in 'human nature'. Over-socializing accounts take an opposite view, emphasizing the role of social pressures in shaping actors' identities. Naturally, this difference in the derivation of action selection mechanisms is reflected in the divergent perspectives on the environment held by the two approaches. Psychologistic approaches place the individual actor in a peculiar autonomous space, detached from his or her surroundings yet subject to a constant stream of invasive environmental stimuli. There can be no such essential autonomy for advocates of the over-socializing view. For them, actors are formed, by some sort of amoeba-like reproductive process, out of the very stuff of social structure; by virtue of these genetic origins, in their activities actors become the perfect representatives of their structural parents.

Action-selection mechanisms once defined, over-socializing and psychologistic approaches can once more converge. With actors securely bound by internal mechanisms to reliable conduct, both sets of action determinists can relax in their accounts of environments. Action determinists need not present the environment as exercising harsh constraints, as must the environmental determinists. Rather, environments are now reduced to mere providers of inputs – often treated simply as information – to which internal mechanisms calmly select appropriate responses. Thus can action determinists of both persuasions agree in their predictions of human conduct. Psychologistic and over-socializing determinists join in the expectation that, other things being equal, actors belonging to the same psychological or social types will respond uniformly to the same environmental stimulus. Accordingly, action determists would explain different strategic responses to recession by equivalently situated managers wholly in terms of the preferences and processing capacities embodied in their action-selection mechanisms.

These, then, are the essential logics of the two fundamental forms of action determinism. I want now to introduce certain particular instances that have been influential in the explanation of enterprise behaviour, both in order to flesh out this rather formalistic general introduction and, especially, to demonstrate their theoretical and practical inadequacy.

Psychologistic action determinism

In the economists' type of profit-maximizing 'Economic Man' (sic), human nature appears in its most simple, one-track and rampantly asocial form. In examining this peculiar type, I do not want merely to set up a target of straw. The concept of 'Economic Man' is important not so much in itself as in the continuing influence of its basic reasoning on the explanation of enterprise behaviour. The rise of the contemporary large-scale, managerial corporation has not yet been enough to dislodge the economists from their habitual – they might say instinctive – reliance upon human nature to ensure regularity of conduct. As this section will demonstrate, the modern manager is either bribed back into conformity with profit-maximization, as in principal-agent theory, or granted a new simplifying drive, as in theories of managerial capitalism. We shall see in the next chapter how such simple conceptions of the human actor still infuse, and compromise, many recent accounts of strategic choice.

The *locus classicus* for action determinism lies in nineteenth century economics. At a time when business enterprise was generally small scale and family owned and controlled, the economists' explanation of firm behaviour was straightforward: the firm was simply identified with the individual entrepreneur. By relying on the entrepreneur, the firm was robbed of internal structure and economists were freed from any need to consider processes of conscious co-operation within firms (Papandreou, 1952, p. 183; Swedberg, Himmelstrand and Brulin, 1987). The motivation of the single entrepreneurial decision-maker, and hence of the whole firm, was assumed to be the unambiguous pursuit of profit; as Senior put it, 'every man desires to obtain additional wealth with as little sacrifice as possible' (quoted in Hutchison, 1984, p. 3). Accordingly, the firm's strategy was derived from a supposed universal drive towards the maximization of profits. The further assumptions of perfect information and rationality protected the entrepreneur from any accidental deviations from the path of profit maximization (Earl, 1984).

This profit-maximizing assumption, as adopted and developed within neo-classical economics, demonstrates what Boland (1982, p. 30) has characterized as 'psychologistic individualism'. As a variant of methodological individualism in general, explanation is solely in terms of individuals, and specifically in terms of their psychological states. These psychological states are treated as irreducible givens, inherent in some mysterious 'human nature'. People are nothing else but 'Economic Men' – by nature profit-maximizing as producers and utility maximizing as consumers (Hollis and Nell, 1975, p. 53). At the level of the firm, strategic conduct is driven by unambiguous imperatives innate in human psychology.

This form of explanation is somewhat frustrating. Reduction to nature pre-empts any examination of the psychological dispositions, from which all actions are supposed to stem, as variables to be explained in themselves (Gellner, 1973, p. 254). However, reliance upon 'human nature' does allow these economists to achieve a necessary simplicity in their model of humanity. By taking operative utility functions as given pre-socially, the possible role of social, political and cultural processes in 'economic character formation' are safely brushed under the carpet (Farmer, 1982; Stanfield, 1983). This denial of the social is vital. It enables the neo-classical economists to atomize the environment into a mere purveyor of discrete stimuli, represented as market signals, between autonomous economic actors. For them, 'households and firms are fundamentally separate from each other and mainly interact through the market mechanism' (Swedberg, Himmelstrand and Brulin, 1987, p. 123) – even though the same human actors populate them both. This detachment of individual actors from society preserves the purity of their action selection mechanisms from the polluting influences of the complex and contradictory social institutions they inhabit. In his economic activities, profit-maximizing 'Economic Man' is kept safe from any possibility of distraction by the contrary logics of the household.

For these neo-classical economists, then, psychologistic individualism is vital to safeguarding the integrity, simplicity and reliablility of the action selection mechanisms governing human conduct. Rescued from the complexity of social being, the human actor is reduced to the simple, reactive atom caricatured by Veblen:

> a lightening calculator of pleasures and pains, who oscillates like a homogeneous globule of desire for happiness under the impulse of stimuli that shift him about the area, but leave him intact . . . When the force of the impact is spent he comes to rest, a self-contained globule of desire as before (quoted in Lukes, 1973, p. 140).

These globules of desire are not wilful pleasure seekers, but slaves to passions imposed upon them by nature. Once endowed with particular drives, the individual decision-maker becomes entirely subject to them. The decision-maker suffers under the imperative that he (or she) 'must choose among the opportunities available to him that one which best achieves his values' (Arrow, 1974, p. 17). For 'Homo Psychologicus', 'the innate psychological factors are antecedent programming devices and therefore . . . the agent, whose conduct is to be explained, is the creature of a programme he did not write' (Hollis, 1977, p. 30–1). The environment provides inputs; actions are just regulated outputs.

The force of these governing drives or programs implies that any two individuals, facing the same situation, will respond in exactly the same way (Boland, 1982, p. 33). Therefore there need be no conflict over strategy within firms and no differences in strategy between them. If it is conceded that some individuals do occasionally disobey their natural imperatives, these deviations are treated as entirely random, free of any systematic relationships to logics other than the purely economic. Thus, as atoms, human actors may be disciplined by the 'law of large numbers' to ensure that, on average, their conduct remains profit-maximizing (Lipsey, [1963] 1979, p. 11; O'Sullivan, 1987, pp. 142–5).

The findings of anthropology soon confused early notions of 'Economic Man'; the motives governing the exchange relationships of Malinowski's Trobriand Islanders appeared sometimes to be economic, sometimes social (Frankenberg, 1967, p. 49). There was no reason, therefore, to assume that capitalist entrepreneurs were always impelled by an innate and exclusive drive for profit-maximization. Indeed, as Nichols (1969, p. 97) noted, the owner manager – unconstrained by outside shareholders and supreme over subordinates managers – was peculiarly well placed to pursue personal goals other than profit. Anyway, the focus on the entrepreneur was becoming increasingly anachronistic by the early twentieth century. The original simple identity between individual entrepreneur and the firm was progressively undermined by the growing size of the modern corporation, the dilution of shareholdings and the rise of professional managers. Reporting the emergence of managerial control in the majority of the top 200 American companies between the wars, Berle and Means ([1932], 1967, p. 114) drew attention to how managerial interests might diverge from those of shareholders. It was plausible to assume that managers would seek personal gain, prestige, power or the gratification of professional zeal rather than profits. This argument was capped in Britain by the Oxford empirical research into what business decision-makers actually did and thought. Hall and Hitch (1939) not only found that decision-makers did not follow profit-maximizing pricing policies; they also concluded that, in prevalent oligopolistic conditions and in ignorance of consumer preferences, they *could* not.

This dose of empiricism placed the economists in an awkward but not irretrievable position. As we shall see later in this chapter, some responded by abandoning their simple psychologism, preserving profit-maximization only by appeal to the harsh disciplines of the environment. Others, the managerial economists, retreated in another direction, sacrificing profit-maximizing behaviour to save their psychologistic individualism. However, principal-agent theorists were the most stalwart, contorting themselves elaborately to defend both psychologism and profit-maximization.

Principal-agent theorists concede the potential divergence in interests between shareholders (principals, in their jargon) and the managers (agents, so-called) to whom they entrust their capital in the modern corporation. These theorists are acutely conscious of the information imperfections that impede principals from ensuring that their agents maximize profits as they should (Jensen and Meckling, 1976; Pratt and Zechauser, 1985). Nevertheless, they do propose two solutions that may perhaps rescue profit maximization while not entailing immediate resort either to market sanctions on the corporation itself or, worse, to the socialization of these troublesome managers. First, principals can impose employment contracts and reward structures upon their managers of a kind designed to reconcile their interests with those of shareholders (Raviv, 1985). Thus, for instance, managers may be seduced into profit-maximizing behaviour by profit bonuses or share option schemes. If this does not work, then principal-agent theorists appeal next to managerial labour markets (Fama, 1980). Managers are reminded that they operate in labour markets just like any other employee, and that if they wish to maximize their value therein they had better attend to profit maximization. Thus, having either shackled managers with golden handcuffs or trapped them into a rat-race of materialistic careerism, principals can relax, confident in the belief that their agents will pursue profit no less single-mindedly than they would themselves – if they could be bothered.

Both these solutions to the managerial agency problem share a common characteristic, that is, a base assumption that managers remain at heart 'Economic Men'. This is reassuring, for it renders managers ultimately pliant to shareholders' interests. Thus, in the first solution, all that needs to be done is to load managers with sufficient material incentives and eventually they are sure to come into line. In the second, managers will play too, for again they are obsessive seekers of the benefits that shareholders graciously dispense to those achieving any position of responsibility. Either way, managers are creatures of avarice, to be controlled simply by the judicious giving or withholding of material reward.

Unfortunately, difficulties arise if – as I shall argue later – managers are rather more tenaciously complex than the simple figures beloved of the economists. To force managers to abandon their interest in the social rewards of prestige and power, shareholders may need to lavish upon them material incentives far greater than the loss due to managerial discretion. The incentives offered through managerial labour markets need be no more effective, for managers may prefer security and the quiet life rather than ruthless careerism. And besides, it is managers who appoint and promote other managers; the complacent or self-interested will quickly reject the ambitious young manager fired with disturbing zeal for profit-maximization. Overcoming such stubborn managerial attachments to their own interests requires the devising of disciplines both highly complex and expensive. But, as Arrow (1985, p. 48) concludes a critical review, economic life is governed by social custom rather than the precise calculation of fees and sanctions demanded by principal-agent theory. In practice, the securing of profit-maximizing behaviour by contracts and reward structures is too complicated, too costly and too disruptive of the social fabric to be widely effective.

Managerial economists take a different course, resigning themselves to the deviancy of managers but still preserving their fundamental psychological individualism. By contrast with the principal-agent theorists' frantic search for elaborate new controls, this approach has an attractive simplicity. In place of the anachronistic profit-maximizing entrepreneur, the managerial economists substitute managers, kitting them out with apparently more realistic psychological assumptions. From his own wide, but casual, observation, Baumol (1959, p. 46) straightforwardly proposed that, for the new species he characterized generally as 'the businessman', 'sales have become an end in and of themselves'. Williamson (1967, p. 32), though more eclectic in what he admitted to managerial utility functions, still equated managers' motivations towards salary, security, dominance and professional excellence with Maslow's psychological hierarchy of needs. Of the managerial economists, Marris (1964) is the most complex. He begins (pp. 49–50) by basing his managerial motivations for growth on managers' psychological drive towards ever-extending personal achievement and the psychological tendency to identify their firms with their own egos. However, he goes on to introduce what he calls 'external' and 'internal' sociological factors. External sociological factors comprise managers' class loyalty to capitalist interests, while internal sociological factors include the need for professional respect from colleagues. Yet Marris (1964, p. 55) at once compromises the external sociological pressure of class loyalty by portraying it, not as an internalized maximand but rather as an external constraint only to be satisfied. At the same time, upon detailed consideration, the internal sociological 'norm of professional competence' as a stimulus to growth likewise reduces to the psychological – 'the desire for professional approbation being one of the most powerful features of middle-class masculine psychology' (Marris, 1964, p. 56).

This reliance upon psychologism has the same rather convenient consequence as it had for proponents of 'Economic Man'. If all managers can be assumed to share the same psychological drives, there is no need for managerial economists to look much inside firms to investigate the possibility of conflict over corporate goals. Since all share the same desire for growth, top management teams can be seen simply as 'basically unitary and indivisible' (Marris, 1964, p. 80). We are effectively restored to the internally unstructured firm of profit-maximizing entrepreneurs. Indeed, there is not even any personal conflict within managers' own psyches: managers are conceived of as being motivated only by growth or security, having no internal identification with the interests of capital. The profit constraint – rather relaxed – operates in a purely external manner through the sanction of the take-over mechanism (Marris, 1964, p. 45).

Thus, in merely updating motivational assumptions, these managerial economists remain attached to the same psychologistic individualism as that characteristic of the neo-classical economists they hoped to supersede. True, to the extent that they had come to recognize different psychological types ('managers' and 'owners') rather than simple universals, they had advanced to what Boland (1982) terms a 'sophisticated psychologism'. However, though again they might deal with tiresome exceptions by invoking large numbers, the managerialists, too, are deterministic in their implications: because their goals are the same, other things being equal, managerially controlled firms are expected to act in exactly the same way.

For all its 'sophistication', this psychologism is no more satisfactory than that of 'Economic Man'. It, too, suffers from an 'infinite regress' that reduces finally to assumptions about 'human nature' (Boland, 1982, p. 35). By sidestepping the issues of how 'managerial' and 'owner' types came about in the first place, and how particular individuals entered them, the managerialists continue to evade the sociological. Yet 'managers' and 'owners' are not fundamental human types; they are social constructs dependent for their existence upon the development of capitalist societies. These social identities are intimately bound together within a social system; capitalists and managers need each other, for the social system which defines them is sustained only by their collaboration. But, in so far as they recognize them at all, managerialists treat social systems as external and impermeable, according individual actors the same kind of demarcated autonomy as someone enclosed within the four walls of a room (cf. Giddens, 1984, p. 174). Thus, Williamson's managers, for instance, are presented as constituting and pursuing their eclectic utilities free from outside intervention, except as they occasionally bump against the limits imposed by market disciplines. The possibility that structural constraints and individual agents are mutually involved in their own creation and reproduction is excluded (Giddens, 1984, pp. 171–4).

However peculiar, this autonomy is important to all psychologistic action determinists, not just the managerial economists. If the predictability of their conduct is to be maintained, then actors must be provided with internal states sufficiently simple and invariable to guarantee regular, standard responses to equivalent environmental stimuli (Bhaskar, 1978, p. 77). They must remain like Veblen's 'homogeneous globules of desire'. It is by constructing their actors as atomistically removed from society that these economists are able to secure this essential simplicity. Economic action in the firm is preserved inviolate from the deviant logics of household or community. The social is prohibited from intruding upon the actor's own psyche. Thus saved from the possibility of any inner conflict between the social and the psychological, or even between one social imperative and another, the human actor is denied the internal complexity capable of generating independent, unpredictable action.

Over-socializing action determinism

The objection that the economists deny the social could hardly apply less to many functionalist and Marxian analyses. Yet they often treat society in a rather peculiarly exploitative fashion, first exalting it, then discarding it. Once society has stamped its indelible mark upon the actor, it may safely be left on one side, as the original social imprint can be relied upon to govern behaviour with complete fidelity. As Granovetter (1985, p. 485) remarks, in effect, over-socializing approaches are hardly less atomistic than the neo-classical economists, for they permit the abstraction of the actor from his or her immediate social context by presuming the complete internalization of the social *within* the individual.

For Parsons (1951, pp. 243–5), the profit motive was emphatically not a pre-social psychological drive but a situationally generalized goal learned by socialization. Values prevailing externally are internalized into the action-selection mechanisms of the actors themselves. Thus Parsons arrives at action determinism by another way. Though he claimed to be creating a general theoretical framework for the analysis of value-orientated human action, since these values are held to derive from an integrated 'cultural system', all consequent actions depend wholly on the system rather than on the autonomous agency of the individual actor. This has rather reassuring consequences. In a well-regulated social system, managers and owners alike, sharing the same systemic values, can all be expected to adopt similar strategies in response to a similar challenge, with no deviancy between firms or dissent within them.

If Parsons makes few open appearances in contemporary organizational theory, that is because this theory generally takes the identity of managerial and capitalist interests as unproblematic anyway (cf. Willmott, 1987). Paradoxically, however, Parsonian logics have been important to the very critics of the consensus that he advanced. Thus, a number of theorists within radical or Marxian traditions have appealed to socialization to rescue their models from the challenge of managerialism. Against Parsons, they would contend that capitalist society is inherently divided by antagonistic class interests; yet, substituting 'ideology' for 'culture', they join him in their reliance on the social. These authors (for example, Mills, 1956; Miliband, 1969; Nichols, 1969; Stanworth and Giddens, 1974; Whitley, 1974; and Useem, 1984) emphasize how managers – at least inner circle ones at the top – are incorporated within contemporary capitalism by rigorous processes of selection, indoctrination and socialization. These social processes – carried out in schools, universities and clubs as well as in the business world itself – are designed to secure on the part of these managers the whole-hearted identification of their (perceived) interests with those of capital. This may be a cruel ideological trick; it is not the less overwhelming. Nichols (1969, p. 146) almost echoes Parsons when he insists that the manager is not simply a psychological man but 'a Social Man, that is a man whose motives . . . operate within a given value structure'.

No doubt, these kinds of Parsonian and Marxian approaches are intended more for the explanation of broad trends in human progress (or lack of it) than for the precise prediction of individual conduct in particular situations. None the less, it would be strange indeed if all these formidable socializing processes, so carefully elaborated, were not to influence the conduct of at least most firms most of the time. And the logic of these socializing arguments leads to the same kind of deterministic expectations as in psychologistic neo-classical economics:

managers and owners alike will strive to maximize profits; strategic decision-makers will therefore be united around the same goals; in so far as they are in the same situation and possess the same knowledge, firms will adopt the same strategies.

Parsonian or Marxian, these approaches adopt over-socialized views that endow the cultural and ideological with awesome and monolithic powers. Society achieves for the over-socializers the same human simplicity as nature does for the psychologistic individualists. As Wrong (1961) complained of Parsons, the individual's personal interests are portrayed as entirely suppressed by internalized constraint, leaving no room for any of the continuing internal conflict to which psychoanalysis draws attention. This internal unity relies moreover upon an external unity that is hardly tenable. Even within the Marxian tradition it is conceded that 'hegemonies' may be plural and contradictory – that for the citizen of Ulster there are the competing forces of religion and capitalism, conflict between which individuals must resolve personally in their own peculiar ways (Clegg, 1979, pp. 87–90). Capitalist structures themselves are riven with contradictory imperatives. As Hyman (1987) observes, the employer desires on the one hand the initiative and creativity of the worker achievable only through co-operation, on the other the passive obedience that must be secured by coercion. Faced with these structural ambiguities, the actor operates under no clear imperative, and must actively choose. Thus the translation from structural 'positions' in society – for example, 'management' – to actions is not necessarily unproblematic, requiring the continuous and creative interpretation by position-holders of their particular situations (Pahl and Winkler, 1974, p. 120; Medding, 1982). Moreover, the collective effect of actors' creative interpretations is to alter – probably incrementally, but potentially radically – the structures that were the original bases for their actions. The relationship between social institutions and actors is therefore reciprocal. People are not simple 'cultural dopes' (Giddens, 1979, p. 71), for it is only by virtue of actors' continuous efforts to interpret them that cultures exist in the first place.

This passive picture of human activity, is the essential characteristic of action determinism, both psychologistic and over-socializing. Whether relying on the original programming of nature or the subsequent pressures of nurture, action determinists imagine people as 'plastic men' – they leave no room for the possibility of 'self-caused', autonomous action (Hollis, 1977, p. 12). This is too oppressive. One view forces pre-social motivations upon social categories; the other crushes all individuality by heavy socialization. Both are reductionist;

neither is plausible. Yet these views do simplify the research process. Except to pause briefly while the managerial economists check whether managers are in control and the principal-agent theorists adjust their contracts, action determinists absolve themselves from contemplating the internal processes of conflict and co-operation by which corporate strategies are resolved. They either appeal to large numbers, from which lofty heights the deviant conduct of any particular individual or firm can safely be disregarded, or they rely upon such tyrannically simplified models of human nature that universal conformity is inescapable. Whether on average or in particular, decision-makers belonging to the same types and faced by the same challenge – for example recession – are simply expected to respond in the same way.

ENVIRONMENTAL DETERMINISM

Environmental determinism relies on the other filter in Elster's (1984) 'two-step' model: exogenous structural constraint. For environmental determinists, the immediate focus is less on individuals than on the context in which they operate. Even so, these contexts are usually rather denuded, generally limited to the economic constraints of product markets, the market for capital and the market for corporate control.

Of course, these environmental determinists are no more homogeneous than action determinists. One crucial distinction is between those who are quite indifferent to the peculiarities and sources of individual behaviour, relying simply on the environment to select; and those who, though viewing the environment as dominant, still grant actors a central role in purposive adaptation to its dictates. There are also different emphases in characterizing the environment. Natural selectionists stress the harshness of an environment in which survival can only be secured by strict and instant obedience. Adaptationists, on the other hand, must assume that the environment allows some time for the processes and learning involved in adaptation – even so, they tend to appeal ultimately to the punitive guillotine of environmental selection to make sure that adaptation does eventually take place. Either way these theorists predict that, whatever the individual's particular actions, the environment will only permit certain pre-ordained outcomes. In the remainder of this chapter, I shall first examine the various environmental determinist positions, elucidating especially their relevance for the analysis of strategic responses to recession; then I shall critically consider just how sharp their market guillotines really are.

Selection and adaptation

Pirated from Darwin, the concept of natural selection took its place besides that of 'Economic Man' to reinforce the deterministic inclinations of nineteenth-century economics. Alfred Marshall ([1890] 1961, p. 495) encapsulated a line of argument that would be vigorously proposed in both economics and sociology for nearly 100 years when he wrote: 'the struggle for survival tends to make those methods of organization prevail, which are best fitted to thrive in their environment.' This appeal to evolutionary notions became especially important as early assumptions about 'Economic Man' came under attack from the managerialists. Neo-classical economists began to realize that faith in the profit-maximizing entrepreneur was redundant in a system in which the environment could be relied upon to reach the same determinate results (Loasby, 1971, p. 884). Competitive markets would now act as the guarantors of profit-maximizing behaviour.

Accordingly, as Alchian (1950, pp. 213–4) classically argued, economists should back away from the trees – the optimization calculus of individual units – the better to discern the forest of impersonal market forces. By thus stepping back, economists will see how the market environment selects some firms for survival, others for extinction. It is of scant interest whether firms hit upon the survival strategy by luck or by rational calculation: 'the survivors may appear to be those having *adapted* themselves to the environment, whereas the truth may be that the environment has *adopted* them' (Alchian, 1950, p. 214). Following Friedman's (1953) famous argument, we can safely assume that business decision-makers somehow profit maximize because it is only those who do – whether by rational calculation or by rubbing lucky rabbits' feet – that the environment allows to survive.

As Latsis (1972, p. 210) observes, in this natural selection mutation of neo-classical economics, 'the decision-maker's freedom of choice is spurious' – he or she must adopt the optimal strategy or face instantaneous liquidation. Economists have constructed a 'situational determinism' in which they need only 'to concentrate on the *logic* of the agent's *situation* and are spared the complexities of the *psychology of the agent* in that situation' (Latsis, 1972, p. 211). This is not to say, as Bourgeois (1984, p. 592) does, that natural selectionists relegate managers to the lowly status of mechanical reactors; only that, for them, the idiosyncracies of individual managerial actions do not matter.

Natural selection economists would themselves disclaim any value in their theories for explaining why particular firms adopt particular strategies. Friedman (1953) and Machlup (1967) readily concede that economists are uninterested in the processes of particular business decisions, being concerned solely for their aggregate effects on prices, production, resource use, and so on. Again, aggregation is adopted as 'the saving grace' of economics (March, 1978, p. 588). The most natural selection theorists will do is predict that, given competitive pressures, firms in the same market will tend towards similar production functions; and that such similar firms, undergoing tightening environmental constraint – as during recession – are likely to have to converge on a still narrower range of strategies in order to survive.

Within contemporary sociology, this natural selection perspective has been adopted most explicitly by the population ecology theorists (Hannan and Freeman, 1977; Aldrich, 1979). Hannan and Freeman (1977, p. 950) epitomize the population ecology approach in their simple statement that 'natural selection maximises fitness'. Again, the selection mechanism is primarily the market – Hannan and Freeman (1977, pp. 958–9) emphasize business bankruptcy rates, while Aldrich (1979, Chapter 6) appeals generally to the evidence of the industrial economics literature in order to assert the continued prevalence of competition. These theorists repeatedly echo Alchian and Friedman: they prefer selection to adaptation (Hannan and Freeman, 1977, pp. 930–1); they stress the role of chance rather than rationality (Aldrich, 1979, p. 39); and their models are most applicable to large populations rather than small ones (Hannan and Freeman, 1977, pp. 959–60).

The allied 'strategy and structure' and 'markets and hierarchies' schools differ considerably from natural selection theorists in that they are not indifferent to the processes by which particular firms adapt to their environments. Accordingly they also accept the need to make some assumptions, however rudimentary, about the nature of human conduct. These schools are concerned primarily with explaining – or justifying – the existence and form of the contemporary large-scale corporation in terms of its efficiency in handling co-ordination or transaction costs. Chandler (1962; 1977) focuses on the long, often confused processes of adaptation by such large firms as Du Pont, General Motors and Standard Oil to the contingencies of diversification; but as a business historian he generally leaves his assumptions rather implicit. Williamson (1975; 1985), the economic theorist, is both more stylized and more explicit: he appeals to supposedly innate human psychological characteristics such as 'opportunism' (self-seeking with guile) and 'bounded rationality' (natural information processing limits to rational optimzation) to explain the necessity for, in different circumstances, markets or hierarchies to organize our economic activities.

Nevertheless, despite a readiness to make some limited assumptions about human nature, in the last instance Chandlerian and Williamsonian perspectives equally rely on competitive markets to enforce obedience to the dictates of efficiency. Thus at Du Pont it was only a dangerous crisis in profitability that finally forced the adoption of a multidivisional structure in 1921; similarly at United States Rubber, the reversal of divisionalization by the incoming Charles B. Segar was followed by near bankruptcy and effective takeover by the reforming Du Pont family (Chandler, 1962, pp. 104–6; 350–1). As du Boff and Herman (1980) sceptically observe, even such large corporations as these are always portrayed as subject to the discipline of competitive markets rather than as being capable of exercising power over them through monopoly or vertical integration. This market supremacy is treated as 'an article of faith' – exactly how these markets actually do regulate increasingly large and powerful corporations is only vaguely specified (Granovetter, 1985, p. 503). This vagueness is particularly marked in Williamson and Ouchi's (1981, p. 364) response to their radical critics, where they concede that market pressures may take as long as ten years to force managerial 'power considerations' to give way to 'efficiency'.

Contingency theorists (for example, Burns and Stalker, 1961; Thompson, 1967; Pugh and Hickson, 1976) follow the Chandlerian emphasis on adaptation rather than selection, but still the reference point is to the demands of the environment. Burns and Stalker (1961, p. 96) posit a simple relationship where 'the effective organization of industrial resources . . . alters in important respects in conformity with changes in extrinsic factors'. Generally these theorists were concerned with the limited problems arising from the adaptation of organizational structures to the exingencies of their markets or technologies – always accepted as exogenously given. However, this type of logic has recently been extended to include the need to align corporate cultures with environments (Davis, 1984; Scholz, 1987) or to appoint appropriately skilled top managers (Godiwalla, Meinhart and Warde, 1979; Hambrick, 1981; Gupta and Govindarajam, 1984). Nevertheless, empirical work has generally been confined in any particular study to the correlation of quite restricted sets of variables with equally limited and crudely defined contingencies. This is inescapable, for with the attempt to apply their logic to the more complex and extensive variables involved in corporate strategies in general, contingency theory collapses into the absurd calculation of 2^{54} possible relevant contingencies (Hofer, 1975). Theoretically, however, the logic of obedience to the dictates of the environment is as ruthless for contingency theorists as it is for natural selectionists: 'organizations do some of the things they do because they must – or else!' (Thompson, 1967, p. 1). Again, only one sort of behaviour is compatible with survival.

Yet committed defenders of contingency theory can find little empirical evidence to support this ruthless characterization of the environment, even when confining themselves to the most limited correlations. Donaldson (1987) has recently tried to refute the critics (for example, Child, 1972) by examining the matching of organizational structures to the new complex environments of Japanese, French, German, American and British firms diversifying during the post-war period. Sure enough, he finds that diversifying firms failing to adopt the more decentralized structures approved by contingency theory did suffer relatively poor profitabilities. Though Donaldson hardly acknowledges it, other results are less comforting. To quote Donaldson (1987, p. 16) himself:

> Thirty three of the forty three corporations that were mismatched in 1959 had also been mismatched in 1949. This may have arisen from diversification in the 1940s or earlier . . . The whole cycle of diversification – misfit – structural adjustment – fit may take a considerable period of time and frequently spans decades.

In short, failure to fit structures to contingencies may exact a penalty upon performance, yet managers can get away with this sub-optimization for decades at a time. This surely grants the average chief executive, at the top for perhaps only five or so years, considerable impunity. Further, over a decade or more, such powerful firms as General Motors or Du Pont have plenty of time to adjust the very environments that are supposed to discipline them.

Another deterministic account of diversification has been provided by the recent theorists of 'strategic groups' (Hatten and Hatten, 1987). These strategic group theorists have addressed themselves to the apparent anomaly for environmental determinism of variations in strategic conduct amongst business units sharing the same industrial environments. The fundamental framework of these theorists is derived from the 'Industrial Organization' school's (Bain, 1968) analyses of linkages between market structure – that is, degrees of monopoly – and market performance. Significantly Bain (1968, pp 329–32) confined himself merely to inferring the conduct link between structure and performance; according to him, even systematic surveys of corporate strategy produced gross classifications which under-estimated the subtleties of conduct and which in themselves could have little application to 'serious analytical pursuits'. However, in amending market structures to include mobility barriers imposed upon subsidiaries by parent companies' degrees of vertical or horizontal integration, the strategic group theorists now claim to be able to explain the conduct of quite small groups of businesses, and even those of single units (Porter, 1981). None the less, to ensure that their mobility barriers do effectively constrain conduct, they are forced ultimately to resort to the primitive assumptions of the action determinists.

According to these theorists, strategic groups contain firms competing within the same industry who share equivalent mobility barriers on account of, for instance, being subsidiaries of multiproduct firms with similar types of diversification or vertical integration (Caves and Porter, 1977; Newman, 1978). A particular industry may contain several strategic groups of businesses, each group characterized by its members' shared patterns of diversification or integration, and each with its own characteristic strategy. Although this account explains diversity within a particular industry, the argument remains deterministic. While arguing that positioning in different strategic groups may endow firms in the same industry with different 'proximate objectives', Newman (1978, p. 418) goes on to insist that ultimately conduct for all will be consistent with 'rational optimising behaviour' – our old friend profit-maximization. Members of the same strategic group are thus driven into meek conformity: 'multiproduct firms with similar rent-yielding assets . . . and similar interdependencies amongst their businesses [will] pursue . . . the same operating procedures in the same market' (Newman, 1978, p. 418; cf. Caves and Porter, 1977, p. 251).

This retreat to profit-maximizing motivational assumptions is not entirely surprising. The model relies on mobility barriers having the same 'objective' value for all actors. If actors differ in their preference functions, their evaluation of mobility barriers will differ also. A barrier regarded as insurpassable by the profit-maximizer may well be considered passable by a sales maximizer. To maintain regularity proponents of strategic group analysis need to introduce the further disciplines either of primitive 'psychologism' – to secure universally equal evaluations – or of natural selection – to ensure that only one sort of evaluation would be viable.

However, the strategic group theorists' assumption of profit-maximizing motivations is casual and unargued. Porter (1980, p. xix), who does not even take refuge in large numbers, relegates the issue to a footnote that begins simply 'Given the premise that managers honestly try to optimise the performance of their business . . .', after which no more is said and everything is left to industry variables. The evidence that the natural selection mechanisms of the markets rigorously discipline parent companies into optimally co-ordinating the conduct of their subsidiaries is no more convincing. The rational global optimizing posited by Newman (1978) would require careful organizational integration. However, Channon (1973, pp. 87–8) has noted the persistence of loose, decentralized holding company structures in the United Kingdom, while Granick (1972, pp. 57–8) has found that head office co-ordination is generally 'quite casual'. Even in the 1980s, despite the strictures of the theorists, holding company structures still survive in over 30 per cent of large UK firms (Goold and Campbell, 1987, p. 147). In short, many British parent companies appear not to feel themselves under any strong imperative to co-ordinate their subsidiaries to secure overall optimization in the way that strategic group theorists suppose. If these holding companies are surviving by environmental adoption rather than by deliberate adaptation (cf. Alchian, 1950), then there are a lot of lucky managers about.

So far, most of these environmental determinists have tended to emphasize product market competition, by which failure to generate maximum profits is supposed to be penalized by bankruptcy. However, attention has been drawn recently to the growth of financial institutions and their capacity to monitor managerial behaviour (for example, Nyman and Silbertson, 1978; Francis, 1980; Cable, 1985; Stiglitz, 1985). Within Marxian traditions, the new role of banks, pension funds and insurance companies has prompted some revision and revitalization of old crude notions of 'finance capital' (cf. Ingham, 1984, Chapters 1–2). This renewal has led some (Mintz and Schwartz, 1985; Scott and Griff, 1985; Scott, 1986) to point to ways in which banking 'hegemonics' or 'spheres of influence' may indirectly structure business decision-making. Advancing beyond simple bank control theories, they argue that banks do not necessarily operate direct control over firms' strategies; instead, banks and the like exercise a general influence towards capitalist interests, both by the provision of finance and through the prevalence of interlocking directorships between financial institutions and industry more generally. According to Mintz and Schwartz (1985, p. 41), 'the behaviours of major corporations are subject to and conditioned by their ongoing capital needs; and they therefore must fit their actions and strategies into the overall patterns determined by the major financial institutions'. Actions may be attempted that are contrary to the interests of the financial institutions – for example, Leaseco's aggressive attempt to take over Chemibank (Mintz and Schwartz, 1985, Chapter 1) – but

these are ultimately doomed to failure by the veto power of capital.
Once more, outcomes are tightly regulated by constraint.

However, as Tomlinson (1982, p. 94) observes, this type of analysis
is still prone to over-heavy reliance on general and imprecise notions
of 'capital' with little detailed examination of how it actually controls
the institutions through which it is supposed to operate. Though brief
case studies may be instanced, in general the exercise of control is
inferred simply from the presence of interlocks or financial involvement. This reliance upon simple, usually quantified indicators of
influence pre-empts any interpretive investigation of banks' actual
motives. It is not clear for instance why the banks themselves should
be any less capable than other firms of falling out of the control of
their shareholders and into the hands of their managers. These
managers may well prefer to enjoy convivial lunches with their
interlocked directors rather than to exhort them puritanically to profit-
maximization. Indeed, Scott (1986) himself points to the way in which
many large financial institutions have slipped out of the control of
majority or even substantial minority shareholders, so that they are
now putatively controlled by rather diffuse 'constellations of interests'.
Anyway, even if capitalists do happen to be in tight control of the
financial institutions, these theorists must rely on the same sort of
assumptions as primitive believers in 'Economic Man' to ensure that
they continue to exercise their influence exclusively and remorselessly
in the cause of simple profit-maximization. Lastly, of course, theories
of bank influence assume that firms do overwhelmingly depend on
external finance an⹁ that they have no means of escaping or mitigating
this dependence.

This is the point of weakness that all these environmental
determinists share. Though their terminologies and emphases may vary
considerably, they rest on the presumption that all constraint really is
so tight that firms can have no effective choice but to profit-maximize.
Particular cases are frequently cited to demonstrate the perils of non-
conformity. Thus, for Chandler's (1962) United States Rubber,
adherence to sub-optimal organizational structures was penalized by
the threat of bankruptcy and the loss of control; in Mintz and
Schwartz's (1985) Leaseco case, self-aggrandizement was stymied by
the boycott of the financial institutions. Moreover, except in the case
of interlocking directors, economic constraint is seen to operate simply
through markets. This section has already cast some doubt on the
effectiveness of market disciplines, but now I want to examine them
more systematically. Following Lawriwsky (1984), I shall analyze
market constraint under three categories: those exercised by competition in product markets; those exercised by the capital markets; and

those operated by the market for corporate control, based on the threat of takeover. I shall argue that there is a great deal of evidence to suggest that the constraints exerted by each of these markets have been substantially undermined.

Market disciplines – blunted or evaded

Taking product markets first, the theory is that non-profit maximizing behaviour will be penalized by bankruptcy. Firms adopting sub-optimal strategies incur additional costs which they cannot pass on to their customers because their more virtuous competitors will undercut them on price. Selling at a loss, the sinful firm faces the empty choice of either returning to the righteous path of profit-maximization or rapidly going out of business. This, in 1921, was the dilemma apparently confronting Chandler's beloved Du Pont. The effectiveness of this discipline relies on product markets being indeed price-competitive. However, if competitors can be excluded and cloudy non-price considerations introduced, then these product market disciplines become relaxed. Managers may raise prices to extract 'surplus' profits for their shareholders; alternatively, they may disperse the potential surplus by pursuing their own particular ambitions or simply by enjoying the Hicksian monopoly profit of 'the quiet life' (Vickers and Hay, 1987). Genuine strategic choice becomes possible.

The measure of corporate power over product markets is controversial, though the most common measure remains simple market concentration (Hay, 1987). With the rise of the large firm over this century, concentration in the UK economy now far exceeds that of the competitive ideal. By 1968 the top 100 firms accounted for 41 per cent of all UK manufacturing net output (Prais, 1976). Since the mid–1970s these top 100 firms' share of production within directly owned units seems to have fallen a little, to around 38 per cent, but been replaced by indirect control through sub-contracting and new forms of power such as franchizing (Shutt and Whittington, 1987). Corporate power reveals itself most clearly at a disaggregated level. Analyzing UK manufacturing in terms of eleven broadly defined industries in 1969, Hannah and Kay (1977, pp. 89–91) found seven of them characterized by top ten firm concentration ratios exceeding 80 per cent. This heavy concentration facilitates domination of particular product markets; Cowling (1982, pp. 80–1) cites the brewing and textile-spinning industries in which the leading companies took respectively 20 per cent and 35 per cent of their UK markets. Increasingly sophisticated marketing and advertising techniques enhance this dominance by obscuring simple price considerations and excluding new entrants (Galbraith, 1967). Further, the growing organization of research and development activities within large technological firms gives them the capacity to *create* the markets they dominate (Karpik, 1972b). For instance, Bauer and Cohen (1981, Chapter 2) tell of how Gervais-Danone was able, by developing new preservation techniques and by constant product innovation, initially to establish for the first time in France a national market for fresh cheeses and yoghurts; then to create a demand for fruit and chocolate-flavoured products that had never existed before; and finally even to persuade the lactophobic Mexicans to become enthusiastic consumers of their monopolistically supplied product. Thus, for many firms at least, there is little 'natural' about the markets that are supposed to select.

Dominance over product markets allows the manipulation of prices and output in order to secure good and easy profits. These profits need not be maximum profits, but only sufficient to preserve autonomy from the disciplines of the markets for capital and corporate control. If the firm can generate sufficient finance internally for its operations, it need make no obeisance to the capital markets. Thus, as Eichner (1976, Chapter 3) argues, the powerful modern 'megacorp' frees itself from the scrutiny of external lenders, naggingly anxious for the security of their loans and interest payments, by carefully adopting sufficiently profitable oligopolistic pricing policies to permit the internal financing of all its investment needs. Such financial autonomy appears extensive. Although there is considerable international variation in self-financing, Jones (1979, pp. 368–70) has shown that, amongst the advanced industrial nations, UK companies were the most independent from the external capital markets during the 1960s; between 1963 and 1965, their ratio of depreciation and retained earnings to gross fixed asset formation was 130 per cent. Herman (1981, p. 357) notes that US corporations planned to finance 90 per cent of their 1979 capital expenditures by internal funds. Moreover, as even Mintz and Schwartz (1985, Chapter 2) concede, large companies such as IBM have considerable bargaining power over lenders, and the relative power of lending institutions generally varies with the supply and demand of funds so that, as during the late 1970s, they sometimes become desperate to lend on almost any terms.

Shareholders need be no more effective in securing profit-maximization than the capital markets. Again, increasing scale has assisted firms in escaping constraint. As firms have become bigger, their shareholders have become progressively more diffuse and, consequently, less and less capable of efficiently monitoring and sanctioning their managers (Stiglitz, 1985). Shareholder dissatisfaction must now be registered indirectly through the market for corporate control. Here, so the theory goes, non profit-maximizing managements may be penalized by falling share prices and the resulting threat of takeover and displacement (Chiplin and Wright, 1987).

But the effectiveness of even the market for corporate control is mitigated by the growing size and sophistication of modern enterprise. The larger the firm, the less easy it is for potential predators to gather the resources to take it over (Marris, 1964; Lawriwsky, 1984). Indeed, Herman (1981, pp. 99–101) observes that it is often large, ailing companies that takeover small, profitable ones. Further, these large firms can afford to hire the advice and deploy the resources to mount increasingly sophisticated takeover defences: Cooke (1986, Chapter 14) details a formidable array of defence tactics that includes such exotica as 'poison pills', 'shark repellants', 'pac-man strategies' and 'crown jewels'. In 1986, a year of 'merger mania', of sixty-five contested UK takeovers, twenty-four targets escaped (Healey, 1987). With this uncertainty of success, and the cost of failure reaching £50 million in the case of Argyll's bid for Distillers (Chiplin and Wright, 1987), potential predators must be tempted to leave in peace all but the most glaringly under-performing companies. Holl's (1977) study of 343 'Fortune 500' firms during the 1960s demonstrates both the extent of freedom from the market for corporate control and the scope it grants for non profit-maximizing behaviour. Holl found that the average profitabilities of the 118 owner-controlled firms and of the 141 managerial firms subject to the market for corporate control (controlling for size and market structure) were not significantly different at respectively 10.98 per cent and 9.89 per cent; but he also found that no less than 84 (nearly 40 per cent) of the managerially controlled firms were effectively free of the market for corporate control and, moreover, were capable of reporting profits significantly lower at 6.73 per cent.

In short, it appears that the disciplines exerted by product markets, the capital markets and the markets for corporate control are not necessarily strict, and that there may be considerable scope for individual firms to evade or even manipulate them. However, I emphatically do not want to dismiss these markets as irrelevant, safely to be ignored, as many of the strategic choice theorists to be introduced in Chapter 3 are inclined to do. It will be my argument later that these markets not only constrain; they actually extend agency by affording certain privileged actors the resources with which to act. My point now is that in analyzing the strategies of particular firms, we should recognize that the pressures exerted by these three types of market are contingent. Consequently, we need to examine in every case exactly how far each firm has succeeded in blunting or evading these market disciplines.

These environmental determinist arguments stem from and have their strongest base in contemporary neo-classical economics. There, at least, researchers have confined themselves to aggregates, employing econometric models that are not expected to achieve complete empirical 'explanation'. Others have been less bashful. Organizational and strategy theorists in particular have engaged environmental logics to describe and prescribe the conduct of individual enterprises. Although they do differ in their degrees of confidence, we can conclude by teasing out the sort of predictions environmental determinists might make if they were so bold as to examine corporate strategies in recession. Assuming tight constraint, they would tend to dichotomize firms into two groups: there is first the group of firms following the narrow, perhaps monotonic, set of strategies consistent with survival; and then there is the group adopting a potentially far wider range of strategies, but all of which eventually lead to failure and therefore are of no subsequent interest. In recession, as constraint is tightened still further, these theorists would expect surviving firms to display very little diversity in either strategy or performance. They would seek to explain any diversity that did exist primarily by reference to variations in the precise nature of the firms' environments. The internal characteristics of surviving firms would be of secondary interest for, whether by conscious adaptation or by accidental adoption they must all somehow have conformed.

But I have argued that constraint need not be so tight. And if constraint is not absolute – for instance, if certain firms do have some control over their product markets and are to some degree independent of shareholders and the capital markets – then the conduct of all survivors can no longer be presumed to accord with the dictates of the environment. It must be conceded that firms may have a margin of discretion in which they can exercise initiative, even to the extent of manipulating the environments that are supposed to discipline them. If this initiative is to be understood, then the analysis should no longer confine itself to the tramlines represented by external constraint, but return inside the firm to the actors themselves.

CONCLUSIONS

This chapter has critically reviewed the implications for the study of recession strategy of a number of influential determinist positions. Though environmental and action determinists have generally concurred in predicting that firms operating in similar environments will tend to adopt similar strategies when confronted by a common threat, for example recession, certain distinctions need to be made. Natural selectionists expect that only those firms paying strict and immediate obedience to environmental demands will survive, and that all others fail; the acutely competitive conditions of recession should make the demands of natural selection still more severe than usual. Adaptationists differ in holding a rather more relaxed view of the environment – for Williamson and Ouchi (1981), selection might take as long as ten years – but they would grant that the pressures for conformity are strengthened by recession. Action determinists have less need to emphasize the punitive or coercive aspects of environmental constraint; for them the environment simply provides inputs which, without dissent, are translated by internal mechanisms into appropriate responses. Aside from distinguishing between such broad 'types' as managers and owners, conformity is unproblematic.

Action and environmental determinists clearly diverge on how to explain this strategic conformity – one set letting the environment do most of the work, the other the internal dispositions of the actors themselves. None the less, the methodological implications of each position are similar. They agree there is little need to delve deeply inside the firm to examine the understandings and motives of particular decision-makers or to seek for dispute between them. For natural selectionists, such things are irrelevant; for adaptationists, internal affairs are secondary and can be subsumed under general assumptions of rationality, whether bounded or perfect; while for action determinists these matters are resolved simply by identifying the prevailing social or psychological type and assuming unity. Thus the research is simplified.

However, this simplicity depends on the assumptions that environment and identities are given and that they tightly regulate conduct. This chapter has argued against both assumptions. Against the psychologistic determinists, it has been denied that human behaviour can be derived directly from innate psychologies with no intervention by social forces; against the over-socializing perspective, it has not only been doubted whether social pressures really do wholly overwhelm the individual psyche but it has also been suggested that these social forces are constituted in the first place by actions stemming from individual actors' own interpretations. None of this would matter if environmental constraint could be counted on to regulate actions anyway. Unfortunately, however, there is plenty of evidence to conclude that the economic constraints represented particularly by the product markets, the capital markets and the market for corporate control are, for many firms, not only loose but controllable.

In sum, neither of the action-filtering mechanisms set out in Elster's (1984) model are sufficiently tight to produce determinate outcomes. The task of the following chapters, therefore, is to propose a theory of strategic choice that ceases to treat internal selection mechanisms or external constraints as given, but instead conceives of actors as reproducing and transforming their environments through their own agency.

Chapter Three

Towards strategic choice

INTRODUCTION

Starting from Elster's (1984) 'two-step' model of human action, the preceding chapter argued that neither those filters embodied in actors' own action-selection mechanisms nor those represented by environmental constraint should be conceived of as given and all-determining. However, Chapter 2 also admitted that an adequate theory of strategic choice would have to ground itself on accounts of both human action-selection processes and environments each capable of supporting non-determinate outcomes. Strategic decision-makers should exercise at least some control over themselves and their surroundings. It will be the chief argument of this chapter that existing accounts of strategic choice have failed quite to satisfy these two criteria.

The chapter begins by introducing two traditions – those of the Carnegie School and of Action Theory – which have been highly influential in recent writings on strategic choice. While allowing that both these traditions have provided significant insights, I shall conclude that they fail to provide accounts of either actor or structure that are wholly adequate to a theory of strategic choice. The chapter goes on to review three recent approaches to strategic choice: the 'Management Types' approach, the French 'Socio-Historical School' and the emergent 'Contextualist' studies. Each of these approaches offers theoretical and methodological advances important to the Realist position that I shall propose in the following chapters. However, I shall contend that their continued reliance on the traditions represented by the Carnegie School and Action Theory tends finally to compromise the human agency essential to strategic choice.

ANTECEDENTS TO A THEORY OF STRATEGIC CHOICE

This part of the chapter discusses the influential work of the Carnegie School and the Action Theorists. It argues that the former, while groping towards a useful conception of the firm's relations with its economic environment, fails to found its position on an adequate theory of human action; and that the latter, in emphasizing action, is unable to provide a convincing account of environmental structure.

The Carnegie School

Stimulated by the implications of oligopoly, Cyert and March (1956, p. 45) wrote that: 'A general theory of the firm will have to contain variables related both to the external environment and the internal organization.' Here they seemed to recognize the dual demands put on an adequate theory of strategic choice: the need for, on the one hand, analysis of the origins of action within the firm and, complementary to this, an understanding of the environment in which this action can be effective. This dual demand was acknowledged in two key concepts – organizational slack and organizational coalitions – that would recur repeatedly in the subsequent strategic choice literature.

The concept of organizational slack draws attention to the firm's relationship with its environment. Although the tendency in recent writings has been to concentrate on slack as an internal phenomenon, consisting of surplus resources accumulated by the organization (Bourgeois, 1981; Marino and Lange, 1983), the concept's significance can be better appreciated if traced back to its origins in Cyert and March's (1956, p. 45) discussion of oligopoly; here they defined organizational slack simply as a firm's 'neglected opportunities for profit'. This definition helps widen the focus to include, as well as the accumulated fat within the organization, the market opportunities beyond it. At the same time, it draws attention to the nature of those economic conditions which release the firm from the imperatives of profit-maximization – for example the oligopolistic domination of product markets – so that they *can* choose whether to pursue or neglect every opportunity for additional profit. Thus organizational slack is certainly a property of organizations but it is also conditional upon the external circumstances in which organizations place themselves. Its significance lies as much in what it reflects as in what it is. In sum, an understanding of the strategic discretion represented by the presence of organizational slack requires analysis of the firm's relationship to its market environment.

If the concept of organizational slack turns attention to the environmental conditions necessary for strategic choice, the concept of 'organizational coalition' provides a step towards understanding the processes by which the goals for strategy are formed in the first place. The emphasis on organizations as coalitions arose from Cyert and March's (1963, p. 23) proposition that only individuals can have goals while collectivities cannot, yet that any discussion of organizational strategy presumes some conception of organizational goals. Cyert and March resolve this paradox by proposing a view of organizations as coalitions of individuals, each seeking to satisfy their own particular goals. These individuals use political processes to create bargains, in the form of policy side-payments as well as monetary rewards, which together represent an agreed definition of the organization's goals as a whole. Thus, for Cyert and March (1963, p. 30), it makes little more sense to argue that the goal of a business is to make profit than to say it is to maximize the salary of the assistant janitor. Thompson (1967, p. 128) develops this view somewhat by distinguishing 'dominant coalitions', that is, those groupings within the coalition whose goals currently have pre-eminence within the organization.

Cyert and March (1963, p. 117) stress that these bargains only achieve a quasi-resolution of conflict. This quasi-resolution is possible because of the bounded nature of human rationality (March and Simon, 1958, pp. 169–71). In a complex world, humans are seen as being constantly confronted by uncertainty on account of the limited and biased ways in which they seek and use information. In order to minimize uncertainty, humans develop and rely on sets of standard operating procedures and decision rules which stabilize organizational goals. They do not fully resolve differences in goals because at any one time they are incapable of attending to all their goals; because they do not notice inconsistencies between their goals and those of others; and because their aspirations towards their goals may well be below the levels actually achievable. However, environmental change can provoke renewed political contest over organizational goals by drawing attention towards previously neglected goals, to inconsistencies between goals or to higher levels of feasible goal achievement. March and Simon (1958, pp. 120–1) specifically cite recession as likely to be associated with intensified intraorganizational conflict. Moreover, environmental change, as it demonstrates their adequacy or otherwise, stimulates adjustment of aspiration levels, operating procedures and decision rules in line with experience – the process of organizational 'learning' (Cyert and March, 1963, p. 100).

This theoretical construction of the firm was important because it revealed and made central internal political processes whose existence action determinists tended to disclaim and whose relevance environmental determinists denied. It was significant, too, in that it proposed a means of understanding the possibility and origins of organizational idiosyncrasy. Each firm's bargaining processes are supposed to produce unique and fairly stable sets of goals which, codified in decision rules, would provide the direction to its own unique strategy. Not only had the Carnegie School thus broken free of the general models typical of neo-classical and managerial economics; by emphasizing the prevalence of organizational slack they had also shown that environmental constraint was not normally so tight as to render a diverse range of strategies impossible. However, important though this contribution was, it did retain a number of limitations – not least that, while producing an account of idiosyncrasy, it had still not achieved indeterminacy.

These limits of the Carnegie School derive from a notion of the individual that is at once exaggerated and impoverished. Irretrievably individualistic, the Carnegie authors abstract their actors atomistically from their social relations (Whitley, 1977, pp. 173–4). Thus, for instance, power is seen as the property of the individual actor rather than of social relationships (Hickson *et al.*, 1971, p. 217); explanation of its exercise is reduced persistently to the narrow terms of socio-psychology (Perrow, 1970, p. 84); and conflict, while being given a central place, is yet portrayed as being merely over individual values and cognitive differences (Pettigrew, 1973, p. 28; Tinker, 1986). The environment is reduced to no more than a source of stimuli, external and uninvolved in the constitution of the organizations and the actors themselves. There is no social analysis of how access to organizations is structured; of the origins of the goals individuals bring to them; or of the foundations of the power they exercise in pursuit of these goals. The key sociological variables of class, gender and ethnicity are apparently irrelevant both to dominant coalitions' membership and to their motivation.   .

But while exaggerating the independence of their actors from society, the Carnegie School also denies them the intrinsic capacity to use this autonomy freely. In the first place, actors' ability to formulate clear goals and to pursue them deliberately is effectively suppressed by the repeated stress upon the inherent limitations of human cognition. Actors are trapped on every side by bounded rationality (March and Simon, 1958), ambiguity (March and Olsen, 1976) and processual limits (Quinn, 1980). Confessing their incapacity to cope with a complex world, actors surrender their freedom of choice and abandon themselves to the reassuring simplicity of standard operating procedures and decision rules. It is with some satisfaction that Cohen, March and Olsen (1976, p. 37) conclude that 'events are not dominated by intention'.

At the same time, the Carnegie authors' individualism encourages them to lapse towards an ambiguous form of action determinism. March and Simon (1958, p. 9) explicitly combine 'the simultaneous influences of nature and nurture' in their psychological postulates of organizational behaviour. According to them, in any particular short period, individuals' actions are explicable in terms of the internal states they bring to their situations and the environmental stimuli generated by these situations. Internal states are functions of individuals' whole previous histories and – as 'memories' – provide the programs for response. In this way, even the creativity of Mozart is reduced to the building and recognizing of established patterns derived from experience (Simon, 1983). Translating to the higher level of the organization, Cyert and March (1963, p. 119) offer a similar dynamic 'feedback-react' system, in which organizations simply await upon environmental stimuli to provide problems according to which they passively apply and obediently adapt their operating procedures and decision rules.

As Allison (1971, p. 67) observes, these accounts explain behaviour less as series of deliberate choices, more as simple outputs of regulated processes. Action is programmed according to past events imposed upon actors by an arbitrary environment. The focus is on purely short-term adaptation (Loasby, 1968, p. 362) – there is no admission that individuals might wilfully choose over long periods to pursue particular goals or to maintain unrealistic aspiration levels in the face of all contrary experience (Crozier and Friedberg, 1977, p. 19). In their simple model of the human actor as detached from society, social identities or loyalties are not allowed to insert any obstacles to pliant adaptation. Without tension between the psychological and the social, there can be none of the internal complexities and antagonisms necessary for either perverse resistance or inspired creativity (cf. Martin, Kleindorfer and Brashes, 1987, p. 71).

In sum, the Carnegie School's individualism is fatal in two respects to the agency that is the precondition for genuine strategic choice. On the one hand, its exclusion of social structure renders mysterious the means by which certain actors attain the power to make and act upon decisions while others simply obey. On the other, the denial of social identities and the emphasis upon psychology – especially cognition – deprives actors of any stubborn internal complexities and conflicts, reducing them instead to endless, though often inefficient, compliance.

Thus, as Machlup (1974, pp. 282–3) comments, the Carnegie School arrives at what he calls a 'behavioural determinism'; in a complex world, and constrained by bounded rationality, it may not be possible to predict them, but actions are nevertheless governed by the two determining independent variables of memory and stimulus. The Carnegie authors fail to interrupt the ineluctable processes of their 'feedback-react' systems by any possibility of autonomous control over either program or environment.

Action Theory

ın contrast to the Carnegie School, with its tendency towards reducing human action to reactive learning machines, the Action positions developed by Weick (1969) and Silverman (1970) insist on the active capacities of human agents. As Silverman (1970, p. 129) puts it: 'The action of men stems from a network of meanings which they themselves construct and of which they are conscious . . . Thus they may respond differently to the same objectively-defined stimulus.' However, these meanings are not wholly idiosyncratic, but become socially sustained, providing actors with shared stocks of knowledge and expectations of conduct. The protection of these shared stocks of knowledge inhibits reaction and adaptation to environmental change. According to Weick (1969, pp. 13–4), actors coalesce around certain shared activities and 'having done so, they retain these attitudes, even if they prove maladaptive, because they *are* shared and they provide a stable basis for shared actions'. Unlike the well-behaved actors of the Carnegie School, those of Action Theory can refuse to 'learn'.

But if the Action Theorists make an explicit and extensively argued case for the intrinsic human potential for agency, in their conception of the environment they actually risk subverting it. On the face of it, they engage in a vigorous repudiation of environmental determinism. Following Berger and Luckman (1967, pp. 106–7), Weick (1969) and Silverman (1970) both abjure the 'reification' of environmental constraint characteristic of the environmental determinists. Weick (1969, p. 28) proposes instead: 'the environment is a phenomenon tied to processes of attention and . . . unless something is attended to it does not exist.' Accordingly, 'Rather than talking about adapting to an external environment, it may be more correct to argue that organizing consists of adapting to an enacted environment, an environment which is *constituted by* the actions of interdependent human actors' (Weick, 1969, p. 23). This voluntarist insistence that constraint is artificial is repeated by Silverman (1970, p. 141): 'The Action frame of reference argues that man is constrained by the way he socially constructs his reality.' Such a view makes a nonsense of environmental determinism, for 'the human actor does not *react* to an environment; he *enacts* it' (Weick, 1969, p. 64).

Although Weick (1985) has recently admitted some (unspecified) temporal limits to environmental enactment, others have seized gratefully on the notion as the stick with which to beat the environmental determinists (for example, Huff, 1982; Smircich, 1983; Smircich and Stubbart, 1985; Ford and Baucus, 1987). In the process, enactment has increasingly lost its social character and become more and more the achievement of small, strangely autonomous decision-making teams or even individuals. As one of the most influential of recent Action Theorists has put it: 'Human actors do not know or perceive *the* world, but know and perceive *their* world . . . People enact their reality either individually or in concert with others' (Smircich, 1983, p. 161). From harsh constraint, environments have been pacified into pliant 'contexts'. According to Smircich and Stubbart (1985, p. 727):

> Environment refers to the ecological context of thought and action, which is not independent of the observer-actor's theories, experiences and tastes. Multiple groups of people enact the ecological context; neither historical necessity nor the operation of inexorable social laws imposes it upon them. From the standpoint of strategic management, strategists' social knowledge constitutes their environment.

Environments do not determine, because they are the creations of the actors themselves.

The constitutive significance given here to actors' own knowledge has epistemological and methodological implications. If each actor enacts his or her own 'context', then in each case researchers should try to establish an interpretive understanding of their personal world-views. They must acknowledge the possibility of 'multiple realities' and, moreover, respect them by engaging in 'empathetic ethnography' (Smircich, 1983; 1985). Empathy is essential, for there exists no 'objective social world' that would enable researchers to judge the realism of actors' own realities (Feldman, 1986, p. 589). The same logic applies to differences within social science itself: social scientists must respect each others' paradigms, forebearing from criticism, for the irretrievably subjective nature of knowledge precludes objective choice between them (Astley, 1985, p. 500). Berg (1985, p. 298) sums up the voluntaristic and relativistic implications of Action Theory for corporate strategy when he proposes:

the enlargement of the environment concept from domains and niches
to contexts, thereby indicating the symbolic and relativistic character
of the reality in which organizations choose to exist.

In denying the independence of social structures from human action,
Action Theorists powerfully refute the absolute tyranny of markets
avered by the environmental determinists. Unfortunately, however,
not all constraint can be swept away into some stock of shared
meanings. At the least, there are certain physical constraints: 'It
matters to social action that we live in a planet with grass and uranium,
rain and volcanoes, baboons and bacteria . . . that our fellows differ in
strength, colour and wits' (Hollis, 1977, p. 187). Action Theory
indulges in an idealist neglect of the material and the physical. Thus
the need for a firm to make a profit in order to survive derives not
simply from arbitrary and artificial meanings or rules, but also from the
material requirements of depreciating capital equipment which, for
action to continue, must be fuelled, maintained and ultimately
replaced.

With this assertion of environmental constraint I do not intend to
give the game away to the environmental determinists – indeed, quite
the opposite. From Elster's 'two step' model I earlier deduced that
strategic choice requires conceptions of both the actor and the
environment that are each capable of supporting human agency.
Action Theory certainly provides a sophisticated appreciation of the
human potential for agency; what it lacks is an account of the means
by which this potential can be realized. Insisting that social structure is
produced only by human activity, the Action Theorists seem to offer a
pleasingly libertarian view of the world, one in which all are equally
agents. The actor is placed before society and agency is independent of
the social. But, I shall argue, this is utopianism of a self-defeating
kind. In their emphatic dismissal of environmental constraint, they also
destroy the structural resources that *enable* action. Action Theorists
risk the same destructuring of society as that of the economists, and
with the same conservative results. Further, this Action Theoretical
derogation of structural constraint not only trivializes agency; it
actually impedes its extension. Let me elaborate.

Certainly – and this is the great insight of Action Theory – society
could not exist without human activity. However, these theorists fail to
recognize the converse, that society also forms the pre-condition for
action (Bhaskar, 1979, pp. 42–3). Human action is organized and its
scope enlarged by existing collective institutions – governments,
political parties, corporations, trade unions and families. Agency is
governed by actors' access to these institutions and by their power to

direct them according to their own purposes. This access and this power are not available equally to all but are socially structured. In capitalist and patriarchal societies, agency is a privilege concentrated in the hands of the wealthy and the male. It is they who 'enact' environments, and they are able to do so because pre-existing social structures have given them the institutional resources – including the labour of other actors – to do so. In short, it is precisely because of structure that some are agents and others are not.

The condition for this narrow concentration of power is that those excluded continue in passive collaboration with, or even blissful ignorance of, the structures that deny them agency. Here Action Theory is in danger of achieving quite the opposite to the voluntarism it intends. Emphasizing the subjectivity and continuous creation of the social world, Action Theorists risk conveying the impression that structural constraint is self-imposed, even the product of imagination. They approach perilously close to the Schutzian fallacy that 'the empirical ego can change the world merely by constituting it in a different way' (Outhwaite, 1983b, p. 95). This is an invitation to arm-chair politics indeed. But the Action Theorists go on to undermine even such a confined politics as this by their commitment to empathetic, interpretive understanding and their denial of any objective social world capable of supporting critical judgement.

Far from promoting free activity, Action Theory's deferential relativism is profoundly disabling. Privileging actors' own understandings, these authors tend towards a 'phenomenological reductionism' (Giddens, 1976, p. 31) that attributes significance only to what their subjects themselves perceive. Unfortunately, however, reliance upon actors' own subjective understandings need give no insight into structures that they do not recognize or, even, acknowledge. Consciously self-serving or not, managers in particular are unlikely to admit that their power depends upon privileged education or merely gender. They would be especially reluctant to expose the conditions for their power to those over whom they exercise it. But Action Theory sets managerial interpretations beyond challenge by subordin-ates and peers alike. By providing no secure, independent basis for legitimate criticism, the Action Theorists deprive actors within organizations of any means for choosing between different interpreta-tions of their worlds. There can be no reasonable grounds for actors to declare the interpretations of their fellows' wrong and to attempt then to persuade them of the validity of their own. Without the right to criticize, reasonable debate is precluded and the possibility of internally generated rational reform foreclosed (Gellner, 1973, p. 61).

Outside observers are no less handicapped. For them especially, without even the status of participants, the principle of empathetic understanding obliges them to defer to their subjects' own interpretations. Rather than arrogantly mediating between right and wrong, the Action Theorists enjoin researchers to retreat to a higher sphere of passive neutrality. But no such detachment is tenable; in refusing to offer the truths capable of extending human agency, the Action Theorists effectively collude with the perpetuation of the ideological errors and oppression that curtail it (cf. Sayer, 1984, p. 43).

Action Theory does have the virtue of consistency. Not content to abandon just its subjects to their own misunderstandings, it embroils social science itself in the same irresolvable confusions. Each paradigm is declared sacrosanct. But Action Theory's relativistic tolerance is inherently self-destructive. By their claim for the exclusivity of rival paradigms, they seek immunity from all external criticism, withdrawing themselves, ostrich-like, from intellectual debate. Yet it is by engaging in critical examination and debate that ideas are advanced and refined; in retreating from the arena, the relativists inflict upon themselves intellectual complacency and decay (O'Sullivan, 1987, pp. 25–9). Though made at the risk of internal degeneration, this withdrawal fails even to secure Action Theory externally. As Tinker (1986, p. 380) warns, there is no 'fair horse race' between competing paradigms. Attractive though its plea for tolerance is, in a world characterized by multitudes of oppressive and self-aggrandizing ideas, relativism amounts to an act of resignation and surrender.

RECENT STUDIES OF STRATEGIC CHOICE

The last decade or so has seen a surge of interest in the issue of corporate strategic choice. Initial stimulus was provided by the publication of John Child's (1972) paper on 'The role of strategic choice', a comprehensive critique of the determinism inherent in contingency theory. For the empirical work that followed, this theoretical paper has been an essential reference point. Unfortunately, however, Child's (1972) own dependence upon the Carnegie and Action traditions would be reproduced in much of the research that he inspired.

Against the statistical methodologies characteristic of the prevailing contingency theorists, Child (1972, p. 2) argued for 'processual and change-orientated' research that accommodated the 'agency of choice'. Following Cyert and March (1963) and Thompson (1967), he focused on the way in which strategic decisions were taken by 'dominant coalitions' within organizations. Stressing that power is unevenly distributed within organizations, Child argued that the key to understanding strategic choices was to examine those with the 'power of initiation'. Thus, the 'dominant coalition concept draws attention to the question of who is making the choice' (Child, 1972, p. 14). Further, dominant coalitions are not subject to their environments (or technologies) because they are capable of choosing them or even, citing Weick (1969), of 'enacting' them (Child, 1972, p. 10). They are therefore able to manipulate or satisfice on performance standards and to pursue other objectives but maximum profit in the form of 'slack' (Child, 1972, p. 12). Child (1972, p. 16) concluded:

> In short, when incorporating strategic choice in a theory of organization, one is recognizing the operation of an essentially political process in which constraints and opportunities are functions of the power exercised by decision-makers in the light of ideological values.

Thus organizational politics become central to the processes of strategic choice.

The three sets of research that I shall introduce in this section pursue the themes that Child identified in 1972. In particular, statistical aggregation has been displaced by detailed, longitudinal case studies demonstrating the idiosyncrasy of strategic choice and change. Studies have tended to focus internally upon the organizational politics and perceptual differences of top management teams, externally upon the economic slack that buffers them from strict obedience to environmental contingencies. But also, just as for Child (1972) himself, all three sets of research remain heavily indebted to the Carnegie and Action Theory traditions. I shall examine first the 'Management Types' approach associated particularly with Miles and Snow (1978); then the less prolific but more independent 'Socio-historical School', confined so far to France; and finally the 'Contextualists', whose careful case study method was firmly established by Pettigrew (1985). Important though all this work has been, I shall argue that none has produced a fully convincing account of either actors or environments capable of supporting a theory of strategic choice.

Management Types and strategic choice

This early generation of research addressed itself primarily to refuting environmental determinism, typically by demonstrating the coexistence of diverse strategies within the same industry. Drawing equally on the Carnegie School and Action Theory, these researchers would typically stress both the organizational slack that permitted strategic choice and the importance of strategic decision-makers' perceptions in guiding choice within their environments (Hambrick and Mason, 1984). Boundedly rational, decision-makers perceptions were generally treated as constrained by their particular sets of experience and expertise. These cognitive characteristics defined basic management types, often described simply in terms of functional background. The ascendancy of particular types within a dominant coalition would be explained by reference to 'coalition bargaining'.

One early piece of work was Miller and Friesen's (1978) factor analysis of eighty-one business case histories yielding ten 'archetypes of strategy formulation'. These archetypes were defined in terms of variables such as managerial tenure, team spirit and decision-making style. Noting that different archetypes – for instance, 'Adaptive Firms Under Moderate Challenge' and 'Innovators' – appeared capable of coexisting in similar environments, Miller and Friesen (1978) concluded against environmental determinism and for strategic choice. Similarly, Gupta (1980), on the basis of a forty-year comparative study of strategic decisions and organizational 'learning' in food-retailing firms, argued that the emergence of different strategies in the same industrial environments confounded the predictions of environmental determinists and demanded explanation in terms of the choices and perceptions of the retailers' senior managements.

However, the most influential formulation of the management archetype approach has been that of R. E. Miles and Snow (1978). Drawing on a large number of illustrative case studies, Miles and Snow (1978, pp. 20–2) propose that there are three basic kinds of problem to which the organization must adapt: the entrepreneurial problem, consisting of the definition and development of organizational domains; the engineering problem, the creation of technology systems for efficient operation in these domains; and the administrative problem, the building of structures and processes allowing constant rationalization of existing systems and the evolution of new domains and systems. Miles and Snow (1978, p. 29) echo the Action Theorists in arguing that firms solve these three adaptive problems according to the particular perceptions of their boundedly rational top management teams:

the dominant coalition largely enacts or creates the organization's relevant environment. That is, the organization responds largely to what its management perceives; those environmental conditions that go unnoticed or are deliberately ignored have little effect on management's decisions and actions.

The potentially idiosyncratic nature of managerial perceptions renders it 'theoretically possible that no two organizational strategies will be the same', even within the same industrial environments (Miles and Snow, 1978, p. 28).

This represents a significant blow against the conformity enforced by environmental determinism. None the less, these two authors do detect certain general patterns of organizational strategy which they reduce to four archetypes: Defenders, with narrow domains and devoted to efficiency; Prospectors, less efficient in existing domains but flexible, continually searching for and experimenting in new domains; Analysers, operating in both stable domains and changing ones; and Reactors, confronted by change but incapable of responding effectively (Miles and Snow, 1978, pp. 29–30). Each of these types possess dominant coalitions of top managers, characterized by different 'distinctive competences' with respect to the entrepreneurial, engineering and administration problems. These distinctive competences are defined in terms of their functional experiences and skills. Thus in Defender organizations, the dominant coalition will give pre-eminence to financial and production experts; in Prospectors, dominance will go to marketing and R & D specialists; while Analysers, having to meet the adaptive problems of both Defenders and Prospectors in their different domains, will be dominated by marketing, applied research and production.

Miles and Snow's (1978) claim that these four archetypes are capable of coexisting within the same industry – in apparent contradiction to the claims of the environmental determinists – has stimulated statistical testing as well as the process, change-orientated research urged by Child (1972). In a questionnaire survey of four industries, Snow and Hrebiniak (1980) concluded against environmental determinism by finding that all four types, as defined by their dominant coalitions' distinctive competences, were capable of coexisting in the same industries. Hambrick (1983), in another large-scale statistical survey, likewise found the four types widely coexisting in the same industries, discovering also quite significant differences in the performances of Prospectors and Defenders. Meyer (1982a; 1982b) went rather further, combining quantitative techniques with case studies in order to analyze how different types of hospital reacted to the same crisis of a threatened strike. He argued that the different 'ideologies' of each type shaped their responses: for instance, the Defender 'Memorial'

hospital was inflexible, while the Analyser 'General' hospital anticipated and adjusted well.

However, the most ambitious attempt to apply this model has been
the historical study by R. H. Miles and Cameron (1982) of American
tobacco companies' adaptation and learning in response to the
common challenge of decline in the cigarette market. Miles and
Cameron (1982) analyzed the relationship between the 'strategic
dispositions' and actual strategies of four of these companies in terms
of Miles and Snow's (1978) strategic types. For example, the two
researchers describe how Philip Morris, the Prospector, was the first of
the tobacco companies to diversify and go overseas. Miles and
Cameron (1982, p. 118) cite such geographical and product diversification as instances of these companies' capacity to 'create' or 'enact'
their 'domains', here giving Weick's concept a far more concrete sense
than the merely perceptual. The two authors are also more concrete
than Miles and Snow (1978) in describing how organizational slack in
the form of oligopoly and financial reserves enhanced the strategic
discretion of these firms. They do not even confine their analysis to
economic slack, but also consider the governmental goodwill and
contacts that gave the tobacco companies sufficient 'political slack'
(pp. 249–50) to stymie and outmanoeuvre increasingly hostile anti-
smoking campaigns.

This interest in the connection between management types and
strategic choices has not been confined to the United States. Indeed,
the English economist Edith Penrose (1980, pp. 79–80) in many ways
anticipated the Miles and Snow (1978) approach when she stressed
how the firm's existing resources, especially those embodied in the
managerial team, would influence the direction of strategy:

> I have placed the emphasis on the significance of the resources with
> which a firm works and on the development of the experience and
> knowledge of a firm's personnel, because these are the factors that
> will, to a large extent, determine the response of the firm to changes
> in the external world and also determine what it 'sees' in the external
> world.

Since first being advanced in the 1950s this Penrosian approach has
recently gained new disciples (for example, Slater, 1980; Odagiri,
1984), with Moss (1981) in particular using it as the basis for
constructing a new economic theory of business strategy. Moss (1981,
pp. 29–30) abandons Penrose's residual commitment to profit-
maximizing assumptions, retaining only the weak assumption that
managers will strive towards whatever goals they have in the way that
best maximizes chances of survival. However, he echoes Penrose with

his emphasis on the 'focusing effects' (1981, pp. 51–9) of resource and administrative imbalances within the firm as determining the direction in which these goals are pursued. Again, the knowledge, skills and experience of managerial and other human resources are important for focusing on particular opportunities. This Penrosian renewal has found empirical expression in Gunz and Whitley's (1985) study of four British firms, which demonstrated how different career structures and experiences shaped their managements' reactions to the recession of the early 1980s. Firms characterized by 'specialist' managements tended to respond by adopting strategies of consolidation and rationalization, while 'generalists', with wider experiences, were more inclined to respond by divestment and new business search.

Boswell (1983) stands a little apart theoretically, but grants a similar importance to managerial characteristics in his substantial account of strategic choices made by three steel companies between 1914 and 1939. He argues (1983, pp. 14–5) that particular individuals express their personal 'deep-seated orientations' (stemming from upbringing, education and career experience) through the various strategies they pursue. Boswell (1983, pp. 8–11) suggests that there are three basic 'dominant pursuits' in these strategies: those of 'growth' and 'efficiency' – closely corresponding with Miles and Snow's (1978) Prospector and Defender types – and the more altruistic pursuit of 'social action'. Company strategies alternate between these pursuits in phases, with occasional periods of 'indeterminacy' (reminiscent of Reactors), according to the orientations of their top management. Rejecting the notion of firms as 'bobbing on the economic waves', Boswell (1983, p. 15) argues: 'If the phases roughly correspond to chief executive tenures, they would often last for 10 or 20 years: longer therefore than most economic cycles'. Thus companies appeared to be under no strong compulsion to adjust their managerial 'orientations' to changing economic circumstances. Citing especially the example of Dorman Long, where even in the depths of the Great Depression the 84-year-old Sir Arthur Dorman could be replaced by the 87-year-old Sir Hugh Bell, Boswell concludes (1983, p. 111): 'the restricted influence of economic fluctuations on the [top management] change-overs is clear. Capital market disciplines were weak. Even top management ill-attuned to the new circumstances possessed a remarkable ability to ride out the depression.'

By demonstrating the potential for diverse strategies within the same industry environments, these authors have gone some way to denting environmental determinism. However, in neglecting the implications of different degrees of diversification and integration, they have not so far allowed for the sort of explanations for industry heterogeneity advanced by the strategic group theorists. More fatal is that, in accounting for the selection of diverse strategies in the first place, these authors do not quite secure themselves from the lingering influence of action determinism. True, they no longer rely upon such crude distinctions as between 'managers' and 'owners'; but it is not clear that the mere proliferation of types according to functional experience – 'marketing managers', 'financial managers' and so on – provides any great advance. Members of these types remain simple beings, like Economic Men, abstracted from their wider social relations and apparently without experience, identities or interests outside the organization. They are 'marketing managers' or 'financial managers', and no more. However far these organizational theorists may have advanced beyond the early crude simplicities of economics, they still hold fundamentally to the same untenable reduction. As Karpik (1978, p. 53) protests, '"Organization Man" is just as much a fiction as "homo economicus". An individual does not go from one world to another when he leaves his private life and enters his work life.' Managers have social identities – in our society, they are mostly male, white and middle-class. The influence of these characteristics, so important to their having achieved managerial status in the first place, can hardly be supposed to dissolve away in all their subsequent activities. Yet this is precisely what these 'Management Type' theorists seem to imply, for they persistently marginalize the social structural identities and resources that motivate and empower actors in their activities, both in their organizations and beyond. The American researchers especially are confined by the Carnegie tradition to portraying actors as asocial beings, busily engaged in functional concerns and constantly prey to bounded rationality. Their stress on bounded rationality – cognition at the expense of values – is ultimately fatal to the agency necessary for strategic choice. Trapped within the limits of their functional experience, these actors do not choose; they do what they do because that is all they know how to do.

The Socio-Historical School

Just as Child was publishing his influential 1972 paper, Lucien Karpik produced his own distinctive declaration in favour of strategic choice. Karpik's (1972a and 1972b) papers have stimulated a school of research whose very title proclaims its concern for the wider implications of strategic choice. None the less, Karpik (1972b) refers to a manuscript version of Child's (1972) paper and, crucially, does not escape the influence of the Carnegie School.

Karpik (1972b, p. 93) echoes Cyert and March (1956) in emphasizing the need to comprehend both the internal and external: 'Interpreting the deliberate activities of the firm cannot be done by partial correlations; one must study simultaneously the internal forces within the organization and the external conditions of the collective activity' (my translation). Internally Karpik (1972b) portrays these enterprises as run by '*gouvernement prives*' ('governing cliques'; my translation), groups of top decision-makers, similar to 'dominant coalitions', who compete amongst each other to impose their particular 'logics of action' on strategy. Karpik (1972b) defines these logics of action in terms of broad, often functional issues – that is production or sales – as well as simple profit-maximization. For the functional managers associated with particular logics of action, the struggle to achieve primacy for their own logic of action over strategic decision-making is not motivated by corporate concerns but by pursuit of narrow sectional self-interest.

While his account of internal political battles between different management functions advances little beyond the Carnegie approach, Karpik does radically break with traditional economistic conceptions of the firm in its environment. Thus externally, the contemporary 'large technological enterprise' has not only secured substantial freedom from market pressures by self-financing and the domination of product markets, it has also organized R & D in order to acquire new, more pervasive powers through an increasing monopoly over knowledge. The importance of knowledge in contemporary life, and its control by these large technological enterprises, suffice to define a new phase for society as a whole: 'technological capitalism'. Under technological capitalism, shareholders, consumers and the state alike are subject to a new 'imperialism' exercised by the unaccountable governing cliques in control of the large technological enterprises of our society. So immense is the scope of these large enterprises that, according to Karpik (1972a, p. 324), they constitute a new object of study, one which must break with old academic distinctions, and combine together all the various insights of economics, political science, sociology and history of science.

The chief empirical outcome of Karpik's numerous theoretical manifestoes have been Bauer and Cohen's (1981) *Qui Gouverne les Groupes Industriels?* and Cohen and Bauer's (1985) *Les Grandes Manoeuvres Industrielles*. Both books address the political implications of corporate strategic discretion, but the first provides the closer focus upon the actual processes of, and conditions for, strategy choice. In this book the two authors studied how the historical evolution of four large French firms revealed what they term '*pouvoir industriel*' – that is, the companies' ability to define for themselves the nature of their activities (Bauer and Cohen, 1981, pp. 37–9). Echoing the proposals of Action Theory, Bauer and Cohen (1981, p. 36) argue that this phenomenon of 'industrial power' should be understood by means of an ethnographic, historical and interpretive approach that establishes each firm in its specificity. In the event, Bauer and Cohen (1981) are only able to present rather piecemeal case studies. In particular, they offer little interpretive understanding of the perceptions and motivations of key decision-makers. None the less, however shadowy in terms of positive motives, their governing cliques are portrayed as constantly battling to safeguard their strategic autonomy against the claims, externally, of banks, shareholders, the state and consumers and internally of their own subordinate managers. Abandoning the pluralism of Cyert and March and Karpik, Bauer and Cohen (1981) describe their governing cliques as constituting a distinct and fiercely exclusive class, ruthlessly manipulating recruitment, promotion, information and organizational structure in order to secure the obedience of their powerless junior and middle managers (Bauer and Cohen, 1981; Bauer and Cohen, 1983a). The environment is no less ruthlessly dominated. Exploiting their control over science and technology, governing cliques manage markets and – a theme picked out at more length in Cohen and Bauer (1985) – bamboozle the state in order to frustrate all attempts at control. Bauer and Cohen (1981, p. 39) emphatically repudiate environmental determinism when they conclude:

> In sum, one should understand its [the contemporary large firm's] environment not as a given imposed on it, but as a system of actors of which it is a member itself, whose rules it can define, and which it can even structure if it is dominant (my translation).

Context and process in strategic choice

However stimulating the sweeping scope of the Socio-Historical School, it has so far failed to substantiate its rhetoric with entirely convincing investigations into the processes of strategic choice. The emergent Contextualist approach, associated particularly with the universities of Aston and Warwick, manages quite the opposite. With their solid empiricism, these Contextualist researchers have penetrated deep into their subjects, achieving detailed and empathetic understandings of their companies. However, the deeper they have burrowed and the greater the empathy of their accounts, the more their concerns have become confined to those of the companies themselves.

Using extensive interviews, given access to internal documentary data and even engaging in consultancy involvements, the Contextualist researchers have been uniquely able to provide substantial and detailed case studies of the processes of strategic choice and change in a number of large British corporations over the last two or more decades. The first and most influential of these studies was Andrew Pettigrew's (1985) study of ICI, *The Awakening Giant*, but this has soon been followed by accounts of Rover (Whipp and Clark, 1986), Cadbury (Child and Smith, 1987), the retailing company Fosters (Johnson, 1987) and the emerging comparative studies of Jaguar, Hill Samuel, Clerical Medical and General Life Assurance, and Longman (Pettigrew, Whipp, Rosenfeld and Pettigrew, 1987). Because in so many respects my own empirical research is similar, indeed indebted to this pioneering work, I need to make my differences very clear at the outset. In brief, I shall argue that, though they are not uncritical of both the Carnegie School and Action Theory, the Contextualists have failed so far to detach themselves sufficiently from these traditions to provide adequate accounts of either the intrinsic human potential for genuine choice or the social structures that make choices realizable. Let me explore these failings further, in as comradely a fashion as possible.

Focusing upon the internal processes of their organizations, the Contextualists repudiate environmental determinism. Pettigrew (1985, p. 453) admits the importance of economic 'context', but concludes his account of strategic change at ICI by declaring:

> No . . . brand of simple economic determinism is intended here. Behind the periodic strategic orientations in ICI are not just economic and business events, but also processes of managerial perception, choice and action influenced by and influencing perceptions of the operating environment of the firm, and its structure, culture and systems of power and control.

This emphasis upon managerial perceptions, together with the very term 'context' for describing environments, clearly echoes Action Theory's repudiation of environmental determinism. Indeed, Johnson (1987), in his account of incremental strategic changes at Fosters, approvingly cites Weick to characterize environments as:

> enactments by managers of the world in which they live; their 'reality' in terms of management action is to be understood not as empirical reality but as a function of management cognition.

However, Johnson is stressing how managers respond only to the environment enacted in their perceptions; he is careful to distinguish an 'empirical reality' existing beyond. Child and Smith (1987, p. 570), though giving their sectoral environments a similar dimension as 'cognitive arenas', also distance themselves from the extreme Action position of Smircich and Stubbart (1985) by asserting the importance of 'real properties' independent of the perceptions and social constructions of the particular actors within them.

Realistic this may be, but by denying themselves the great Action Theory alibi against environmental determinism, the Contextualists are left with the problem of how agency is possible in the face of environmental constraint. Child and Smith (1987, p. 570) offer no more than to say that the scope for strategic choice is a matter of degree, but in adopting the structuration theory of Giddens (1979), Pettigrew (1985) and Whipp and Clark (1986) suggest a more satisfactory solution. Following Giddens (1979), environmental structures are portrayed as both enabling and constraining human action:

> In the past structural analyses emphasising abstract dimensions and contextual constraints have been regarded as incompatible with processual analyses stressing action and strategic conduct. Here an attempt is being made to combine these two forms of description and analysis. First of all by conceptualising structure and context not just as a barrier to action but as essentially involved in its production . . . and second, by demonstrating how aspects of structure and context are mobilized or activated by actors and groups as they seek to obtain outcomes that are important to them (Pettigrew, 1985, p. 37).

This appeal to an elaborate sociological framework is not quite fulfilled, however. The Contextualists define their contexts too narrowly. Though these authors may sometimes refer to national cultural characteristics – as, for instance, in Pettigrew's (1985) linking of Organizational Development's success within ICI in the 1960s to a general cultural atmosphere of liberalism and tolerance – they fail to connect such factors to any systematic account of wider social structure. The tendency is to adopt an economistic atomism. For Johnson (1987, p. 232), 'the business environment is seen as a complex, atomistic mix of potentially divergent and ambiguous signals'. Thus the ways in which social structures of class or gender may be mobilized by managers in obtaining important outcomes are systematically ignored. Defining environments largely in economic terms, the focus is set – particularly with the 'firm-in-sector' approach (Child and Smith, 1987) – on immediate industry sectors. Accounts of industry sectors are richly descriptive but, except perhaps for appeal to dubious life-cycle analogies (Child and Smith, 1987; Whipp and Clark, 1986), generally unanalytic (cf. Starkey, 1987). There is for instance no systematic analysis of the companies' scope for strategic discretion in terms of positions within product markets, capital markets and the market for corporate control.

This atomism extends to the Contextualist conception of their actors. Though Johnson (1987, p. 236) might refer to one character as 'patriarchal' and Child and Smith (1987) acknowledge the continuing influence of the Cadbury family, the Contextualists leave unexamined the social sources of their actors' powers and motivations. The deference enjoyed by the patriarch derives from society's ideology of paternalism; the power of the founding Cadbury family is supported by capitalist structures. Accounts that abstract individual actors from such social relations are incomplete and superficial, for they omit the preconditions for the conduct they describe.

This atomistic reduction of the human actor is all too characteristic of the Carnegie tradition. Here, for all its promises of rich understanding, Action Theory fails to provide the Contextualists with sufficient safeguards. In their commitment to the interpretive method (Pettigrew, 1985; Johnson, 1987, p. 38), these researchers defer too readily to actors' own explanations for their behaviour. The principle of interpretive empathy deprives them of the critical distance that would allow them to challenge the individualistic accounts offered by the subjects themselves. As a result, actors emerge from the Contextualist studies as asocial beings; in accounting for their behaviour, they appear to have no capital, no gender, no generation. This promotes a second reduction, again characteristic of the Carnegie School. Denying their actors interests, powers or even internal conflicts derived from social identities, the organizational struggles that the Contextualists so vividly describe are rendered somehow antiseptic. Organizational politics are reduced to the level of Cyert and March's (1963) coalition bargaining, the issues confined to competitive performance and managerial careerism all somehow detached from wider social-structural tensions (cf. Willmott, 1987).

This is not the limit of the Carnegie School's influence. Even within the confined realms of organizational politics, these authors constantly deprecate their actors' capacity either to formulate goals independently and clearly or to pursue them purposefully and effectively. Agency is smothered by the Contextualist emphasis upon complexity and cognitive limits. Pettigrew (1985, p. 441) specifically distinguishes his process account of strategic change from the 'rational-analytic' schemes that allegedly dominate the literature, while Johnson (1987 p. 17) denounces the rational model of strategy as saying:

> little about the the problem of management. Specifically it does not
> address such issues as the limitations on analytical and rational
> behaviour, the interaction of managers and stakeholders in the

location and definition of strategic problems or the exercise of choice
and the management of change at an inter-personal level. In short it
is a de-personalised model of management, which equates management with analysis and rationality.

At one level the behaviours these authors describe do indeed appear
confused and largely irrational. If one assumes that the fundamental
goal of these firms is profit-maximization – as these authors generally
do, though they might dress this up in terms of 'survival', 'efficiency',
'competitiveness' or even 'awakening' – then their overall corporate
strategies certainly appear to be burdened with confusion and
irrationality. Analysis of the motivations of powerful individual actors,
on the other hand, might reveal that corporate strategies in fact reflect
the rational and successful pursuit of personal interests other than
corporate profit maximization. Stubborn strategic conservatism or
sudden rushes of corporate adventurism, however irrational from the
point of view of shareholders, may express the very rational defence or
pursuit of factional interests.

We can only appraise the rationality of such conduct by thoroughly
understanding the motives of the key actors with influence upon
strategic decisions. This is where the Contextualists let us down. In
focusing upon individuals' cognitive limits and fixing on a criterion of
rationality at the corporate level, the Contextualists fail to illuminate
such actors' private values and ambitions. To take one instance, in
Pettigrew's (1985) massive account of ICI, the figure and motives of
future chairman Harvey Jones is always left in the shadows. The
degree to which he was engaged in the rational pursuit of his own
particular career interests, separate from those of ICI as a whole, is
not examined. Thus, while the strategic evolution of ICI may show few
signs of rational planning, Harvey Jones' personal manoeuvring may
have done. After all, he got the top job in the end.

My complaint against the Contextualists, then, is that their accounts
of human agency are at the same time too eclectic and too limited.
They remain trapped by the Carnegie and Action traditions into both a
narrow focus on human cognition and an atomistic conception of the
environment. Moreover, interpretivistic relativism seems to have
sapped their critical defences. Pettigrew (1985, p. 41) warns against
'theoretical ethnocentrism'; Child and Smith (1987), eschewing the
extremes of both voluntarism and determinism, lamely decide that
strategic choice is a matter of degree; while Johnson (1987, p. 300) less
than ringingly concludes that alternative theories are no more than
'metaphors', each valid because each capable of illuminating different
facets of human behaviour. The point of the last two chapters,
however, is that these alternative theories are more than metaphors
that can be picked up and put down like different sets of magnifying

glasses; each involves fundamentally opposed conceptions of human nature. An indifferent eclecticism that refuses to affirm any fixed beliefs about human nature risks at best intellectual inconsistency, at worst a basic disrespect for humankind. In the case of the Contextualists, moreover, these 'metaphors' are not merely irreconcilable; they are actually subversive of each other. The Contextualists fail to provide a convincing account of strategic choice because, still rooted in both the Carnegie School and Action Theory, they have no conceptions of either the actor or structure capable of supporting human agency.

CONCLUSIONS

Many common themes emerge from this review of recent North American, French and British studies of strategic choice. These authors have rejected environmental determinism by portraying environments as dominated (especially Karpik, and Bauer and Cohen), chosen (Miles and Cameron) or enacted (Child, Johnson and Miles and Snow). They have confounded the expectations of simple environmental determinists – though not those of the 'strategic group' theorists – by demonstrating the equal viability of different strategies within the same industries or environments (for example, Miller and Friesen, Gupta, Snow and Hrebiniak, and Hambrick). Though some of these studies have been statistical, most have relied on longitudinal and processual case study research, with some (for instance, Gupta, Miles and Cameron, and Boswell) adopting deliberately comparative approaches. Many have stressed the importance of top management knowledge, experience and other characteristics for the direction of strategy (for example, Miles and Snow, Penrose, Hambrick and Mason and Boswell). Several have emphasized the internal politics of organizations, colouring their accounts with sometimes rather casual references to such concepts as 'power' and 'ideology' (for example Child, Boswell and Pettigrew). But only a few have extended their scope to consider the political and economic implications of strategic choice for the wider society beyond the confines of the firm (for instance Karpik, and Bauer and Cohen).

The readiness of the majority of these studies to confine themselves to the bounds of the organization and its immediate market environment reflects a lack of concern for the wider structural conditions in which action takes place. In particular, there is a common failure to seek systematic understanding of how certain individuals happen to gain power. Thus Boswell's (1983) discussion of family controlled steel firms ducks any examination of the property relations that defined the acceptability of various leaderships and strategies, while Miles and Snow's (1978) discussion lacks any analysis of how the particular managerial 'distinctive competences' are acquired, legitimated and gain primacy. Relying too heavily either on the Carnegie School's restricted notion of environment or on the insubstantial picture provided by the Action Theorists, these studies exclude from their accounts consideration of how the power to decide strategy is structured, especially through access to wealth and education, by the wider society.

Most of these studies also fail to establish adequate conceptions of actors as potential agents. The behaviourism of Simon, Cyert and March persist in references to 'learning' (for example Gupta, Miles and Cameron) and 'adaptation' (for instance Miles and Snow) in response to environmental stimuli. There are few attempts at the sophisticated understanding of individuals' meanings and objectives advocated by the Action Theorists. Instead, Miles and Snow (1978), with their influential concept of 'distinctive competences', reduce the personalities that guide strategy to simple ensembles of skills and perceptual biases that are crudely derived directly from functional backgrounds. Even Bauer and Cohen (1981), for all their professed commitment to interpretive and ethnographic methods, in practice fail to elaborate the particular motives or interests of any of their actors; their governing cliques are left to appear as seekers of power merely for power's sake. Though Pettigrew (1985) and Johnson (1987) certainly provide rich understandings of managerial perceptions, they allow their readers little access to the personal goals that shaped them. It is Boswell (1983), with his pen-portraits of key actors' upbringings and experiences, who offers most sense of his characters as private individuals possessing personal motives for the particular strategies they adopted.

The following two chapters will introduce a Realist approach to corporate strategy that both insists on the interpretive understanding of individual actors and recognizes the implications of structure for their agency. However, though going beyond the limits of the Carnegie School and Action Theory, this Realist approach does not entail a complete repudiation of these earlier studies of strategic choice. Indeed, it shares and draws heavily upon their rejection of environmental determinism; their concern for the internal politics of organizations; and their preference for longitudinal and comparative case-study research. Where Realism differs is in its aspiration to go deeper and wider into the circumstances of strategic choice.

Chapter Four

Realism and agency

INTRODUCTION

I have claimed that a Realist approach can offer a superior perspective on business strategy. What then is Realism? This chapter will introduce the Realist position, developed particularly by Roy Bhaskar. It is Bhaskar's general philosophical foundations – augmented by the social psychology of Harré and the sociology of Giddens – that will form the basis for my accounts of strategic choice that follow in later chapters. The significance of Realism, I shall argue, lies in its conception of real social structures as essential to both human actors' intrinsic potential for agency and their external capacity to actualize this potential. To bring out the distinctive value of this Realist approach, let me begin by recapping the main arguments of the two last chapters.

My basic thesis is that any adequate theory of strategic choice must be established upon a non-deterministic account of the human actors who make the decisions in the first place. In Chapter 2 I distinguished two basic forms of determinism, each of which contained two sub-categories of their own: action determinism, both psychologistic and over-socializing; and environmental determinism, natural selectionist or adaptationist. Typically, action determinists explain human action in terms of fixed internal mechanisms that dictate regular responses to environmental stimuli; these stimuli, for the psychologistic action determinists in particular, are generally regarded as chaotic and discrete. For the environmental determinists, on the other hand, it is the environment that dominates, so much so that, especially for the natural selectionists, the motivations of human actors hardly matter. I argued that neither basic form of determinism is capable of providing a satisfactory account of corporate strategic action. The human actor of action determinism is too simple, denied individuality by the over-socializers and denuded of social identity by the psychologistic determinists. Deprived of internal complexity either way, these actors lose any intrinsic capability for initiative or choice. Conversely, the environmental determinists propose an absolutism for their environments that is too oppressive: they do not acknowledge the extent to which environments are the productions of the very actors they are supposed to control, nor do they demonstrate that their constraints really are so tight as to squeeze out all scope for the exercise of human discretion. The inadequacy of both forms of determinism led me to conclude in favour of an account of corporate activity that allowed for genuine strategic choice.

Recalling Elster's (1984) formulation, I opened Chapter 3 by arguing that an account of strategic choice would require theories of both the human actor and environmental structure capable of supporting human agency. Unfortunately, I found that neither of the two traditions that inform current accounts of strategic choice – the Carnegie School and Action Theory – actually fulfil this dual requirement. In their exaggerated reaction to environmental determinism, the Action Theorists indulge in so emphatic a dismissal of environmental constraint that they leave mysterious the social origins of the motivations and powers of the agents they celebrate. Action Theory arrives finally at a utopian voluntarism and a disabling relativism. The Carnegie School, on the other hand, remains fatally indebted to the simplified, asocial actor of psychologistic action determinism, portraying the individual as a hapless reactor to environmental stimuli and an ineffective pursuer of tiny atomistic interests. I went on to demonstrate the damaging influence that these Action and Carnegie perspectives continue to have on recent accounts of strategic choice.

But my picture was not all bleak. The strategic diversity and organizational idiosyncrasy discovered by recent researchers has, to say the least, left the determinists with a lot of explaining to do. Moreover, these strategic choice researchers have developed, especially in the careful studies of the Contextualists, valuable models for how empirical work should now proceed. However, such further empirical work needs to build, not on the inadequate foundations of the Carnegie School and Action Theory, but rather upon a theoretical perspective that is capable of fulfilling Elster's dual requirement. This is my task here; by introducing the sociological, I hope to endow the human actor with both the internal complexity and the external resources that together are essential for the possibility of genuine strategic choice. It is by recognizing, not denying, society that decision-makers can be given at least some control at once over their environments and themselves.

Accordingly this chapter will take three parts. I shall begin with an overview of the Realist conception of society, indicating the importance it accords to social structure as precondition for human agency. This relationship between structure and agency will then be explored from two directions. First, I shall outline how social structures grant certain actors the external powers necessary to agency – control over both material resources and the labour of other actors. In this respect, the capitalist enterprise, combining labour and capital, potentially constitutes a particularly important instrument for agency. But capitalist structures alone rarely dictate how these corporate powers are actually used: the plural and contradictory nature of the social structures embodied within the firm precludes unambiguous determination and allows sufficient autonomy for individual actors to choose which powers to use and how. Quite how actors can genuinely choose the manner in which they deploy their structural powers forms the second approach to this relationship between structure and agency. Again, the intrinsic capacity for genuine choice between actions will be founded upon the complexity of the social structures from which the actor is constituted. There is no such person as the 'pure' capitalist or the 'simple' manager. Internally complex, and acting within a plural and contradictory society, the human actor is able to choose how to act and with what. The various structures that actors exploit in their strategic choices, and the constraints under which they operate, are the subject of the following chapter.

REALISM AND SOCIETY

Genuine strategic choice can only be exercised by agents, that is, by people whose conduct is neither internally nor externally determined. It is the core of the Realist argument that any plausible claim for such human agency must be founded upon accounts of both actor and environment that explicitly recognize the social. For, as Bhaskar (1979, p. 43) insists:

> All activity presupposes the prior existence of social forms. Thus consider *saying*, *making* and *doing* as characteristic modalities of human agency. People cannot communicate except by utilizing existing media, produce except by applying themselves to materials which are already formed, or act save in some or other context. Speech requires language; making materials; actions conditions; agency resources; activity rules. Even spontaneity has as its necessary

condition the pre-existence of a social form with (or by means of) which the spontaneous act is performed (italics in original).

In short, society, as provider of the means for agency, constitutes its pre-condition.

Society does not, of course, just drop from heaven, perfectly and immutably formed. Rather, society is the product of the human activity it makes possible. As actors draw upon its structural properties, they actually work on it, reproducing and – occasionally and usually incrementally – transforming it. To take the example of language again: while its effectiveness as a mode of communication clearly depends upon the collective acceptance of certain established grammatical rules, these social rules do not determine the actual words we employ (Bhaskar, 1979, p. 44). To the extent that we conform to established grammatical rules in choosing our words, then we reinforce the linguistic structures prevailing in society; on the other hand, as we strive to communicate novel ideas in novel ways, we actually develop these structures into new forms. Bhaskar (1979, pp. 43–4) epitomizes this relation between actors and society in two dualities – first of structure, then of praxis:

> Society is both the ever-present *condition* (material cause) and the continually reproduced *outcome* of human agency. And praxis is both work, that is conscious *production*, and (normally unconscious) *reproduction* of the conditions of production, that is society (italics in original).

Here Bhaskar (1979) acknowledges the influence of Giddens' (1976) concept of structuration, which proposes a mutual dependence between society and actor. However, Bhaskar (1983, p. 84) is wary of accepting the forms of dependence between the two as exactly equivalent:

> It is because the social structure is always a *given*, from the perspective of intentional human agency, that I prefer to talk of reproduction and transformation rather than of structuration as Giddens does (although I believe our concepts are very close). For me, 'structuration' still retains voluntaristic connotations – social practice is always, so to speak, *restructuration* (italics in original).

By no means does this suspicion of voluntarism reflect a disdain for the human potential for freedom – quite the opposite. As the following sections of this chapter will demonstrate, the 'stronger ontological grounding' Bhaskar (1983, p. 87) claims for social structure is essential to the possibility of the emancipatory social science that is Realism's object. The real and enduring nature of structures provides a standpoint for social criticism independent of personal subjectivity.

Nevertheless, I shall rely upon Giddens' (1984, pp. 16–33) conception of society making available to actors certain social rules and resources, whose structural character derives from the stable and accepted manner in which they are employed over time and through social systems. These social structural resources might be material – for instance capital – or authoritative – for instance, the managerial power to command. For those with privileged access to these resources, each kind is capable of enhancing their individual power to act. Yet each is socially reproduced – in the case of capital, by the exploitation of labour; for managers, by society's inculcation of obedience and respect for exclusive expertise. These resources are deployed by actors according to the rules society provides for the guidance of action. Such rules are not law-like in the sense of imposing definite courses of conduct; rather, they simply afford procedures or principles capable of generating action. They are like codes in that they rely on mutual understanding and conformity. Thus rules are followed because other actors' recognition of the same sets of rules assures the efficacy of the actions they guide. For example, a manager acts as a manager because confident that subordinates will be obedient to his or her managerial authority. The manager may break commonly accepted rules for conduct, but in doing so risks ineffectiveness because other actors are unwilling or unable any longer to co-operate. In short, a world without social rules would be an anarchy in which actors would be free, yet lack the capacity for effective agency.

It is important, too, that rules can easily be translated into resources. Ideologies of all sorts exemplify this dual character of rules. In so far as managerial claims to 'a right to manage' indicate deferential behaviour to subordinates, they are rules for conduct for the worker; in so far as they secure obedience, they constitute a resource for the manager. Thus power involves more than resources *tout simple*; it is also about access to, and manipulation of, the social structural rules that determine their allocation and usage.

This is no more than an introductory sketch of the Realist conception of society. The next section of this chapter will examine in more detail how social structures empower people to act on each other. I conclude the chapter by considering how social structures are implicated in the very constitution of people as agents.

STRUCTURE AND POWER

Action Theory's subordination of society to the actor was inspired by a voluntaristic fear of law-like social determination and reinforced by an interpretive trust in actors' own accounts. Realism, however, both insists on the need for structural resources to empower actors as agents and finds in the reality of these structures an independent basis for the critical and therefore emancipatory appraisal of interpretive understandings. Thus for Realists, structure is not antipathetic to but rather precondition for agency. Without social structure, actors would not possess the means to agency; with it, Realism can undertake the critique of structural constraint by which agency can be extended.

Inseparable from the capacity for agency is the possession of power. Thus for Giddens (1984, p. 15):

> To be an agent is to be able to deploy (chronically in the flow of daily life) a range of causal powers, including that of influencing those deployed by others. Action depends upon the capability of the individual to 'make a difference' to a pre-existing state of affairs or course of events. An agent ceases to be such if he or she loses the capability to 'make a difference', that is, to exercise some sort of power.

But this power is not simply an intrinsic property of the human actor as biological individual. Within society, the actor needs more than just physical strength. To 'make a difference' to the flow of events, to be effective in influencing the conduct of other individuals, the actor must be able to apply the resources and manipulate the rules that habitually organize human activities. However, not everyone has access to the same rules and resources, neither are they equally capable of deploying them. The powers society grants are highly structured – some have more than others – and it is those with privileged access to social powers who are best able to 'make a difference'. Thus social structures do not necessarily inhibit human agency; for those with control over their rules and resources, they substantially enhance it.

This point is reinforced by analyzing the structural resources that form human powers a little further. Bhaskar (1986, p. 175) distinguishes two types of power that together constitute what he terms the 'dynamic bases of action'. On the one hand, there are 'competences', which comprise intrinsic practical capabilities, skills and abilities of various kinds; on the other, there are certain extrinsic 'facilities', including political, economic and normative (moral, legal, idcological,

etc.) resources. For example, as a manager one may possess both
, competences in the form of professional skills and facilities in terms of
the normative support accorded to 'managerial prerogative'. Quite
clearly, access to political, economic and normative facilities is
governed, in almost all societies, by relatively stable social structures:
in a purely capitalist society (an ideal type) these facilities would be
concentrated in the hands of the owners of capital; in a purely
patriarchal one, they would be the monopoly of older men. Less
obvious is the socially structured character of human competences. For
all their apparently intrinsic nature, these competences are far from
being simple individualistic properties (Giddens, 1979, p. 89); both
their acquisition and their value depend finally on the structure of
society as a whole. Thus superior intrinsic competences, in the form of
work skills, for instance, may be gained by socially structured access to
privileged education. Further, it is society that defines the relevance of
such skills (or other intrinsic competences) and social change can easily
render them redundant. In short, the extent to which actors are also
agents depends upon the powers society affords them.

This insistence upon social structure implies no reification. Structural
powers are only made concrete as they are deployed in action;
otherwise they merely exist in the minds of actors as remembered sets
of rules for conduct and rights over resources (Giddens, 1984, p. 25).
Structures, then, manifest themselves in the systems of interaction
through which human actors organize their activities (Giddens, 1984,
p. 17). These systems become regularized as institutions – families,
firms or markets – as their participants develop continuities in their
interactions. Each system is characterized by certain structural
properties – established distributions of resources and rules of conduct
– and actors draw upon these as they pursue their particular ends.
Thus in economic life, actors pursue their ends by deploying their
particular competences (entrepreneurship, for example) or facilities
(capital perhaps) in such institutionalized systems as corporations and
markets. Likewise, older actors draw upon their superior normative
facilities to transmit certain intrinsic competences (speech, work skills,
deference to authority) to younger actors through family and
educational systems of upbringing.

Thus institutionalized systems afford actors, by their structural
properties, certain definite powers which they deploy, expend,
augment and transmit in their interactions. However, these systems of
interaction are neither tidily discrete nor governed by neat symmetries.
It is essential to the enabling rather than determining aspect of
structures that the systematic translation of particular, superior powers
into corresponding achieved actions be denied any smooth inevit-

ability. Mere possession of capital should not dictate that the entrepreneur deploys it to a particular end; inferiority in normative powers must not guarantee the obedience and receptivity of the pupil to the teacher. The potential for agency requires that actors' powers and motives within a particular system be autonomous from any single structural logic.

Unacceptable, therefore, is Lukes' (1974) proposal that social structure endows actors with definite 'real interests' according to unambiguous structural location – for instance, a member of the working class has a real interest in the overthrow of capitalism – and that, if actors could only know them, these structural interests would supply the motives for their action. Though Lukes (1974) stresses the frequent rupture between the two, his framework allows for a potential connection between structure and action that is too deterministic; it carries the implication that, once rid of ideological blinkers, the actor has no alternative but to act in accord with externally defined 'real' interests. To preserve the possibility of choice, interests must be detached from structure and instead be defined by the objectives that actors formulate for themselves (Benton, 1981, p. 173). Agency requires that motives for action should not be imposed by simple structural position.

Just as there should be no necessary connection between structure and 'interests', neither should powers be automatically translated into achievements. Hindess (1982) warns against deterministic 'capacity-outcome' accounts of power, whereby the mere possession of superior power guarantees the attainment of desired objectives. To be agents, actors must be left with the ability to forbear from exercising their power to the full or to maximum effectiveness. Thus, as Hindess (1982) argues, there is little doubt that during the Vietnam War the Americans were far more powerful than the guerrilla forces of the Viet Cong, yet somehow they allowed themselves to be defeated. Victory in Vietnam required a commitment of resources that the United States chose not to make. The intervention of choice thus breaks the deterministic link between 'capacity' and 'outcome': there is no necessity that apparently 'more powerful' actors will always triumph over others.

This detachment of particular powers from both necessary motives for and success in action is possible by recognizing the plurality of the systems in which actors interact and the diversity of powers they have available in each. In their systemic activities, actors are not confined to the logics of just one set of structures. Within contemporary society, actors participate in a multitude of systems and, as they move from one to another, they import various structural powers and independent motives. As Hindess (1982, p. 507) asks, why should one structural characteristic, such as class, demand priority over any other structural characteristic, say gender or ethnicity, in all the various 'arenas' in which actors participate? As members of capitalist enterprises, families and ethnic communities, actors occupy diverse structural positions and have available a range of rules and resources for action. Further, following Bhaskar (1978, pp. 110–1), these structures are not arranged in some tidy base-superstructure relationship, with one social characteristic hierarchically defining the rest. Rather, Bhaskar (1978) insists, the relations between structures are complex and potentially contradictory. This complexity frees the actor from any unique structural determination and offers the possibility of choice. As Bhaskar (1978, p. 111) writes:

> The theory of complex determination, in situating persons as comprehensive entities whose behaviour is subject to the control of several different principles at once, allows the possibility of genuine self-determination (subject to constraints) and the specific power of acting in accordance with a plan or in the light of reason.

Actors are not faced with just one set of structures from which to draw their rules and resources; rather, they are confronted by the confusing and ambiguous array presented by all the many systems of interaction in which they participate. Subject to no singular structural determination, the actor must constantly choose. Thus at work the family businessman can exercise power over his children either as employer or as father; and at the end of the day he carries a residue of his authority as boss back to his own fireside.

So far, I have emphasized how action depends upon, yet remains relatively autonomous from, social structure. Now I wish to argue the converse – that, though they are themselves only produced and reproduced by virtue of human action, none the less these structures too retain a certain independence. This independence forms the basis for granting structure a 'reality' separate from the interpretations and actions of actors themselves. Far from imprisoning actors within some 'reified' structural cage, acknowledging the 'real' nature of structure opens the possibility of freeing actors from the narrow constraints of their own interpretive understandings.

Action Theory is correct in asserting that social structure can only exist by virtue of the activities of human actors. As actors draw upon structural rules and resources in their activities, they effectively reproduce and reinforce them. The tiny efforts of individual capitalists in pursuit of profit not only augment private capitals but combine to perpetuate capitalist structures as a whole. However, such reproduction of structure is rarely deliberate; it is usually the unintended consequence of independently motivated actions. 'People do not marry to reproduce the nuclear family or work to sustain the capitalist economy', yet these are the effects of their combined activities (Bhaskar, 1979, p. 49). Rather than the conscious creation of individuals, therefore, structure is the unintentional product of collective actions.

Not only are actors often unaware of the consequences of their actions; they need have no understanding of the 'totality' of structures that make them possible (Bhaskar, 1979, p. 55; cf. Benson, 1977). The insider trader may be wonderfully knowledgeable of the processes and opportunities involved in takeover battles, yet still be ignorant – or careless – of the deeper political and economic structures that underlie them. Making a buck does not require sophisticated understanding of political economy. In relying upon the interpretive understanding of the actors themselves, then, the Action Theorists expect too much of their busy agent. For, as Bhaskar (1986, p. 162) puts it, 'what an agent does not make (what it must take to make) it can have no privileged understanding of'. While providing the essential preconditions for insider trading, the vast totality of structures that permits takeover battles is quite independent of the activities of any single trader. In sum, traders may be quite unaware of both the structural conditions for, and productions of, their activities.

Indeed, social structures do not depend upon continuous enactment by traders at all. As accepted distributions of resources and recognized procedures for action, structures may remain latent in the minds of actors during periods of inactivity. As such, moreover, they may be learnt by education and socialization, even before activity begins. Thus structures are like schools: latent during holidays, but enduring ready for pupils new and old to reactivate them at the onset of term (Harré, 1979, p. 38). In just the same way capitalism fails to disappear over weekends.

It is this 'ontological gap' between underlying structures and particular events (Bhaskar, 1986, p. 33) that gives the social its real character independent of immediate human activities. The world is 'stratified' (Bhaskar, 1978, p. 66), so that the events accessible to empiricism are merely the surface manifestations of underlying and enduring structural mechanisms. Science does not require that these structures can be empirically identified – after all, in proposing the circulation of blood, Harvey had to posit a capillary system that could only then be imagined (Harré and Secord, 1972, p. 72). Likewise, for the social sciences, capitalism is not a concrete thing easily to be pinned down, but its existence and form must none the less be assumed if such events as takeover raids are in any sense ever to be explicable. Capitalist structures are real in that they are necessary for the multitudinous activities of our everyday economic life. Thus the social constitutes 'a most peculiar type of entity; a structure irreducible to, but present only in its effects' (Bhaskar, 1979, p. 50). Society is no less real because we cannot know it directly; society continuously shows itself in the actions it renders feasible.

It is these social structural conditions for, and constraints upon, action that are the proper concern of social science. As Bhaskar (1979, p. 45) puts it, social scientists are less interested in Christmas shopping itself than in the economic processes which make it possible. Accordingly, social science should engage in 'retroductive' investigations of the hypothetical structural preconditions for particular events, employing hindsight for selecting or rejecting alternative explanations (Bhaskar, 1986). This 'retroductive' process should penetrate ever more deeply into the strata of structural mechanisms generating any particular event. Bhaskar (1986, p. 63) summarizes the Realist process thus:

> Its essence lies in the *movement* at any one level from knowledge of manifest phenomena to knowledge, produced by means of antecedent knowledge, of the structures which generate them. As deeper levels of reality are successively identified, described and explained, knowledge at more superficial levels is typically revised, corrected or more or less drastically recast, issuing in a characteristic pattern of description, explanation and redescription for the phenomena understood at any one level of reality (italics in original).

Thus, as the retroductive elaboration of structural conditions proceeds through its successive iterations, earlier explanations are subjected to constant amplification. Contrary to the interpretive tradition of Action Theory, therefore, the actor's own account of his or her activities is never final and definite; he or she provides no more than a provisional starting point for explanation. The next stage is to explain not only the conditions for his or her actions, but also the origins of his or her own beliefs about them. There is no need to sink into relativistic deference to the actor. As Bhaskar (1979, p. 80) argues, we can confidently prefer our Theory T over the actor's proto-scientific beliefs P if we can show first that P is false while T provides a more complete explanation, and, second, that T can explain why P is falsely held.

From a Realist perspective, therefore, dependence upon actors' own interpretive understandings unnecessarily trivializes and confines research. Actors may not understand either the conditions for or the consequences of their actions. But while Action Theory credulously resigns itself to these limits – and the Carnegie School triumphantly finds confirmation of bounded rationality – Realism undertakes the criticism that can actually advance understanding. This preference for the observer's explanation does not imply any arrogant authoritarianism over the actor – rather the opposite. As Bhaskar (1979, p. 81) goes on to argue:

> If, then, one is in possession of a theory which explains why false consciousness is necessary, then one can pass immediately, without the addition of any extraneous value judgments, to a negative evaluation of the object (generative structure, system of social relations or whatever) that makes that consciousness necessary (and, *ceteris paribus*, to a positive evaluation of action rationally directed at the removal of the sources of false consciousness).

The point of social scientific research, therefore, is not to accept human cognitive limits, whether complacently as in the case of the Carnegie School or timidly as in Action Theory; rather it is to enlighten actors as to the conditions for and constraints on their actions. There is no need to defer to a woman's own explanation for engaging in low-paid casual employment as only natural, because 'this is women's work'. Realist explanation would demonstrate the structural constraints – gender bias in education, unequal family responsibilities – that lead to women's concentration in certain kinds of work. By making these constraints explicit, rather than colluding in their obscurity, a Realist account would enable such a woman to engage in actions to remove them:

> In as much as social science may reveal a discrepancy between social objects and beliefs about those objects, and may come to socially explain such a discrepancy, then we may and must pass to a critical assessment of the social causes responsible for it. Such a critique . . . facilitates the development of emancipatory practices orientated to emancipated (free) action (Bhaskar, 1986, p. 159).

Thus identifying those structural constraints that the actors themselves fail to acknowledge implies no condescending confirmation of their incapacity for agency. In offering critical illumination of structural constraints, it pays respect to actors' potential to enact change themselves. Consequently – and here again Bhaskar (1986, p. 182) diverges from Giddens (1976) – the social sciences are not necessarily value neutral. In an unequal world, it is the privileged few who have most to lose from the revelation of their structural advantages. And, as social scientific knowledge augments their capacity for actively transforming society, it is clearly the structurally oppressed many who have most to gain.

But the transformation of embedded and extensive structures is not to be achieved individually; actors must apply themselves in 'mass' action (Bhaskar, 1986, p. 176). Collectively produced and reproduced, social structures can only be transformed collectively. This collective action might be organized through trade unions or political parties, but by no means necessarily. Recalling Giddens' (1987) warning in Chapter 1, the capacity for mass action is not the exclusive property of the labour movement. Indeed, the capitalist enterprise represents at least as potent a means for mobilizing collective activities, and may be superior. The possible superiority of the capitalist enterprise in collective action is founded on its crucial difference from either trade unions or political parties, that is its essentially undemocratic character. Unfortunately, this undemocratic character ensures that the collective activities of its employees are not directed towards self-emancipation, but rather to enlarging the agentive powers of its dominant actors.

STRUCTURE AND ACTOR

So far I have tried to demonstrate how social structures, far from being antagonistic to agency, both provide the resources and afford the autonomy that make it possible. However, this is only half my task. Harré (1979, p. 246) points out that environmental autonomy is a necessary but insufficient condition for agency. After all, electrons possess exactly this autonomy and so, in a more limited sense, did the atomistic beings of psychologistic action determinism. What the electrons of physics and the atoms of action determinism lack is an intrinsic potential for agency. To fulfil their potential for agency, human actors need not only some control over their environments but also control over themselves. Rather than the pliant internal simplicity of the electron, this reflexive capacity demands the internal structure and complexity that can provide the stuff of resistance and choice. Thus Harré (1979, p. 246) distinguishes people from electrons:

> People on the other hand are internally complex. Their inner structures and processes endow them with the possibility of initiating action and internally transforming the effects of the environment and other people and things.

The task of this section, therefore, is to endow the human actor with sufficient internal structure and complexity to transform it from reactive atom to reflexive agent. Again, Realists derive this agentive potential from the complex structures of society.

Realism conceives of the human actor as structured internally in three separate ways. Against the idealism of Action Theory, Realism insists on recognizing physiology; to the emphasis upon cognitive psychology characteristic of the Carnegie School, Realists add the sociological. The actor is thus the subject of not just one set of principles, but rather is constituted as the locus for a complex junction of physiological, psychological and sociological strata (Bhaskar, 1979). Just as for society as whole, none of these strata provide any unique or dominant determination, but each presents a range of courses according to which actors can direct their activities. At the dinner table, guests are torn between the physiological drive of hunger, psychological tendencies toward greed and social pressures for delicate good manners.

Such social pressures are not themselves unambiguous, for the diverse and contradictory nature of social structures provides actors with a range of alternative structural rules by which to steer their activities. As they participate in society, actors are offered a plurality of 'social selves' – for example, parent, capitalist, community leader – each carrying different principles for action (Harré and Secord, 1972, p. 151). This complex character of the society without adds powerfully to the complexity of the actor within. Physiological principles, centred relatively coherently around imperatives towards physical survival and reproduction, add to human complexity simply by virtue of their potential oppositions to psychological and sociological principles. Incorporating social structural rules, on the other hand, multiplies internal complexity not only through its oppositions to the other strata, but also by introducing all the conflicts and self-contradictions characteristic of society as a whole.

Moreover, it is this complexity, especially in the diversity of social selves, that frees the actor from any unique internal determination and provides the range of options that permits genuine choice. As an actor one feels internal conflicts – between one's social identities as capitalist, parent, community leader or whatever – and one is forced to choose between each of their particular logics. It is here that Harré (1979, p. 254) roots the human potential for agency:

> Actors act by striving to interpret (imperfectly) the principles for action available to them and they can choose to turn to or ignore some of them. We are agents because we have turned from action according to one principle to action according to another.

Thus the internal complexity essential to agency is not simply innate in people, but rather a quality to a great extent dependent upon the structural complexity of society at large.

However, mere importation of contradictory structural rules into the human actor is not in itself sufficient for agency; the actor also needs to develop the capacity for genuine choice between the alternatives they present. Here again actors depend upon society, for to exercise genuine choice between the many social selves they have available they must also possess a theory that they *can* choose. Harré (1983, p. 29) puts it thus:

> To be a pure agent is to conceive of oneself as (hold a theory that one is) a being in possession of an ultimate power of decision and action. A pure agent is capable of deciding between alternatives, even if they are equally attractive or forceful. A pure agent is capable of overcoming temptations and distractions to realize its plans. It can adopt new principles and it can curb its own desires.

Harré's argument is that the capacity to choose between principles, to resist distractions, relies first upon the actor believing him or herself able to do so. For transformation from actor bewildered by the diversity of available options into agent capable of genuinely choosing between them, the person requires a 'theory of self' that gives him or her this confidence.

To conceive of oneself as an agent, therefore, requires access to a theory of agency. However, actors develop their self-conceptions through their interactions within society and must draw upon the 'local theory of selves' (Harré, 1983, p. 257). Harré (1983, p. 193) elaborates the nature of a theory of agency and the social processes by which it might be acquired:

> In possession of a *theory* that I am an agent capable of acting against the tide of my inclination, capable of getting myself up and going etc., I have the means to readjust the means-end hierarchies which are involved in the preparation of action. And I have a way of explaining how my mental life (with others) appears to me the way it does. By being forced to listen to the exhortations of others, I learn to exhort myself, and by watching others push each other into action, I bestir myself (italics in original).

Unfortunately, however, societies are not equal in the extent to which they grant their members theories of their own agency. For example, ascetic Anglo-Saxon cultures promote agency by preaching stern resistance to spontaneous passions: in Latin cultures, however, impulses towards grief, joy and violence are deemed irresistible (Harré

and Secord, 1972, p. 259). Societies also differ internally in the extent
to which they allow agency. The spoilt aristocrat blithely expects to
fulfil every whim, while the poor are taught by harsh experience and
pious teaching to be 'meek and mild'. Thus once again, society is the
essential precondition for human agency. The social not only provides
a diversity of structural rules between which an actor can choose for
action; it also provides the confidence by which he or she may choose
between them.

This, though, provides a further basis for argument against Action
Theory, with its constant emphasis upon empathetic, interpretive
understanding. If actors' conduct is guided by socially produced
principles of action, then their own explanations cannot be wholly
personal and subjective. Actors must draw on theories of being in their
accounts as well as their selection of actions, and are liable to do so in
only a partial, even incorrect fashion. Thus an actor may explain a
particular managerial decision in a way meaningful to her, yet still be
mistaken. She might say: 'I did this because this is what marketing
managers do.' At a very simple level, we can correct this actor,
because we have available a well established theory of what marketing
managers do, and she has plainly misunderstood this theory. We might
then seek out an alternative theory of why she did what she did. But
we can go still one step further by observing that this is all very well,
but what is interesting are the structures (the delegated capitalist
power to command, hire and fire) that allowed the actor to carry out
this particular action, even though she was wrong. Thus actors' own
accounts should be treated seriously, yet also as statements that may
be corrected and amplified (Bhaskar, 1986, p. 166).

Nevertheless, as Chapter 6 will admit, there does exist some
convergence between Action Theory and Realism. Let there be no
doubt that Realism shares Action Theory's commitment to the
importance of human action and interpretive understanding. For
Bhaskar (1986, p. 147), 'human history consists, as Marx put it, in
nothing but the *activity* of men in pursuit of their ends' (italics in
original). Realism's difference is in taking interpretive understanding
only as a starting point, and one not immune from critical
commentary. Realism is prepared to intervene to ensure that human
activities are effective and that ends are genuinely chosen. In their
common recognition of the agentive potential contained in human
activity, Realism and Action Theory are also led to a shared
repudiation of predictive social science. In a world subject to the
activities of agents, the pattern of events cannot be determinate; at any
time regularity may be ruptured by choice. But again this does not
entail a collapse into a complete reliance upon immediate understand-

ings. Bhaskar's (1986) commitment to retroductive explanation, subjecting the past to successive analyses in order to reveal at ever deeper levels the preconditions for particular events, makes possible an understanding extending far beyond that available immediately to the actors themselves. Informed by this retroductive penetration, Realism can offer a critical commentary that actually contributes to agency, rather than taking it for granted.

CONCLUSION

In this chapter I have argued that it is because of, not despite, social structure that people may be agents. I have also stressed, however, that we are not all equal in our agency. Only some are granted access to plural structural rules and resources; only some possess the social confidence and competence to manipulate them. A structurally founded critical social science can and should contribute to extending these agentive capacities further. In the meantime, agency's concentration in the hands of a small elite has rather peculiar consequences – especially when exercised through control over the strategic choices of the capitalist enterprise.

Commanding potentially vast human and material resources, the firm's dominant actors can apply massive power upon society. It is my argument, to be extended in Chapter 5, that those in control of these resources need not devote them entirely to the reproduction of capitalist structures through faithful pursuit of profit. Capitalism gives the firm's dominant actors enormous resources; it is unable to determine what they do with them. The structural complexities of society permit deviation from profit-maximization and provide the conditions for strategic choice. These conditions include, at the least, that the firm's dominant actor's be able to command the obedience of subordinates, pay suppliers, fend off lenders and satisfy outside shareholders. As they direct the activities of their employees to their own personal ends, they must also ensure the reproduction of these conditions. If they wish to engage their firm in still more ambitiously idiosyncratic strategies, dominant actors must actively deploy their resources to transforming the structural constraints upon their actions. Their personnel experts will groom obedient managerial cadres; their marketeers will apply themselves to product differentiation and exploitation of market share; their financial and public relations staff will warn shareholders and bankers against 'short-termism'; their

corporate planners will pick off troublesome competitors by acquisition. Transforming the immediate structural conditions for their
actions in all these ways, dominant actors enlarge their personal scope
for strategic choice. And, just as all the dedicated efforts of individual
profit-maximizers contribute to the reproduction of capitalism as a
whole, so do the strategic choices of less single-minded strategists
combine to subvert it.

Chapter Five

Social structure and strategic choice

INTRODUCTION

The argument of the previous chapter was that the possibility of
agency depends upon social structural complexity. Without social
structure, actors would have neither the tools nor the will preconditional to agency. And without structural complexity, actors would
lack the range of powers and motives enabling them to exercise this
potential for agency in choice. In this chapter I will introduce three
sets of structures – capitalist, patriarchal and ethnic – each in tension
with each other and thus each affording opportunities for independent
action. But before examining these structures further, let me sketch
how structural complexity permits strategic choice within the firm.

In this book I shall conceive of the firm as a particular
institutionalized system of interaction possessing certain structural
properties derived from the larger capitalist structures that imbue
economic activities within our society. These structural properties give
certain actors – owners or managers – not only control over the capital
embodied in the firm but also the right to organize the labour of other
less structurally advantaged participants. For the holders of this power,
command over the firm's resources substantially enhances their
capacity for action. The actions of dominant actors – owners and
managers – are not, however, dictated simply by the capitalist logics of
their class position. Owners, managers and workers participate in a
plurality of social systems – families and communities as well as
capitalist enterprises. Each of these systems possesses structural
properties of its own, conferring different sorts of authority and
indicating different modes of behaviour. As they move from one
sphere to another in the course of their everyday lives, actors carry
with them the diverse structural properties of all the social systems in
which they participate. Thus dominant actors need not depend upon

any single set of social logics, but can avail themselves of a variety of structural rules and resources with which to inspire and justify their conduct. Even at work, the firm's dominant actors may refuse to conform narrowly to their roles as stereotypical capitalists, modelling their behaviour instead on alternative patriarchal or ethnic principles. By the same token, subordinate actors, participants too in these other social systems, can be persuaded to defer not just to the rights of capital, but also to patterns of authority drawn from the community and the household. It is this harnessing of diverse structural principles that allows dominant actors to construct personal objectives free from any singular structural determination; and it is this exploitation of plural sources of structural power that enables them to enlist the energies of other actors to their particular cause. In short, dominant actors exercise strategic choice by virtue of the skilful pluralism with which they manage their various social structural advantages.

This chapter has two main parts. The following section examines some of the structures from whose diversity and contradictions actors derive their power and autonomy. The subsequent section considers first how the firm's dominant actors mobilize these divergent structures internally by the construction of 'local ideologies', and then how they maintain their powers externally by the management of their market environments.

COMPLEX STRUCTURES

This section introduces three sets of structures – capitalist, patriarchal and ethnic – demonstrating the complexity of both their internal formations and their interrelationships. Though these are not the only ways in which society is structured, I shall demonstrate in later chapters that these three structures are particularly important in explaining the recession strategies chosen by dominant actors in my eight case study firms.

Capitalism

The contemporary business enterprise is founded upon certain capitalist principles so basic that they are, too often, taken for granted within organization studies. Without the privately owned capital supplied by shareholders, the firm would not exist. Yet without the labour and creativity captured within the firm, capital would stagnate and deteriorate. Despite the symmetry of this dependence, within a capitalist society it is the suppliers of capital who dominate. Capitalist structures give owners control not only over the labour of their employees, but also over the products of their work. Owners renew and augment their capital by engaging their employees in the production of goods and services which they can exchange in the market-place for profit. Thus capital is reproduced in a self-perpetuating circular movement: capital organizes and enlarges the activities of labour by providing it with equipment and direction; in return the profits earned by these activities replenish and expand the original capital.

Capital's reproductive need to hire workers in labour markets and to earn surpluses in product markets endows capitalist structures with an abstract determinacy. However, this structural logic is no more than a rule, to which the individual possessor of capital need not defer entirely. Marx's (1954, p. 151) own account of the circular reproduction of capital seems to recognize this distinction between structural rule and actor's behaviour:

> As the conscious representative of this movement, the possessor of money becomes a capitalist. His person, or rather his pocket, is the point from which the money starts and to which it returns. The expansion of value . . . becomes his subjective aim, and *it is only in so far as the appropriation of ever more and more wealth in the abstract becomes the sole motive of his operations, that he functions as a capitalist, that is, as capital personified and endowed with consciousness and a will* . . . The restless never-ending process, of profit-making alone, is what he aims at. This boundless greed after riches, this passionate chase after exchange value, is common to the capitalist and the miser; but while the miser is merely a capitalist gone mad, the capitalist is a rational miser (italics added).

Thus capital possesses law-like requirements for its reproduction, yet need not determine the conduct of the owner. Simple ownership of capital does not define the actor as capitalist; the actor is a capitalist only to the extent to which he or she *acts as* capitalist.

Of the eight firms whose strategies I shall be examining, four were dominated by active owner-managers. In another two firms, owner-managers had been dominant until quite recently. None of these actors functioned wholly as the pure capitalist of Marx's caricature. Economic class position alone did not exhaust their personalities – they possessed internal complexities that afforded them plenty of other motives for action. Besides, as I shall argue in this section, capitalist structures themselves contain too many complexities of their own to provide any

simple rules for conduct. The imperative towards profit maximization
is confused on the one hand by the growing sophistication of enterprise
and on the other by the proliferation of managerial and entrepreneurial ideologies originally intended to support it. Moreover, as
the following sections will insist, these capitalist structures exert no
monopolistic hold upon their owner-managers; they must compete for
influence with the distinct and potentially contrary logics of patriarchal
and ethnic structures. First, though, I wish to demonstrate that these
owner managers are far from unusual.

Examining the evidence from corporate America, Zeitlin (1974)
emphatically dismisses the so-called managerial revolution as a
'pseudo-fact', and asserts instead the continuing influence of
'kineconic' family ownership patterns. Evidence from the United
Kingdom confirms the continuing influence of family owners upon
strategic management. In the UK, Nyman and Silberston (1978)
estimated that at least 56 per cent of the top 250 British firms had
proprietorial groups owning sufficient shares (more than 5 per cent) to
exercise effective control over their managements. More recently,
Scott (1985; 1986) has revealed the continuing activity of a substantial
'business class' dominating the conduct of many of Britain's largest
companies: 49 of the top 250 UK companies were under the majority
control of a single family or closely inter-married group of families; a
further 27 had families who were the largest but not majority
shareholders; and another 35 contained influential families amongst
their twenty largest shareholders. More than half the families Scott
identifies contain true 'entrepreneurial capitalists', in the sense that
they were represented on their companies' boards of directors rather
than simply being detached and passive shareholders.

However, mere ownership of capital neither dictates the direction of
conduct nor guarantees its effectiveness. Capitalism, beset by its own
internal contradictions, affords few unambiguous guides to action. In
the governance of labour, as Hyman (1987) demonstrates, capitalists
are torn between the alternatives of coercion and incorporation –
discipline to ensure control, discretion to allow scope for creativity and
initiative. Strategic planning likewise is bedevilled by the conflicting
demands of short and long term profit-maximisation, dynamic and
static efficiency (Silberston, 1983). As the modern corporation grows
larger and more sophisticated, as it broadens its scope into new
activities and regions, these dilemmas become even more imponder-
able. The very success of contemporary capitalism in creating the
complex large-scale enterprise of today has generated an information
overload that increasingly undermines the ability of capitalist logics to
provide any clear direction for conduct (Kay, 1984). Unable to

determine the consequences of their actions, capitalists grope uncertainly into the future, choosing between courses that they can only hope will lead towards profit maximization. But whereas uncertainty is discomforting to the profit-maximizing capitalist, owner managers applying the resources of their firms to ends other than maximum profit may actually welcome this ambiguity. The inherent confusion of modern enterprise enlarges the potential for choice by camouflaging deviation from the strict course of profit-maximization. The more obscure the profit-maximizing course, the harder it is to judge and penalize strategic actions that diverge from it.

If there is not sufficient complexity here, then further sources of tension and potential contradiction can be found in the techniques and ideologies capitalists have themselves developed, originally in their own support – namely, entrepreneurism and managerialism. From its outset in the Industrial Revolution, capitalism had to bolster its claims for 'free enterprise' against the constricting traditionalism of aristocracy and peasant. By invoking the ideological figure of the 'entrepreneur' – depicted as pioneering risk-taker and source of all prosperity and progress – early capitalists sought to legitimate the unfettered pursuit of profit (Bendix, 1963; Scase and Goffee, 1982, p. 126). Today, in late twentieth-century Britain, this entrepreneurial ideology is being reasserted once more, this time to justify an assault on the alleged constraints of the welfare state and its replacement by a new 'enterprise culture' based on individual initiative and self-reliance. Thus, whether in protest against feudalism or 'socialism', the entrepreneurial figure has repeatedly been projected as the individualistic champion of economic license and the opponent of consensus and constraint. But this endorsement of entrepreneurial freedom contains a paradox. The entrepreneur is not bound to behave like Marx's 'rational miser', for the ideology is liberating rather than constraining. It is the essence of entrepreneurial freedom to be able to disregard even the constraints of cautious calculation.

This risk-taking, opportunistic aspect of entrepreneurism is, however, in direct contradiction to the alternative ideology of managerialism. Managerialism, both as phenomenon and idea, was also the creation of capitalism, but one which has gradually escaped its control. As their enterprises grew beyond the bounds of their will or capability to manage directly, capitalists were increasingly forced to delegate their economic responsibilities to managers. In so doing, they imported yet another contradictory force, for these managers occupy a deeply equivocal position within capitalist structures (Wright, 1985; Willmott, 1987). As delegates of capitalists, the managerial claim to a 'right to manage' is ultimately merely derivative of capitalists' 'right to do what one likes with one's own' (Storey, 1983, p. 103). Yet managers also seek independent legitimation for their practices on the grounds of 'economic efficiency' based upon professional training and impartial expertise (Storey, 1983). This managerial self-image – managers as disinterested and professional servants of efficiency – is not easily reconciled with unfettered autocracy based simply on property rights. While the supremacy of the owner may be the consequence of business luck or even just inheritance, the manager regards his or her authority as achieved through the steady cultivation of skill and hard-earned promotion. Managerial success is the result of discipline rather than chance or opportunity. This contrast between managerial restraint and entrepreneurial risk is captured in Channon's (1979) study of strategies within service industries, where typically founding entrepreneurs would enthusiastically embark upon campaigns of aggressive conglomerate diversification, while managerially controlled firms cautiously restricted themselves to related diversification.

Indeed, post-war managerial ideology has increasingly displaced capitalists from their former central position within the firm. Managerialism now proposes an 'organic' conception of the firm in which capitalists are just one of many 'stakeholders' and profitability only one of several needs to be satisfied (Child, 1969; Alvesson, 1987, pp. 160–2). Against the arbitrary authoritarianism of naked capitalism, managers invoke the notion of the firm as 'team', with all united around the same goals just as in football or cricket (Child, 1969, p. 124). Very likely this organacist conception of the enterprise was originally intended to strengthen capitalism, not by changing it but by obscuring it (Nichols, 1969). Yet repeated invocation of team ideologies must, by creating norms and expectations, eventually hedge capital's former absolutism.

Capitalist structures, then, are deeply fractured in both the rules and the resources they offer actors. Simple ownership of capital rarely provides either sufficient resource for, or unambiguous guide to, action. From the outset, capitalist property rights have required reinforcement by an entrepreneurial ideology; ironically, this ideology now legitimates radical departures from careful, rational profit-maximization. The problems of reproducing capital in the form of the increasingly large and complex enterprises of today possess no simple resolutions, and perforce have stimulated the growth of a managerial class whose commitment to professionalism and organicism may actually conflict with, and constrain, the whims of the owner. In sum, capitalist structures, while they provide the material and ideological resources necessary for action, are incapable of imposing determinate rules for how they are actually used in practice.

Patriarchy

To the confusions internal to capitalism must be added the complexities of the wider society. Owners, managers and workers do not exist in some separate sphere, isolated from all other forms of society. These actors are bred, fed, and loved in households characterized by an altogether separate set of structures: patriarchy.

I shall use the term patriarchy in the Weberian sense, referring to the authority and rights exercised by older males over the activities of both women and younger males, originally within the household but also potentially beyond it (Weber, 1964, pp. 346–7). As Walby (1986) and Hartman (1979) allege – though confining the concept to the domination of men over women – patriarchal structures have always operated in tense but close articulation with capitalism. Patriarchy, by restricting women's capacity to claim full value for their labour, creates a potential pool of cheap labour ready for capitalism to exploit. Yet in practice, as during the Industrial Revolution or in the immediate post-war period, the capitalist demand for cheap female labour in the factories has repeatedly clashed with patriarchal concern for maintaining established authority within the household. It is such tensions between capitalist and patriarchal structures that older actors within certain of the case study firms were able to exploit. I shall concentrate on the way in which the patriarchal ideology of paternalism (Lawson, 1983) enhanced dominant actors' scope for strategic choice, both by mapping alternative rules for conduct and by providing them with the additional authority necessary for securing the obedience of their younger managers.

The claim of paternalism is that patriarch and subordinate are united in a 'organic partnership', in which interests are shared and authority natural (Newby, 1975). The patriarch's authority is not without obligations: paternalism is governed by a 'deferential dialectic' according to which the patriarch admits a duty of protection while in return expecting his dependents to accede completely to his domination and to accept his interests as their own. Though learnt in the household, this deference can be exported beyond. Thus Lawson (1983) describes how paternalistic ideologies were drawn upon to support the still shaky legitimacy of early capitalists during the Industrial Revolution: George Courtauld portrayed his workforce as his 'family', with him as 'father' and 'patriarch'. Again surprising perhaps to those with faith in the emergence of a professionalized management, this paternalistic idea survives not only in small family enterprises (Scase and Goffee, 1982), but also in such large corporations as Marks and Spencer, ICI and British Petroleum (Anthony, 1986).

In these instances, paternalism may endorse little more than a conventional exchange of employee loyalty for employer protection. However, as Weber (1964, pp. 341–54) suggests in his classic discussion of patriarchial authority outside the household – 'patrimonialism' in his terms – paternalist ideologies can license practices far more sharply opposed to capitalist rationalities than simple care for labour. The ideal-typical patriarchal chief disdains the disciplines of capitalist calculation. Scorning professional bureaucracies, he assembles his retinue from kin, dependents and favourites often raised from the lowest ranks. Recruitment, promotion and organization of this band of retainers is highly informal, subject to the arbitrary whims and favours of the chief himself. These retainers obey the commands of their chief absolutely. In the pure form of Weberian patrimonialism: 'Obedience is not owed to enacted rules, but to the person who occupies a position of authority . . . The obligations of obedience on the basis of personal loyalty are essentially unlimited' (Weber, 1964, p. 341). The activities of the chief, even in economic spheres such as taxation, are wont to be chaotic, uncalculating and traditional. Though precedent may restrict certain actions, patrimonialism allows a space where 'the chief is free to confer "grace" on the basis of his personal pleasure or displeasure, his personal likes and dislikes, quite arbitrarily' (Weber, 1964, p. 342).

This is a model of behaviour that, if transferred to the contemporary enterprise, would operate a significant release from the disciplines of profit-maximization. For the patriarch, power is personal, action arbitrary. And, indeed, this patriarchal model can be transferred from one system of interaction to another. As they clock on at work in the morning and then return home in the evening, actors do not cross some Lethean divide that strips them of all memory of their other lives. Everyday participants in the patriarchy of their family life, actors remain responsive to its divergent appeals during their working day. This is not to say that, in harnessing the licence of patrimonialism in pursuit of personal objectives, the patriarch is entirely unconstrained. As Martin and Fryer (1973) demonstrate in their study of the Lancashire textile industry in the 1960s, adhesion to paternalist traditions in the face of international competition may lead the firm to bankruptcy or takeover. Patriarchal economic conduct is possible, but does require some shelter from the full brunt of competitive forces.

In short, patriarchal structures, though the product of the household, offer both rules and resources that can potentially be extended beyond it. Within the firm, the patriarchal ideal may both provide the older male with codes of conduct starkly opposed to strict capitalist disciplines and endow him with sufficient legitimate authority to follow them. But while giving power with one hand, patriarchy takes it away with the other; paternalism's own internal dialectic insists that patriarchal authority should not be exercised too brutally according to personal whim.

Ethnicity

Ethnicity, too, provides rules for action that at the most are only contingently supportive of capitalist logics. As Rex (1986, p. 81) maintains, ethnicity enjoys no harmonious or determinate relationship with economic structures. Ethnic groupings sometimes coincide with, sometimes reinforce, the class groupings derived from relations to the means of production; yet, as in South Africa, they can also cut across and disrupt them. Indeed, ethnicity itself works in a highly indeterminate fashion. Ethnicity is not an innate biological characteristic imposed by nature; rather, it constitutes an identity, providing access to activities shared by other members of the ethnic grouping, that is social and may be chosen. Thus the oppressed Bengali Asians of Bow rely more on their ethnic identities than the Asians of more tolerant Battersea (Wallman, 1986). Ethnicity, then, provides structured resources and codes of conduct that are embraced more fervently by some than by others, and which may support or impede capitalist economic activities.

Here, though, I wish to concentrate upon how ethnic identities provide rules for conduct in business interactions outside immediate community systems. The two case study industries – office furniture and domestic appliances – are parts of the wider furniture and electrical consumer goods sectors which, because of their low barriers to entry and rapid growth up until the 1960s, have historically attracted many Jewish entrepreneurs (Aris, 1970, pp. 109–10; Pollins, 1982). Given these industrial characteristics, it is not surprising that two of my case study firms were dominated by Jewish businessmen explicitly drawing upon ethnic codes of conduct; in two more, Jewish influences were present but less immediate.

Community values deeply penetrate Jewish economic activities. For the various groups of Jewish immigrants flying racial persecution in Europe from the late nineteenth century onwards, business success became essential both for material livelihood and social status within a caste-ridden English society. In her account of Jewish businessmen, Kosmin (1979, p. 53) observes: 'Their whole sense of identity – indeed their whole life – is involved in business and work'. These Jewish entrepreneurs bring to their work certain characteristic approaches learnt from their communal experiences. Survival of terrible oppression has inculcated a stubborn, almost perverse, optimism, epitomized in the Hebrew phrase 'hiyé-tov' – 'it will be good, it will come right' (Kosmin, 1979). Although business success is to be the instrument for regaining social standing within the wider society, traditions of ghetto community and collective support in adversity render status at work less important. Relations between employers and employees are traditionally informal and personal, with workers often on first name terms with their bosses (Aris, 1970, p. 237). In emergency, the typical Jewish boss is always ready to *schlap*, that is, to join in physical or dirty work (Kosmin, 1979). In return, however, the Jewish boss expects complete obedience, often acting in domineering and autocratic fashion (Aris, 1970, pp'. 21–2).

Of course, the various generations of immigrants were not all the same. In particular, Berghahn (1984) notes how the German and Austrian refugees of the inter-war period – from amongst whom two of the case study entrepreneurs were drawn – often possessed high professional qualifications and skills. Thus, while earlier inflows had tended to concentrate initially in the primitive and labour-intensive 'sweated' trades, this generation has been able to penetrate the more highly skilled chemical and jewelry industries and also to introduce new methods and products (Berghahn, 1984, p. 108). Moreover, although many of this later generation still retain a nostalgia for their German *Heimat*, some embrace their adopted country with an unqualified enthusiasm, claiming to be 'more English than the English' (Berghahn, 1984, p. 175).

For the Jewish businessmen I shall introduce later, their ethnicity imposed no inescapable patterns of conduct, but rather made available rich reserves of rules and resources upon which they could draw selectively in their economic activities. Yet the relation between Jewish ethnicity and capitalist logics remains complex. On the one hand, dedication to hard work and the capacity for innovation clearly contribute to capitalistic success. In the circumstances of recession, however, informality, personal loyalties, blithe optimism and auto-cratic management styles could easily lead to business catastrophe.

STRATEGIC CHOICE AND CONSTRAINT

In the preceding section I introduced three sets of structures – capitalist, patriarchal and ethnic – each independent and each capable of generating different patterns of conduct. This social structural complexity leaves no room for the simple actor of action determinism; rather, the human actor becomes the nexus for diverse and conflicting structural principles. Possessing not only physiology and individual psychology, the actor also has access to a plurality of social selves. Thus for the businessmen I shall describe later, social structures offered at once the capacity to act as capitalists, as patriarchs or as Jews. Picking and mixing from these diverse social opportunities, these actors were able to synthesize personal aims and modes of action unique to themselves and independent of any single structural determination.

However, this independence in the formulation of their purposes is not sufficient alone to establish these actors as agents. To be true agents, actors require the powers necessary to be effective in their actions. They must be able to harness material resources and the activity of other actors to the achievement of their own objectives. Here lies the singular attraction of the capitalist enterprise. As collections of administratively co-ordinated human and material resources (Penrose, 1980, p. 24), firms represent peculiarly potent instruments for action. Organizing factories, equipment and people, stretching perhaps across the world, capitalist firms agglomerate resources on a scale that equals, and often surpasses, that of whole nation states. These firms are not, moreover, static or dependent organizations; as economic units they possess the mechanisms for near limitless self-expansion. But the most significant feature of the capitalist enterprise for human agency lies in its government by hierarchies of administrative authority. Access to hierarchical authority is not available to every one, of course, but dependent upon social structural privilege, whether it be the ownership of capital acquired through entrepreneurial effort, inherited wealth due to the sheer accident of birth or hard-won recognized managerial skills. However, those ascendant over these hierarchies enjoy a capacity to dispose resources on a scale and with a freedom from subordinate challenge without parallel within democratic society. Neither party politician nor trade unionist exercises such great power with so little internal accountability. Thus, as a means for enlisting material and human resources to the narrow purposes of its elite, the capitalist enterprise is uniquely able to extend the agency of a few, at the same time as restricting that of the many.

Nevertheless, simple command over formal hierarchies of authority within the firms does not confer unbridled powers. I shall concentrate here upon two sets of constraint, within and without the firm. First, in the system of interaction represented by the firm itself, dominant actors cannot rely on mere possession of formal authority but must act continually to maintain and extend it. As we saw in the previous section, property rights alone were inadequate to the early capitalists such as George Courtauld, and today managerial claims may circumscribe the arbitrary rule of the entrepreneur. The more idiosyncratic dominant actors seek to be in their business activities, the more careful they must be to protect their internal legitimacy. Second, the resources combined in their firms must be reproduced and safeguarded, at least to the extent necessary to the fulfillment of dominant actors' objectives. Labour must be rewarded, machines fuelled, materials bought, shareholders recompensed. Thus the need to reproduce and protect the resources under their control constrains dominant actors to achieve at least adequate levels of business efficiency within the market systems in which their firms interact. These two sets of constraints – internal legitimacy and external markets – will be examined in turn.

Local ideologies

Though the hierarchies of managerial authority within the firm offer a uniquely effective means of mobilizing the labour of other actors, they do not give absolute power. Dominant actors must carefully manage their interactions with the subordinate actors whose activities they seek to direct. So long as these subordinates operate in other systems of interaction, and retain the option of abandoning entirely the particular system of the firm, mere managerial command will never be capable of exacting complete obedience. Able to appeal to rules and resources independent of their immediate work situation, subordinates may defy or defect from an organizational structure that they perceive as oppressive or illegitimate. As Zald and Berger (1978) put it, top managers exceeding the bounds of organizational legitimacy risk provoking 'organizational coups d'etat' or 'bureaucratic insurgencies' on the part of managers immediately below them. The alternative to revolt, especially for those with managerial or other valued skills, is simple 'exit' (Hirschmann, 1970) – a haemorrhage of the actors whose labour is essential to the achievement of dominant actors' objectives.

If, therefore, dominant actors want to pursue personal objectives beyond those endorsed by capitalism in security, they, too, must appeal to alternative structural sources of legitimacy. To extend their scope for legitimate activity, dominant actors may construct, from whatever other social structural rules and resources are available to them, 'local' ideologies enshrining those personal objectives for which the firm is their instrument. Exactly the same divergent social structures that confine their power as capitalists (actual or delegated) may be conscripted to enhance their power to achieve personal ends. Thus, a dominant actor need not depend solely on his status as major shareholder or chief executive: as oldest male, he may demand the deference of younger subordinates to him as patriarch; as Jewish entrepreneur, the same actor may justify boldly optimistic conduct as only natural. It is by skilfully weaving local ideologies from diverse structural rules and resources that dominant actors free themselves from the constraints on legitimate action imposed by any single set of social structures.

These 'local' ideologies, then, are beliefs concerning the organization and its relation to its environment that both embody the objectives held by dominant actors and serve to secure the compliance of other actors important to achieving them. As such, local ideologies can exert a threefold influence upon the strategic actions of the firm: evaluative, cognitive and legitimatory (cf. Shrivastava, 1985). In their evaluative function, these ideologies establish the objectives towards which actors should direct their activities, excluding others. Cognitively, ideologies introduce consistent biases, shaping conceptions of what is important or possible, and thereby limiting actors' (both dominant and subordinate) perceptions of opportunities for strategic action. Finally, local ideologies discipline actors by determining for them legitimate practices. There is some irony in this last aspect: local ideologies actually constrain the actions of dominant actors, for, unless they are prepared to risk dissent, they, too, must confine their strategic choices to what has already been defined as ideologically legitimate (Green, 1987a).

Though this concept of local ideologies covers similar phenomena as that discovery of the 1980s, 'corporate culture' (for example Peters and Waterman, 1982), its intention is very different. The missionaries of corporate culture, even when opportunistically claiming for themselves the notion of ideology, rely too heavily upon social psychology and functionalist assumptions of organizational harmony (Pascale, 1985; Weiss and Miller, 1987). One notable exponent, Edgar Schein (1985, pp. 50–2), explicitly invokes Parsons and Merton to assert that the function of organizational culture is to promote adaptation and integration. According to Schein, organizational cultures epitomize organizational members' shared conceptions of their 'ultimate survival problem' and embody a consensus on the 'core mission' necessary to meet this problem. Trapped within the concerns of cognitive psychology, Schein is quite unable to recognize the social structural inequalities that render any such internal consensus entirely bogus. Organizational members may come to accept certain shared conceptions, but these will be imposed by dominant actors. It is only the few who enjoy privileged access to diverse social structural sources of legitimacy and exclusive control over organizational hierarchy who are able to construct and propagate 'cultures' embracing the whole firm (Alvesson, 1987, p. 213). Though these dominant actors may like to think of their 'cultures' as 'corporate', in so far as they maintain their power and serve their ends, they remain narrowly ideological. Thus, local ideologies are not the means of managing a survival problem for the members of the firm as a whole; rather, they enlist the labour of the firm's employees to the service of dominant sectional groupings. What the organizational literature generally describes as culture, and here will be termed local ideology, is an instrument of control, not consensus (cf. Lebas and Weigenstein, 1986).

Ideological control is not simply and easily secured, however. Here hierarchical position does confer a crucial initial resource. While formal authority is limited in what it can achieve directly, the access it gives to structures of command, communication, hiring and firing, payment and promotion can, if skillfully employed, be used to extend control through ideological incorporation. Following Mintzberg's (1983) typology, ideological incorporation of key actors can be achieved in three ways: by 'calculated identification', by 'evoked identification'; or by 'selected identification'. Calculated identification is the weakest of the three, according to Mintzberg (1983), being based merely upon the self-interested assessment by actors of potential rewards and punishments. Calculated identification corresponds to the ways in which Bauer and Cohen's (1981; 1983a) 'governing cliques' manipulate their middle managers with salaries and perks into acceptance of their subordination. Evoked identification is obtained by socialization and indoctrination, as in Mills' (1956) and Bendix's (1963) accounts of the training of managerial elites at General Motors and General Electric. However, identification can be evoked more informally, for instance, by cultivating inspirational organizational 'stories' of the sort described by Wilkins (1983b) and Martin and Powers (1983) or through the rituals of 'Fosterization' discovered by Johnson (1987) at Fosters Menswear. Then there is selected identification, emerging from the manipulation of the mechanisms of recruitment and promotion in order to ensure that only those who fit the prevailing ideology are allowed to enter into positions of authority. Dahrendorf (1959, pp. 46–7) classically epitomizes the predicament for the aspiring manager subject to selection: 'to be successful means to be liked, and to be liked means, in many ways, to be alike'.

However skilled the manipulation of incentives, training, recruitment and promotions, ideological incorporation is unlikely to be complete. Incorporation may only be necessary for that small group of key actors whose positions within the hierarchy of formal authority give them sufficient access to understand the idiosyncratic nature of dominant actors' conduct and renders their co-operation essential to securing the compliance of subordinate actors (cf. Abercrombie, Hill and Turner, 1980). For the rest, for whom the rationales of top management decision-making are impenetrably obscure and whose scope for discretion is anyway tightly constrained, administrative co-ordination will probably suffice. Indeed, dominant agents will very likely fail to achieve the complete ideological incorporation even of senior echelons, and will have to tolerate a number of competing local ideologies (Beyer, 1981; Starbuck, 1982). The plural and contradictory nature of the broader social ideologies upon which dominant actors must draw, and the constrained powers of hierarchical position, limit the extent to which coherent local ideologies can be assembled and imposed. These other senior managers participate in other systems too, and their exposure to alternative ideologies and their capacity to defect gives them a basis for independent actions which cannot be entirely expropriated. Thus, local ideologies will rarely be totally hegemonic and there will always be some room for contest and dissent. Where local ideologies are least cohesive and secure, the consequences for corporate strategic choice may be the same instability and inconsistency as characteristic of Miles and Snow's (1978) Reactor organizations.

In sum, while the capitalist properties of the firm will support authority exercised in the direction of profit-maximizing activity, dominant actors who too obviously seek to turn the firm's resources towards other objectives must actively manage the consent of subordinates. Failure to remain within the bounds of legitimacy risks provoking on the part of subordinate actors either internal revolt or debilitating defection. These dominant actors will therefore exploit their access to alternative structural sources of legitimacy – perhaps patriarchal or ethnic – and, by manipulating their administrative controls, create from them local ideologies capable of supporting their conduct. This may suffice to suppress internal dissent; however, the capacity for effective strategic choice depends as well on the management of market environments.

Market systems

Ideological manipulation may divert the firm from capitalist logics, but it cannot free it entirely. The resources embodied within the firm do not live by ideas alone. Labour and materials must be paid for. To obtain the resources necessary for corporate action, dominant actors must enter factor markets; to pay for their resources, they must generate income in product markets. Thus the firm's dominant actors are inextricably involved in markets, and must carry out their market transactions with at least some regard for business efficiency, as measured by profit.

However, markets do not impose this profit constraint in some objective and ineluctable fashion. Action Theory is right in objecting to the 'reification' of market constraints so typical of environmental determinism: markets are nothing but the products of human activities. This insight needs to be retained. Like any other system of interaction, the participation of human agents renders its patterns of activity indeterminate, subject to the choices of its members. However – and here, as always, Realism departs from Action Theory – markets are also like other systems in that action remains subject to structural constraints. In their market activities, actors can only draw on the social structural rules and resources available to them. As elsewhere, these constraints are real; if not determining, they certainly set limits on possibility. But constraints can be negotiated. By careful choice of objectives, selection of particular relationships and skillful manipulation of transactions, actors can combine to steal from the interactions that constitute their markets complete determinacy.

This conception of markets as non-deterministic social systems is very distant from that of conventional economic theory. As Hodgson (1988, pp. 177–83) observes, economists tend to regard 'the market' as a natural order, operating within some abstract, ethereal sphere, and populated only by momentarily colliding and interacting economic atoms. Well-ordered, determinate outcomes are assured by the pure, impersonal and undistractable nature of these atoms' interactions. In reality, of course, this market ideal cannot protect itself from the polluting intrusions of the social world. Examining the historical development of market economies, Polanyi (1944, p. 250) concluded that, far from being natural to human societies, markets only achieved their modern pre-eminence – first in industrializing Britain and later throughout the world – by the deliberate and often violent deployment of state power. Even once established, markets remain dependent upon a whole web of supportive social institutions – customary, legal and political – without which they could not work with any reliability at all (Hodgson, 1988, p. 174). At the same time, the curt impersonality supposed to govern market interactions is constantly undermined by our human tendency to construct continuing social relationships amongst those with whom we deal (Granovetter, 1985, p. 481). Market relations are often direct, enduring and selective. Baker (1984) shows that stock exchange members will choose their trading partners according to friendship, enmity or even sycophancy, and they will form 'crowds' capable of collectively refusing to 'hear' the bids of opportunistic, unparticipatory traders.

Embedded within a plural social world, market transactions frequently depart from narrow economic rationality (Granovetter, 1985, p. 506). Managers and entrepreneurs enter markets not just to accumulate profit, but also to agglomerate the capital and labour necessary for all sorts of different ends – social prestige, political influence or even power for power's sake. Participation in markets is no more than an unfortunate condition for enjoying the use of other people's resources. Thus markets enable by providing access to the means of action; they constrain in so far as actors must obey prevailing rules of exchange in order to get from them what they want. Once the basic needs of existence are satisfied at least, markets contain no imperative; the extent of participation, and the profit required, are the result of choices dependent upon personal objectives.

These choices emerge from the complex, even contradictory social identities of market actors (cf. Swedberg, Himmelstrand and Brulin, 1987, p. 176). In the market-place – as in any other system of interaction – actors need not operate exclusively according to the rules 'belonging' to that particular system. Rather than being simple asocial atoms, market actors are members of families, communities and religions. Having available diverse social codes of conduct, actors may choose therefore to defy the full logic of capitalist rationales in particular market transactions. Monopolists may mercifully fail to extort the last drop of profit from their customers; small business people may deliberately ignore opportunities rather than expose themselves to alien and potentially threatening suppliers or clients; norms of friendship and community may displace capitalist rationalities in transactions between long-established family businesses in local backwaters. In making these various choices and acting upon them, these actors are effectively defining the extent and nature of their markets. Markets do not exist where actors refuse to participate; markets operate according to the rules which their constituents actually use.

Thus markets can be transformed from systems governed by the invisible hand of determinism into systems characterized by social relationships subject to choice. Indeterminate themselves, it cannot be markets that determine conduct. This is not to give in to the idealist voluntarism of Action Theory. Markets remain the mechanisms for satisfying quite basic material needs. Capitalist structures afford actors more or less resources to start with: the less marketable property or skill one possesses, the more one has to concentrate one's efforts in the market-place exclusively on earning one's keep. In other words, structural privilege defines the extent to which actors can turn the market to objectives other than merely meeting the basic needs of existence. Moreover, the market environment is not just a subjective, personal construction, but rather the playground on which very real actors can be brought into often dangerous interaction (Child and Smith, 1987). Actors can only play according to their own rules so long as they are able to protect themselves from opportunistic rule-breaking and the incursion of other actors operating according to quite different rules. Whether economically – by constant innovation and the raising of investment requirements – or socially – by cultivating trade associations, state protectionism and 'old boy' networks – participants must work to 'close' their markets against potential disruption (Cawson *et al*, 1989).

Where markets bring together actors of unequal powers – say, multinational corporations and peasant farmers – there always remains the potential for determination. In order to pay the taxes of authoritarian governments and repay the loans of usurious money-lenders, peasants may be driven into the exclusive cultivation of cash crops and forced to sell their produce at the prices set by monopsonist buyers. But here it would be powerful actors, not abstract markets, that dictated conduct to the weak; and the dictates of the powerful are a matter for their own discretion. Social structural inequalities would define what was possible between powerful and powerless in the market-place; they could not determine what actually happened.

Markets, then, are not determining in themselves, but do provide the mechanisms through which determination can be exerted by powerful actors. Thus they constitute yet another set of relations which a firm's dominant actors must strive to manage as far as their structural powers allow them. Market activity makes an ambivalent contribution to their agency. On the one hand it maintains and extends the resources under dominant actors' control, on the other it entails a dull treadmill of profit generation that distracts from final objectives, while also exposing them to the threats of powerful corporate actors (ruthless predators, tough customers) with quite contrary purposes. In the market-place, just as internally within the firm, actors' success in applying adequate resources to personal objectives requires the skilful exploitation, manipulation, selection and sometimes evasion of particular interactions. I shall deal here with the three spheres of interaction delineated by Lawriwsky's distinction between product markets, the market for capital and the market for corporate control.

Fundamental are transactions in product markets. If revenues earned in product markets are essential to maintaining the fabric of the enterprise, these should be earned with as great as efficiency as possible. This does not necessarily imply profit-maximization, for that would involve a dedication of resources to the exclusion of other objectives. Rather, the aim would to achieve that happy equilibrium at which resources adequate to dominant actors' objectives could be earned with the least possible diversion of effort. Though this might entail a ruthless exploitation of labour internally, the resulting surplus would not necessarily be translated wholly into profit but in part at least into activities and resources meeting the personal objectives of the firm's dominant actors. Securing this surplus against the competing claims of other actors would, however, require power in the market-place. If dominant actors are to earn the necessary surplus, they must eschew product markets already crowded with other powerful corporate actors – multiple retailers, single suppliers – and they must carefully erect barriers against the entry of powerful new actors playing to different rules and with their own demands on the available surplus.

These ideal product market conditions describe, of course, the position of the classic monopolist of economic theory. Monopoly power, with the consequent capacity to raise product prices above competitive levels, can be exploited in two ways: either to maximize profits, or, by many a free agent, to earn just sufficient easy profits to allow the diversion of at least a part of the firm's resources towards activities more congenial to personal inclinations (cf. Vickers and Hay, 1987). Dominant actors seeking to enlarge their scope for strategic discretion will, therefore, carefully select product markets where they can concentrate sufficient structural resources to ensure superiority over other participants (customers, suppliers, competitors) and where they can secure as much protection as possible from more powerful interlopers.

Successful exploitation of product markets also permits the evasion of potentially constraining relations operated through other markets, especially the markets for capital and corporate control. With good profits – not necessarily maximum profits – dominant agents can rely on self-financing rather than going outside either to the banks or to the stock markets to raise their capital (Eichner, 1976). The adoption of deliberately cautious strategies, with modest financial requirements, will reinforce this independence. There is no need to expose product market surpluses to the avaricious claims of such powerful actors as the financial institutions. Thus, so long as the surplus earned is secure, steady and sufficient for both the firm's reproduction and the satisfaction of personal objectives, exploitation of cosy product markets frees dominant agents from the disciplines otherwise exerted in both the markets for capital and corporate control. The potential for constraint remains however; failure to keep within the bounds of economic prudence will jeopardize dominant agents' control over their firm's resources. For the quoted company, poor performance risks precipitating shareholder revolt or merciless takeover; for the heavily indebted company, a default in interest payments will provoke the unforgiving intervention of the banks.

Thus the three markets – for products, capital and corporate control – do combine to constrict the freedom with which dominant actors can dispose of the resources embodied in their firms. Dominant actors must be for ever managing a delicate compromise between both the powers and the dangers that markets offer. Participation in product markets is vital to reproducing the resources they need to meet their personal objectives, yet at the same time dictates at least some regard for the rules of capitalist exchange; external finance may be necessary to gain still further resources, but endangers dominant actors' autonomy against the claims of the financial institutions and outside shareholders. However, there need be no inevitability about the market interactions dominant actors enter. Actors seeking most independence in strategic choice would seek monopolistic or niche markets, ignore the blandishments of the banks and, if possible, avoid the equity markets, keeping ownership exclusively for themselves.

CONCLUSIONS

The last two chapters have proposed a Realist account of strategic choice based on a strong affirmation of human agency. Strategic decision-makers *can* choose because they draw from society both sufficient internal complexity and external resources for agentive action. Moreover, by skilfully exploiting structural advantages and carefully managing constraints, certain actors are capable of transforming the capitalist enterprise into a particularly potent instrument for this agency. It is this conception of actors and the firm that will underly the presentation of recession strategies in Chapters 7, 8, 9 and 10. First, however, I want to outline some methodological principles and problems and introduce the two industries from which my case study firms come.

Chapter Six

How and where the research was done

INTRODUCTION

The theoretical discussion of the last four chapters establishes the basic grounds for deciding how strategic choice should be researched and in what sorts of firms and industries. Thus, against the determinists, I asserted in Chapter 2 the importance both of examining the conduct of individual firms and of investigating the internal processes from which this conduct emerges. Research should therefore proceed by case study analysis, rather than by large-scale statistical survey. This discussion also suggested empirical procedures for adjudicating between determinist and strategic choice accounts of corporate strategy. Environmental determinists' claims for the merciless nature of market constraints dictate that the possibility of strategic choice must be tested in the harshest environments available; while the action determinists' expectation of stereotypical behaviour indicates the importance of comparing actors' responses to equivalent stimuli. Chapter 3 went on to introduce some recent approaches to strategic choice, particularly applauding the historical, comparative and 'cultural' methods they have developed. However, this chapter also lamented the prevailing dependence on empathetic interpretive methods and neglect of wider social structures. Accordingly, the last two chapters have proposed a Realist approach to strategic choice which insists on the recognition of social structure and the possibility of critical analysis. It is with the methodological implications of this Realist approach that this chapter will mainly deal.

The following section establishes some of the broad methodological principles entailed by a Realist approach and introduces some of its problems. It begins, therefore, by showing how the interpretive understanding of actors' behaviours urged by the Action Theorists should be supplemented by an analysis of the social structures that empower them. It goes on to outline two important identification problems and to indicate how they might be overcome: first, what are the choices; second, who are the choosers? The third section of the chapter is concerned with more concrete research procedures, in particular, the selection of appropriate industries for testing strategic choice and the techniques of data collection. That done, the fourth and fifth sections examine the UK domestic appliance and office furniture industries, which together formed the immediate contexts for my eight case study firms. These sections will demonstrate that both industries, in any event pretty competitive, endured recessions of particular severity. The following four chapters will show how the eight case study firms not only responded to recession in highly idiosyncratic ways, but also survived largely unscathed.

METHODOLOGY

Briefly, this section has three parts. The first suggests how structural analysis should be combined with interpretive understanding; the second considers how moments of strategic choice can actually be captured; and the last explores the ways in which those with the power to choose should be empirically identified.

Analysis of institutions and strategic conduct

The Realist reconciliation of structure and agency imposes a dual requirement upon empirical research. If, as Bhaskar (1986, p. 147) insists, human history is produced by people pursuing their own ends, then any adequate account of their activities and their products should be founded upon an interpretive understanding of the motives which inspire them. However, the fact that human activities happen – or do not happen – also presupposes the existence of certain structural conditions. Though actors rely upon these structural preconditions, they may not always recognize them. Simple interpretive understanding of actors' motives for their actions is therefore not enough. In adding an analysis of structure, Realist research amplifies the scope of explanation by demonstrating how and why any particular action *could* happen.

The need for this dual approach is incorporated in Crozier and Friedberg's (1977, pp. 197–8) distinction between *le raisonnement strategique* and *le raisonnement systematique* and Giddens' (1979; 1984, pp. 288–93) similar contrast between 'the analysis of strategic conduct' and 'institutional analysis'. *Le raisonnement strategique* and the analysis of strategic conduct share equally a respect for people as potential agents, capable of constructing their own objectives and meaning systems and of acting in accordance with them. That is, people both formulate strategies and enact them. As Reed (1985, pp. 141–6) elaborates, this conception of the human actor requires as its corollary analyses that combine the 'cognitive mapping' of actors' frameworks of beliefs and assumptions with an 'interpretive understanding' of the relationship between these cognitive maps and their actual conduct. Thus examination of the corporate strategies of the firm as a whole entails not just a detached narrative of business actions but also an attempt to penetrate the consciousnesses of the actors making the decisions.

Clearly, this analysis of strategic conduct must rely considerably upon the tools of 'empathetic ethnography' advocated by Smircich (1983). The researcher should mine the rich material provided by actors' own accounts, both as explicitly argued by them and as revealed in the symbols, metaphor and rhetoric they employ. Indeed, it follows from the discursive and reflexive capacities they have as agents (Giddens, 1984) that decision-makers should possess and be able to express considerable understanding of their own motives and actions. Nevertheless, some distance and independence should be maintained. As Bhaskar (1986, p. 167) warns, it remains 'incumbent upon the social student to avoid both the pitfalls of arrogant dismissal of and fawning assent to first-person accounts'. Firms are not democratic organizations, and their resources are subject to diversion towards exclusive ends. Their dominant elites deliberately propagate local ideologies mystifying and justifying the workings of the firm. Particular accounts must be checked, both against those of others and also retrospectively for their consistency with the structural conditions necessary for their actions. Here institutional analysis takes its part.

To rely solely upon the analysis of strategic conduct is to undertake an artificial methodological 'bracketing' (Giddens, 1979, p. 80) that, as in Action Theory, treats structure as given or irrelevant and trusts overmuch in actors' own accounts. A complete account of action would also include an 'institutional analysis' – Crozier and Friedberg's (1977) *raisonnement systèmatique* – that acknowledges structure both as constituting the rules and resources on which actors must draw in their activities and as continually reproduced or transformed by those activities. Institutional analysis continually asks what conditions must have existed for a particular series of events to have taken place, and what now are the constraints and opportunities governing future events. Institutional analysis of structural conditions does not, therefore, confine itself to the particular local structures embodied within the firm but extends beyond it in space, to include wider structures of domination (such as class or patriarchy) and in time, to incorporate the historical production of these structures.

Thus institutional analysis inescapably refers both to the historical processes which precede action and to the totality in which it takes place. This concept of 'totality' (Bhaskar, 1979, pp. 54–5; Benson, 1977, p. 4) compels recognition that even the minutest event is implicated within a vast network of relations that encompasses the whole of society. That firms are dominated by particular agents, that their strategies are directed according to some objectives rather than others, even that firms exist in the form that they do, all reflect the ordering of the entire social world. The process of 'totalization' in research powerfully enlarges the researcher's capacity for explanation. Equipped with an understanding of this totality, the researcher can, for instance, qualify actors' dissimulating attributions of their powers to claimed qualities of managerial 'excellence' or 'professionalism'. Domination might be traced back, in the case of a major shareholder, to capitalist structures or, in the case of older male actors, to patriarchy. Naturally, the process of totalization in describing a particular conjuncture may be more or less complete – each time we explain a strategic decision, we need not reconstruct the origins of capitalism – but the existence of totality remains: 'Although it is contingent whether we require a phenomenon to be understood as an aspect of totality (depending on our cognitive interests), it is not contingent whether it *is* such an aspect or not' (Bhaskar, 1979, p. 55). Corporate strategies, therefore, should not be treated as isolated in their conditions or in their effects.

The concept of totality also recognizes the historical precedents for strategy. Bhaskar (1979, pp. 39–45) specifically counterposes his Realist account against Berger and Luckman's (1967) 'dialectical' conception of society as the *continuous* creation of individual actors. According to the Realist approach, people act within structural conditions which are the product of past actions. To understand the formation of these conditions, analysis needs to introduce history; to understand their transformation, it needs to incorporate the processes of change (Bhaskar, 1979, p. 47). Or, as Abrams (1982, p. 8) encapsulates his argument for an 'Historical Sociology', the research should treat ' . . . what people do in the present as a struggle to create a future *out* of the past'. Insight into this struggle is provided by the analysis of 'critical situations' (Giddens, 1979, pp. 228–9), 'events'

(Abrams, 1982) or 'turning points' (Whipp and Clark, 1986, p. 18).
For Abrams (1982, pp. 199), events provide methodological 'points of
entry' into the processes linking action and structure:

> The great events mark decisive conjunctions of action and structure;
> they are transparent moments of structuring at which human agency
> encounters social possibility and can be seen most clearly as
> simultaneously determined and determining.

For the firms that form my case studies, the recession of 1979–81, the
worst in the post-war period, constitutes exactly such a 'great event'.
Faced with crises often threatening their very survival, these companies were forced to take strategic decisions which exposed,
challenged and sometimes revolutionized their whole *raisons d'être*.

In sum, research into corporate strategic choices should proceed
from two directions. Fundamental is an analysis of strategic conduct –
an attempt to understand how the decision-makers see the world and
what they seek from it. However, this understanding must be
tempered by a more detached institutional analysis. Institutional
analysis should be directed at amplifying actors' own accounts by
establishing the structures upon which their actions both depended and
worked. It should fear neither amending actors' accounts nor
extending them, both beyond the bounds of the firm and beyond the
particular moment of decision. The problem now, though, is to
identify these opportunities for genuine strategic choice.

Comparison and choice

For Giddens (1984, p. 9), the notion of agency involves the real
possibility that 'the individual could, at any phase in a given sequence,
have acted differently'. In other words, to be an agent an actor must
enjoy the capacity to choose between different courses of action. This
capacity involves not the 'empty' choices characteristic of environmental determinism, in which the decision-maker must choose the
profit-maximizing course in order to survive; rather, the capacity for
agency implies that the actor has available a range of 'feasible rivals'
for action (Shackle, 1979, p. 12). The problem then is to find out, at
any particular instant of decision, whether feasible rivals existed and
what they were. Or, as Kennedy and Payne (1976) describe the task in
reconstructing business histories, we need to know what firms *could*
have done, other than what they actually did do.

Identifying these opportunities for genuine choice is no easy matter.
It is not enough to rely simply on actors' perceptions of available

alternatives for action (Benson, 1977) – they might be wrong. Yet the full range of feasible options cannot be established by trial either, for it is an unfortunate feature of the 'unbearable lightness of being' (Kundera, 1984) that actors can never experience the same moment of decision twice. It is impossible to test alternatives because the experiment can never be repeated in exactly the same circumstances. There is no perfect solution to this problem, but approximations do exist. Following the Weberian procedure indicated by Hollis (1982), one might attempt an imaginative reconstruction of the options available. Another more empirical approach would be to examine similarly placed actors and search for differences in conduct. As Spender (1980, p. 133) argues, it is by seeking out the contrasts between firms that one discovers their idiosyncrasies.

Thus the strategic alternatives available at recession can be reconstructed by comparing the strategies of firms operating in like circumstances. Of course, even a large group of firms may not empirically test the whole range of possible strategies – indeed it is just possible that they might voluntarily converge upon a single strategy. However, the presence of strategic diversity is certainly suggestive of strategic choice, even if its absence does not necessarily rule it out. But such diversity is not enough on its own. If choice is to be meaningful, it must be about ends as well as means. My claim for strategic choice is not made merely in the fairly trivial sense of 'functional equivalents' or 'equifinality' (Child, 1981; Hrebiniak and Joyce, 1985), but rather in the strong sense that different strategies will yield different performance outcomes yet still be compatible with survival. Genuine strategic choice reveals itself, therefore, in the phenomenon of like-situated firms pursuing a range of strategies, all viable but producing varying performances.

Accordingly, the empirical analysis of this book attempts to standardize the circumstances of its case study firms, in terms of their industrial environments, and to test them with an uniform challenge, in the form of severe recession during the early 1980s. The eight case study firms were drawn from just two industries – three from domestic appliances, five from office furniture. The rival firms in each of the two industries were not, of course, exactly alike (the very fact of their diversity may be taken as suggestive of previous strategic choices). None the less, within each industry the selected firms were as near comparable as possible, all being amongst the industry leaders and experiencing similar severe recessions in their markets. Though the firms did not all have precisely the same product ranges, they did compete substantially with each other. Where they did not compete directly, the firms remained 'potential competitors' (Baumol, Panzar and Willig, 1982) in the sense that market barriers to entry and exit were generally quite low. Thus, as will be shown, the prevalence of factoring and 'badge engineering' in the domestic appliance industry rendered it quite easy for manufacturers to enter new product fields, especially as distribution channels were merging. In the office furniture industry, the emergence of 'systems furniture' was rapidly blurring the traditional industry distinction between wooden and metal furniture. In effect, then, the sample firms within each industry enjoyed very similar strategic options at the onset of the recession.

Models for this comparative approach include Barna's (1962) study of 'aggressive' and 'defensive' firms in the electrical engineering and food processing industries; Miles and Cameron's (1982) account of the divergent tobacco companies' responses to the common challenge of increasing health awareness; Boswell's (1983) contrasts between three steel companies during the fluctuations of the inter-war years; Pettigrew's (1985) comparisons of success and failure in organizational development between divisions within ICI; and the statistical tests of Miles and Snow's (1978) types carried out by Miles and Cameron (1982) and Meyer (1982a; 1982b). In each of these studies, the comparison of the different strategies adopted in the face of similar challenges revealed a range of 'rivals' for action and illuminated the idiosyncratic factors involved in the final selection of strategy.

Who chooses?

If, as I have argued, corporate strategic choices are made by a small, exclusive minority in pursuit of their particular ends, how should these dominant actors be identified? Power within organizations does not correlate neatly with hierarchical position (Dahl, 1961, p. 122; Daudi, 1986, p. 175). Senior and subordinate actors alike confuse the simplicity of hierarchy by their capacity to appeal to other structural sources of power than rank. The result, as in Miles and Snow's (1978) Reactor organizations, is that power frequently becomes diffused and contested. Once more there is no perfect solution to this problem. However, the political scientists investigating 'community power' within North American towns and cities have faced equivalent complexity and in the controversies surrounding their research they have generated a number of useful approaches.

The 'community power' researchers have developed four chief methods of investigation: the 'who gets what' approach; the 'decisional' approach; the 'reputational' approach; and the 'non-decisional' approach. All of these methods are relevant for the analysis of power within organizations as well as communities. Significant, too, is that the methodological controversy which surrounds them has also resolved itself in an emphasis upon comparative studies.

The 'who gets what' approach infers actors' powers from the resources and similar benefits they accumulate. Martin (1977, pp. 117–9), for example, argued that the increasing share of GNP going to earnings rather than to profit indicated a gain in the relative power of workers at the expense of employers. Against this type of approach, Polsby (1979) has pointed out that the distribution of resources need not precisely reflect actual powers because people may benefit from windfalls or even from the deliberate generosity of the powerful. This objection may be less relevant to conditions within firms, where resources are perhaps more tightly controlled than in the community as a whole and where the systems of authority through which they are allocated are more definite. Certainly, promotions to senior management positions, and the resources accruing to them, are not likely to be gained by chance or charity. This should reinforce our confidence in managerial rank as one indicator of relative power.

The 'reputational' method, first used by Hunter (1953) in his study of power within Regional City, relies on the opinions of presumably informed persons to assess the distribution of power. Thus Hunter (1953) asked a number of recognized community 'leaders' to rank the city's ten most powerful citizens. However, this approach attracted strong criticism from Dahl (1961) on a number of counts. In particular, he argued that Hunter's reputational approach made no distinction between the ability to exercise power and its actual exercise; that it gave no common definition of power; and that it presumed that there existed a small group of leaders in the first place, whose power would be similarly recognized by all. We shall return to the first two of Dahl's points in discussing the 'non-decisional' methodologies that have emerged in response to Dahl's critique, but on the last one we can note again the different circumstances of firm and community. Within an hierarchical organizations such as the capitalist enterprise, it is not unreasonable to presuppose both that, to a considerable extent, power will be concentrated and that its holders will be well known.

In his own New Haven study, Dahl (1961) insisted upon the use of several methods; most distinctive, however, was his 'decisional' methodology. With this 'decisional' approach, Dahl hoped to overcome the weaknesses of the reputational method by measuring individuals' powers according to the number of successful initiatives or vetoes they enacted in certain controversial decisions. But this method too has its faults. To start with, as Bachrach and Baratz (1962; 1963) and Crenson (1971) point out, Dahl's decisional method relies on the unlikely assumption that that all observed decisions are of equal importance. Moreover, Dahl risks inconsistency for, in identifying specifically controversial decisions, he had no other means than to depend upon local opinion – in other words, reputation. However, these authors' main objection was to the behavioural focus upon observable conduct. Dahl's concentration upon actual decisions excluded the power expressed precisely in the fact of no decision ever taking place (Bachrach and Baratz, 1963). Such may be the power of 'anticipated reaction' that the weak may never dare or bother to test the might of the powerful by actually advancing certain issues for decision in the first place. Alternatively, so strong may be dominant actors' control over the agenda that challenging issues never reach it anyway. In either case, the behavioural basis of the decisional method fails to capture the power reflected in 'non-decisions'. As Bachrach and Baratz (1962) argue, powerful actors deliberately 'mobilize bias' to ensure that certain issues are never aired.

It is as important to allow for such mobilization of bias within the firm as within the community at large. Indeed, management teams, relatively select and compact, are perhaps even more vulnerable to bias through the imposition of local ideologies. For the firm's dominant actors, the security of their strategic choices is best served by narrowing debate rather than widening it. The whole point of ideological incorporation, therefore, is to ensure that attention is safely channelled exclusively to activities consistent with dominant actors' particular objectives. In short, for community and company alike, recognition of this covert 'second face' of power (Bachrach and Baratz, 1962) demands a more subtle approach than simple decision analysis.

Crenson's (1971) study of air pollution policies in North American cities seeks to overcome the problems of non-decisions and anticipated reactions by combining reputational methods with comparative analysis. He began with a detailed comparison of the historical development of pollution controls in the adjacent and similar cities of East Chicago and Gary, using both interviews and documentary data. By comparing the promptness of controls in East Chicago, where US Steel was absent, with the tardiness of Gary, where US Steel was a major employer and polluter, Crenson was able to infer that, despite the company's careful abstention from declaring its view, US Steel nevertheless exercised considerable power over policy. Crenson went on to survey a large sample of cities in order to link progress on pollution to power dispositions as measured reputationally. He justified this resort to the reputational approach at some length. Its chief advantage is that, in contrast to the behaviourism of the decisional approach, reputations can indirectly take into account the powers of non-decision-making and anticipated reactions. The reputational approach need not assume a small group of leaders; Crenson carefully gave respondents the option of answering that there were no leaders at all. Crenson allowed for the variability of power over different issues by specifying a single type of issue (pollution control). He also acknowledged the danger of respondents' diversity in defining 'power' and 'influence', but argued, bearing in mind the power of anticipated reactions, that 'for our purposes, whatever an informant regards as influence is influence' (Crenson, 1971, p. 112).

Clearly the reputational approach is well-suited for capturing the ideological celebration of dominant actors. However, Crenson's comparative analysis of matched pairs, as in Gary and East Chicago, offers another significant advantage. The contingency theorists have argued that relative departmental powers (Hinings *et al.*, 1974; Hackman, 1985) or the importance of particular functions (Godiwalla, Meinhart and Warde, 1979; Gupta and Govindarajam, 1984) will depend upon the firm's particular industrial or market environment. According to this environmentally determinist argument, an organizations' most powerful actors will be those most capable of, and devoted to, securing profit-maximizing outcomes. The claim for strategic choice, however, implies that people often seize power precisely in order to divert the companies' resources away from profit maximization and towards their own personal objectives. Strategic choice theorists, therefore, would not expect power to be distributed consistently within the same market environment; rather, they would expect that even two similarly situated companies would reveal quite idiosyncratic distributions of power and that these differences would be reflected in the diverse strategies they adopted. Thus again, by examining the power distributions in like-situated firms, the comparative method can test the possibility of strategic choice.

The potential value of Crenson's comparative approach has been accepted even by Polsby (1979), assistant to Dahl in the New Haven study. However, he raises two further problems. First, he criticizes the assumption that the non-raising of an issue necessarily implies suppression rather than genuine consensus. Second, he points to the possibility of consensus arising from free trade-offs between different goals; some communities may genuinely consider steel industry jobs as possessing greater utility than clean air. In the context of the firm, however, these reservations apply less forcefully.

To start with, firms are authoritarian, not democratic, institutions. In this context of unequal authority, the participation in, and the scope for, free trade-offs is bound to be limited. Although decision-makers in firms operating in conditions of perfect competition are necessarily compelled by mutual self-interest to unite around the single goal of profit maximization, in most firms there is only the need to make sufficient profits to ensure survival. This leaves a considerable margin for dispute between different objectives. But this potential for dispute is rigorously controlled because those people admitted to positions of decision-making authority have first to undergo careful processes of selection, socialization and ideological incorporation. In these circumstances, consensus is artificial; or, at the very least, the grounds for reaching it are severely biased. Thus – whatever force they may have in the context of city politics – Polsby's (1979) remaining reservations over Crenson's (1971) methodology have less relevance to the case of the firm.

All these various measures of power and influence have been used in organizational studies. The reputational method in particular has tended to prevail, as exemplified by Perrow's (1970) study of departmental powers in twelve manufacturing firms and Tannenbaum's (1974) analysis of the reputed powers of managers and workers. Hinings *et al.* (1974), as well as using a reputational method, employed a crude decisional measure to investigate, *inter alia*, the relationship between departments' participation in various types of decisions and formal positional authority in seven companies. Bauer and Cohen (1981) rely chiefly on decisional methods for defining membership and power in their 'governing cliques'. 'Who gets what' assumptions underlie Salancik and Pfeffer's (1974) study of power and resources in university departments, and Pettigrew's (1973) use of changing salary levels in his account of power struggles in a computer department.

As Cox, Furlong and Page (1985, pp. 31–9) conclude, the essentially contested nature of the concept of power suggests that the wisest approach is to remain open to the insights offered by all of these approaches. Accordingly, I have been flexible in attempting to identify dominant actors within each of my case study firms. The obvious starting point was organizational rank, both on the grounds of the hierarchical authority it accords and, following the logic of 'who gets what', in the power its attainment reflects. However, it was soon clear that chief executives did not all exercise the same amount of power and that marketing directors and production directors, though formally peers, often varied radically from firm to firm in the relative respect they enjoyed. It was important, therefore, to grasp reputationally how senior managers judged their own and their colleagues' powers, looking for some sort of consensus. This reputational evidence could be corroborated, to some extent at least, by asking managers' to suggest and discuss particularly significant decisions that exemplified these powers. Comparisons were made between firms operating in similar environments in the hope of discovering tell-tale differences. This eclectic bundle of measures could not, of course, be combined to form any precisely calibrated and consistent index of relative powers; none the less, the case studies do appear to yield quite strong convergencies.

One last point should be borne in mind. Recalling Hindess (1982, p. 505), it is in the nature of agency that agents may choose whether or not to exercise their powers fully or consistently. Accordingly, the absolute disposition of power cannot simply be read back from outcomes – whether reflected in reputations, rewards or decisions – only its exercise in particular struggles. Therefore, the case study research has to discriminate between agents' deployment of their powers from issue to issue.

RESEARCH PROCEDURES

Though a number of the recent studies reviewed in Chapter 3 (for example, Pettigrew, 1985; Johnson, 1987) have achieved impressive and convincing degrees of detail by concentrating on single firms, I have preferred to investigate strategic choice within eight firms in two industries. Besides the advantages of comparison already outlined, by examining a range of firms I hope to demonstrate that the power of strategic choice is fairly general, something not to be easily dismissed as the property of just one or two exceptional companies or a particular industry.

The office furniture and domestic appliance industries were selected for the research according to a number of criteria. To start with, the two industries had the advantage of being independent, in the sense of having different sorts of customer, industrial or consumer. Additionally the fragmented nature of each provided fairly large sampling pools for the research to draw upon. However, the most important criterion was that, in order to provide as rigorous a test of strategic choice as possible, the selected industries be characterized by particularly harsh competitive environments. Though neither the office furniture nor the domestic appliance industries was perfectly competitive, both possessed plenty of the sort of product market competition that environmental determinists would expect to enforce conformity to profit-maximization. Indeed, as we shall see, these environments were rapidly deteriorating under the impact of new technologies, changing distribution structures and international competition. Even more significant, however, was that the two industries endured particularly sharp recessions during 1979–81 – if anything could, these collapses in demand should have squeezed out the scope for strategic choice. Evidence that decision-makers in similarly placed firms might respond idiosyncratically to the same stimulus of recession would, at the least, be confusing to the action determinists; while evidence that firms could survive the worst recession of the post-war period by pursuing diverse and non-optimal strategies should certainly stretch the environmental determinists.

To give the environmental determinists a fair chance to discover the possible fatal results of strategic choice, the research also follows up the strategies and performances of the companies during the recovery period, with the last formal interviews taking place in all the companies during 1985, four years after the trough of the recession (further follow-up telephone interviews took place during the autumn of 1987). The additional benefit of this recovery research is that it allows some comment on the performance outcomes of various recession strategies: were firms really emerging leaner and fitter, or was it better in the medium term to have adopted 'holding' rather than 'cutting' strategies? Eight case studies from two industries in one recession will, of course, provide only suggestive, not conclusive, evidence on the effectiveness of various recession strategies.

Before contacting any firms in the two industries, a small pilot study was carried out in a Manchester chemicals company. The two industries were also thoroughly researched using published data such as government and trade association reports and statistics, company annual reports, press commentaries, market research reports and stock brokers' analyses. In addition, interviews were carried out with five senior industry observers from the relevant trade associations, an electrical appliance retailer and a government body closely associated with the domestic appliance industry.

Next, leading firms in the two industries were contacted by an introductory letter (addressed to the chief executive by name) which briefly explained the purpose and methods of the research and asked for their co-operation. Summaries of the eventual research results were promised to participants. The letters were followed up two or three days later by a telephone call to explain the research more directly. Out of six firms approached in the domestic appliance industry, three agreed to co-operate; in the office furniture industry, five out of eight agreed.

The case studies made use of both documentary and interview data. Such public materials as sales brochures and house magazines were always sought. Five companies also made available – always on a selective basis – a variety of more confidential documents including management minutes and memoranda, detailed sales figures, management accounts, or consultants' reports. In one case admission was granted to the annual management conference. In all firms, tours were made of factories and offices, providing the opportunity to observe significant symbols of internal politics – for instance, office geographies (Pettigrew, 1973) – or corporate 'cultures' – dress and office decoration (Wilkins, 1983a).

However, the chief research tool was interviews with (mostly senior) managers. These interviews had a dual purpose: first, to elicit accurate accounts of each firm's recession strategy and subsequent recovery performance; second, to gain insight into why these particular strategies were adopted, especially in terms of internal politics, ideologies and histories. Interviews generally lasted at least one hour, and would occasionally extend through an entire morning or afternoon. Almost all the subjects were senior or middle managers, including in every case the present chief executive. The emphasis was on the senior managers because, however much they might contest power between themselves, it is finally from amongst them that decisions emanate and therefore their objectives, capacities, and cognitions which are most influential upon strategic choices (Wilkins, 1983a).

The interviews were conducted broadly according to the principles of the 'focused interview' as developed by Merton and Kendall (1946) and applied in similar research by Spender (1980). Interviews were therefore carried out with a minimum of guidance, with mostly unstructured questions. Semi-structured questions would usually be introduced towards the end as subjects tired and in order to fill in specific gaps. Interview guides were prepared before each interview according to the stage of the research and the position of the subject; but rather than being 'straight-jackets', following Merton and Kendal (1946), they only specified areas of interest and left the interviewer free to follow subjects' lines of thought. In this sense, the interviews had what Merton and Kendal (1946) call 'range', permitting the subjects themselves to raise unanticipated areas of concern. The interviews also had 'specificity', that is, they encouraged subjects to fully express their own definitions of situations and actions. Importantly, 'depth' was also sought, in order to maximize 'self-revelatory comments concerning how the stimulus material [here the recession] was experienced' (Merton and Kendal, 1946, p. 555). This depth especially enhanced subjective understanding of the actors' strategic conduct.

Following the procedure of Bate (1984), Pettigrew (1985), and

Johnson (1987) most of the interviews were taped and transcribed verbatim. Occasionally, the interview circumstances were too noisy or too informal to permit tape recording; sometimes, too, subjects would request that no recording be made or that the recording should be temporarily interrupted. Most subjects were little concerned by taping. Johnson (1987, p. 72) observes that managers tend to be less inhibited the more senior they are, and this was generally my experience too. Indeed, as Daudi (1986, p. 57) found in similar research, many managers appeared to enjoy the interviews as an opportunity to review crises and triumphs with a flatteringly attentive listener. Anyway, in case there was any inhibition, I would generally switch off the tape recorder towards the end of the interview in order to allow more relaxed discussion; this rarely elicited a different quality of information and occasionally appeared suspiciously artificial. When recording was not possible, notes would be taken during the interview or immediately afterwards.

The verbatim transcripts were invaluable to the process of historical reconstruction. Long-hand notes are inescapably less full and more selective than any complete recording. Reviewing the transcripts some time after the interview frequently revealed points the significance of which had not been properly appreciated at the time. The verbatim records also facilitated detailed cross-checking of different inter-viewees' accounts of the same incidents (cf. Johnson, 1987, p. 67). This cross-checking was important not so much because of any suspicion of widespread deliberate deception on matters of fact, but rather because it helped correct lapses of memory and, often, would expose variations in emphasis that reflected significant internal political differences. The impression gained in this research was generally of a frankness born of a sincere desire to help. As Spender (1980, p. 32) asked: 'What reasons do we have to suspect hardworking managers of wasting time cooking up false evidence for some minor academic researcher?' Anyway, it was possible to corroborate much of the interview material with documentary data.

As well as facilitating accurate historical accounts of events necessary for institutional analysis, the interview transcripts were vital for the analysis of strategic conduct. These transcripts permitted detailed textual analyses, revealing through their choice of key words, symbols and metaphors, how senior managers subjectively understood the events they described, and, by the presence or absence of commonalities, the extent to which these understandings were shared by management teams as wholes (Thompson, 1980; Huff, 1983). Such material also provided insights into the 'rhetoric of control' and the construction of legitimacy involved in the 'management of meaning'

Table 6.1 *Formal Research Interviews*

	Recorded and transcribed	Notes only
Industry observers:		
Domestic appliances	–	3
Office furniture	–	2
Case studies:		
Domestic appliances		
Exemplar	8	–
Homecraft	6	1
Rose	10	5
Office furniture		
Castle	6	1
Fenwood	3	1
Kremers	8	2
Shilton	4	2
Barton	4	–
Totals	49	17

(Gowler and Legge, 1983; Pettigrew, 1985, p. 44). Thus the significance of many of the stories managers told lay not simply in the events they recorded, but also in how they legitimized internal power relations, rationalized organizational practices and expressed prevailing management philosophies (Wilkins, 1983b; Martin and Powers, 1983). Where managers expressed themselves consistently, it was possible to adduce the existence of fairly coherent local ideologies in which the goals and options for strategic action were commonly accepted and established authority was beyond doubt. Having established these local ideologies, it would, of course, be possible to trace them back to their various social structural foundations.

Table 6.1 provides details of the number of interviews carried out in each firm, broken down according to whether or not they were recorded. A total of 66 formal face-to-face interviews were carried out, with 61 in the firms themselves. On average, therefore, just under eight interviews were carried out in each firm. However, the amount of interviewing varied widely between firms according to both size of management team and the degree of co-operation. For instance, Barton's management team was only four strong. At Fenwood, co-operation was quite limited, the most extensive interview being with Charles Fenwood, chairman and major shareholder; it soon became clear that he was the dominating influence upon everything of importance within his firm. Rose, with divisions and factories scattered around the country, was a much larger and more complicated company and demanded many more interviews. All the interviews recorded in Table 6.1 were carried out during 1984 and 1985, except for a further interview carried out at Kremer's in 1987. The table does not record numerous casual conversations with managers and other employees – over lunch, on factory tours, etc. – which were also often very informative. Nor does the table record a series of follow up telephone discussions which were carried out during 1987 to check on the progress of all of the companies since the original research was carried out.

These, then, were the procedures by which the research was done. It is time now to examine the two industries within which the research actually took place.

THE DOMESTIC APPLIANCE INDUSTRY

In 1979, after a decade of severe challenge, the British domestic appliance industry remained highly fragmented. The largest British manufacturing operations were carried out by the subsidiary companies of the newly created Thorn EMI. Strongest in gas and electric cookers, Thorn EMI's domestic appliance divisions enjoyed a combined turnover of about £200 million. Next came Hotpoint, jointly owned by Schreiber and GEC, with a turnover of more than £100 million, mostly from refrigeration and laundry products. After Hotpoint came the Tube Investments subsidiaries; competing with Thorn EMI across the range, but especially in gas and electric cookers, these companies' combined turnover exceeded £60 million. Other British companies, all much smaller, included LEC and Kelvinator, both specializing in refrigeration, Servis, specializing in laundry products, and Belling, specializing in electric cookers. Hoover, which still combined British and American shareholdings, dominated the vacuum cleaning and laundry products markets with a total turnover of about £200 million. The Dutch company Philips and the Swedish Electrolux also had substantial manufacturing operations in the UK. As well as producing traditional electromechanical 'white goods' domestic appliances, Philips, Thorn EMI and GEC also had divisions producing consumer electronic 'brown goods' (that is, televisions, radios and, later, video recorders).

The weaknesses of the British domestic appliance industry were deep-seated. Although the original GEC had begun manufacture in 1889, it was not until the 1930s, after the abandonment of the Gold

Standard and the adoption of tariffs, that companies such as Hoover, Hotpoint and Belling had established substantial manufacturing capacity in this country (Corley, 1966). Then the end of the Second World War propelled new companies such as Thorn, LEC and Kenwood into a booming market, fuelled by pent up demand for replacements, massive house-building and full-employment. During the 1950s, the sales of washing machines, for example, grew at an average annual rate four times greater than total consumer expenditure (Green, 1987b). This boom period of the late 1940s and 1950s was to engrain certain characteristics into the industry which were to have prolonged consequences.

A booming home market and old-established strength in the colonies permitted British manufacturers to ignore European markets. The difficulties of meeting ever-expanding demand under conditions of material and component shortages imposed by post-war controls and then the Korean war encouraged an emphasis on the problems of production rather than marketing. However, Government regional policy dictated that increases in production should be made largely by the incremental addition of new plants dispersed around Scotland, Wales and the North. Long-term planning and investment in large-scale production were discouraged by the government's 'stop-go' demand management policies, to which domestic appliances, as deferrable purchases frequently made on credit, were especially vulnerable (cf. Dunnet, 1980). Failure to establish dominant brands or significant economies of scale depressed barriers to entry, thereby allowing a continuous infusion of small manufacturers right up until the early 1960s. As late as 1963 there were still 140 British companies, and the top four shared only 25 per cent of the UK market (Corley, 1966).

These conditions had contributed to the development of two characteristics noted by academic commentators of the time. Barna (1962) characterized the industry as dominated by a 'defensive' strategic orientation based on short-sighted policies of ruthless cost-cutting, sustained by intensive production and simplicity of products. Complementary to this, Rogers (1963), in his psychological study of management teams in the industry, noted a prevailing contempt for the consumer and a preference for engineering values. The exception to this was Hotpoint between 1956 and 1963, when under the leadership of the dynamic marketeer Craig Wood (Corley, 1966; Jones and Marriot, 1970). However, Craig Wood's calamitous fall under the impact of Bloom's price-cutting incursions served to reinforce the dominance of 'defensive' and production-based orientations. Two decades later, Senker (1984, p. 27) would still describe the British

Table 6.2   Domestic Electrical Appliance Industry: 1973–86[1]

	UK establishments: sales and work done £m	Exports £m	Imports £m	UK market £m	UK market Index (1979 = 100)[2]
1973	412.2	69.8	98.2	440.6	95.0
1974	452.0	90.1	114.4	476.3	86.1
1975	658.8	107.1	138.4	597.1	98.1
1976	644.8	134.8	163.8	673.8	92.1
1977	743.5	177.4	221.0	787.1	88.8
1978	858.3	185.1	252.1	925.3	93.6
1979	969.1	178.6	303.7	1,094.2	100.0
1980	1,036.8	198.8	326.6	1,164.6	92.6
1981	1,021.3[3]	n.a.	433.5	n.a.	n.a.
1982	1,019.8	151.9	466.6	1,334.5	102.9
1983	1,250.9	157.8	601.6	1,694.7	126.8
1984	1,303.0	163.6	734.2	1,873.6	136.0
1985	1,412.1	190.0	834.4	2,056.5	142.5
1986	1,582.0	201.1	930.3	2,311.2	153.7

[1] Sources: *Business Monitors* PQ368 (1973–81) and PQ3460 (1982–6).
[2] UK market deflated by industry Producer Price Index.
[3] PQ3460 figure; £1,044.2 million.

manufacturers' policies as typically 'tactical' and 'reactive'.

Despite a number of acquisitions in the 1960s and early 1970s, the major British manufacturers failed to rationalize or concentrate manufacturing capacity, so that, by comparison especially with Zanussi or Indesit, they were burdened with factories that were small, dispersed and multi-product, many still based on pre-war or wartime armaments facilities (Owen, 1981). By the early 1980s, none of the top seven European manufacturers – Zanussi, Electrolux, Siemens-Bosch, Philipps, AEG-Telefunken, Indesit, and Thompson-Brandt – was British (*Financial Times*, 12 June 1984).

During the 1960s exports to the Old Commonwealth had already been drying up as Australia, Canada and South Africa developed their own industries. At the same time the Italians were establishing a foothold in this country based on greater price-competitiveness (Senker, 1984). Finally, the British industry's accumulated weaknesses were unmistakably exposed by the coincidence of entry into the Common Market with the Barber Boom in the early 1970s. From 1973, imports climbed steadily ever further above exports (see Table 6.2), with the Italians claiming the bottom end of the market and the Germans taking the top end. The British manufacturers capitulated in many segments by joining the major retailers in 'badge engineering', whereby imported products were sold under British brand names. In a generally stagnant market, import penetration rose from 22.2 per cent in 1973 to 27.8 per cent in 1979 (Table 6.2).

Table 6.3   Distribution Structure for Major Domestic Appliances, 1979

% Sales	Gas cookers	Electric cookers	Fridge freezers	Auto washing machines
Gas boards	90	—	—	—
Electricity boards	—	40	27	19
Multiples)		18	14	21
Independents)		12	9	15
Department stores)	10	10	15	13
Discounters)		10	12	20
Other)		—	—	12

Sources: Monopolies and Mergers Commission, 1980; Keynote, 1979; Mintel, 1980.

Nevertheless, British companies retained some advantages, however eroded. The UK market was peculiar in several respects. In cookers, for example, continental products had to overcome or adapt to the special need for compactness imposed by typically small British kitchens and also the unique British partiality for grilled foods. Moreover, the retail structure was still dominated by the Gas and Electricity Boards, who were very closely meshed with their British suppliers (Monopolies and Mergers Commission, 1980). Thus, at the beginning of the 1980s, three British manufacturers held 85–90 per cent of the electric cooker market (Keynote, 1981) and two British companies together held 60 per cent of the gas cooker market (Monopolies and Mergers Commission, 1980). This strength in cookers, combined with production in highly depreciated old manufacturing plant, helped yield relatively high profits for several of the leading manufacturers up until the recession.

However, technological and market changes were beginning to threaten even the traditional cooker. The new Conservative government's policy of privatizing the Gas Board show-rooms was an immediate threat, and left the Electricity Boards insecure as well. Meanwhile, more than a decade of decline since the abolition of resale price maintenance had reduced the High Street independent retailers to a tiny share of the market for most products. In their place, multiples such as Curry's and discount stores such as Comet were emerging with considerable bargaining power and an increased readiness to put their own labels on the products of both domestic and foreign manufacturers goods (see Table 6.3). As Green (1987b) notes, British manufacturers, defensive and production-orientated, did little to resist this emergence of concentrated retail power.

At the same time, after two decades of stability, a host of new technologies was beginning to come available by the end of the 1970s. Computer Aided Design (CAD) provided opportunities for enhancing design and production flexibility; pre-painted steel offered the chance to raise quality and eliminate expensive paint-plants; plastic components would enable the production of lighter and cheaper appliances; and micro-electronic controls promised at this stage at least a marketing advantage. However, with almost all these new technological opportunities, it was European manufacturers who were the first to seize the advantage (Senker, 1984). Candy, for instance, had installed fifty-seven robots by the mid-1980s (*Financial Times*, 18 July 1985).

Though behind in production technologies, new products were giving the British manufacturers a chance both to escape the mature, replacement-type market conditions that had characterized the UK since the end of the 1960s and to exploit the emergence of more discriminating consumers. The emergence of built-in kitchens brought a new emphasis on colour (rendering the traditional generic term 'white goods' anachronistic); stimulated the rise of the 'kitchen centre' as a new retail outlet; and, perhaps most important, created a demand for 'built-in' and 'slip-in' cookers in place of the traditional free-standing 'tombstone' type. Built-in kitchens, combined with the threat to the Gas and Electricity Boards, were also increasing the demand for dual-fuel cookers, long a technological possibility. Likewise, the popularity of the 'two-door' fridge-freezer, the gradual penetration of the dishwasher and the potential of the automatic washing machine all presented British manufacturers with new opportunities. Most radical of all was the microwave oven: based upon a completely new technology, it provided a new product that complemented, rather than competed with, traditional cooker technologies (Market Assessment, 1981a). While most of the rest of the market was severely depressed, the value of microwave sales trebled between 1979 and 1982 (Euromonitor, 1985). However, most ominously for the conservative British manufacturers, as a small electronics 'brown good' produced to world standards, microwaves blew away the traditional technological and retailing idiosyncrasies that had long protected the British cooker market.

These opportunities were only hesitantly taken up by the British manufacturers. Only one UK manufacturer had begun even small-scale production of microwaves by 1979, while in 1978 Colston had closed down the country's only dishwasher manufacturing operations. Even where British manufacturers did compete with the new products, they suffered much higher import penetration than with their old. Thus, in 1979 import penetration for traditional electric cookers was only 3.7

Table 6.4 Domestic Electrical Appliance
Industry, Deflated by UK
Manufacturer's Price Index[1] 1979–86

	UK establishments: index of sales and work done (1979 = 100)	UK market index (1979 = 100)
1979	100.0	100.0
1980	93.8	93.3
1981	84.4	n.a
1982	78.2	90.6
1983	91.0	109.2
1984	89.3	113.7
1985	94.8	118.2
1986	98.2	122.5

[1] *Source: Economic Trends*, various issues.

per cent, but for built-in electric ovens it was 28.7 per cent; for old-fashioned refrigerators import penetration was 33.1 per cent, but for the booming fridge-freezer market it was 65.4 per cent (Euromonitor, 1985).

Consequently, British manufacturers faced considerably more than recession in 1979. Their retail structure was threatened by revolutionary change; new technology was transforming production methods and introducing new products to satisfy an increasing sophisticated consumer market; foreign manufacturers were undermining their old preserves from above and below. Moreover, the recession was particularly severe because of the combination of high interest and exchange rates. As Table 6.2 on p. 132 shows, the index figure for the UK market as a whole registers a collapse of 7.4 per cent between 1979 and 1980, with an apparent recovery by 1982 (unfortunately the 1981 UK market cannot be calculated because of missing export figures for that year). However, this 1982 recovery is almost certainly illusory, as the domestic electrical appliance Producer Price Index actually records a fall over the year, reflecting severe discounting by desperate manufacturers. Deflating by the general UK Manufacturers' Price Index demonstrates that real demand probably remained depressed even in 1982, 9.4 per cent below the level of 1979 (see Table 6.4). The full impact of the recovery was probably not felt until 1983. Even then, as Table 6.4 also shows, British manufacturers had not recovered to their 1979 levels of output (adjusted by the general Manufacturers' Price Index) even by 1986. Import penetration rose to 35.0 per cent by 1982, and to 40.3 per cent by 1986. A measure of the severity of this recession was that, while total UK manufacturing output fell by 14.2

per cent between 1979 and the trough of 1981 (*Economic Trends*, December 1982), UK domestic appliance manufacturing output fell by 15.6 per cent in the same period and by 21.8 per cent by 1982 (Table 6.4).

It is hardly surprising, then, that the three leading manufacturers were all forced to close down substantial capacity, with severe redundancies; that Servis lurched from rationalization to rationalization as it passed through two changes of ownership; that Kelvinator succumbed to Candy in 1982; and that Hoover, after losses of £39 million between 1980 and 1982, was taken over completely by its American parent in 1983, while two other major British manufacturers experienced periods of takeover threat. None the less, there were some achievements. By 1985, two British companies had invested in substantial microwave production, and imports had been halted or reversed in some sectors, notably fridge-freezers. Moreover, the British industry largely avoided collapses on the scale of those of Zanussi, Indesit and AEG – despite the lack of government support that the Italian manufacturers allegedly enjoyed. Substantial restructuring did not come until 1987, six years after the recession.

THE OFFICE FURNITURE INDUSTRY

The UK office furniture industry shared several characteristics with the domestic appliance industry of the post war period: in particular, preoccupation with a growing but cyclical home market; product conservatism suddenly challenged by technological and market change; and persistent fragmentation.

By the early 1980s, there were still over 200 manufacturers serving the UK market. Only four companies – Arenson International, Project, Twinlock and Vickers – had turnovers in excess of £10 million in 1979–80. Several, however, were subsidiaries of large conglomerates (for example, Sheerpride was owned by Lonrho, Tan-sad by GEC). Leading family controlled companies included Arenson, William Vere and Abbott Bros., all within the top dozen manufacturers.

Despite this multiplicity of manufacturers, competition was contained to some extent by a tendency to specialize in one of the three main sectors: storage, seating or desking (desks, tables and allied products). Another traditional distinction within the industry was between metal and wooden manufacturers. On the one hand, because of its increasing cost advantage and its relative flexibility, metal was taking an ever increasing share of office storage and seating products; on the other hand, because of its greater attractiveness and prestige value, wood was increasingly dominant in the desking sector (Furniture Industry Research Association, 1983). Many manufacturers had production facilities and expertise concentrated in one or other material, and therefore tended to focus on the appropriate products. Thus, although the industry was highly fragmented overall – no manufacturer had more than 10 per cent of the total market (Keynote, 1983) – in particular segments there was greater concentration. For example, Abbotts and Arenson, though with wide ranges, were both strongest in wooden desking, while Vickers, Sheerpride and Harvey were strong in metal storage.

The wooden furniture industry had originally been craft based, with a plethora of tiny workshops clustered around the traditional skill centres of East London and High Wycombe. During the 1960s, rapid expansion and the opening of satellite factories in the regions stimulated the larger companies to eliminate craft methods in favour of large batch production. However, the wooden furniture manufacturers failed to establish sufficient economies of scale in either production or marketing to squeeze out a persistent fringe of tiny, marginal producers. The metal office furniture companies had different roots, often being associated with larger general engineering companies. Again, because of the easy availability of components, they were not able to rid themselves of competition from small assembly type operations. Seating manufacture in particular was described as predominantly a 'cottage industry' (Market Assessment, 1981b, p. 34).

This fragmented backwardness was supported by the survival of perhaps 1,700 specialist High Street office equipment and furniture retailers (Market Assessment, 1984). Although multiple retailers such as Rymans, Wildings and Universal were developing, and the Property Services Agency (later Crown Suppliers) dominated public sector purchasing (see Table 6.5), these small retailers continued to exert a strong influence on the industry. They were characterized as highly conservative and usually loyal to their traditional, often local suppliers. However, these retailers' emphasis on price competitiveness made them ruthless in demanding heavy discounts, especially during the mid–1970s recession, and prone to accepting cheap and shoddy products from often transient 'railway arch' producers. One senior industry observer accused them of 'selling discounts, not furniture'. With direct sales personnel each having to generate roughly £1/2m sales annually simply to break-even, even quite large manufacturers were forced to rely heavily on the retail trade. However, a few of the

*Table 6.5 Distribution Structure for
Office Furniture Manufacturer's
Deliveries to Outlets*

	%
Wholesalers/major stockists	40.0
Direct to end-user (private)	17.2
Direct to end-user (public)	11.8
Retail	15.7
Other (e.g. mail order)	15.4
	100.1
Total value (£ million)	140.0

Source: Furniture Industry Research
Association, 1983.

larger manufacturers did maintain 'flagship' retail showrooms in London.

For the office furniture industry, the 1975–6 recession had followed, with a slight lag, the collapse of the office building boom of the early 1970s. Although many office furniture companies had originally moved out of the domestic furniture market to escape its seasonality and fashion-consciousness, the office furniture market, tied to the building cycle and dominated by easily deferrable replacement purchases, had always been liable to severe fluctuations. However, the mid–1970s recession was the worst of the post-war period so far, and also coincided with the beginning of a period of radical product and market change.

The traditional desk, the core office furniture product, followed a simple basic design whose essential features had barely changed in twenty five years (Keynote, 1983). Although there were numerous subtle differentials according to the grade of user, within all but the market for boardroom desking there was little scope for significant product differentiation. Even the introduction of 'flatpack' furniture (that is, knock-down kits) in the 1960s had not altered the basic parameters. For the major manufacturers, there was, therefore, a strong inducement towards capital intensive volume production of standard products. This well-established pattern was challenged during the mid–1970s by two new developments in the nature of office work.

The first was the trend towards large 'open-plan' office areas. The second, often connected with the first, was the spread of new computer and communications technologies. The response to these was the development of 'systems furniture' – in the United States, primarily 'screen-based'. The American manufacturer, Westinghouse, had originally developed screen-based furniture for its own vast open plan offices during the early 1960s, and only later turned to selling it to other customers (Keynote, 1983). However, following this, a host of screen and partition suppliers had sprung up, with upwards of 600 separate companies in the UK by the early 1980s – many, such as Unilock and Dexion, attracted from outside the furniture industry (Market Assessment, 1983). However, it was the more sophisticated manufacturers who took the next step of combining screens with furniture into systems specifically adapted to the new office technologies such as computers, word processors and telecommunications.

These new technologies created numerous novel problems. VDU operators required ergonomically designed seating and careful lighting. Computer printers had to be mounted on special tables or trolleys, while their discs and their voluminous print-outs – far from fulfilling the dream of the 'paperless office' – demanded new types of storage on a massive scale. Moreover, computer and telecommunication systems, with their numerous cables, generated complex problems of 'wire management'. For all these special needs, traditional office furniture was completely inadequate.

The adaptation of the furniture, the solution of lighting and cable safety problems and the introduction of co-ordinated colour schemes for office 'land-scaping' all required tailor-made and integrated designs. The introduction of artificial materials and greater use of colours, together with the integrated nature of the furniture blurred traditional distinctions between metal and wooden sectors. These challenges were heightened because many of the orders for systems furniture, unlike the piecemeal orders for traditional products in the past, were large-scale contracts from major companies engaged in complete reform of their approach to office furnishing. These major companies, keen to cut out intermediaries and finding many dealers too small and too conservative to cope with systems contracts, would now often insist on purchasing direct from manufacturers. With contracts often exceeding £500,000 some also preferred to lease rather than to buy outright.

Thus, by contrast with traditional furniture, systems furniture required close co-ordination with customer architects and specifiers, production to order and high regard for service. Entry into systems furniture by British manufacturers would entail much greater sophistication in sales, marketing, finance and design, while forcing a revolution in production.

The systems concept gave foreign manufacturers their opportunity to break into the British market, hitherto protected by the high bulk to value ratio of traditional products and the fragmented and conservative nature of the retail network. From the mid–1970s, it was Westinghouse, Steelcase and Herman Miller from the United States, Mausser

Table 6.6   Wooden Desks and Desking Industry, 1978–86[1]

	UK establishments sales and work done £m	Exports £m	Imports £m	UK market £m	UK market index (1979 = 100)[2]
1978	25.4	n.a.	n.a.	n.a.	n.a.
1979	31.0	1.1	2.0	31.9	100.0
1980	28.5	1.2	2.6	29.9	81.7
1981	24.4[3]	n.a.	2.8	n.a.	n.a.
1982	31.7	0.9	2.9	33.6	78.1
1983	39.8	1.4	4.6	43.0	95.1
1984	53.8	1.1	3.4	56.1	117.5
1985	61.4	2.1	7.2	66.5	130.3
1986	66.5	0.9	9.0	74.6	139.9

[1] Sources: *Business Monitors* PQ372 (1978–81) and PQ4671 (1982–6). NB: these figures substantially understate the true extent of the UK market because they exclude a large number of very small establishments, the assembly of imported components and the refurbishment of second-hand furniture.
[2] UK Market deflated by industry Producers' Price Index.
[3] PQ4671 figure: £24.4 million.

from Germany and Castelli from Italy who were the main pioneers of systems furniture in the United Kingdom. The specialist Herman Miller, with a world turnover of $175m in 1979–80, two factories in Bath and sophisticated leasing packages, emerged as market leader with 34 per cent by the early 1980s (Furniture Industry Research Association, 1983). With a few exceptions such as Hille, the British manufacturers were either too small, too enmeshed with the conservative retailers or too distracted by the recession of 1975–6 and subsequent strong recovery to embark on the lengthy, expensive product development and organizational change that systems required.

Consequently, when the recession came in 1980 (see Tables 6.6 and 6.7), the majority of British manufacturers still had no presence in the most dynamic sector of the market; by 1982 systems furniture was estimated to account for 23 per cent of the whole office furniture market (Table 6.8). Meanwhile, the overall market was suffering the worst recession since the 1930s, exacerbated by severe public expenditure cuts and weak overseas markets hit by a high pound and difficulties in the Middle East and Nigeria. As the index figures show, the real value of the UK wooden desk and desking market (Table 6.6) fell by 21.9 per cent between 1979 and 1982, while the metal filing cabinet and containers market (Table 6.7) crashed by a catastrophic 49.2 per cent over the same period. Perhaps surprisingly though, import penetration did not increase rapidly, even during the recovery. Between 1979 and 1985, import penetration for wooden desking rose from a mere 6.3 per cent to 10.8 per cent; for metal filing cabinets, the

Table 6.7   Metal Filing Cabinets and Containers: 1978–86[1]

	UK establishments sales and work done £m	Exports £m	Imports £m	UK market £m	UK market index (1979 = 100)[2]
1978	26.1	7.2	3.8	22.7	85.0
1979	32.6	6.8	4.7	30.5	100.0
1980	29.7	7.7	4.4	26.4	70.6
1981	25.3[3]	n.a.	3.1	n.a.	n.a.
1982	26.2	8.2	4.2	22.2	50.8
1983	28.1	7.0	5.2	26.3	58.0
1984	34.2	7.9	7.7	34.0	73.3
1985	49.7	7.3	8.3	50.7	105.6
1986	55.1	7.2	8.9	56.8	n.a.

[1] Sources: *Business Monitors* PQ399.1 (1978–81) and PQ3166 (1982–6). NB: these figures understate the UK market because of the large trade in second-hand filing cabinets.
[2] UK Market deflated by industry Producers' Price Index.
[3] PQ3166 figure: £25.3 million.

increase was only from 15.4 per cent to 16.4 per cent (see Tables 6.6 and 6.7).

Thus, many major British companies were forced to finance system furniture developments and launches at a time when foreign manufacturers were already well entrenched and the market as a whole was heavily depressed. Against this background, it was not surprising that many of the British ranges met with limited success, and that many companies were compelled to declare heavy redundancies during the recession. However, none of the major companies went out of business (although Twinlock was taken over by Acco from the USA), so that little industrial rationalization was achieved. Chapters 9 and 10 will

Table 6.8   Structure of the UK Office Furniture Market, 1982 (% of sales value at manufacturers' sales prices)

			%
Seating	:	conventional	27
		systems	7
		Subtotal	34
Desking	:	conventional	23
		systems	10
		Subtotal	33
Storage	:	conventional	28
		systems	6
		Subtotal	34

Source: Furniture Industry Research Association, 1983.

describe the strategies of five of the leading British manufacturers – four of whom launched systems ranges, and one of whom chose not to.

CONCLUSION

The last two sections have described the domestic appliance and office furniture industries from which the eight case studies are drawn. I have stressed the competitive and turbulent natures of both these industries and the severity of the recessions they endured. It was my argument earlier that these types of environment should provide ideal conditions for testing the notion of strategic choice. However, I have also stressed the difficulties involved in identifying both moments of strategic choice and those agents capable of exercising it. The task of the next four chapters, therefore, is to try to capture empirically the elusive phenomenon of strategic choice.

Chapter Seven

The domestic appliance companies

INTRODUCTION

Here at last we start with the empirical material proper. The last chapter provided a general background to the domestic appliance industry during the 1979–85 recession and recovery. In this chapter and the next I shall focus on three leading British domestic appliance manufacturers – known pseudonymously as Rose, Homecraft and Exemplar. This chapter will begin by briefly introducing the three companies, giving basic data on their products, factories, ownership, management and markets. In this my aim will simply be to establish the broad similarity of their positions as they approached the recession. From here I shall go on to explore the internal characters of these companies, describing their top managements and the ideals that motivated them in their business activities. This section will reveal that superficial similarities in ownership, products and markets in fact conceal very radical differences in the internal characters of these three companies. It is to these internal differences that I will ascribe the divergent strategic choices to be described in Chapter 8. But before examining the companies' recession strategies, I shall conclude this chapter by considering the degrees to which the three companies had cultivated sufficiently strong positions in their various markets in order to enjoy the freedom of strategic choice.

In all the following case studies, company and personal names will be pseudonyms. A few superficial company characteristics (such as locations) have been left deliberately vague or even slightly altered in order to help conceal identities. All quotations are verbatim tape recorded statements, except where otherwise stated or occasionally where minor changes have been necessary to protect the speaker's anonymity. The particular status of a speaker is usually specified only when it is important to distinguish between successive quotations;

when the speaker is not a senior manager in the company; or when this
has particular significance for interpreting the quotation and the
speaker's position can be stated without revealing his identity (all
interviewees were male). It should be noted that it was impossible to
interview two key figures: Jo Stone, chairman of Exemplar, and Sir
Ben Rose, founder of Rose. Both were dead by the time the research
took place. However, as we shall see, these two men were very vividly
remembered by their managers.

THE COMPANIES

Exemplar, Homecraft and Rose were three of the foremost British
domestic appliance manufacturing companies. This section outlines
their basic organizational and market characteristics immediately
before the recession (see Table 7.1 for a summary). In particular, it
will draw out the degree to which they shared similar environmental
conditions.

Originally founded in 1920, Exemplar had been taken over in 1967,
after several years of decline, by Universal Engineering Holdings.
Universal was a successful manufacturing conglomerate, engaged
chiefly in heavy engineering, telecommunications and electronics and
with a turnover in 1979 of nearly £3 billion. However, Universal failed
to reverse Exemplar's decline. In 1974, as a last resort, Universal's
Chairman, David Bernstein, brought in Jo Stone to engineer a
recovery. Jewish and originally qualified as an architect, Jo Stone had
fled Vienna for England in 1938. During the war he had worked in a
factory building wooden-framed Mosquito aircraft and had built up a
very successful domestic furniture business in the South of England.
Exemplar was now merged with Stone's furniture business to form a
joint company between Universal, with a 62.5 per cent shareholding,
and Jo Stone's own company, Stone Furniture Industries, with 37.5 per
cent. Jo Stone was to remain chairman and managing director of this
joint company until 1983, when it was dissolved.

After substantial losses in 1975 and 1976, Jo Stone restored
Exemplar to a position of rapidly improving profits, and by 1979 had
more than doubled turnover to beyond £100 million. There were two
chief activities: refrigeration, some factored and the rest manufactured
at the main Midland site; and the manufacture of laundry equipment at
the Welsh plant. In the UK, Exemplar held relatively small market
shares in both markets (see Table 7.2), and exported only about 6 per
cent of total turnover. Small amounts of factored cooking equipment

Table 7.1 The Domestic Appliance Companies

Name and status	Key personnel	Relative turnovers[1]; export %; and employment[2] (1979)	Main products
Exemplar (jointly owned by Universal and Stone)	Jo Stone (Chairman and Chief Executive to 1983)	0.48 5.7 5,500	refrigeration; laundry
Homecraft (subsidiary of AEL)	Bill Tarling (MD from 1971)	0.21 5.4 2,400	electric cookers laundry; heating
Rose Domestic Appliances (subsidiary of REE)	Cyril Bowden (Divisional Chairman to 1984)	1.00 11.5 13,200	electric cookers; gas cookers; refrigeration; laundry; microwave; small appliances; heating.

[1] Relative turnovers expressed as a proportion of Rose Domestic Appliances in 1979.
[2] For the sake of confidentiality, employment figures are given to the nearest 100.

Table 7.2 Exemplar, Homecraft and Rose: UK Approximate Market Shares for Major Electrical Domestic Appliances, 1970 (%)

	Exemplar	Homecraft	Rose
Electric cookers (free-standing)	—	33	40
Washing-machines	20	5	5
Tumble-driers	15	50	10
Refrigerators	12	—	20

Sources: Market research reports (especially Keynote, 1979) and manufacturers' own estimates. (These figures should be treated with some caution.)

and vacuum cleaners were also sold. But the original North cooker factory had been transferred to Universal by Stone soon after his arrival, and was finally closed down in 1979. Lastly, there was a small appliances company based at another Midland site, with largely separate management.

Homecraft had been founded at the end of the last century and in 1919 had been one of the founder members of its present parent company, Amalgamated Engineering Limited (AEL). By 1979 AEL was a large diversified holding company, with activities spread through automotive engineering, smelting, and various consumer durables, giving a total turnover of over £1 billion. AEL's Domestic Appliance Division, of which Homecraft was the largest part, also included a gas cooker company and a small appliances company. Homecraft had enjoyed rapid growth and high profits throughout the 1970s, based on three core products: electric cookers, heating and laundry.

Electric cookers, built at its main Midland plant, were the mainstay of Homecraft's business, accounting for roughly 60 per cent of total turnover, and holding a substantial share of the UK market (see Table 7.2). Allied to this, Homecraft also factored a small amount of American microwave cookers, with about 5 per cent of the market. Laundry equipment was made at both Homecraft's South site and at a second smaller Midland site. Homecraft was currently the leading tumble-drier manufacturer in the UK though its new washing machine operations were so far much less successful. In electric heating, still mostly made at a small North factory, Homecraft also held market leadership in a fragmented market that before 1978 was severely depressed by the Electricity Boards' adverse tariff structure. Exports were low.

With a turnover in 1979 approaching £200 million, Rose Domestic Appliances was the largest of the three companies and Homecraft's chief rival in the electric cooker market. Rose also held 40 per cent of the gas cooker market and, with mostly factored products, 20 per cent of the microwave oven market. As Table 7.2 indicates, Rose was an important refrigeration manufacturer and factored a substantial amount of laundry equipment. About one third of Rose's refrigeration and most of its laundry goods were sold through Rose's own High Street retail chain. The Division also contained a small appliance company, whose food-mixer held 40–50 per cent of the market, and a gas heating company. Almost all Rose's exports came from the small appliance company.

The Division's original parent company, Rose Electrical Industries, had been founded before the Second World War by the Austrian Jewish immigrant Ben Rose, later Sir Ben. Ben Rose had begun selling electric lamps and radio valves from street stalls in 1926; in 1932 he acquired his first factory. It was only in the 1950s, as part of a wider post-war diversification, that he first started manufacturing domestic appliances. None the less, the appliances division grew rapidly, both organically and by a number of acquisitions. These acquisitions contributed to the dispersed character of the division's operations: major electrical appliances were made at the North site; small appliances at the South site; and gas appliances at one site in London and another in the Midlands. However, in 1976 Ben Rose retired as chairman and was succeeded by Jim Donald. Donald's reforming strategy culminated in the takeover of Imperial Electronics and Entertainments in 1979, just before the beginning of the recession. From contributing 12 per cent of the old parent's turnover, the Domestic Appliance Division was reduced to only 6 per cent of the new group, Rose Electronics and Entertainments (REE). Embracing activities ranging from defence and medical electronics to leisure and with a 1980 turnover well over £2 billion, the new Rose group was now aimed ambitiously at global, high growth markets.

In sum, superficially these three leading domestic appliance manufacturers had much in common as they faced the challenge of the recession. All operated in similar environments. They competed directly in a number of segments and had the facility, especially by factoring, to join in competition in other segments. All three companies concentrated on UK markets, in several areas of which they were dominant. All were multiproduct, with a number of dispersed factories. Finally, although precise relationships differed, they shared a common position as subsidiaries of large, diversified companies, all predominantly based in manufacturing. Yet the following two sections will show that these surface similarities conceal many important differences in both the companies characters and their external relations.

INTERNAL CHARACTERISTICS

In a sense, the three companies' internal characters represent a continuum. At one extreme was Exemplar, firmly dominated by the Jewish entrepreneur Jo Stone; at the other was the tranquil consensus of the Homecraft management team; and languishing somewhere in the middle was Rose Domestic Appliances, whose demoralized and aging managers still hankered after the regime of Sir Ben, their founder and another Jewish entrepreneur. I shall discuss each company in turn.

Exemplar

From 1974 to 1983, Exemplar was forcefully, even eccentrically commanded by Jo Stone. However, David Bernstein, Universal's chairman, well knew what he was buying when he appointed Stone to run his troublesome subsidiary. The two had first done business together in the 1950s, when Stone supplied the wooden cabinets for Bernstein's fast-expanding radio and television operations. To serve this dynamic, consumer-orientated sector, Stone had made use of his war-time experience constructing Mosquito fighter aircraft to develop an innovative method of mass-producing moulded woods. The careers of these two young entrepreneurs had then diverged – Bernstein going on to build his vast Universal empire by a series of controversial takeovers, while Stone was to be the first to escape the primitive small-scale traditions of domestic wooden furniture manufacture by creating a company based upon mass-production and a strong brand name in the High Street. By 1974, however, these two successful businessmen needed each other once more. The highly-geared Stone Furniture Industries was straining under the pressure of recession, while Bernstein was finally running out of patience with the chronically weak Exemplar. Stone Furniture needed the financial backing of Universal; Bernstein needed the managerial talent of Jo Stone.

For the next nine years, then, Jo Stone would dominate Exemplar. The company's strategy over these years, and particularly during the recession, cannot be understood without appreciating Stone's auto-cratic, entrepreneurial style, the highly personal relationships he enjoyed with his hand-picked management team, and the keen patriotic enthusiasm Stone inspired for manufacturing investment and the capture of home market share. However, his dominance was not easily achieved.

Exemplar in the mid–1970s was described as 'a political animal'. This represented a severe challenge to Jo Stone. Only visiting the main Midland factory and headquarters once a week (sometimes less), and without experience in domestic appliances, Stone's initial authority was precarious. Used to running his own show, moreover, he was unpractised in the politics of large bureaucracies. One manager described Stone's predicament thus: 'He [Stone] found a large organization, with independent managers going off in all directions, quite confusing. And because he was an entrepreneur, he would not have been able to cope with that sort of situation.' For Stone the solution was a ruthless purge of the bloated and scheming administrative complex that he had inherited.

The story of how Stone dismissed the forty seven strong marketing department was particularly widely recalled. Within six months he reduced the department to a mere four members; six months later there were none. One of his first actions, the way this episode was recounted ten years later, reveals much about both his decisive style and the respect in which his managers held him. One manager remembered with only slight exaggeration:

'In a meeting they [the marketing staff] demonstrated that they knew less about a particular product than Mr Stone himself had learnt by staying over night in [Midland town] and walking down the High Street and looking in Curry's window. So the whole department was got rid of overnight.'

The message was clear: Stone knew what he was doing and he did not want people getting in his way.

By 1979 administrative staff had been reduced to one-fifth of its former peak and the former management was almost entirely replaced. From early on his own son was brought in as sales director and his deputy at Stone Furniture was appointed finance director. But Stone also promoted internally a group of young managers still in their late twenties and early thirties. One director described this new team thus:

A personalised team was created. Not really like forming a Praetorian Guard, in that respect, the Stone men as opposed to the non-Stone men. There wasn't that sort of thought in mind – to form a gang loyal to Stone. But it develops that way of course, because Number Twos promoted are obviously very loyal. It was a very virile team, very young.

This youthfulness is important to the complex relationship Stone developed between himself and his new managers. Stone was described by one of these managers as 'very autocratic, very difficult', and by another, more charitably, as 'an enlightened dictator'. Stone's relative age supported his autocratic manner. By 1975, Jo Stone was 57 years old: the average age of his ten senior managers was 33, with five still in their twenties. By 1980, although there had been two departures and replacements, the managers' average age was still only 38. These young managers themselves recognized the paternal style in which Stone governed them – and indeed the workforce more generally. Remembered one, 'He ran it [Exemplar] on a very patriarchal basis'; for another, Stone was, 'that odd mixture of paternalist and autocrat'; and for yet another, the Stone regime was 'a benevolent paternalism . . . He was the man in charge . . . He was the father figure.'

Consistent with this paternalistic style, Stone's relationships with his managers were direct. Remembered one director: 'He had – because he was this type of patriarchal figure – he had quite personal relationships with people. They weren't the impersonal relationships you get in some businesses. And his likes and dislikes would show when he was talking to the person.' Some of these managers recalled this relationship somewhat wryly – in retrospect at least – but all had acquiesced. For the younger managers especially, Stone's autocratic ways could be quite easily accepted. They felt they had a lot to learn from his greater experience. One put it this way:

> He was very difficult to work with because his ideas had to be the dominant ideas. He'd got to have his own way. But I found it a tremendous experience, basically because of my age . . . If I'd been 44, maybe I'd have said, 'Well, I don't really want to sit down and be told how to do it'. But in my particular situation it was fantastic, because, I mean, I'd only been out of college [a very few] years, learning all the theory, and then you come along and meet someone who has never read a textbook in his life, but probably personifies what in many ways the textbooks were trying to tell you . . . I mean, he did have difficulty with people who were older than me who were here, because they didn't want to be told how to do it . . . Say ten years on, having had ten years experience, then maybe you'd want to be a little more your own man.

It was not only the younger managers who felt they could learn from Stone's management skill. In particular, all respected his entrepreneurial talents. It was as an 'entrepreneur' that Stone was most often characterized. Thus, in the words of one manager, he was 'an entrepreneur, a self-made man'; for another, 'he was a natural, seat-of-the-pants businessman, entrepreneur – that was his greatest strength'. Described as a 'genius' by two directors, by another as 'charismatic' and by another as 'the saviour' of Exemplar, Stone was seen as almost infallible: 'You're in the presence of a genius. Now genius's can make mistakes; they can go up a wrong alley and get destroyed. But it so happened that all the things he tried to do at Exemplar, every single one of them clicked.'

Respecting him though they did, these managers none the less perceived themselves as possessing strengths very different to those of Jo Stone. There was about them a sense of self-conscious professionalism. One manager contrasted the pre-1974 management with Stone's new team, of which he himself was a member:

> There was a fairly typical 'political' style of management [before 1974] where the people who were in charge tended to be politicians first, 'doers' – I think is the word – second. These people very quickly left [laugh!] . . . Fortunately there was a very good second line team there who were mainly better qualified than the previous bosses, better trained and more professional.

Another manager put the same emphasis on professionalism, but this time drew the contrast between Stone and his appointees, while rather gushingly insisting that their differences were complementary: for him, the new team was 'professionally based, because Exemplar only went for the professional people and the result was a first class team of professional executives with an entrepreneur of frankly outstanding ability to give them the guidelines and the inspiration'. More blunt was a third: 'I'm a professional manager, and he [Stone] was an entrepreneurial manager of what I might call the untutored school.'

Stone's management methods were far from those demanded by the standards of professional management. There were few bureaucratic controls or procedures. Stone himself didn't keep a filing cabinet and 'the meticulous financial and market analysis were for the birds'. As one director demonstrated:

> As far as he [Stone] was concerned, management is a question of face-to-face human relationships. Although he wrote memos, he had no files at all, but he had a brain like a computer. But he had no paperwork, no files. This was his office [gesturing] – no file cabinets, nothing . . . The only files he carried were those he was forced to carry, the immediate papers that he was dealing with for the individuals. But no files, nothing.

This informal management style was partly natural to Stone as an entrepreneur but was also imposed by the strain of running two businesses – Exemplar and Stone Furniture Industries – at the same time. Another manager explained:

He was here [the main Midland factory] often only every two weeks
or once a month. So he insisted that vast reports weren't created; that
he had personal touch particularly with the main areas, with
marketing and with personnel and industrial relations; and that he
expected things to be discussed in a fairly short period of time. And
once he got the feel of it, he would then make the decision.

This entrepreneurial informality quite frequently came into conflict
with the norms of managerial professionalism that prevailed lower
down the organization. Stone resisted cautious management advice,
however well-founded: 'He was a born optimist and one interesting,
one rather endearing characteristic was that he only wanted to hear
good news . . . He did not want to hear about the bad news because it
disturbed him emotionally.' Another manager expostulated: 'It was
quite reasonably organized at one level below the actual interface with
Stone. The Stone interface, no. It was really Stone versus the rest, in a
very unsatisfactory way. But, I mean, he succeeded. Who are we to
damn?'

Whatever the tensions, ultimate authority remained with Stone on
account of his formal positions as chairman, managing director and
substantial shareholder. One manager exclaimed: 'How do you
disagree with the man? He's the boss!' Another, also asked what it was
like to disagree with Stone, laughed: 'It could be bloody stormy. You
could see your P45 sliding over the desk on many occasions. But you
either agreed to differ and go off and do it his way or you agreed to
differ and got out. It was as simple as that!'

In the first year or so, many had 'got out' – some jumping, some
having been pushed. Those remaining, however, were generally more
than merely deferential to Stone's rank or grateful for early
promotions; they came to have a strong personal identification with
him. There were three values in particular to which Stone inspired his
managers' commitment: hard work, lean administration and a patriotic
faith in the future of British manufacturing.

Stone himself worked notoriously hard: 'He was dedicated to getting
it right . . . He certainly gave his all to the two companies [Exemplar
and Stone Furniture] . . . He didn't seem to have any other interests in
life' (Stone died within a year of Exemplar's de-merger from Stone
Furniture in 1983). The work ethic was reinforced by the lean structure
he had imposed on the company: 'He cut this company right down to
the bone, then he cut some more. There's no fat in this company at all.
Managers *work*. Directors *work*. Everybody *works*.' As another
director put it: 'The eleven working directors – who are in name only
directors, they are very much operational – they are all *doers*. None of
the departments have a lot of back-up staff who produce all the doing,

while they do the thinking. Each one is actually operational.' Two directors described themselves as 'Chiefs who work like Indians'. Now there were no politics:

> If you look around at my colleagues and I now, I think the shortest time probably anybody has been in is about ten or twelve years . . . It's one of the strengths of Exemplar, that each one of us knows how the other one ticks. And we've knocked all our rough edges off each other a long time ago, and there's no bloody in-fighting or factions at the top.

Although a substantial shareholder, Stone's mission for Exemplar was by no means simple profit-maximization. One director indicated the careful balance Stone had to keep between profit and his own more personal objectives.

> Profitability was always needed to be high because we weren't wholly owned by Universal but they are pretty hard task-masters in terms of return on capital invested. So profitability naturally is always a priority. But he [Stone] wanted this through penetration, volume as opposed to making Rolls Royces at low volume and making a nice big profit. He wanted to be the biggest and the best.

This pursuit of growth was more than mere ego-mania. Stone also had a strong personal commitment to the future of British manufacturing. Two more directors described his goals thus: 'He was an industrialist at heart. He got his satisfaction, not needing to work for money, in wanting to create something for the future . . . He wanted to set the company up for the next ten years'; and: 'His real interest was not in making money. His real interest was in production, the British economy and the people who worked for Exemplar.'

Stone's managers identified strongly with this mission: 'We perhaps get a little emotional about it. But yes, our competition predominantly was not [two leading British companies] . . . It was the Italians.' Describing Exemplar's strategy in 1984, one manager identified the success of Exemplar with that of the United Kingdom as a whole: 'We want to attack by building more effective capacity in the UK and push back the imports. We will consider in due course exporting, but at the moment there is far more to be gained – both from a company point of view and the country's point of view – by pushing back imports.' Even after Stone's retirement in 1983, Exemplar's advertising retained its patriotic flavour and the August 1984 employee report was headlined: 'Exemplar pushing back imports.'

Accordingly Stone had embarked upon a heavy investment programme in refrigeration at Midland site which he justified in a long memo to Bernstein, Universal's chairman, entirely in patriotic terms. Against the advice of his managers, his first new refrigerator plant was to be a 'small box' one, the lowest margin segment of the market, but one where Exemplar could most directly confront the Italians. However, while working for the new factory, Stone did decide to factor Italian refrigerators from 1976 to 1979 in place of Exemplar's own. This decision was perceived as a stinging rebuke by Stone to his production and technical staff: 'We were all, manufacturing and design, we were all shattered. We didn't want to see the factory, which was our livelihoods, to cease [sic]. And also it brought into stark relief, if you like, the fact that we had failed, because we hadn't got the right product at the right time.'

For all his commitment to manufacturing investment, tensions between the engineers and Stone would persist. One engineer put it thus: 'Stone was *not* an engineer, didn't understand us and was therefore rather anxious to keep us at arm's length . . . because he knew he wouldn't know whether we were trying to bamboozle him'. On at least one occasion, he openly accused his senior engineers of 'collusion'. Though Stone reserved the right – often exercised – to override the advice of his engineers on strategic issues, in practice they were allowed considerable day-to-day autonomy.

On the other hand, Stone did involve himself heavily in personnel and marketing. In operational detail, Stone's 'first love was people, his second was marketing.' Though on his first arrival at Exemplar Stone had had to be ruthless, he soon introduced the same strongly paternalistic personnel policy that he had earlier developed in his furniture company. Consistent with his suspicion of bureaucracy, the focus was upon the factory personnel. One director characterized Stone thus:

> He seemed to have an almost God-given responsibility to look after the hourly-paid workers, and he was very, very interested in the well-being of the hourly-paid. And he attached very much more importance to *their* well-being than he did to his overhead [i.e. staff].

Although he reduced the work force by almost 45 per cent between 1974 and 1979, he also introduced, gradually and with careful consultation with the unions, a paternalistic package that included profit-sharing, generous sick pay jointly administered by management and unions, on-site hairdressing, wedding presents, and the abolition of clocking-in. By 1978–9 the profit-sharing scheme delivered to all personnel, including management, a bonus worth the equivalent of just under fifty three hours pay. Stone's recognition that his paternalist style could only with the greatest difficulty be extended to the North cooker factory, notorious for bad industrial relations, contributed to his decision to transfer its management to Universal.

Stone likewise put his own imprint on marketing – he deliberately never appointed a marketing director. Before his arrival, Exemplar had been locked into price competition with low quality, unreliable and poorly serviced products. For Stone, as one director put it, 'discounting was a dirty word'. Accordingly, Stone had revamped the entire product range and galvanized the service organization. Additionally, he carefully cultivated the small independent retailers, rather than the discount chains, in order to encourage more retail price discipline. In 1979 Stone launched the innovative 'Exemplar Sales Point' scheme specifically for the independents, which rewarded loyalty and firm pricing by giving member retailers preferential manufacturers' sales price discounts, support for staff training, local advertising and shop displays, and absolute priority with deliveries. By 1981, this package would be further strengthened with the introduction of 'margin support', a clever means of getting round retail price maintenance restrictions by granting special subsidies to retailers having difficulties in sustaining what Stone called the Maximum Retail Price.

Marketing considerations always had priority for Stone: 'We've always run our business on a sales-led basis . . . [A lot of companies] are what I call "accountant-led". Our business is never led on that basis. I mean, it's very much a sales and marketing based company.' One of the production managers readily conceded: 'You can talk about volume, productivity and so on – this is my direct responsibility – but the fact that we are favoured in the market place above the Zanussis of this world, which was the target that we aimed for, has been the result of the customer coming first . . . Without the customer, we have no business.'

Homecraft

Homecraft, too, was marketing orientated, but in almost every sense far more moderate in character than Exemplar. Unlike the unusual joint venture agreement between Stone and Bernstein, Homecraft was a wholly owned subsidiary of AEL and locked into a conventional divisional structure that included gas cooker and small appliances operations. Nevertheless, over the years Homecraft's close-knit team of managers had developed a highly distinctive character of their own. Successful manufacturers of just three ranges of products (electric cookers, laundry equipment and heaters), their constant anxiety never to jeopardize the profits upon which their relative autonomy depended committed them to caution and consensus.

Bill Tarling, managing director since 1971, had built a stable and cohesive top management. He himself had originally joined the company in 1963 as production director. This had been just after Homecraft's crisis with the Venus cooker, whose innovative design had been undercut by disastrous quality and reliability problems. Tarling's marketing director, and deputy from 1983, had first joined Homecraft a year before him, specifically with the brief to rebuild the then devastated cooker range in the market place. The production director during the recession period had originally been Tarling's works manager in his previous company, transferring with Tarling to fulfil the same role at Homecraft during the 1960s before elevation in 1971. The R & D and finance directors, too, had first taken their roles in the early 1970s.

As one director remarked in 1984, when this team was still intact: 'The management consistency is very, very substantial – a relatively young team which has grown old together.' Cohesion was carefully protected: 'We're not a ruthless company . . . but if someone is clearly out of phase with everybody, than we get rid of them quickly.' For instance, a new sales director was got rid of during the recession. Apart from this, senior management was well integrated: 'the inner team . . . works very closely together, and rarely – there's a lot of luck in this – in fifteen years I've not seen a fundamental clash in personality between the four people [production, marketing, R & D and financial directors] whoever they've been.'

Senior directors all made frequent use of the 'team' metaphor. This was how three expressed it: 'At the end of day, as Homecraft, we are a very small decision-making team, who live on each other's doorsteps'; or, 'We're all in together *here* and that produces a very good team'; and, 'Really it's about people, getting together and making a team, and making it work. I think that, if you say, "have we got a recipe for what success we've had?", I think it is that: this business of really getting your feet on the ground, getting down to it, and pulling together, and working together.'

Striking, too, is how all four senior directors repeatedly employed the term 'balance'. This might be used to describe relations between directors: 'by and large, the balance between those four [R & D, marketing, production, and finance] has been well maintained on this site. It all hinges in the end, of course, on personalities. I mean, never mind the policy, what actually happens is to do with who the people are. And generally the balance has been well held on this site . . . It is a balanced team in that sense.' Or: 'One of the great things about Homecraft is that we are a good team, we have a good team spirit . . . And I think we like to think we are a good balance in the team.' The same word might be applied to strategy: 'It's all a matter of balancing the risk . . . It's all a matter of getting your balance right . . . There is no simple touchstone. It's a matter of getting the act together, getting the right balance . . .' Another director appealed: 'You've got to strike a balance . . . You've got to strike a balance. You've got to balance your business at any given time, haven't you?'

The strategy was basically marketing-orientated. It was stated as a self-evident truth that marketing must take priority in the domestic appliance industry: 'Its marketing led, not production. That's how its got to be in this industry.' Another manager was a little more nuanced, but concurred: 'I suppose that all manufacturers in the appliance industry are marketing-orientated. And it depends I suppose to some extent who you're talking to. But I cannot see a company like us being production-orientated. It's going to be more market-orientated.' But again this commitment to marketing was balanced: 'It's no good being market-orientated', continued the same director, 'unless for the products that you design, the products that you innovate with, you have the equipment and the manpower and the technology to build them. So it's never in the end a solely marketing-orientated company'. As yet another put it, with the characteristic Homecraft concern for consensus: 'We don't have a marketing-dominated or a production-dominated or a design-dominated or a finance-dominated company. We have a market-led company.' The company also cherished a reputation for innovation, but this was far from reckless: 'We have probably brought out more product innovations than most companies, so we are certainly not saying "lets be stodgy and ultra-conservative and never be making anything", because that's equally a road to ruin. Its all a matter of getting your balance right.'

The nature of the main Midland plant was closely bound up with the Homecraft creed. Tarling's original promotion from production director to managing director had been based on his success in reforming a plant that was old, cramped and multiproduct. Another director commented: 'Whoever became boss of this operation . . . needed to have a fairly good understanding of production because fundamentally it is a big production plant, and one that is very complicated because we are a multi-product plant, which is unusual.'

However, the multiproduct nature of the factory reinforced the balance in Homecraft's business: 'Well, the fact that it is a multi-product plant – with all the disadvantages in terms of inventory, in terms of logistics, management control, production scheduling, all the complications that mean you lose economies of scale – in highly volatile markets, it is a major advantage because whenever something is crashing to the floor, something else is on the rise.' Even the cramped nature of the plant was made into a virtue. Another director put it thus: 'Over the years, this company has had a success record which in part has been based on utilizing its square footage to a greater and greater extent and getting more out of the same basic overhead. There's a saying that as long as the walls of Homecraft are *that* shape [making a bulging gesture with his hands], bulging, then all is well [laugh]!'

Close proximity on the same site also reinforced the team spirit: 'Here its across the corridor and there they are.' The marketing department was immediately next door to the managing director's office, and the design department was just below – the relationship between marketing and design was described as 'almost incestuous'. So, far from being a constraint, the compact nature of the site was seen as integral to the style and strategy of the company. One director mused:

> You do have to say sometimes: OK, there are things that perhaps we have got to do strategically, but which will inevitably make a bigger, more diffuse sort of structure that maybe will be much more difficult to capture with this kind of team spirit. That's the sort of thing we wonder. If we were to change dramatically in any kind of way, that, I think, we would lose.

The company therefore chose to concentrate on just three key products: cooking, laundry and heating. 'Its a three legged stool, and each leg is important. So that was a decision – not to chase sheer volume for the sake of volume by going into, say, refrigeration.' In each of these products, Homecraft commanded relatively high market shares and enjoyed close relations with the Electricity Boards, the company's biggest customer. Homecraft was not eager to venture outside these strongholds:

> You see, we're brand leaders in many of the things we're in. I don't think we start off with the philosophy that our number one objective is to be brand leaders, thereby destroying the opposition, thereby increasing our market . . . We say, let's get the money in [laugh] and then we'll worry about the rest. So we are fairly cautious in our philosophy.

Rose Domestic Appliances

While Homecraft was characterized by cohesion and stability, by the late 1970s Rose had become a company in uncomfortable transition. The product of rapid growth by acquisition, Rose was the most diverse of the three domestic appliance companies, with products ranging from small appliances to gas cookers and manufacturing plants scattered all over the country. Up until 1976, unity amongst senior management had been maintained by loyalty to the commanding figure of Sir Ben Rose, the company's founding entrepreneur. However, after Sir Ben's retirement to a mere figurehead position within the group, the loyalists' hold over their disparate empires came under increasing threat from tightening economic pressures and a new breed of managers with little respect for traditional methods. Thus, as the company approached the recession, Rose was still struggling to find a means of restoring the vigour and integration it had enjoyed in the 1950s and 1960s under the leadership of Sir Ben.

At the end of the 1970s there were five main sites, of which the North Site was the most important (see Figure 7.1). Manufacturing major electrical appliances, the North Site had originally been built up by Cyril Bowden in the early 1950s, and his success there had been the basis for a career which took him twenty-five years later to the chairmanship of the Domestic Appliances Division and deputy managing directorship of the Rose group as a whole. Thus, the North site 'was always cherished and recognised as something special in the Rose [main] board, the panoply of Ben Rose's contemporaries.' Its management was cohesive and long serving; by 1980, there was only one manager who had not done twenty-five years continuous service on the site. One outsider caricatured these managers thus: they had 'started as boys and are now [1984] around fifty years of age and have spent around thirty odd years together and are still operating together . . . knowing one another's intimate secrets and no doubt chasing the same girls over the same rooftops.' Although constrained by production schedules set by Sales at the South site – referred to dismissively as 'down South' – these North site managers had always enjoyed considerable operational autonomy. It had only been in 1977 that they had lost their separate company name and status.

The gas cooking and heating side was very separate, too: 'There was undoubtedly, of course, a tremendous in-built belief that you were a "gas man" or an "electric man".' Ben Rose had originally entered gas cooking by acquiring two well-established companies, one based in London, the other in the Midlands. By the end of the 1970s, the

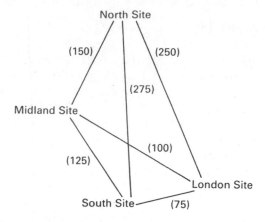

Miles between sites – in brackets – are approximate; relative positions are deliberately distorted.

North site: Major electrical appliances: manufacturing, design and development.

Midland site: Gas appliances: manufacturing, design and development.

London site: Gas appliances: manufacturing, design and development, sales and marketing, finance and service.

South site: Small electrical appliances: manufacturing, design and development, sales and marketing, finance and service.
Major electrical appliances: sales and marketing, finance and service.
Export sales company.

Figure 7.1 Rose Domestic Appliances: Main Sites, 1979

London site was being run down, and investment was concentrated on the Midland site of the old Bright and James Appliance Company. Apart from the site director, most of the management at the Midland factory pre-dated the original takeover in 1971. As late as 1984, one manager commented: 'They're not all Rose men here, they're all Bright and James men here.' The old BJA logo still eclipsed the Rose one at the main entrance to the Midland site. A so-called 'Committee of Five' – middle managers from before the takeover – remained powerful. Although the ranges of the two original gas companies were now almost exactly the same, and both companies' cookers were being built increasingly on the Midland site, even in the early 1980s they retained separate brand names and sales forces.

Even if each of the sites remained highly independent and distinctive in character, Rose's senior management was tightly bound by personal loyalties. The philosophy, according to one of the newcomers, was simple: 'Sir Ben very much believed in developing his mates in the business. He was very much against bringing people in from the outside.' At the same time, Ben Rose would always stand by his men. One of his managers remembered:

> He virtually never sacked anybody – he never sacked anybody who had been with the company a long time, I should say more accurately. And his attitude was: "that chap's been with us twenty years – we should have found out long ago he wasn't the right guy – its too late now, we shouldn't throw him on the slag heap." I think that attitude cost the company a bit of money, but boy oh boy, it made people feel that here was a man with a heart.

As another newcomer observed, '[Ben] Rose would operate on a kind of loyalty bonding between himself and his staff'.

Thus relationships between Ben Rose and his loyalists were very personal and sometimes highly emotional. Founder of the company, still an 11 per cent shareholder in 1976 and 77 years old upon his retirement, Sir Ben was both father-figure and entrepreneurial model to his managers. This is how one senior director remembered the relationship between Ben Rose and his managers:

> You can have many husbands, but you can have only one father; you can have many chairmen and managing directors of a company, but you can have only one founder. And you have this almost unique sort of ability when you are the boss. It is your idea, you have created it. You become very much the *father* of not only the company . . . but also you are the father of all the people in it. And his [Ben Rose's] was a very strong paternal attitude . . . He regarded everybody as sort of children. "They are very good lads," he would say, "They are marvellous lads." But you were never more than a lad.

Another director made the same use of the 'father' image, again referring both to Sir Ben's role as progenitor of the business and to his relationship with his managers:

> It was a personal relationship; he didn't forget people. I suppose we saw him as a paternal figure, as somebody that had built up a very big business, and had made a lot of important decisions and was responsible at that time for employing 75,000 people – and that was from, you know, literally from selling lamps off a stall in a market. I mean, it was the proverbial . . . rags to riches and success to those who go out and look for it. We believed in him.

Ironically, the family spirit engendered by Sir Ben would later be turned against these managers. By the early 1980s, the common

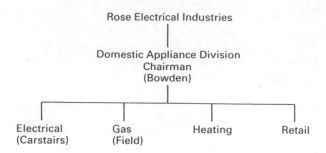

Figure 7.2   Rose Domestic Appliances: Structure, 1979

accusation against the 'Rose Men' was that they were 'incestuous' and 'inbred'.

At the time of the recession all the key positions – within domestic appliance manufacturing at least (see Figure 7.2) – were still held by managers who had made their careers under Sir Ben Rose. Bowden, chairman of the division as a whole, was particularly closely identified with Sir Ben, having joined as early as 1946: 'he [Bowden] was extremely close to the man at the top; he had been with the company since he was a boy really, and had moved almost from shopfloor level to [deputy] managing director of Rose.' Carstairs, chairman of the electrical appliances part, and Field, chairman of gas appliances, were more protégés of Ben Rose's trusted lieutenant, Jo Teal, the dynamic salesman who had originally built up the domestic appliance division after the war. The system of insider patronage that Ben Rose had created undoubtedly produced close and longstanding relationships. Thus, like several other managers, Carstairs had been recruited from the same company that Teal had first come from; Carstairs and Bowden had been in brown goods together; and Teal, Bowden and Field were the team that had established the original Rose electric cooker business during the 1950s. It was this dense network that would be threatened by the gradual invasion of a new management breed that began in the late 1970s, almost simultaneous with the onset of the recession.

Personal loyalty appeared more important to these managers than financial reward. Three directors independently stressed the low salaries Ben Rose paid, managers had been well rewarded by the career opportunities offered by rapid growth. One senior manager commented: 'in the thirty years I've been with the company, the turnovers have gone up from roughly £300,000 to £300 million – don't take these figures precisely, but in that order . . . I couldn't see another company in domestic appliances who were doing any better.

In fact I couldn't find a company which was doing as well . . . So why move?' The rewards were not simply careerist; managers were genuinely excited. Another manager recalled the 1960s and early 1970s: 'Morale was extremely high and the spirit of the company under Sir Ben was without doubt . . . without question, extremely high. People were not working for salaries.'

Though Ben Rose had effectively retired in 1976 and Jo Teal in 1977, for many managers they still epitomized 'the old Rose', 'the Rose way' or 'the Rose men'. Teal's favourite phrase – 'I steer by the seat of the pants' – was much quoted. To the old Rose managers, this meant that he did not *need* to carry out formal analyses: 'When Jo said, "I steer by the seat of my pants", what he really meant was: "I have – and he undoubtedly did have – a *feel* for the business. Don't ask me why; I just sense this is what we ought to do."' Thus, apart from budgeting and investment appraisals, control was informal: 'It was never sort of technical stuff. It was entrepreneurial in the extreme.' Or:

> There was no management 'talk', no management jargon, no clear organisational chart where people knew precisely what the job was, who they were responsible to. There was a lot of by-passing of any formalities which might have existed on a chart. But they didn't matter, because this was Rose, and we were dedicated to the products. It worked.

Another senior manager, seeking to epitomize Teal's lack of formal skills, affectionately recalled a subsidiary board meeting which he attended: 'he [Teal] gazed at a set of figures for a long time and then looked over at me and said: "What's J. F. M. A.?". And I said: "January, February, March, April". "Oh", he said.'

This 'seat-of-the-pants' management style also favoured production. One newcomer put it thus: 'It was seat of the pants, to some extent it was sort of *manufacturing* driven, rather than sort of marketing or product development driven. And the culture was that if you weren't running around hitting bits of iron with hammers, with spanners in your hand, then you weren't a *man*.' This manufacturing emphasis was a legacy of the rapid growth of the 1960s, reinforced by Ben Rose's personal bias. 'It was all from that period of consumerism, and so the problem was not of sales or marketing; the problem was how to meet an insatiable demand.' Sophisticated marketing was disregarded; volume production of simple products was seen as the key. Another manager recalled the formula: '[we] just knew that the cheaper you produced the product into the market, the more you were likely to sell. The more you sold, providing the price was reasonable – and you've already spread your fixed overheads – the more money you made, and the more money the company could invest into itself.'

Ben Rose aimed for dominance of the UK market. According to one of the 'Rose men',

> Like a lot of people who are not British but who come to Britain and then become more British than the British, his whole concentration was on the United Kingdom . . . He saw himself very much as a man who wished to grow within the United Kingdom. His primary interest lay in market shares. He was a man who believed that if you had a large market share, you would succeed.

Success was measured not in terms of maximizing returns, but in making what was roughly conceived of as reasonable profits. Remembered another: 'We were not measuring our profitability by the usual criteria of capital employed and that sort of thing. I mean, the companies were run pretty informally . . . It was *profit* for the sake of *profit* – I mean, a profitable company.'

The appointment of Jim Donald from outside as chairman of the Rose Group in 1976, the subsequent takeover of Imperial Electronics and Entertainments, and the severe recession which followed all represented sharp shocks to the old 'Rose men'. One of the 'Rose men' measured the extent of the contrast between Sir Ben's regime and the new Donald style thus:

> I think it is fair to say that the changes we introduced were almost parodied by the two gentlemen. One [Rose] was about five foot four inches and the other [Donald] about six foot two. One weighed about eight stone and the other about twenty stone. So you couldn't have had two more opposite characters. And I think Jim Donald came over as a rather distant heavy-weight – and I use heavy weight in the complimentary sense.

The arrival of Jim Donald brought sweeping changes and the first challenge to the old 'seat-of-the-pants' traditions. These changes were summed up by the word 'professionalism'. One of the 'Rose men' remembered the impact of the new chairman thus:

> In came R.O.C. [Return On Capital] and cash flow as the new gods. Market share was seen not as unimportant but not as important as the other two. He introduced planning . . . We move from the natural flair to the planned economy, with all the merits and the disadvantages that went with that. The merit I think was that we became more professional – I think that would be the right word – we became a much more professional activity.

Jim Donald himself drew the contrast between Ben Rose's entrepreneurial leadership and his more professional management style. Thus another manager vividly remembered how Donald first introduced himself to his managers upon taking over the chairmanship:

> He is a professional manager and later at the handing over ceremony he expressed that very clearly. And he said: 'OK gentlemen, I'm Jim Donald and I've been around and met a few of you. I've seen you in your locations. I'm now officially taking over. I've got to impress upon you that there is a significant difference between Sir Ben and myself.' These are not his exact words, but something like this. 'You have been used to operating with an entrepreneur of high quality and a man of genius. I am a professional manager. My style, of necessity, is completely different to Sir Ben's. You've reached the end of an era. There will be much change, much gnashing of teeth.'

The same man continued, re-emphasizing the distinction between professionalism and entrepreneurship:

> I mean, he said he was a professional manager, and the age of the entrepreneur had gone. He wouldn't even try to be an entrepreneur, because he wasn't. And he had a style which he considered to be a professional style.

Jim Donald regarded domestic appliances as a 'mature' industry, with low technology and trapped inside a saturated UK market. The 1979 takeover of Imperial, involved in defence and medical electronics as well as global entertainments, was intended to take the Rose Group into high technology, world markets with potential for fast growth. The 'old Rose' men immediately recognized a downgrading of their status: under the new regime:

> It [domestic appliances] lost its privileged position to some extent, and of course with Imperial coming in, which was a very vast organization, it lost its position further down the line again. Whereas Rose was always about lighting, television and television rental and domestic appliances, these became a very small part of the piece. And whereas because *that* was Rose and domestic appliances would always be continuing, in the new Rose Electronics and Entertainments situation, it's a question of: 'is it a business? Is it better to invest money into appliances instead of putting it into defence or entertainment?' The whole attitude and ethos of the company became different.

Although as yet they retained their senior management positions within the domestic appliances businesses, the 'Rose men' were not immune from alien interventions. Return on capital employed criteria were rigorously applied. A detailed review of the product-line profitabilities revealed unsuspected losses in refrigeration manufacture. The 'Rose men's' natural instinct to fill an underutilized satellite plant with new products of doubtful profit was emphatically denied, leading to closure in 1978. But perhaps most ominous, the appointment for the first time of two young and professional personnel managers, both from outside the division, threatened the old career networks.

The 'Rose men' recognized the need for change, but struggled to cope. Asked in 1984 whether it was difficult to adapt to the new management style, one 'old Rose' manager agreed:

> Yes, yes, I think its difficult to adjust for people who've been with the old Rose for a long time and therefore to that extent are old and their minds tend to be rigid and in the past – yes, difficult. For younger people, easier, and then the new input of management trainees and the like come to something that's always existed as far as they are concerned. Yes, it's difficult to adjust, certainly.

Moreover, there were considerable doubts, which mounted particularly in the early 1980s, about the way the changes were being carried out. By 1984 the 'old Rose' managers would perceive themselves to be irredeemably stereotyped as 'incestuous' and 'inbred':

> This is change, and it's change that managers have got to get used to. And one way that you can achieve that change – its not the best way, but it is the easy way – is to change your managers . . . You know, get rid of the old order. You have what is currently referred to as an 'incestuous' management, right. And so, because we've been around a long time, by inference, that is a bad thing. It means that we are inbred and incapable of taking on board change. And if we do take on board the change, then we are less than capable in making it work because we came up the wrong way.

Let me sum up this section. These three companies, although competing in many of the same markets, approached the recession with very different internal characteristics. Exemplar was firmly dominated by the charismatic, entrepreneurial Jo Stone, dedicated to long term growth on the basis of good industrial relations and sound marketing. Rose Domestic Appliances had recently lost its similarly domineering entrepreneur, and was struggling to replace its old manufacturing based informality with a new unity and purpose centred around professional and rigorous performance criteria. Lastly, Homecraft's stable and cohesive team had built up a consensus around the need to achieve steady profits by the careful but committed marketing and development of just three core products.

The creation and maintenance of these firms' individual characters were neither accidental nor effortless. Stone had had to transfer the cooker factory and purge the old Exemplar management; Tarling had built up a close knit team that deliberately protected itself from dissidents and radical organizational change; the 'Rose men' had been carefully cultivated by Ben Rose and Jo Teal. However, at Rose the old divisional leadership was being challenged by new financial controls from above and the appointment of new outsider managers below. At Exemplar and Homecraft, by contrast, the prevailing management and orientations were secure from internal challenge. Stone combined the authority of office and ownership with the legitimacy of success and the loyalty of a hand-picked group of subordinates; Homecraft's management was cohesive, exclusive and cautiously successful. The next section examines the extent to which these managements were secure from external challenges to their discretion.

THE SCOPE FOR STRATEGIC CHOICE

So far, we have seen that all three companies possessed managements that held very distinct aims and which, in two cases at least, were strongly entrenched. But however divergent their natural trajectories, these aims would all be for naught if environmental pressures were so fierce as to deny them any scope for effective strategic choice. To what extent, then, did the managers of these three companies enjoy sufficient autonomy and security to pursue recession strategies, each according to their own particular objectives?

Recalling the discussion in Chapter 5, I shall consider the companies' latitude for strategic choice in terms of Lawriwsky's (1984) distinction between the constraints exercised by product markets, capital markets and the market for corporate control. Each of these markets exerts external pressures upon company managements for profit-maximization, to the exclusion of strategic choice. Thus, the extent to which Exemplar, Homecraft and Rose managers would be able to pursue strategies consistent with their distinctive characters would depend upon the ease with which they could generate adequate, not necessarily maximum, profits from their product markets; upon their independence for finance from the disciplines of the capital markets; and their freedom from the scrutiny of exigent shareholders or the threat of predatory takeover.

Exemplar

At first glance, Exemplar's product market position at the onset of the recession appears weak. The company had deliberately got out of the electric cooker market, instead concentrating on the much more competitive and import prone refrigeration and laundry markets. In none of its present markets did Exemplar command more than a 20 per cent share (see Table 7.2). However, this gloomy picture neglects the company's marketing skills. In particular, Jo Stone had carefully cultivated the loyalty of the independent retailers, who still accounted for roughly one-third of refrigeration sales and about one-fifth of laundry sales nationally. Because small retailers never build up large stocks and therefore need a constant dribble of supplies, they were not so liable to savage destocking as the large retailers. Moreover, through margin support and the Exemplar Sales Point schemes, it was easier to discourage them from discounting. Thus, though competing in inherently more difficult markets, Exemplar had succeeded in building itself a relatively protected niche. In the words of one Exemplar manager, the independents: 'gave us a sort of base to see us through hard times.'

Exemplar was unusual, too, in being jointly owned by Stone Furniture Industries – Jo Stone's family business – and Universal Engineering. Stone and his wife personally owned 17 per cent of the joint company (the only one of his managers who also owned a significant stake was the finance director, with a tiny 0.25 per cent stake). Although the furniture company was to suffer persistent difficulties throughout the recession, Jo Stone himself had a personal fortune by now largely independent of short-term fluctuations.

Nor did Universal depend greatly upon Exemplar's performance. Exemplar represented a tiny part of its vast and diverse engineering operations – less than 4 per cent of a total turnover approaching £3 billion. Universal's size rendered the risk of takeover highly remote. Besides, its shareholders were diffuse: an insurance company, with 6 per cent of the equity, was the only substantial single shareholder, though chairman David Bernstein himself held about 2 per cent. Moreover, its financial reserves (around £1 billion at the start of the recession and rising) made it effectively self-financing while, at a time of high interest rates, also providing a substantial revenue to offset the dip in manufacturing profits. This financial strength was reflected in a share price that actually rose during the recession, only beginning to come under some pressure during the recovery.

This by no means meant that Universal's management was lax.

Subsidiary company financial ratios were examined closely each month and Exemplar entered the recession still burdened with heavy debts of £21 million, mostly to Universal itself. None the less, Stone was gradually reducing Exemplar's gearing, and so long as performance continued to improve, Universal was prepared to allow Stone considerable operational autonomy. Remembered one Exemplar director, he 'was basically making the main decisions. Universal act as an interested shareholder in that they give the business a lot of license and, provided the business is being run satisfactorily, then there is considerable freedom. When things start going wrong, then, like the prodding shareholder, they will prod quite hard if need be.' But Stone was able to exercise a more than normal autonomy.

First, he enjoyed the respect and friendship of Universal's chairman, David Bernstein, another Jewish entrepreneur who had first done business with Stone in the early 1950s. Before being brought into rescue Exemplar in 1974, one manager explained 'Stone had demonstrated a very personalised style of management in Stone Furniture which Bernstein respected as an individual and knew about, and therefore nobody was doing anybody any favours'. So close did the relationship between the two seem that an unfounded rumour started that the two were family relations. Second, Stone was always fierce in protecting his freedom: according to one director, he and Bernstein 'were at daggers drawn on some occasions'. Lastly, there was the unique advantage of the Stones' personal shareholding. One manager observed of Stone's relative strength by comparison with other Exemplar managing directors, before and after:

> As he was part owner of this company, he was in a very different position to [the present managing director] or any of his predecessors, who were wholly dependent on a head office to finance the thing. Stone could say: 'Thirty per cent [sic] of this company is mine and I'm going to do it.' He just did it. When he'd done it, he told people he'd done it.

Another manager laughingly recalled Universal's predicament in dealing with Stone: 'They [Universal] couldn't ride roughshod over him, because they couldn't get rid of him. Every three legged stool, he owned one leg and Bernstein had two. But there was no way Bernstein could get that bloody leg off him!'

Homecraft

As for Homecraft, its 'three-legged stool' of electric cookers, laundry and storage heaters was firmly based. In cooking, Homecraft held a third of the UK market, second only to Rose (see Table 7.2). In tumble-driers, Homecraft held half the market. As for storage heating, Homecraft's strategy, of retaining manufacturing capacity and continuing product development, was well rewarded during the boom at the end of the 1970s and early 1980s that followed the Electricity Board's reversal of its tariff policy; at one stage the company was temporarily able to capture half the market. For all three products, Homecraft's major customers were the Electricity Boards, who were carefully cultivated. Moreover, after years of good profits and moderate investment, Homecraft had accumulated substantial reserves of over £7 million.

However, Homecrafts' position was complicated by its relationship with its parent, AEL. The Group did not interfere in the strategic direction of its subsidiaries. As one director exclaimed in some frustration, 'I've no idea what AEL's philosophy is – they've never told me. I've not the faintest idea what they want. They've been wandering around for twenty years so far as I'm concerned.' The domestic appliance divisional board did not intervene either: Tarling was deputy chairman and Homecraft contributed the largest part of the profits.

Paradoxically, however, Homecraft's financial strength imposed constraints. Between 1981 and 1983, AEL was to make heavy losses and undergo severe rationalization. The group's gearing reached 50 per cent in 1981. By 1982, Homecraft would be making cheap loans to the Group and fellow subsidiaries of £4 million, while accounting for 32 per cent of its trading profits and increasing its share of AEL's total turnover from 3.9 per cent in 1979 to 8.1 per cent. Thus, Homecraft was under considerable pressure to keep providing the profits that were, to a large extent, propping up the rest of the group. This was expressed sardonically: 'If Homecraft catches a cold, then AEL gets pneumonia.' Reflecting these troubles, AEL's share price fell in 1981 to less than 20 per cent of its 1979 peak.

AEL's shareholders were highly dispersed and takeover rumours began to circulate in the early 1980s. None of Homecraft's directors held Group shareholdings excess of £2,000, but, trapped within their ailing parent, they certainly recognized Homecraft's special attractiveness to potential predators: 'when you've got a successful operation within a leviathan like AEL, whcrc you've got a particular piccc of the

cake being very profitable, and obviously operating well in difficult
conditions, then you'll obviously have people looking at it – you're
bound to have investors looking at it, or the City men.' Yet to some
extent these attentions might be regarded as flattering – Homecraft's
successful management could regard their prospects after any takeover
with some complacency. In fact, it was not until 1984 that AEL faced
its first open bid.

Rose

The chairman of Rose Domestic Appliances, Cyril Bowden, had
traditionally enjoyed a position that was described as 'baronial'. Over
his long career with Rose he had built up a personal share holding far
greater than any of his managers, and by 1979 he was the second
largest shareholder on the main board with a stake worth between
£80,000 and £150,000 during the year (in a company as large as Rose
Electronics and Entertainments, however, this represented less than
0.02 per cent of the voting equity). Despite the changes since the
retirement of Sir Ben, he remained a dominating figure in the Rose
group as a whole. Bowden's unique status was summed up thus: 'He
had a lot of autonomy. He had also been Chairman of the brown
goods company; he'd also been in charge of Lighting. And in his
capacity as sort of deputy managing director of Rose [group], he had
authority and power, which could be translated into the Domestic
Appliance division.' But by the late 1970s, under the Donald regime,
this autonomy could no longer be guaranteed.

For the first time, Rose Domestic Appliances was coming under
pressure to meet rigorous performance criteria – one of Donald's first
acts had been to expose the unprofitability of two satellite refrigeration
plants which soon after had been closed. Old Rose managers now
perceived the division as reduced to a 'cash cow', turned to servicing
the heavy debts incurred by the Imperial takeover and funding further
high technology and global ventures. Between 1979 and 1980, debt
increased eight times and profit coverage of interest payments
collapsed from a formidable fifty times to only twice. Under these
conditions it was not surprising that Donald should show a sharpened
concern for return on capital employed. The discontent of the 'Old
Rose' managers expressed itself in the way they treated 'R.O.C.E.' as
the symbol of the new regime. One manager pointedly pretended to
forget the precise meaning of these despised initials. Another
commented: 'its all about return on capital now . . . If I might be a

mite controversial, I think I am more of a Ben Rose man than I am perhaps a R.O.C man.'

But the division's ability to generate the required profits was under challenge. Hitherto, Rose had relied on volume production of conventional products to achieve dominance of markets. Emphasizing price competitiveness, the actual marketing of these products had been weak. The company had retained a multiplicity of brand names (as exemplified by the failure to integrate the marketing of the two gas cooking companies) and had always been ready to supply retailers with products to sell under their own labels. This marketing weakness left Rose in an exposed position as, by the end of the 1970s, markets began to change rapidly. Refrigeration had always been a cut-throat business, but Rose's other traditional strengths were now under attack too. In small appliances, Rose's dominance of the traditional food-mixer market was being eroded by the new fashion for imported 'food-processors'. Even in the cooking area, traditional products were being superseded by Continental built-in and slip-in styles, while the British Gas showrooms, which traditionally took 90 per cent of Rose's gas cookers, were threatened by privatization. Thus Rose could no longer count on sustaining profit margins simply by economies of scale in production and high UK market shares.

By 1979, Rose Electronics and Entertainments had a highly dispersed shareownership: one institution owned fractionally more than 5 per cent, while Ben Rose had by now largely shifted his investment. However, shareholders' concern following the Imperial takeover was registered in a 47 per cent drop in the Rose group's share price between 1979 and 1980. By the recovery period, takeover rumours were becoming rife. But even then it would be difficult to galvanize some of the company's management. One of the newcomers summed up the atmosphere in general in 1984 thus:

> One of the greatest problems is to convince the boys and girls out there that we may be part of the great Rose Electronics and Entertainments who turned in £130 million [profit] or whatever it was. But [-] cookers don't make money. Rose will shut it. No doubt they will close it or they'll sell it off and if they sell it they'll sell it to somebody who will turn it inside out to make it successful. And its very difficult: there's an air of absolute security. 'It can't possibly happen here.' It bloody well will happen here if we don't do something about it!

Thus, of the three companies' managements, Rose Domestic Appliances' was probably the least independent of external pressures. The recession would provide a severe test of the extent to which

Bowden's high influence and the oligopolistic hold over the cooker markets could still protect the division's idiosyncratic ways against the externally imposed disciplines of return on capital employed.

Exemplar and Homecraft had more leverage against such external pressures. Jo Stone, having consolidated his position internally by the purge of the old management and disposal of cookers, had eased Exemplar's former dependence upon the powerful multiple retailers and reassured Universal by restoring profitability and gradually reducing gearing. His trump card, of course, remained Stone Furniture's 37.5 per cent share. Homecraft's position was more complex, for its very financial strength entailed, within a faltering AEL, heavy obligations. However, with market dominance in a range of products and substantial financial reserves, Homecraft too could expect to be cushioned, to some extent at least, against most upsets. We shall see in the next chapter how far these three companies actually proved able to exploit their varying degrees of discretion in their responses to the recession.

Chapter Eight

The appliance companies in recession and recovery

INTRODUCTION

In the last chapter I introduced three leading domestic appliance companies: Rose, Exemplar and Homecraft. Superficially these companies had much in common. All three were subsidiaries of large British manufacturing conglomerates; they competed directly in several sectors; and all concentrated on home markets that were under increasing threat from foreign competition. On these grounds alone, one might expect them to adopt very similar strategies in the face of the common challenge of the 1979–81 recession. However, the previous chapter also revealed the widely different internal characters of these three companies. Rose remained in the grip of a generation of managers still loyal to the 'Rose way' of 'seat-of-the-pants' decision-making and mass production of cheap, standard products. At Exemplar, the domineering Jo Stone was dedicated to the rebuilding of British manufacturing through paternalistic care for workers and clever marketing. Homecraft's managers too were committed to marketing, but, ever-mindful of the need for 'balance', had none of Stone's fanatacisms. Thus beneath the surface similarities each of these companies had very different instincts for strategic action. Moreover, as the last chapter concluded, none of these companies – except perhaps Rose – appeared to be under sufficient market pressures to force them to ignore their instincts.

This chapter, then, will examine just how far the dominant actors in these three firms actually were able to choose their responses to the recession according to their own inclinations. The next section will begin by providing simple narrative accounts of the three firms' strategies during the recession and through into the recovery. The third section will examine the consequences of these strategic choices, both for financial performance and for the careers of the decision-makers. The chapter will finish by investigating several key strategic issues on which the three firms took very divergent approaches.

RECESSION STRATEGIES

As indicated by the quotations with which this book began, in general Exemplar responded to the recession by 'hanging on' while Rose 'cut back' severely. Homecraft took a midway course, neither investing substantially nor rationalizing very greatly. This section outlines the companies' recession strategies in more detail.

Exemplar

At Exemplar, the severe cuts of the mid–1970s, and Stone's deliberate cultivation of a trim but market sensitive management had left the company well prepared for the sudden collapse of demand in 1980. One director compared Exemplar's position to its competitors thus:

> The fact that we had trimmed our ship a little bit and had reviewed our policies made it easier for us to respond. As I say, it's not to say we didn't go through a rough period. If you look at our results, they weren't very clever in the early 1980s. But I think we were more alive to the requirements of the market place. We hadn't been sitting back and being complacent, as I think a lot of companies had who were successful in the 1970s.

Thus for Exemplar, according to another director, the recession was 'more of a hiccough than affecting our long-term policy, which didn't change'. The company remained true to its policies of supporting the independents, resisting discounting and, but for a temporary interruption, continued investment in production facilities. In 1981, at the depth of the recession, Stone launched his margin support scheme for the struggling independent retailers. Jo Stone was given all the credit within Exemplar for dreaming up this ingenious device for maintaining price discipline, and when one of the major discount retailers responded fiercely by taking Exemplar to court, he himself handled the case in person. But even though Exemplar maintained its strong face in the market place, the company could not be entirely spared from economies and rationalizations internally. Nevertheless, these too bore the unmistakeable stamp of Jo Stone.

It was only in April 1980, as retailers suddenly entered a bout of radical destocking, that Exemplar began to feel the first effects of the recession. For three months the company took heavy losses but in July Stone was forced to make 150 people redundant. Another 150 redundancies followed later that year. None the less, the paternalistic Stone insisted that all these redundancies were confined to indirect workers rather than direct factory workers. The design department, for instance, lost 40 per cent of its staff, while in the factory losses were confined to maintenance, stores and quality control staff. However, both staff and works were put on short-time for a spell during 1980. Moreover, Stone was forced to curtail some of the less central fringe benefits he had introduced – for instance, personal loans and credit at the factory shop and the withdrawal of hairdressing facilities during working hours. Industrial relations also came under strain for the first time since Stone's early rationalizations. To the stress of redundancies and a determined productivity drive, Stone added the provocation of a unilateral factory 'smoking ban'. Motivated by his own personal distaste for smoking and his unlikely fear that Exemplar refrigerators might arrive in showrooms with cigarette ash inside, this ban was imposed against the advice of his managers. A short strike in September 1980 soon brought a compromise: the smoking ban was rescinded, though non-smokers were given the automatic right of transfer to no-smoking areas.

There were other areas of rationalization. Exemplar had never been strong in exports, preferring to concentrate upon the defence of the home market and rather resenting the inconvenient product modifications required for overseas sales. As high exchange rates reduced export margins, Exemplar was not loathe to withdraw from most of its foreign markets, concentrating instead on just a few relatively protected areas such as Malta and the NAFFI. Another area of chronic difficulties had been the small appliance company, which had been managed separately until the arrival of Stone, and whose high seasonality and different distribution channels were alien to the experience of most Exemplar managers. As difficulties mounted during the recession, the small appliance company was sold in 1982 for £5 million. This helped Stone with his balance sheet, laden with heavy debt and high inventories: interest payments amounted to nearly £3 million in 1979–80. By year-end 1981, £8 million had been repaid to Universal.

The pressure from Universal remained heavy none the less. Instead of the usual monthly basis, detailed reports were required weekly. At one stage, Universal stepped in to forbid all advertising. However, Exemplar's managers had a strong champion in Jo Stone. As one remembered: 'Without having the strength of the individual, Stone in this case, saying: "Well, you know, if you put a stranglehold on me like that, you'll kill my business", we may have gone through a tougher period than we did.' However, Stone was not able to stave off Universal's most important intervention, the veto on the new Welsh factory.

As the second new refrigeration plant neared completion, Stone planned to begin work in 1979 on a new £9 million washing machine factory at Damnar in Wales. However, even before the recession, the European market had suffered surplus production capacity; besides, Exemplar was already in heavy debt. Although Stone's own sceptical managers could not dissuade him, Universal decisively refused funds for the project.

Stone did not surrender, persistently arguing for this major new investment until, in late 1980, he at last secured approval. But this was not all. Stone went on to add still more controversy by insisting that the new factory should be the first washing machine factory in the UK to adopt pre-paint production technology. Again his management, especially the production and technical directors, advised strongly against this additional risk. Failure to master the untried technology, when Exemplar was wallowing in a depressed market and burdened by heavy debt, might well jeopardize the very survival of the company. When Stone began pre-paint production in 1982, against the warnings of the engineers who wanted six more months development work, initial scrap rates were indeed high; but within fifteen months of opening, scrap was down to 1 per cent and the factory was breaking even after less than a year's operations.

Homecraft

There were no such rash projects at Homecraft. Though the recession was in fact to be a period of continued economic good fortune for Homecraft, the company would not allow this success to distract it from its traditional caution. Profits were protected by rationalization; long-term positioning of core products was safeguarded by continued, but narrow, investment and innovation.

Homecraft's rationalizations did not, in fact, have to be very severe. The company closed down half its Southern factory and brought forward the closure, anyway planned, of its smaller Midland site. The transfer of washing machine production from the closed site to the main Midland site helped keep it fully stretched. However, the main site's chief boon was the revival of the storage heater market, which doubled between 1978 and 1981 following the Electricity Board's introduction of Economy 7 tarrifs. As Homecraft took around 50 per cent of the UK market with its new slim-line heater, the company's perseverance and continued investment in what had been the weakest leg of its three-legged stool during the mid–1970s was resoundingly vindicated. Recalled one manager triumphantly: 'We were the first out with it [slim-line heaters], so we had a field day. We had three years of making money like drunken soldiers.' Good industrial relations permitted the easy switch of workers from cooker production to new storage heater lines. Thus, although lay-offs and short-time working had to be introduced temporarily in 1980, the main Midland site was spared any redundancies. Total employment actually rose in each year between 1980 and 1982.

Homecraft also strived for greater efficiency, in particular reducing its rather high average credit period by more than a third. Investment, such as there was, emphasized areas which could save space and labour in the cramped main plant – for instance, three robots and an automated washing machine testing station – or where it could speed up the design process – for instance, Computer-Aided Design. An experiment with Quality Circles rather petered out. Disappointing, too, was an effort to boost exports, which raised the proportion of overseas sales by 30 per cent between 1979 and 1981, before being punctured by the severe difficulties of the company with which Homecraft had engaged in a joint export promotion campaign.

At home, Homecraft continued to protect its core products by continued development. In 1980, the company introduced a new range of built-in cookers, with the top-of-the-range cooker utilizing micro-chip controls for the first time. In 1981 came the first slip-in cookers, designed to meet the new Continental challenge and only a little behind the first British company into the market. Particularly important was the launch of a second generation of even slimmer storage heaters, which would keep the resurgent competition at bay a little longer. One omission, however, was the continued reliance on American factored microwave ovens, despite reliability problems and a failure to gain substantial market share. This neglect of microwaves stood in stark contrast to the manufacturing lead seized by its chief rival in the cooker market, Rose.

Rose

For Rose, the initiative in microwaves was to be the exception in a period that was otherwise marked by introverted rationalization and reorganization. Both the company's traditional disunities and the new pressures of incoming professional management contributed to the bloodshed. The old physical and cultural distance between sales and production rebounded at last on the manufacturing sites. One major appliances manufacturing manager complained that the sales managers, detached at the South site, did not care enough to respond vigorously to the slump in demand:

> It was easier for Sales to say, 'We're not selling, therefore we don't need to make so many, therefore we must make people redundant, cut back production, and lay people off and put them on short-time working.' You know, it was easier for them to say that rather than 'We're not selling. How can we sell more?'

But the new financial controls also bit sharply as markets became more difficult. Observed one 'Old Rose' manager on the effect of Donald's profitability criteria during the recession: 'If you take the view that you must never produce less than x per cent return [on capital employed], then you go through periods of cutting, cutting, cutting. And sometimes you damage your long term prospects by going through that procedure.'

At the small appliances company the rise in Sterling crippled important export markets, while at the same time letting in American and European imports on a large scale for the first time. Despite an extraordinary offer by the workforce to take a £10 a week pay cut and a joint management-union protest to the then Minister for Trade and Industry over exchange rate policy, small appliances had to make 750 redundant in September 1980 and close one satellite plant. On the gas cooker side, the gradual run-down of the London site was abruptly ended by closure in the hope of quick cash from sale and redevelopment; this entailed 1,200 redundancies by 1982, though staff functions were provisionally retained at the site. Transfer of cooker production from London saved the Midland site from redundancies. The major electrical appliances North site was less fortunate, however. The first 400 compulsory redundancies came in the spring of 1980, and by 1982 the workforce had been slimmed down by a total of 1,500. A determined productivity drive brought improvements of 30 per cent between 1980 and 1982, with resistance in the press shop being firmly broken after mass dismissals and a four month strike. A major programme of renewing the old electric cooker lines was halted, even after the delivery of three of the new presses. The separate major electrical appliances design and development centre was closed, with only two-thirds of the staff retained to be transferred to other locations.

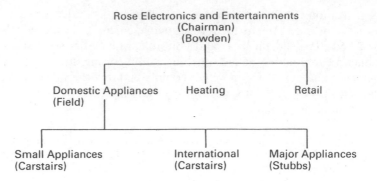

Figure 8.1   Rose Domestic Applainces: Structure, 1983

The North site struggled to maintain volumes to fill its vast capacity. The general response was to seek cost savings in order to sustain substantial price-cuts. In refrigeration, for instance, although Rose's models were already based on a simple 20-year-old German design, the production engineers embarked on a rigorous 'value analysis'. Recently decimated, the design and development engineering group could offer no resistance. The new 'Economy' refrigerator range, considerably despecified, achieved reductions in transfer prices of, typically, 10 to 15 per cent. It was also sold to discount retailers under their own labels – at some sacrifice to Rose's marketing position.

More positive measures at the North site included a deal to manufacture refrigeration compressors both for itself and a foreign manufacturer; the very tentative introduction of a new 'cooking by light' technology in 1982; a late entry that same year into electric storage heating, to take advantage of the booming market; and, most important, the manufacture of Japanese-designed microwaves. This Japanese design replaced the earlier unsuccessful venture with Rose's own design. With an investment of £2 million (40 per cent paid for by the Department of Industry), Rose converted a redundant chest-freezer factory so that it became the first UK volume microwave manufacturer. Neglected, however, was the new slip-in cooker market; although a slightly adapted electric built-in was promoted from 1982 as a stop-gap, it would not be until 1984 that Rose fully committed itself with large-scale production of properly designed slip-ins. In this area it would be three years behind its main cooker rival, Homecraft.

The recession also reinforced the pressures towards organizational change within the appliances division. In 1981, one of the new personnel managers instituted 'Walking/Talking' weekends in order to bring managers from different sites and functions together informally.

For the first time, managers began to be sent on outside training and development courses, specifically intended to extend their understanding beyond narrow functional areas. Another attempt to achieve greater co-ordination between sites and functions was the experiment with Business Area Management Meetings from 1981. All this culminated in the radical divisional re-organization of 1982–3 (see Figure 8.1). Planned informally, and with little consultation outside the trio of Bowden, Carstairs (Electricals) and Field (Gas), this reorganization brought large gas and electric appliances together for the first time within a single Major Appliances Division, headed up by one of Bowden's protégés from gas heating, Stubbs. International and Small Appliances Divisions were set up at the same time, both under Carstairs. All three new divisions were to be presided over by Field. The basic intention was to create a unified organizational structure capable of integrated manufacture of gas and electric cookers sharing the same basic chassis and parts, thereby realizing massive production economies of scale.

However, this Bowden reorganization provoked considerable resistance. The proposal to centralize all marketing, finance, personnel and design and development functions first at the South site and later at a new headquarters in Windsor, entailed moves that would be very disruptive to the families of several senior managers and besides appeared to have a dubious business rationale. One manager expostulated about centralization: 'It doesn't make the slightest sense to me frankly. Its just a perpetuation of the self-interest of the people who are located there [the South site]. You know, if you stand back from the business, the only place for design and development, just as for your sales and marketing, is at the sharp end where the units are actually being built.' The traditionally separate gas and electrical managers disliked amalgamation too: 'Neither party found the other party a particularly welcome bedfellow because traditionally they had been very different parts.' Though Field had begun his career on the electrical side, many electrical managers noted the predominance of 'gas men' in the new Major Appliances Division management: the impression was that 'Major Appliances had been given as a trophy, as it were, to the gas side'. Finally, those managers who did actually care for marketing were concerned that the rivalrous Gas and Electricity Boards would resent dealing with the same unified organization. Much ironic significance was to be attached to the acronyms for the new small and major appliance divisions: S.A.D. and M.A.D.

To sum up, the three companies each adopted different responses to the recession. Even the two heaviest rationalizers, Rose and Exemplar,

-differed substantially in emphasis. Certainly both cut back, but Exemplar disposed of one whole activity and protected the rest, while Rose spared none of its business from rationalization, though ultimately holding on to them all. Likewise, neither Rose nor Exemplar were innovative in developing new products or new markets. In both cases, such innovation as they did attempt was largely confined to manufacturing operations – in Rose's case, the production of a foreign designed and established microwave oven; in Exemplar's case, pre-paint. However, this pre-paint innovation was part of a major investment in new capacity on a scale that clearly marked Exemplar out from the other two companies.

Homecraft rationalized, too, of course. None the less, its closures and redundancies were on a much smaller scale than Rose's, and, unlike Exemplar, it retained all its activities. In this, Homecraft did display a degree of conservatism. However, the company also kept faith with its traditions of innovation by continuous development within its three core product areas. In particular, it retained its technological lead in slim-line storage heaters and, in stark contrast with Rose, was early into the burgeoning slip-in cooker market. Additionally, Homecraft was unique among the three Companies in at least trying to develop new overseas markets.

CONSEQUENCES OF RECESSION STRATEGIES

We have seen that Exemplar, Homecraft and Rose each responded to the recession very differently. Exemplar had invested; Homecraft had consolidated; Rose had rationalized. What, then, were the consequences of these various strategies for the three companies' financial performances, both during the recession and during the recovery? What, too, were the consequences for the managements of these companies?

Figures 8.2, 8.3 and 8.4 present the turnovers (indexed), profit margins and returns on capital employed for the three companies for financial year-ends between 1978 and 1985 (precise figures are provided in Appendix 1 on p. 300). These graphs thus encompass both the end of the recovery from the previous economic cycle and the petering out of the last recovery in 1985. The graphs also include, for the sake of comparison, the (unweighted) averages for four other leading UK domestic appliance manufacturers (see Appendix 1). Amongst these four comparison firms, one specialized in electric

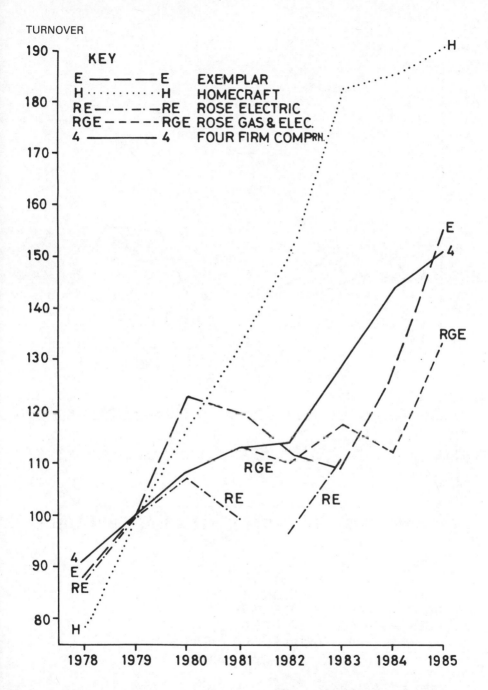

TURNOVER

KEY

E ———— E	EXEMPLAR
H ············· H	HOMECRAFT
RE—·—·—RE	ROSE ELECTRIC
RGE————RGE	ROSE GAS & ELEC.
4 ————— 4	FOUR FIRM COMP^RN.

Figure 8.2   Domestic Appliance Companies' Turnover Indices, year-ends 1978–85

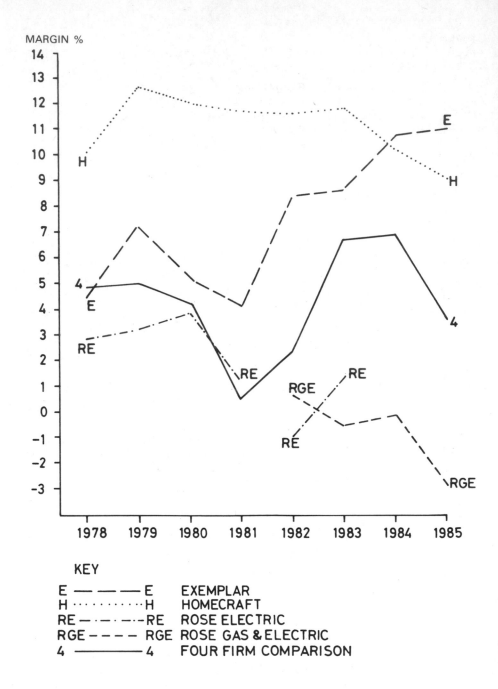

MARGIN %

KEY

E — — — E   EXEMPLAR
H ·········H   HOMECRAFT
RE —·—·—RE ROSE ELECTRIC
RGE — — — RGE ROSE GAS & ELECTRIC
4 —————4   FOUR FIRM COMPARISON

Figure 8.3   Domestic Appliance Companies' Profit Margins, year-ends 1978–85

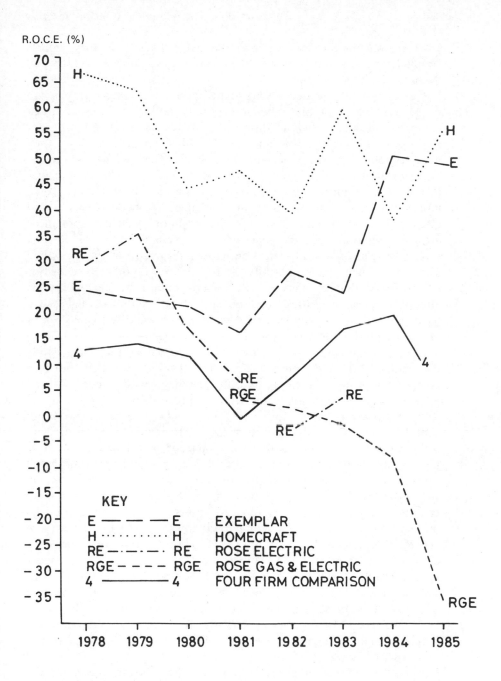

Figure 8.4   Domestic Appliance Companies' Returns on Capital Employed year-ends 1978–85

cooking, one in refrigeration and the two others had fairly diverse product ranges, one strongest in refrigeration, the other in laundry and vacuum cleaning.

The quality of the accounting data upon which these graphs are based requires that they be interpreted rather cautiously. Each company's accounts include different activities, several use different year-ends and – especially significant for subsidiary companies – they tend to follow different accounting policies. Because of its various reorganizations and its traditionally decentralized style of manage- ment, Rose's figures are particularly unreliable. The company's own internal management accounts are plagued by inconsistencies and discontinuities over time. Results for Rose Major Electrical Appliances are given separately for the years they are available, 1978–83. Results for all Rose's gas and electrical activities are given for 1981 to 1985. There is a further discontinuity in the figures in that Rose Major Electrical Appliances' figures only include manufacturing operations after 1981. Despite all these inadequacies, these are the best figures we have. So long as the above caveats are borne in mind, we can attempt broad longitudinal and cross-sectional comparisons.

Before examining the performance of our three case study companies, I should comment on the averages for the four-firm comparison group and the extremes represented within them. At first glance, Figure 8.2 appears to show that the recession hardly dented the average turnovers of the four companies, which increased by 50 per cent between year-ends 1979 and 1985. However, comparison with Table 6.2 on p. 132 reveals that this apparent growth was made up in part by inflation and in part on the back of a rapidly growing home market with which the companies were unable to keep up; in unadjusted terms, the UK market as a whole grew by just under 90 per cent in this same period. Moreover, profits – whether measured by margins (Figure 8.3) or return on capital employed (Figure 8.4) – were severely depressed by year-end 1981, though only one company actually dipped into the red. The strength of the subsequent recovery is reflected in a profits peak higher in 1984 than the previous peak of 1979 immediately before the onset of the recession. The profit drop of 1985 indicates the slackening of the recovery in general. Within these averages, the best performer of the four was the refrigeration specialist. This company exactly doubled its turnover between 1979 and 1984, while its return on capital employed ranged from a low of 17 per cent in 1982 to a high of 34 per cent the following year. On the other hand, the laundry and vacuum cleaning company underwent the most severe difficulties. By 1982, its turnover was more than 10 per cent down on its 1978 peak, and even in 1985 it was still only 10 per

Table 8.1   Exemplar, Homecraft and Rose : Approximate UK Market Shares for Major Electrical Domestic Appliances, 1984 (%)

	Exemplar	*Homecraft*	*Rose*
Electric cookers (free standing)	—	33	30
Washing machines	25	4	4
Tumble driers	10	30	10
Refrigerators	13	—	16

Sources: Market research reports (especially *Euromonitor*, 1985) and manufacturers' own estimates. These figures should be treated with some caution.

cent ahead of its pre-recession level. Moreover, the company had made severe losses in 1981 and 1982, though by 1985 it had recovered to become the second most profitable of the four-firm comparison group. These four firms provide a benchmark; how, then, do our three case companies compare?

Already the weakest of the three companies before the recession, Rose became a chronic loss-maker from 1982. During 1981 and 1982, the profitability of gas cookers, following the London site closure, balanced the electrical side's losses; by 1983, however, electricals were recovering and it was the turn of the gas side to drag the whole group down. Return on capital employed – that scorned symbol of the new professionals – actually worsened as the recovery progressed (Figure 8.4). Sales were no better. Heavy discounting – reflected in the low and disappearing profit margins (Figure 8.3) – did not save Rose from continuously depressed turnover. Between 1979 and 1983, Rose Electric consistently trailed the four-firm average, while the gap between the four-firm average and Rose's gas and electric turnovers combined widened steadily between 1981 and 1984, only beginning to close in 1985 (Figure 8.2). Market share in electric cookers fell from 40 per cent before the recession to 30 per cent in 1984 (compare Tables 7.2 and 8.1 on p. 146 and above). This loss of market leadership had been the penalty particularly for failing to introduce slip-in cookers until three years after leading rivals such as Homecraft. However, investment in manufacturing microwaves cookers did enable it to preserve its third place in the UK market despite mounting competitive pressures. Rose had also been fairly successful in defending its market shares in laundry equipment, though rather less so in refrigeration (Tables 7.2 on p. 146 and 8.1).

Clearly the Rose group's concern for return on capital employed was merited on more than symbolic grounds. With some of its new, higher technology ventures in persistent difficulties, and coming under increasing takeover threat, the group desperately needed to exact better performances. When Bowden retired in 1983 he was replaced by an outsider who was a relative newcomer to the Group as a whole.

The new divisional Chairman regarded the 'Old Rose' managers as 'incestuous', a term much repeated and resented by the managers themselves. Accordingly, he brought in more new managers (many of them holding MBAs), promoted management training schemes at outside institutions, and employed many external consultants. The new regime was epitomized by the 1984 Rose group 'Corporate Values Statement', which pointedly emphasized 'customer orientation', 'unashamed career meritocracy', 'tight standards' and 'effectiveness'. The Bowden re-organization, seen as typifying the old production bias, was partially reversed so that the gas and electric sides once more presented separate faces to the Boards. Bowden's nominee for the managing directorship of the division departed swiftly. But if the 'Old Rose' era was over, Rose's troubles were not. Far from reversing Rose's decline, the Electrical and Gas division's losses actually increased to year-end 1985, while turnover faltered before making a slight gain.

At Exemplar, the story was very different. Years of heavy investment were rewarded when, in 1982, 'overnight the market changed . . . [and] for the first time in the history of this company it was equipped to meet that. It had *never, ever* before been able to react to a buoyant market because it had never invested enough. So overnight . . . we suddenly found we could make everything we could sell.' In Figure 8.2 on p. 183 the disposal of the small appliance company in 1982 – which had accounted for 10 per cent of total turnover – conceals the strong sales growth in core products that began in 1982–3. Despite the disposal, Exemplar's total turnover had edged ahead of the four-firm average by 1985. The most significant contribution came from the new Damnar factory, which enabled Exemplar to push up washing machine market share to 25 per cent (see Table 8.1 on p. 187), where it was now level with the former market leader. In refrigeration, a market increasingly penetrated by imports, Exemplar was able to hold its share steady, promoting it from number five before the recession to number two. This sales success was not achieved by simple discounting; even including the lagging small appliance business, profit margins remained comfortably above the four-firm average throughout the recession, and in 1984 and 1985 were even edging above Homecraft's (see Figure 8.3 on p. 184). By 1984, Exemplar's return on capital employed more than matched Homecraft's, though it slipped behind again the following year (see Figure 8.4 on p. 185). As profits improved, the pay-out to managers and workers alike on the profit-sharing scheme rose from a low of 12 hours of annual salary in 1980–1 to 90.25 hours in 1982–3.

In spring 1983, Stone finally retired. The domestic appliance and furniture companies were demerged, with Exemplar reverting wholly to Universal's control. Stone took his financial director back with him to Stone Furniture Industries, though he himself remained as chairman of Exemplar. However, as they themselves remarked, Stone had failed to cultivate any natural successor amongst his team of young managers. Accordingly, Universal was forced to appoint an outsider who had senior management experience with a large multinational and expert knowledge of microelectronics. Exemplar's strong recovery performance did not suggest an urgent need for a radical redirection of strategy, so that the new managing director made few changes. The new managing director's chief initiatives were to push microelectronics with rather more enthusiasm than Stone had done, to court the multiple retailers more actively and to investigate once more potential export markets. These were all actions which Stone's managers had desired for some time, but which had been suppressed for as long as he had remained in control. All of Stone's senior managers remained in their former positions, with the first departure not coming till 1986.

At 90 per cent between 1979 and 1985, Homecraft enjoyed the most rapid growth of our three case companies (see Figure 8.2 on p. 183), with cooker sales taking over the baton as the storage heater boom finally eased during 1983. As Rose collapsed, Homecraft edged very slightly ahead in the free standing electric cooker market, while it retained leadership in the tumble- and spin-drier markets. However, years of modest investment were finally beginning to catch up with Homecraft, as the recovery stretched capacity and delivery times lengthened. Growth actually slowed during 1983–5. In the fastest growing appliance sector, microwaves, Homecraft was handicapped by its persistence with factored products. In 1984, the company still had less than 5 per cent of the microwave market, a strong contrast with its leadership in conventional electric cookers. By the time Homecraft did finally begin microwave manufacture in 1986, two of its sister companies within AEL were already committed to factoring other manufacturers' microwaves; this lack of co-ordination would retrospectively be justified as 'the three brands strategy'.

Homecraft's continued high profits during the recession and recovery (see Figures 8.3 and 8.4 on p. 184 and p. 185) were both vital to supporting AEL as a whole and, ironically, a tempting object for unwelcome but repeated takeover bids and rumours. During 1984 a leading continental domestic appliance manufacturer was one among several companies that made threatening share purchases. The pressure on Homecraft mounted still further when a new divisional chairman both referred back Homecraft's profit forecasts for 1984–5 and pressed for more ambitious investment plans. At the same time, the long-established team began to disintegrate, as both the financial and production directors retired in 1984. It was recognized that, after a long period of stability, 'we're at another break point'. During 1984 and 1985 profit margins sank below those even of the recession period.

Thus the performances of the three case study firms varied widely during both recession and recovery. Significantly, performances did not converge on some profit-maximizing ideal even under the heightened pressure of recession. The differences in returns on capital between the best (Homecraft) and worst (Rose) performers hovered consistently in the rough range of 30 to 40 per cent between 1978 and 1982; differences in profit margins actually increased, from 7.2 per cent to 12.6 per cent. On both measures, the gaps between best and worst performers amongst the four firm comparison group substantially widened during the recession. For all seven monitored domestic appliance firms, the range in returns on capital employed rose from 60.9 per cent in 1979 to 92.2 per cent in 1981 (see Appendix 1 on p. 300).

Overall, Exemplar's strategy of disposing its weakest operations while investing in the strongest appears to have reaped the most gains over the recession and recovery period. By the mid–1980s its profitability had attained the same heights as Homecraft's, while market share had been boosted in at least one crucial sector. Homecraft's caution had protected profits, while not preventing strong sales growth in core products, but there were signs that this might not continue for ever. Rose's performance, however, was clearly lagging behind not only the four-firm comparison group's average performance, but even behind that of the worst performer amongst them. The old 'Rose way' was superseded by the accelerated management and organizational changes following Bowden's retirement, but by 1985 the company had still not been turned round.

STRATEGIC CHOICES

In the last two sections I have demonstrated the variety of strategic responses to the recession adopted by the three domestic appliance companies and the wide range of their subsequent performances. In this section I will re-examine particular strategic choices in order to elucidate the factors behind them. The section will focus especially on two areas where the companies diverged: the different innovation strategies of Homecraft and Rose, and the different investment strategies of Homecraft and Exemplar. These different strategies were rooted in particular internal and external relations which powerful actors had deliberately built up in preceding years in order to promote and protect their freedom of action.

The different approaches to microwave epitomize the differences between Homecraft and Rose. For both companies, cooking was the single most important business, and together they dominated the UK market. Moreover, while the conventional cooker market was stagnant, the microwave market grew threefold between 1979 and 1982. This new cooking technology should, therefore, have been of equal interest to both companies. However, Rose began its first manufacture as early as 1978, while Homecraft waited until 1986.

A number of reasons contribute to explaining Rose's manufacturing lead. First, there was the personal enthusiasm of Carstairs, stemming in part from his experience in the brown goods company. Rose was also advantaged in that its consumer electronics division had already got agreements with the same Japanese company that would eventually license them them microwave technology. Further, there was the abundance of unused capacity at the North site, for which no alternative employment readily offered itself. Finally, there was the old Rose confidence in mass production for British markets. Rose managers were convinced that, with heavy freight costs and a rising Yen, they could achieve significant cost advantages. Anyway, as one director put it:

> It was natural to manufacture. That was our style. We are a manufacturing company. Rose is a manufacturing company. There may be less emphasis on manufacturing now – I'm sure there is – but the strength of Rose was its manufacturing resource and its facilities. Sir Ben [Rose] would never sell a product unless he made it. He didn't factor. Factoring was not his business. To factor product was an exception rather than the rule.

Thus the decision by Rose to manufacture microwave was made partly on account of its managerial and production resources and partly because it chimed so well with the company's manufacturing tradition. But the particular resources were not entirely accidental. Carstairs was a protégé of Teal and the production director at the North site was a protégé of Bowden. The massive production capacity of the North site owed its existence to Bowden and his team as the expression of their manufacturing bias. This capacity now served to support a decision to manufacture microwaves that was anyway their inclination.

In the same way, production resources influenced Homecraft's decision in a more than simple way. Both the design and marketing departments had been keen to enter microwave production, yet they acquiesced quite easily to the delays. Admitted one enthusiast: 'It would be false to give the impression that there is this little tower, ivory tower, with marketing in it, who keep shouting through the window, you know, "microwave! microwave! microwave!" and everybody ignores them.' Homecraft's managers advanced several reasons for their hesitation. Microwaves were seen as a brown good, alien to their traditional products and requiring different distribution channels. Homecraft would have to familiarize itself with a new and fast developing technology. Microwaves were standard products aimed at world markets in which a relatively small company like Homecraft could never achieve the volumes or keep up with the research of the large, well-established American and Japanese manufacturers. But all these obstacles applied in much the same way to Rose, who had chosen to overcome them by licensing agreements.

There were special circumstances, however. AEL's continued difficulties put Homecraft under a subtle, but unspoken constraint. It was frequently insisted that AEL encouraged innovation – 'There's always been encouragement for innovation, even going back to that [recession] period' – and, indeed, it had willingly supported Homecraft's development of its own microwave prototype. Likewise it was emphasized that AEL had never turned down a request for investment. Rather, as one director put it: 'I'm not criticising AEL that we haven't spent any more; its not AEL's fault – its ours for not asking for it.'

Yet there remained a subtle pressure that inhibited Homecraft from asking in the first place. Another director explained when probed on the microwave issue:

'[long pause] . . . Yes [laugh]. You're getting near to a very sensitive part of our philosophies. Its a dilemma, you see. This is the most successful company in this division and I think its probably the most successful in AEL. You obviously have, you know – that everybody in AEL is looking at you because you are the generator of quite a lot of profit and its been a very difficult time for AEL. And you want to keep that up. I think there is an *unsaid* sort of pressure, but pressure that you realize is there because in actual fact if we were to stop producing profit for any reason, like next year, it would be a pretty unfortunate thing for AEL as a whole . . . There is a degree of obligation to the whole division and to the whole Group that, you know, you don't let wild flights of fancy take you into a situation where for a few years you might become significantly less profitable because you were doing some venture in a very great and grand way but which didn't bring home the bacon too quickly. That would be a disastrous thing to do.

Thus, Homecraft did feel externally constrained against entering microwave manufacture; crucially, however, it never actually tested the precise degree of this constraint by advancing a formal proposal. Forcing the issue might have prompted anxious interventions by the AEL main board. Further, as a break with the 'three-legged stool' tradition of concentrating on core products in which Homecraft as manufacturer and the Electricity Boards as retailers held high market shares, microwave might in the long term dilute the high profitability upon which Homecraft's special status within the division and the Group depended. Homecraft's managers tightened the financial straight-jacket themselves.

Lastly, there was the nature of the main Midland plant. As one director pointed out, Homecraft did not have either the problems or the opportunities that Rose had with its vast surplus capacity at North site. However, Homecraft's cramped factory was the result of a deliberate policy of maintaining full loadings and managerial proximity. Entering microwave production would endanger the close-knit consensual team if it meant rapid expansion or opening a new factory. One director worried: 'If you make any dramatic changes like building new factories all over the place and expanding like mad, it would be a thing where you'd find the difficulty in translating all that organization – the compact team spirit sort of working that you get working in an organization like this.' For Homecraft's managers, the consequences of a runaway success were to be feared nearly as much as those of failure.

Even if delaying with microwaves, Homecraft had not been complacent in other respects. The company did not baulk at launching the second generation of storage heaters only eighteen months after the successful launch of the first. This action was argued for strongly by the design and marketing departments, despite the reluctance of especially finance, who cautioned against the expense, and production, who were averse to the disruption. The decision was controversial:

> Production's reaction was: 'For God's sake, we've only just got this one going nicely just now; why do you want to change it?' Finance said: 'Well here we are, we're falling into recession, it's going to get worse before it gets better, and you want to spend a lot of money on a product that's not necessarily going to pay back in the short-term.'

However, continued development was vital to retain market leadership and central to the company's innovative tradition. As another director described the decision, it was:

illogical from the production point of view; from service, from spares, from every point of view like that. But perhaps very logical from the point of view of keeping in the forefront of the market and presenting to our main customer, the [Electricity] Boards, that, you know, 'Homecraft were the greatest; they were the innovators'.

Here, then, marketing and design did prevail. The protection of dominant market shares and cultivation of the crucial Electricity Boards remained paramount.

At Rose, of course, production interests had prevailed in product development. With nearly a third of the design engineers dismissed, it had been the production engineers who had taken the lead in producing the despecified 'Economy' range of refrigerators. They had taken considerable satisfaction in eliminating all the troublesome frills which they regarded as having been unnecessarily imposed on previous models by marketing and design. For the 'Rose men', this episode represented a triumphant reassertion of the old production values:

> We really had to get our fingers out and get something done . . . That is just an example of what can be done and what was achieved by a group of people who have the knowledge and the ability, the will, the dedication, enthusiasm, motivation – they all count – to pull a company round when its got products that are too bloody expensive and in a bloody difficult market, a really difficult market.

But the disastrous failure to launch a slip-in was equally character-istic of Rose's production engineering bias. For Homecraft, it had been a routine response to the pioneering efforts of a smaller rival. However, the Rose production engineers saw the slip-in, with its replacement of the practical eye-level grill by one at waist height, as functionally retrograde, not appreciating its marketing appeal. For the engineers, the slip-in had none of the technological fascination of microwave or 'cooking-by-light', their other innovation. The marketing department was too weak, too distant from the factories, and too passive after years of dependence of the Gas and Electricity Boards to overcome the conservatism of the engineers. Indeed, for many of Rose's marketeers, the slip-in represented a dangerous Continental fashion, whose promotion would only encourage imports and the discount retailers who had seized on it from the start. All this was exacerbated by the problems of rationalization and reorganization: 'It was a fairly bloody period . . . Once you take management attention away from the things it *should* be doing – development and marketing and running the business sort of *outwardly* – and once you've turned yourself in and looking *inside* the business, there is a sort of spiral.'

In investment strategy, Exemplar stands out as being the sole company actually to add to capacity during the recession. For Rose, burdened with surplus capacity and in financial straights, the failure to invest in new factories was hardly surprising. The choice of the London gas site for closure was dictated not by its productivity record, which was better than the Midland site's, but because it was more likely to raise quick funds. At Homecraft, even though there were ample financial reserves and capacity at the main Midland factory was already stretched, large-scale investment was ruled out at least in part for fear of jeopardizing managerial cohesion and the company's special status within AEL. Stone, however, insisted on building his new laundry factory at Damnar. The Damnar episode exemplifies Stone's predominance over his managers, particularly the engineers, and his fierce commitment to the long-term future of his company.

Opposed by both Universal and his own managers, Stone's decision was hard to justify on rational grounds. The European industry already suffered from excess capacity and Exemplar was strapped for funds. One manager described the investment as 'marginal', and two called it 'an act of faith'. But Stone would not allow a recession to divert him from his long-term strategy. One director summarised his argument:

> If Exemplar has got to be made efficient, if it has got to be developed, if the existing plant is not in the long term an asset to be developed, to make modern things, then there must be a new asset, and that's got to be Damnar [bangs table]. And if when you're building it you go through recession, its all the more reason to build it quicker.

But if the logic of this argument did not persuade Bernstein at Universal, Stone's strong personality and personal shareholding eventually won through. Asked how Stone finally overcame the opposition, another director laughed, and then went on: 'By sheer force! And by a certain commitment on his own part, both morally and financially.'

The decision to introduce pre-paint at Damnar was equally idiosyncratic. Although the company had gained pre-paint experience at its new refrigeration plant, pre-painting washing machines was a very different matter. Unlike refrigerators, washing machines are subject to the severe stresses of hot water and vigorous vibration. Additionally, the consumer demand for flush doors on front-loading washing machines meant that Exemplar would have to do what no one else had so far done, that is, draw pre-painted steel into a curved indentation. The sceptical design and production departments attributed Stone's preference for pre-paint to his experience in wooden furniture: 'There he was with a sort of ready-made, finished plank. All he'd got to do was cut it to size and glue it. And he couldn't see why you couldn't do domestic appliances in exactly the same way.' Stone's commitment to pre-paint was not based on any understanding of the very real problems and risks involved: 'He was not an engineer in his own right and therefore didn't appreciate the problems – which was just as well because if he had he might have had second thoughts.' As it turned out, of course, Stone's faith was entirely vindicated.

The sale of the small appliance company contrasts strikingly with the investment at Damnar, and indeed with the policies of Rose and AEL towards their small appliance subsidiaries. Stone's son had initially wrestled with this troublesome subsidiary until his departure in 1978. With a separate history and different product markets, Exemplar managers dismissed small appliances as 'not in our chemistry'. However, other factors operated. With the £5 million proceeds, the sale enabled Stone to reduce considerably his dependence on Universal at a difficult time. Moreover, it completed a process of consolidation, beginning with the disposal of the electric cooker business, that was at least partly determined by the limits of Stone's willingness to delegate. The small appliance company's sales organization had always been difficult, and the problem for Stone had been compounded by the departure of his son, an expert in sales organization. One director speculated:

> He [Stone] probably felt, and here I'm probably putting words into his mouth, he probably felt that he was *stretched* . . . I don't think he felt he could spread himself to cope with small appliances as well . . . . Then his son, for reasons I don't know about, set up his own business and went to Israel. And I think that set him back, because, overnight he'd lost his right hand man on the sales side.
> Question: So he needed someone he felt he could trust?
> That's right.

So long as Stone remained reluctant to delegate, persistence with the small appliance company risked the dissipation of his managerial energies and, in the case of continued failure, the confidence both of his managers and of Universal. Stone disposed of the Company because he was not prepared to compromise his own personal power.

CONCLUSION

It is by no means clear from the last two chapters that, in the strategies they followed during the recession, these three companies were guided by the shining star of profit-maximization. Rather, the case studies suggest that companies, even when competing in the same or very accessible markets and confronted by the same stimulus of recession, are able to choose quite contrary strategies. My contention is that the direction of these strategies were determined neither by environments nor by rigid action selection mechanisms; rather they stemmed from the deliberate and independent actions of agents who had, as individuals or groups, carefully exploited initial positions in order to enlarge their margins of discretion. I shall elaborate this argument in Chapter 11, but let me now briefly review the evidence of these two chapters.

At Exemplar, Stone, dedicated to the regeneration of Britain's manufacturing base, persevered in building first two new refrigeration plants and then, in the teeth of opposition from Universal and his own managers, the new Damnar washing machine factory. His capacity to implement his personal vision for Exemplar depended upon the careful development of his originally somewhat precarious position. In his relations with Universal, Stone had not rested on his shareholding. By producing steadily improving results and by slowly reducing Exemplar's gearing, he had consolidated the personal respect of Bernstein and striven to relax the majority shareholder's detailed supervision. In the market-place, by restoring Exemplar's reputation for quality and cultivating the loyalty of the independents, he had prized himself off the treadmill of shoddy products and competitive price-cuts.

Internally, Stone had built a nearly unchallengeable position. He had ruthlessly purged the old Exemplar management, installed his deputy and his own son in two key directorships and developed a new team of young managers who, dominated by his forceful and charismatic personality, regarded him with a mixture of gratitude, affection and awe. Yet still Stone would not delegate except on operational detail – and not always even that, especially in the areas of industrial relations and marketing. In order to cope he had to concentrate the extent of his responsibilities. Thus the drastic reduction of administrative staff, the transfer of electric cookers and the sale of the small appliance company were all, in part at least, determined by Stone's need not to dissipate his managerial energies on bureaucracy or intractable side-shows.

At Homecraft too, Tarling and his management team had developed a position where they could pursue their course steadily and without interference. Within the team a decade of close working had produced consensus, while outside Homecraft's rapid growth gave them the legitimacy of success. High market shares and the carefully nurtured relationship with the Electricity Boards ensured high profit margins and the steady augmentation of financial reserves. With a spread of three core products in the main Midland factory, Homecraft was insured against disaster in any particular area. So long as Homecraft could be relied upon to continue providing sufficient profits, neither the division nor AEL main board had any cause to intervene. Thus Homecraft's decision not to manufacture microwaves is entirely intelligible. To build a new factory, besides providing occasion for internal controversy, would carry the risks of opening up or dispersing the existing management team, of provoking detailed queries from an anxious AEL, and of interrupting the high profits on which Homecraft's prestige and autonomy within the group depended. Far better, then, to persist with the well-established strategy of steady development within the three core areas.

At Exemplar and Homecraft, therefore, powerful agents had clearly used the years preceding the recession to build up positions from which they would be able to pursue their own objectives, or at least to interpret those of the firm in the light of their own, even during the severe crisis of the 1979–81 recession. At Rose, however, management was more constrained. Yet, though under mounting pressures, the 'Old Rose' managers were still able to negotiate these constraints according to their old habits. One more time, the production engineers asserted themselves to despecify refrigerators and stymie slip-ins. But the reversal of the Bowden reorganization and the infusion of new professional managers from outside, all against a background of declining performances, demonstrate that anachronistic strategies cannot be pursued with impunity for ever. In 1983, declining Group profits and the increasing threat of take-over finally compelled a new top management to impose reform. Here – at last – the market for corporate control fixed the limits of managerial discretion.

Chapter Nine

The office furniture companies

INTRODUCTION

In the last two chapters I examined the recession strategies and subsequent performances of three domestic appliance companies. In the next two chapters I want to do the same for five office furniture companies. Again, I shall be trying to show that the diversity of strategies adopted during the recession demonstrates that these firms' dominant actors enjoyed a very substantial scope for strategic choice. This freedom for strategic choice was all the more remarkable for the office furniture companies because, as was shown in Chapter 6, their industry suffered an even more severe down-turn than domestic appliances.

These two chapters follow very similar structures to the two preceding chapters. In this chapter, I begin by introducing each of the five companies, with the emphasis on establishing the degree to which they competed in the same or similar markets. The following section focuses on the internal characteristics of the companies as they approached the recession. This chapter concludes by examining the extent to which the had developed sufficient leeway from external pressures to allow them to exercise strategic discretion during the recession. Chapter 10 will then go on to describe first the companies' actual recession strategies and then their consequences, both for financial performance and for strategic and management continuity. Chapter 10 will conclude with a detailed comparative re-examination of several significant decisions that particularly illustrate the idiosyncrasy of these firms' strategic choices.

THE COMPANIES

This section briefly introduces the five office furniture companies: Barton, a small independent manufacturer; Castle, precarious subsidiary of a troubled conglomerate; Fenwood, family-run and successful; Kremer's, an expansionary public company, but effectively under family control; and, lastly, Shilton, recently transferred from family control into the hands of the ambitious holding company Field Investments.

Barton Ltd was founded before the First World War as a small rural manufacturer of traditional Windsor chairs by the present joint managing directors' grandfather. During the 1930s the company diversified into other types of domestic furniture and after the Second World War began to manufacture office seating as well. The two brothers, David and Michael Barton, took charge of the business after the sudden and unexpected illness of their father in 1965. David Barton, then 22 years old, had only recently completed his furniture training course at a local college; Michael, then 18, had to cut short his own course. Both brothers pitched in to what was then a small family company, but soon a rough division of responsibilities emerged, with David more involved in the factory, design and sales while Michael concentrated on accounts, buying, stores and administration. After the death of their father in 1979, the brothers owned equally all the ordinary shares in the business.

During the 1960s the brothers completed the company's shift out of the domestic furniture market, with the aim of escaping the uncertainties of fashion and increasing price competition. Instead, Barton concentrated on office seating (80–85 per cent of turnover) and executive wooden desks and cabinets. After a decade of rapid growth, by 1979 Barton was the largest UK seating manufacturer and, though doing little export, held around 7 per cent of the home market. None the less, it remained quite small, with less than 200 employees on one site.

Castle Office Furniture provides a stark contrast to Barton. The declining subsidiary of the mini-conglomerate General Engineering Holdings (GEH), in the late 1970s Castle Office Furniture still shared a large London site with Castle's metal manufacturing and wooden library equipment companies, and together they all made up the Castle Engineering and Furniture division. In addition, Castle Engineering and Furniture had a satellite factory about sixty miles to the south. Castle was still one of the leading metal storage and desking manufacturers in the country, with a long tradition of quality products which dated back to before the Second World War. However, apart from an ambitious and ill-fated screen-based wooden office furniture range (launched in 1972 and abandoned two years later), the company stagnated through the 1970s, suffering several loss making years.

In 1976, GEH had finally intervened by appointing a consultant with a marketing background, Ron Simpson, as managing director of Castle Engineering and Furniture. His rationalization entailed the closure and sale of the London site, the rundown of general engineering, the transfer of remaining manufacturing activities to the South site, the closure of provincial warehouses, the ending of direct sales and an export drive in the Middle East. By 1979, Simpson had returned Castle to profit, holding about 15 per cent of the UK metal storage market and with 25 per cent of turnover exported.

Fenwood was more like Barton, being an old established family firm. The original company had been founded by the present chairman and managing director's grandfather more than a century ago. Fenwood began to make wooden office furniture after the Second World War, ceasing to make domestic furniture in 1950. Charles Fenwood, chairman and managing director today, first joined the company in the mid–1930s and became managing director in 1940. His younger brother, Derek, had begun at Fenwood in the 1930s too, but had left for the War and then to emigrate before returning in the mid–1950s to run the newly acquired seating business. Derek later became sales director for the whole company.

Under Charles Fenwood's leadership, the business had grown steadily since the Second World War with a series of acquisitions. By 1979 the company had seven factories scattered around the country and its activities included wooden desking, office seating, metal furniture and drawing equipment, metal furniture components and filing systems and occasional subcontracting work for domestic furniture manufacturers. In addition, the company had its own West End dealership which took between 5 and 10 per cent of turnover. Between 1974 and 1978, turnover had nearly quadrupled, while profits had multiplied twelve times. The company probably held about 10 per cent of the wooden office desking market in 1979.

Kremer's, the largest of the five companies, was a major competitor for Fenwood. Kremer's was the creation of Bernie Kremer, the son of an East End Jewish immigrant. Bernie began in 1952, selling domestic furniture out of the back of a garage. Expansion was rapid and, although nearly wiped out by a factory fire in 1961, by 1979 Bernie Kremer had built the biggest wooden desking manufacturing business in the country. The rapid growth of the 1960s had been based on an innovatory range of 'knock-down' desking (that is, kit) which was so successful that it was to remain the company's core product right up to the 1980s. This success had allowed Kremer's to abandon domestic furniture in 1964, to go public in 1971 and from that same year to develop a big manufacturing complex just outside London.

However, the opening of the third works on this site came just before the severe 1975 slump in office furniture. To fill capacity, Kremer's had been forced back into the domestic market with a contract to supply 'flat-pack' (self-assembly) furniture to a leading retailer. By 1979, domestic furniture would account for about one third of total turnover. At the same time, Kremer's had been developing overseas markets, with sales companies in France and the United States. Between 1971 and 1979, total turnover had risen by more than six times and profits had nearly quadrupled. Exports accounted for slightly more than 10 per cent of turnover and the company held about 12 per cent of the home market in wooden desking.

A challenger to both Fenwood and Kremer's was Shilton Furniture. Although originally founded in the East End of London immediately after the First World War, the third-generation brothers Harry and Alex Shilton had reinvigorated the business since taking over control of the business as joint managing directors in 1968. The company had gone public in 1972 and added to its activities by going into office seating and making expanded plastic moulded shells to supply domestic furniture manufacturers (the Plastform subsidiary). Since 1974, Plastform had been involved in a joint venture in Canada, which was Shilton's only significant overseas activity and which became wholly owned in 1978. Plastform also produced plastic foam for office seating and supplied shells for Shilton's latest venture, a domestic furniture range launched in 1977. These new activities were based at a second factory in the Midlands.

Since going public in 1972, Shilton's turnover had trebled by 1978, though profits lagged somewhat. The launch of a basic range of knock-down office desking, enthusiastically adopted by Taylor's, a leading national wholesaler, helped take the company's share of the market to roughly 6 per cent, not far behind the industry leaders amongst which Fenwood and Kremer's numbered themselves.

However, in July 1979, Shilton Furniture was bought by Field Investments, a rapidly expanding holding company led by the entrepreneurial Maurice Field. Immediately after acquisition it was decided to close the old London site and move desking up to the Midland factory, with consolidation and redundancy costs of £2 million. The disruption and expense was exacerbated by the discovery in December 1979 that Shilton's stocks had been over-valued by £1

Table 9.1 The Office Furniture Companies

Name and status	Key personnel	Relative turnovers[1]; Export %; Employment[2] (1979)	Main products
Barton (family owned)	David and Michael Barton (joint MDs)	0.39 1.6 200	seating; executive desking and storage.
Castle (subsidiary of GEH plc)	Simpson (MD to 1980); Alderton (MD to 1982); Baxter (MD thereafter)	0.68 19.3 450	metal storage and desking; library furniture; systems furniture.
Fenwood (family owned)	Charles Fenwood (chairman and MD) Derek Fenwood (sales director)	0.61 8.7[3] 400	wooden desking; office seating; metal furniture and filing.
Kremer's (plc; family own 33%)	Bernie Kremer (chairman); Chris Kennedy (MD to 1980); Harold Levey (MD thereafter)	1.00 10.5 600	wooden desking; office seating; domestic furniture.
Shilton (subsidiary of Field Investments plc)	Bernard Gold (marketing supremo, 1981); James Turk (chief executive, 1981 onwards)	0.60 3.0 400 plastic furniture.	wooden desking; office seating; domestic furniture;

[1] Relative turnovers expressed as a proportion of Kremer's turnover in 1979.
[2] For the sake of confidentiality, employment figures are given to the nearest 50.
[3] Export percentage and employment figures only relate to Fenwood's main wooden furniture activities.

million and that profit forecasts had been over-optimistic beyond all reasonable justification. The Shilton brothers, together with their financial director, were forced to resign immediately, and legal proceedings were begun against them. Thus Shilton entered the recession in a state of production, managerial, financial and legal chaos.

The basic characteristics of the five companies are summarized in Table 9.1. Although the companies differed markedly in terms of size and ownership, they all competed in the same or similar markets. (Comprehensive market share data are excluded because of their extreme unreliability in the office furniture industry.) Fenwood, Kremer's and Shilton competed head on in wooden desking, the main product of all three companies. Barton held off from outright competition in the mass desking market, but competed with with Fenwood, Kremer's and Shilton in both executive desking and seating. As a metal manufacturer, Castle stood slightly apart from the other four, but its products competed indirectly with the wooden products of the others. Anyway, supported by the continuing expertise of its wooden library furniture company, Castle had shown its capacity to launch a direct challenge with its screen-based wooden range. The diversified activities of Fenwood confirmed that the barriers between metal and wood were by no means insurmountable. Of course, all these distinctions – between wood and metal, between seating, storage and desking – would soon be jeopardized by the emergence of systems furniture.

The next chapter will deal with how the five companies met the threat of systems furniture, and much else. Meanwhile, the following sections of this chapter will examine first the companies' internal characteristics and then their external relations in more detail.

INTERNAL CHARACTERISTICS

Typical of the craft origins of the wooden furniture industry, four of these companies were – or had been until recently – family run and controlled. Barton and Fenwood were still under complete family control. At Shilton the family management had just sold up and then retired in haste; while at Kremer's rapid growth had entailed some widening of the top management and a dilution of the family shareholding by public flotation. Even Castle had some family residue; although the Castle family's shareholding was now negligible, one representative still sat on the GEH Main Board. The following pages will examine the internal characteristics of the five companies further: first, Castle Office Furniture, declining and demoralized despite attempts at reform; then Shilton, newly taken over but chaotic; next Kremer's, with its expansionary Jewish and East End management; and lastly the two cautious family businesses, Fenwood and Barton.

Castle

For Castle the 1970s had been a decade of stagnation and failure: 'The company had rested on its laurels too long; old out-dated products; old out-dated managers.' This was despite the arrival of a new managing director, Simpson, in 1976. An outsider and former consultant, Simpson's brief when he arrived in 1976 was to restore Castle to profits by radical rationalization: 'He was brought in to get rid of some of the factory space, generally to carve and dismember.' However, Simpson's rationalizations did not restore confidence or purpose to the company. As another senior manager put it:

> Castle had survived by asset stripping its own business. When they made a loss they'd sell something to balance the books. So the company got smaller; it survived and it survived and it survived . . . Generally the company was run-down, the product was out of date and the people were too old.

The middle ranks, still 'full of dyed-in-the-wool old soldiers', were nostalgic for the company's grander general engineering past and, after having seen so many outsider directors and consultants come and go, becoming increasingly sceptical about the prospects of any revival. Another manager said of the company at the beginning of the 1980s: 'It had pride in its history but not much pride in its products.'

When Simpson was promoted to the GEH Main Board in 1980, yet another outsider, Brian Alderton, was appointed managing director. Described as a 'marketeer' (with audible inverted commas), he was the third managing director in succession with a marketing background. Alderton tried to strengthen this orientation still further with new recruits to his top management team; soon only one of six directors had been with the company for more than five years, and only two were without any sales or marketing experience. But this grafting of outsiders and marketeers on to the remains of the traditional metal bashing management achieved only superficial change. One manager recalled this period:

To tell the truth, I think the vast majority of people . . . had written
it off. They were marking time – calculating what their redundancy
was worth . . . Alderton was a great inspiration, and he encouraged
the broad-minded employees that there was a future. But the
hardcore had decided it was a waste of time.

Shilton

Shilton was another company which had lost its sense of direction.
Before the take-over, the company was 'very much a Jewish *family
business*', with the Shilton brothers' mother and sister closely involved.
Autocratic and with extravagant lifestyles, the Shiltons excluded their
operational managers from policy making or financial responsibilities.
Thus, the hasty departure of the brothers, together with their financial
director, left the company's middle management sharply exposed,
especially as it coincided with the onset of the recession and a
haemorrhage of skilled desking personnel and managers unwilling to
be transferred from London to the Midlands.

These difficulties were compounded by the decision, for economy
reasons, not to appoint an overall chief executive in place of the two
brothers. So confused was the management structure that the
managing directors of the seating and Plastform subsidiaries reported
to the managing director of desking, only to discover their mistake
upon his subsequent demotion. With nobody in clear command,
Shilton suffered fierce political in-fighting as each part fought to secure
its own survival and disclaim responsiblity for the overall decline. It
was not until December 1980, when the flamboyant Bernard Gold was
seconded from Field Investments' main board to take charge of the
marketing side, that any sense of direction was restored. In the
meantime, the company's depleted and confused management
struggled to cope with the problems of wooden desk manufacture,
financial control and strategic direction for which they had no
preparation.

Kremer's

By contrast with Castle and Shilton, Kremer's was a company that
perhaps suffered from an excess of confidence. Heavy investment in
plant and machinery, expensive ventures on the Continent and in the
United States were all part of what was admitted to be their 'expansion
dream' or 'ego trip around the world'. 1979 was jubilantly proclaimed
in the Annual Report as the year that the company had passed its

'psychological milestone' of £1 million pre-tax profits. The nature of this confident commitment to growth needs some examination.

It was partly fired by the forceful and ambitious personality of Bernie Kremer himself:

> Growth is what we all want in business . . . Run a small business? That wasn't me . . . One wanted the business to grow, one was young and ambitious, and having smelt a bit of success, you wanted a bit more, let the thing develop.

Bernie's career was described by his managers as 'the usual rags to riches story' and in creating and running a large public limited company he had fulfilled his youthful personal ambitions. Going public was:

> Bit of an ambition I suppose; it's an ego trip. If you run a public company, if you're managing director or chairman of a public company, it's a bit of an ego trip. It's a bit of pride – that you've arrived. It's an ambition. Why do we do it; why do you want to be successful? It's not a question of more money, because in the end you can't use the money you might get from it. It's just a question that you have made a success of things.

But his own commitment to growth was reinforced by the nature and character of his extraordinary team of managers.

As late as 1985, there were still nine men in management positions who had been with the company since before the first move out of London in 1962. Some of these remembered Bernie Kremer's early days when he would load the lorries himself. Many of them were East Enders, with long experience of the furniture trade starting out from the shop-floor. For them, the company's rapid advance had brought chances for promotion: 'We grew together; we grew, we moved up the line together; . . . we've all grown up together.' Another manager reminisced in the same way:

> You came in here as a wood machinist; you came in here as an upholsterer; you came in here as an assembler; you came in here as like a general hand; and you shone at your job . . . You had pride of occupation, which you shone at; you were a good operator, with a chance of becoming a chargehand. If you took the initiative with your opportunity, you got a bit higher up the ladder – by your own performance, and it would only be by performance . . . You would get there and you would hold it. You would take on more responsibility. You'd be thirsty, not so much necessarily for the money side of it, but for making a personal ego. You were now a manager or director, as opposed to chargehand.

These managers would still identify themselves as 'Danny's men'. Danny Kremer, Bernie's brother, had been production director until his death in 1968. While Bernie Kremer was seen as relatively sophisticated, Danny was described as a 'furniture man', 'the old Jewish type of governor, who got involved'. One director remembered how Danny 'would chase me round the factory with his shoe in his hand to hit me, because he saw me doing something that he told me I was wrongly doing'. Autocratic, instinctive, hard working and hard swearing, Danny's abiding influence was well recognized: 'a lot of his dust has rubbed off on a number of people.' Loyalty to his memory and to each other gave 'Danny's men' a sense of familyness which, while embracing the Kremer family, was not simply identified with it. One manager put it thus: 'We're still very much a sort of close-knit team, working well together – almost, very much a family affair, family business, although there's only two members of the family in the business.' Two other managers tried to explain further. The first: 'I still think its based on a family business here. I think that's got a lot to do with it, I think. Don't you think that's got a lot to do with it?' The second: 'The family is a family of people working together as a team. That's what Jim means by family . . . Kremer's is a family.' The first: 'You might not understand, but the family [the Kremer family itself] probably get more stick from people like us than they would in an ordinary business.' Another manager put the sense of identification another way: 'They used to say that when a Kremer's man died, if you cut him through the middle, they were like a stick of rock – "Kremer's" written all the way through.'

There was, therefore, a devotion to each other and the company that was intense and often explosive. From the main board down, managers shouted and swore easily – Jewish managers sometime lapsing into Yiddish in the excitement. Except towards Bernie Kremer, there was little respect for rank or privacy: 'We have extremely good relationships amongst the directors and senior managers, and down to the foreman level . . . Its all Christian [sic] names here. Everyone says his piece, without being rude. They might shout, but nobody walks around with a chip on their shoulder.' One of 'Danny's men' made the same point particularly about his fellows: 'We'll kill each other and then bring them back to life again – there's no hard feelings.' Yet another manager explained, again using the family metaphor: 'We fight like brothers and sisters. That's how we fight.' But, the same manager insisted, referring to a recent 'terrible argument': 'We only rowed because we wanted to do what's right for Kremer's!'

The character of these men influenced both strategic orientation and the decision-making style. Thus the predominance of people with craft origins contributed to a self-confessed 'production orientation': 'Like Caesar had his Praetorian Guards, Hitler had his SS, we had Production.' Years of expansion in highly competitive markets and heavy investment in automation had set a premium on economies of scale through volume production. Kremer's was 'a production orientated company. We had said that if you produce at efficient levels, you'll make a profit. What we'd been trying to say is that so long as you produce at high volumes, your production costs go down.' In the words of another manager: 'We worked on a philosophy that if you maximise a factory so that you produce to get efficiency, put it into a warehouse and distribute it to a requirement. So basically we *made* to get efficiency, and you put it into your warehouse . . . Production used to set the pace for everything.' There was no sales or marketing director.

Since going public in 1971, Kremer's Main Board had consisted of the same small team of four. It was dominated by the chairman, Bernie Kremer, by force of his strong personality, his continued hard work and close involvement and his 15 per cent shareholding. Kremer's 'was still very much a one-man band'. Bernie Kremer was 'the Governor.' His supremacy was described in a matter of fact, yet strangely moving sort of way:

> He's obviously captain of the ship . . . He's just Bernie Kremer. You know, what can one say? He built the company. He had help, to be generous about it. But there is no one like him and that is it. He can be hard; he can be soft; he can be gentle; he can be persuasive; he can be friendly; he can be tough; be generous; he can withdraw a little bit. You know: he is the chairman of the company; he built the company up.

The other three board members were the production director, Sammy Cohen, the managing director, Chris Kennedy, and the finance director, Harold Levey, who was also the chairman's son-in-law and a 5 per cent shareholder. Especially after Bernie Kremer's severe illness in 1977, Kennedy was clearly being cultivated for succession to the chairmanship.

Kennedy had a unique role on the Kremer's board: 'a lot of people around here blow their top, and he had a sort of calming influence.' Another manager put it laughingly: 'he used to be known as the Gentile on the board of mad Jews – with all the Jews shouting at each other, he was there in the middle.' In any event the team worked hard, closely and with great spontaneity. 'We were all in the same building and worked very closely together. And we all worked very long hours – we still do – and we'd start talking very early in the morning and go on late at night, talking over the weekend and this sort of thing. Very close.' Decision-making took place within what was called a 'free-wheeling structure'. The company's informality was perhaps epitomized by the director who welcomed visitors with a hole in his shoe and the stuffing coming out of his office chair (presumably one of Kremer's own products). As another director remembered, with the benefit of hindsight: 'the advantage of being less structured is that Kremer's does things very quickly. If it decides to do something, it can do it very fast. But the danger is that it could do something bad as well as good.'

Fenwood

Fenwood, although another family firm, was very different. After forty years of successful and centralized leadership combined with a 90 per cent shareholding, Charles Fenwood was at least as commanding a figure as Bernie Kremer. Thus, though well past normal retirement age by 1985, he would still be described as 'the beginning and the end of everything in the organization'. Charles and Derek Fenwood visited all the scattered plants at least twice a year and monitored them by highly-centralized purchasing and financial systems. Unlike Kremer's, however, Fenwood's philosophy was one of cautious safeguarding of profit rather than reckless pursuit of growth. The formula was summed up thus:

> The thing is to manufacture whatever you *are* manufacturing efficiently and – hopefully – profitably . . . There is a feeling in this industry that the great thing to go for is turnover. That's a thing we've never been for. We are quite happy to see a drop in turnover if we can improve our efficiency.

Except for a burst of rapid growth towards the end of the decade, Fenwood's turnover had grown relatively slowly throughout the 1970s; on the other hand, this caution had produced profit margins that were consistently high by industry standards.

Barton

Barton was similar to Fenwood in its cautious – but successful – family management style. David and Michael Barton were more than joint owners or ordinary managing directors; they had saved the company after their father's sudden retirement and since then been the architects of its unchallenged success. The two brothers were very closely involved in the running of the business. As one of them said:

> I've never quite understood why people get so excited about building
> ivory towers and going away from the general flow of the business as
> they get bigger . . . As you know, [the other brother] is there, I am
> here; that door [the speaker's] is always open . . . I can hear what is
> going on out there. I need to be that close to it.

Michael Barton still saw every piece of post that came into the
business; David would be consulted about a mislaid invoice. The
philosophy was that 'it is crucial to know what is going on and being in
the heart of the business all the time'. However, the two brothers
always consulted their production and sales directors. One of the
directors protested:

> Although we know they are the major shareholders, they will consult
> you about anything and they will sit down and talk it over with
> you . . . Never once have I known them to say: "Its a managing
> director's decision; that's it, you'll have to go along with it" I've never
> known that. They'll always sit down. O.K.: they may make up their
> own mind if they want to do something at the end of the day and one
> has to go along with it, but its always done in the right way.

David and Michael had developed a group of managers that worked
hard, as a team and with enjoyment. The production director had
previously run a small furniture business of his own; the sales director
had always worked for small, family companies. One expressed their
homogeneity thus:

> Remarkable as it is, we're all on the same wavelength. Sometime's it
> doesn't happen with people . . . Probably that is David and Michael's
> policy – no doubt. The people they've selected, myself included, they
> want people that are on the same wave-length; that, O.K. they can
> talk work, they can talk football, they can talk social things. And
> that's very much the emphasis on which David and Michael have
> gone about things.

All stressed the long hours, but also that they enjoyed their work:
'We're happy; we work hard; and we enjoy what we're doing.' David
Barton himself was described simply thus: 'He's a workaholic –
thoroughly enjoys himself.'

The team was united around the objectives of steady growth within a
specialized niche that would preserve the security and independence of
the family business. As one of the brothers put it:

> We've fortunately been in a position that we've been able to generate
> sufficient funds of our own to satisfy the expansion we've wanted to

keep. And we prefer to keep expansion on a regular incline rather than suddenly shooting up and then maybe staying on a plateau or dropping down. So really it is, being a private company, the elimination of risk as far as possible.

To sum up, these five companies differed considerably in their leaderships and objectives. At Barton, Fenwood and Kremer's, senior managements were all well entrenched, bolstered in each case by substantial shareholdings and demonstrable and longstanding success. At Barton and Kremer's – two single site companies – strongly cohesive management teams had developed to reinforce the prevailing leadership orientations. Thus Kremer's was characterized by a vigorous and self-confident commitment to volume production; while Barton, like Fenwood, preferred cautious growth and the safeguarding of profits. By contrast, Castle and Shilton – incidentally the two companies without family managements – were both confused. Shilton was leaderless, while GEH was vainly trying to superimpose an alien marketing direction upon a management that was aging and demoralized. Chapter 10 describes how these diverse leaderships and objectives were expressed in the five companies' recession strategies. First, however, the last section of this Chapter will examine the extent to which each of these companies was either sufficiently free from outside pressures to permit consistency in strategy or so constrained as to compel change.

THE SCOPE FOR STRATEGIC CHOICE

Although all of these companies were competing in fiercely competitive markets in which none held commanding market shares, remarkable is the extent to which the more successful had consciously cultivated positions safeguarding their profitability and independence. To start with, three – Barton, Fenwood and Kremer's – had deliberately chosen to move from their domestic furniture origins in order to specialize in the more stable and potentially less cut-throat office furniture industry. Even within this same industry, the companies adopted varying strategies to reinforce their positions. I will deal first with their financial strategies and then with their market strategies. Barton and Fenwood will present strong contrasts with Castle, Kremer's and Shilton.

Financial positions

Crucial to Barton and Fenwood – the two family companies – was the preservation of financial autonomy. As has already been seen, Barton stressed the importance of steady growth within the limits of the company's ability for self-financing. Barton invested little in new machinery, preferring to build up its financial reserves and to spend on land adjacent to its existing site. The company made no borrowings of any sort: 'That will be the danger signal when we have to borrow . . . We wouldn't be very happy if we had to borrow.' Indeed, Barton entered the recession with £2 million in its reserves. In the same way, the brothers had avoided going public: 'We are not really very interested in, you know, the USM [Unlisted Securities Market] or in larger share float. We don't really want to be a subsidiary to other people, you know, to answer to them all the time. No: we would rather do our own thing as much as possible.'

Similarly at Fenwood, although they had contemplated going public in the late 1960s:

> Ever since, we're very glad we didn't . . . We like to have complete control of what we do. When you go public, you don't have control of what you do. Being private, it enables us to take a longer term view and perhaps do things in the short term that would not be acceptable to an outside shareholder who's looking for short term results.

Fenwood had been equally independent in its attitude to debt: despite its many acquisitions during the 1950s and 1960s, 'never at any time have we bought anything that we didn't own. In other words, nothing we bought with a bank loan. Everything was bought with cash and profits, if you like. Therefore, we only expanded when we could afford to expand, expand soundly.' The company had also avoided heavy spending on automation. Thus, by the end of the 1970s, Fenwood had accumulated very substantial financial reserves – £3 million in the main wooden office furniture company alone.

Both these two family companies emphasized how this financial strength freed them from short-term considerations. One Barton director commented on the predicament of competitors who had gone public:

> They always feel that they have got to be either taking over another company, opening another factory, or doing something in a flamboyant way to be able to influence the market, the financial market – whereas we don't need to do that, you know, so long as we are satisfying ourselves and we're doing right in the long term.

This was echoed at Fenwood:

> Being private, we don't have to produce good news every six months, which our friends who are publicly quoted do. And if there isn't any, they have to manufacture it, or you have to change your policy and slow something down because you really have to tell the shareholders something. We haven't got that problem. We're much more concerned with what we're going to achieve over the next five years.

Castle, Kremer's and Shilton were less careful to ensure their financial independence. Both Castle and Shilton were weighed down by financially over-stretched parent companies. Shilton's holding company, Field Investments, was paying the price of rapid but ill-digested growth during the 1970s. Group borrowings trebled in the three years to 1980 – when interest payments were three times higher than trading profits. Maurice Field owned only 10 per cent of the equity and by 1982 Field Investments' share price had collapsed to 6 per cent of the 1979 high. Maurice Field was forced into a desperate programme of rationalizations and disposals that would eventually leave Shilton as his sole manufacturing subsidiary.

As for Castle's GEH, its generally lax financial management was typified by its tolerance of Castle's poor performance through the 1970 – as one director observed, leaving little doubt which proposition he thought was true, 'either they were generous or they were slow on the draw'. The Group did not enjoy the confidence of the City, forestalling a take-over attempt in 1977 only with the greatest difficulty. The gradual disposal of the London site did not inhibit a continuous rise in borrowings – interest payable trebled between 1978 and 1981. With losses before tax in all three years 1981 to 1983, the company would be forced into a severe rationalization programme. By 1981, GEH's share price had slipped to a sixth of its 1978 high.

Kremer's was different in that it was a public company in its own right. Kremer's management recognized the pressures this put them under: 'When you become a public company, you get pushed. You've got to grow, got to grow, got to grow. You've got to have better figures every year . . . otherwise you become a has-been. So you've got to develop.' None the less, as it entered the recession the company appeared to be strong: debt was negligible, the family – including Harold Levey – held 35 per cent of the otherwise dispersed shares, and profits and share price were at all time peaks. Not surprisingly, the company seemed highly credit-worthy so that by the time of the recession it had been able to acquire facilities from no less than eleven banks. As we will see later, the problem would be how to control this financial cornucopia.

Product market positions

This potential financial vulnerability on the part of Castle, Kremer's and Shilton was compounded by their weaknesses in the market place. Granted, in the highly competitive office furniture industry, no one firm could hope to gain dominating market shares, but these three companies exacerbated their weak positions. For Shilton, the botched transfer of desking production to the Midland site had destroyed the dealers' faith in the company's reliability and quality; the company became popularly known as 'Shit-on'. Moreover, without a direct sales force, the company was heavily dependent on one major wholesaler, Taylor's, who accounted for roughly a third of total turnover in 1980. Similarly, Kremer's had no direct sales force and relied on only one retailer for its domestic furniture sales – one third of total turnover – and on just two important dealers for 20 per cent of its office furniture sales. In some mitigation, Kremer's had been developing overseas markets while it enjoyed close relations with the two office furniture dealers – in the case of one, based on a family friendship dating back to before the war. Though with perhaps only 12 per cent of the market in the early 1980s, Kremer's was also the largest wooden desking manufacturer.

At Castle, Simpson had only just abandoned direct sales, but in retrospect this was perceived to be a mistake: 'We found ourselves trapped, in the sense that you lose control of your market place. You are selling to the guy who sells. You don't know what's going on at the end where the buyer is buying.' The chief exception to indirect sales was the 25 per cent of turnover tied to the government's Property Services Agency. Exports took a further fifth of turnover. However, both at home and abroad the company was competing against rivals who had invested heavily in new improved manufacturing capacity and competed fiercely on price:

> There's so much over-capacity – that's caused the crunch. People . . .
> are coming on the scene and putting a huge investment in and
> stamping out filing cabinets at very low rates. In a declining market,
> its just dog eat dog . . . We were just busy fools, just carrying on
> bashing out tin boxes with very little return.

Trapped in a commodity-type market, Castle could only compete on price.

Barton provides a sharp contrast. Concentrating heavily on home markets, all Barton's UK sales were through an assiduously cultivated network of 200 dealers – 'it was a partnership with them from the start'. Loyalty was encouraged by special discount schemes. However, the company's policy was that no one customer should account for more than 5 per cent of total turnover. 'We would hate to be answerable to someone like MFI [a very large retailer] or something because its 40 per cent of turnover.' Property Services Agency contracts averaged only about 1 per cent of total turnover.

Barton had decided to concentrate on the specialized niches of seating and executive desking rather than taking on the big desking companies. By the early 1980s, the company could credibly claim to be the largest UK seating manufacturer, albeit with a market share of just 7 per cent. Barton's senior management explained their strategy thus:

> We felt that as we were only in it in a relatively small way, we would be better suited to producing executive furniture rather than main line commercial desking, which then meant that we avoided head-on conflict with any of the major office desking manufacturers at the time . . . It meant that we had a niche of our own, rather than trying to compete with them.

On the other hand, especially in seating, competition with the small cut-price manufacturers was avoided by keeping to the top end of the market:

> On the cheaper lines we had no way, apart from trying to compete on price, of competing with smaller manufacturers with lesser overheads and a smaller market area . . . We could never compete with them on price anyway, so we chose not to, but to move up market with really better quality and better designed products.

Independence was cherished even in design: 'David [Barton] is very much involved with the design of everything – he controls his own destiny really.'

Fenwood, likewise, was chary of taking on big contracts from private companies or the Property Services Agency: 'We couldn't afford to take the risk.' Instead, it relied on a nationwide network of forty or fifty dealers, with some of whom the company had had links since before the Second World War. Fenwood also owned a small West End dealership, which took a little over 5 per cent of its total output by the late 1970s, but which had originally been bought mainly to act as a showroom and to provide a means of monitoring other dealers' costs. Additionally, Fenwood had taken a 26 per cent stake in its biggest dealer, with around a third of total output, in order to help fund its expansion. Risk was further reduced because all of Fenwood's factories made two or three out of a deliberately wide range of products: 'We make a very big range of furniture and we wouldn't want to have much tied to one particular range . . . The wider range you have, the more market you aim at. As one market goes down, another goes up.'

Thus Barton and Fenwood had carefully developed positions in the market place – one by specialization, the other by diversification – that might protect them from the full shock of recession. Moreover, both had safeguarded their independence from outside shareholders, the banks or any particular customer. Insecure financially and weaker in their markets, Castle and Shilton were likely to be more vulnerable and more constrained during the recession. Kremer's position – strong in finance and dependent in sales – was more ambiguous and might require careful management. In the next chapter we will see how far the differing external constraints on each of these companies allowed them to pursue recession strategies consistent with their diverse internal characters and objectives.

Chapter Ten

The furniture companies in recession and recovery

INTRODUCTION

The last chapter introduced the five office furniture companies as they entered the recession. Each possessed very different internal characters and all varied in the extent to which they had built up scope for strategic discretion. Thus Barton, committed to independence, had deliberately cultivated niche positions in seating and quality desking and strictly avoided any resort to outside finance. Castle, by contrast, was dependent on its ailing parent and faced the full rigours of the price competitive metal storage market. The company had not, moreover, yet succeeded in resolving its rift between incoming marketeers and demoralized old guard. No such divisions troubled Fenwood, where Charles remained firmly in control and substantial financial reserves and a diversified product range promised to buffer the company against most foreseeable threats. The emotional Kremer's was the most expansionist of the family companies – and least chary of taking on debt to exploit its opportunities. Lastly there was Shilton, in chaotic transition from London-based Jewish family business to provincial subsidiary of the dynamic but highly geared Field Investments.

As we shall see, these five companies adopted very different strategic responses to the recession. The following two sections of this chapter provide a broad overview of these strategies and their repercussions. The chapter finishes by investigating several particularly significant strategic decisions. I shall then have completed my presentation of the case study data from the two industries. Chapter 11, therefore, will proceed to re-examine the empirical evidence in the light of the competing theoretical perspectives introduced in earlier chapters.

RECESSION STRATEGIES

The five companies undertook a wide range of strategies. This section begins by describing in more detail the cautious strategies of first Barton, the only company not to launch a systems range, and then Fenwood, whose systems range was very modest; the section deals next with Shilton, another tentative entrant into systems, but a company where the new management was at last replacing chaos with a determined bid to restore volumes and reputation; finally it considers the over-confident strategies of Castle and Kremer's, both with highly ambitious new systems ventures.

Barton

Protected in its carefully developed niche, Barton did not allow the recession to divert it from its existing course: 'we never did anything dramatically different during the recession, let's say that . . . I'm sure that's been a strength really, its continuity of policy.' Accordingly, the company avoided entering any discount wars: 'We never have been a discount company . . . We would have preferred that [short-time working] if necessary to discounting in order to get turnover. We certainly didn't buy turnover at that time at all.' At most, a few of the larger accounts were allowed discounts of 1 to 2 additional per cent. There were, however, a number of developments along the lines of existing policy.

Thus the company continued to introduce several new ranges during the recession in order to reinforce its shift to the more resilient top ends of the market. Chief of these innovations was the launch of a German-designed range of ultra-sophisticated executive seating in 1982. However, except to supply seating to complement other manufacturers' ranges, Barton did abstain from entering the systems market. Moreover, after getting rid of the export manager in 1979, the company retreated from most overseas markets. The biggest changes came on the works side, where the new works manager (promoted to director in 1981) instituted a radical shake-up of the factory's supervisory and working practices. All the existing foremen were changed and payment by results was introduced. In addition the company strove to upgrade the skills and commitment of the workforce by recruiting younger workers and training the existing ones. The apprentice scheme was expanded to train six new workers a

year. There were no redundancies during the recession, and employment was held steady at just under 200 throughout. Although
expenditure on new equipment was minimal, between 1979 and 1985
the factory's floorspace was steadily doubled by no less than five
successive expansions.

Fenwood

Fenwood's traditional policy of sound finance was to be vindicated
during the recession. One senior manager pointedly contrasted the
wisdom of Fenwood's management with that of newer, upstart
companies:

> A lot of old companies with continuing sort of family management
> have learned a lot of lessons from the [1930s] Depression, so that
> when a recession comes along now they know how to behave and
> they know how to prepare for it. Whereas a lot of younger companies
> that have grown up since the War, they've had such a gravy train
> since the end of World War Two that they just went on thinking that
> it was never going to stop. You know, the sun's going to shine for
> ever and all they had to do was to produce more and sell more and
> make bigger profits, and when it suddenly hit them briefly, they threw
> their hands up in horror . . . We established a sound financial base so
> that we'd be able to withstand that sort of thing.

Characteristically, Fenwood responded to the recession not by
discounting to sustain turnover but rather by reducing capacity to
maintain profits:

> Well, the recession resulted in excess capacity and we just cut it
> down. We reduced capacity and we were able to continue to trade
> profitably. Other people had desperate problems in trying to compete
> for what business was available at prices that were not attractive, and
> as you know, many of them did not trade profitably.

In all, capacity was cut back by about 20 per cent, mostly by renting
out half the space of the metal furniture factory and by the closure of
one small and long rather inconvenient wooden furniture factory. The
workforce was gradually slimmed down by about a third between 1979
and 1983, though this was mostly by natural wastage and there were no
major redundancies. Fenwood's strategy was not just defensive. In
1982, the company launched a simple range of systems furniture, based
on existing products but supplemented by wire management and for
sale through the existing network of dealers. The company insisted
that systems only represented an 'evolution' in the market and was

content that it accounted for little more than an eighth of total turnover by 1985: 'if systems furniture drops off, well, we're not terribly worried because we're making everything else as well.' Fenwood remained a firm believer in the future of traditional furniture, launching a new budget range, again a development of an existing range, but which was amongst the first to make use of melamine finishes.

Shilton

If the recession failed to divert Barton and Fenwood, those companies which had not in preceding years taken such care to develop managerial, financial and market strengths would all, in their different ways, be devastated. At Shilton, Bernard Gold had saved the crucial Taylor's contract by revamping the old knock-down range during the summer of 1981. Such was Shilton's dependence by then that according to one manager 'if he [Gold] hadn't held Taylor's, and done the product right, I doubt if it [the company] would still exist'. Shilton's heavy loss making domestic furniture company was sold in July for a nominal £1, with forty-five redundancies. However, Gold was not able to prevent the core office furniture business from slipping into the red for the first time in year-end 1981 and he himself had to depart in November on account of a scandal unconnected with the company.

A new team of young outsider managers was appointed during 1981, capped by the arrival in December of 36-year-old James Turk as chief executive. Faced with mounting crisis throughout Field Investments, Chairman Maurice Field put the new team under immediate pressure: 'a lot of pressure, a lot of pressure – because, I mean, he was in a straight jacket himself.' Field imposed the toughened regime indirectly through tight financial controls and performance linked management-incentive schemes. One senior manager expressed Field Investments' philosophy thus:

> They do not believe in running the businesses. They invest in businesses and say: 'Well, there's the capital and I want a minimum return on funds of 25 per cent and an objective of 40 per cent return on funds. And how you do that, what you make and all the rest of it, so long as its legal, is up to you.'

The management changes and subsidiary divestments elsewhere in the Field group made abundantly clear the likely fate of Turk's new team if they failed to meet these performance targets. This discipline was reinforced by the nature of the incentive scheme, which was based exclusively on the corporate measure of return on capital: 'Every manager is in the cart together, in that it [the scheme] is not based on sales input, it is not based on debtor days or creditor days, or anything else – we are all in it together.'　Therefore, if Turk was formally free to implement his own recovery strategy and to build his own management team, he was very aware that this freedom depended upon him satisfying stringent and constricting performance criteria. Failure to meet these would lead either to the imposition of a new management team or the addition of Shilton to Field's long list of businesses for closure or disposal.

One of Turk's first actions was to dismiss eight of the old Shilton management – some accused of being 'political animals'. None the less, two long-serving senior managers were retained on the production and technical side and, after this initial purge, Turk worked hard to create confidence and cohesion. He met with some scepticism initially from the remnants of the old regime – his early sales targets were thought to be just 'telephone numbers'. As for the three new directors, two had already been recruited before Turk's own appointment. Yet, though each of the top four managers differed strongly in personality, all stressed how they had come to work as a 'team': 'You couldn't actually put the four of these people together in a pub and say, "Well, they're a group of friends or whatever". But we are.' It was emphasized that the old 'politics' had been abolished, allowing informality and delegation in an atmosphere of mutual trust: 'James [Turk] lets us all get on with it. And therefore only occasionally do we need to get together for whatever policy decisions we need to take.'

The new management team faced a rapidly deteriorating situation at the end of 1981. Two of the newly appointed directors admitted they seriously considered resigning as soon as they understood the true situation. Since 1979, the company had made more than £1 million pre-tax losses, and by 1982 turnover had fallen to less than half the pre-slump record. Accordingly, tight financial controls were imposed for the first time – surviving old Shilton managers referred to 1982 as 'the year of learning about numbers'; the London showroom, famous for its extravagant drinks account, was closed; sales and accounting staff were reduced by 50 per cent. By year end 1982, total employment was almost exactly half that of 1979.

Formerly a production director with a domestic furniture manufacturer, Turk applied his expertise to improving quality and delivery times. Desperate to fill the factory, he also made a determined assault on the public sector market, first winning a £1/3 million contract from the Department of Health and Social Security and then a vital contract with the Property Services Agency. This PSA contract was soon developed into a guaranteed minimum of £1 million a year for five years; by 1984 this sum had more than doubled. A simple 'wire tidy' range of systems furniture was launched in June 1982, for distribution through dealers; a new seating range was introduced in March 1983; and there was a short-lived venture into manufacturing office fittings.

Castle

Alderton, with his new sales and marketing dominated team, took charge just as the recession was pushing Castle back into losses. Nearly 200 redundancies (40 per cent of all employees) were necessary during 1980. Even in these unpropitious circumstances, Alderton remained committed to launching the ambitious 'Fortress' range of systems furniture. A prestigious outside consultant was commissioned to design a high quality range that would exploit the colour potential of metal and meld the best features of American and Continental systems fashion. A team of four more young outsiders was recruited to manage development, direct selling and office planning for the new Fortress range. The Fortress team was to be based in a new showroom situated near the City of London.

However, the initial Fortress launch of autumn 1982 was hampered by inadequate sales literature, production delays, and poor communications between the factory and the London showroom. For the first six months, Fortress sales proved to be less than a sixth of the original projections. Meanwhile, between 1981 and 1982, the Property Services Agency had cut its crucial orders for conventional storage products by 50 per cent and the high value of Sterling was restricting export markets.

As Castle's losses continued to increase, morale collapsed and staff, even directors, began to desert. Alderton was left isolated and over-stretched. Desperate for sales, Alderton was forced to pursue Castle's remaining customers himself – 'dashing around the country like a water-spider' and giving away substantial discounts. For all his energy, Alderton found it hard to cope:

> Brian Alderton was a marketeer. His discipline, his profession was marketing. And I think Brian would be good for a business that was doing well and expanding – he had plenty of flair and ideas. But when he found himself in a position where the business had to contract quickly and contain its resources and ensure its cash flow was maintained – and indeed achieve some small level of profit – Brian wasn't really the right guy for that sort of situation.

This was a generous comment; others complained he spent too much time worrying about the Fortress colour scheme. Alderton had recruited new sales and production directors and had just begun work on a further retrenchment plan when he decided – unresisted by the GEH Main Board – to take a job with another company.

Meanwhile, GEH, with losses amounting to over £3 million for year-end 1982, had been forced into still more rationalizations and site disposals – including even its prestigious London headquarters – in order to keep its debts under control. Threatened by persistent take-over rumours, in July 1982 the Main Board was convulsed by what the financial press termed a 'Board Room court martial'. One of the victims was Simpson, Castle's chairman and former managing director. A new GEH chief executive was appointed: an accountant, he was described as 'exceptionally *tough*, well educated, well disciplined'. One of his first acts was to ask Baxter, due for early and demoralized retirement the next month, to take charge of Castle Furniture.

Baxter had originally joined Castle as an apprentice thirty-six years before. Since then, he had acquired a wide experience in design and in both home and export sales. He had first been appointed to the Castle board in 1979 as design and marketing director, but then lost his marketing responsibilities in 1980 to one of Alderton's appointees. Though certainly a product of the old regime at Castle, Baxter was nevertheless experienced in marketing and an enthusiast for the Fortress range. But now the GEH chief executive's injunction to him and his management team was unequivocal:

> Get me some money, because that's what I need; otherwise we're going to have to close this business. I need money on core-line business. If you haven't got a core-line business, you can't do anything; you can't afford Fortress or anything else. You've got to generate profit.

Thus it was abundantly clear to Baxter and his team that the survival of the whole company was at stake.

Baxter at once implemented Alderton's retrenchment plan, with a further twenty-two redundancies and a 20 per cent reduction in overhead costs as a proportion of the whole. On the sales side, Baxter was anxious to escape 'the tonnage game' – high volumes at low margins – into which Alderton had desperately let the company slip. This entailed a measured withdrawal from the increasingly competitive Middle East market and a gradual levering up of prices on traditional products at home. In order to diversify, a new business services division was launched in 1983, but this was terminated after losses within a year. The sudden revival of sales to the Crown Suppliers (formerly the Property Services Agency) towards the end of 1982 provided a welcome bonus.

As both an enthusiastic supporter of systems from the first, and an advocate of direct sales, Baxter also persevered with Fortress – despite continued scepticism from GEH. In 1983 a new marketing director was appointed from the library furniture company who, applying his expertise in large contracting, also took charge of Fortress. The depleted Fortress sales and planning teams were rebuilt and proper sales literature was produced for the first time ready for the product's relaunch in autumn 1983. This was the range's last chance:

> You get to the stage when you've invested a lot of money and you want to see some returns before you put more money into it . . . It was taking too much of the resources from the company and too much of the effort . . . Although it was never said – nobody ever admitted it – but we had got to that stage and had to make up our minds which way to go.

Kremer's

Kremer's, like Castle, did not allow catastrophic performance during the recession to distract it from entering the systems market on a grand scale. After all, the company had a well-established policy for dealing with the periodical down-turns characteristic of the office furniture trade:

> We took the view that no, you can't follow the pattern; you've got to even it out and ride with it . . . We're not going to take these ups and downs. What we're going to do is, we set the pattern for production, we're just going to make. Bong . . . So when the market opened up, we could start deliveries straight away; up went our prices; bong, we were away. Now this worked for five or six down-turns – fantastic – and we were the clever boys . . . Now that was fine. Come the '79/80 recession, when everybody thought it was another of these down-turns again, in fact it was not so. It was something completely different.

At first, Kremer's persisted in its usual confident strategy, investing a further £0.5 million in automation, launching two new seating designs, revamping the executive desk range and, perhaps most important, producing its first systems furniture range in October 1981. But difficulties mounted: there was an expensive recall of factored filing cabinets; finished goods stocks kept accumulating, until they reached twice pre-recession levels; the United States subsidiary dipped into losses, while the French subsidiary required substantial stock building; and – most catastrophic – just at the end of 1980 Kremer's lost its large domestic furniture contract. As one senior manager remembered:

> A lot of chickens were coming home to roost at that time and a lot of problems that we suffered in '82–83 were the result of decisions that had been taken a number of years before – with production levels being kept at too high a level, stocks being allowed to build up and the company being too production orientated.

In October 1980 Chris Kennedy, managing director and heir apparent, died unexpectedly at the age of 48. Harold Levey, an accountant still in his mid–30s and with no sales or production experience, was suddenly propelled into the managing directorship. Kennedy's calm and caution were sorely missed at this critical moment for the company. As one director put it: 'Twelve years we had worked together. We were a very close knit group of people, and with the checks and balances, the right sort of balances between us . . . When Chris died, if you like, one of balances was taken away.'

Thus Kremer's pressed on without restraint, with occasional reservations expressed only by Bernie Kremer himself:

> We applied our very successful formula – very successful [said with some irony]: let's keep making, boys! We set the pattern and kept making. We set that steady level through the year, but of course we get into Year One, and then suddenly we find ourselves in Year Two, and what the hell do we do? This sudden upturn hasn't come; do we carry on? Yes, we'll carry on again. I mean, the banks lent us money as fast as we could get, as we wanted. No problem. So you get lulled into a false sense of security, and we were taking this money until all of a sudden, we turned round and we didn't have any space!

As finished goods stocks built up, Kremer's was even forced to rent more warehousing. Bank loans and overdrafts were allowed to escalate from nil in 1980 to roughly £6 million in early 1983; by year-end 1983, gearing exceeded 200 per cent and interest paid was more than ten times trading profits.

The final crisis was precipitated by the collapse, in 1982, of Johnson's, the retailer and wholesaler who accounted for 8 per cent of total sales. This failure cost the company £400,000. That year, Kremer's made heavy pre-tax losses and the share price fell to a fifth of the 1979 level. Having already sold the majority share of its cash-hungry French subsidiary, Kremer's was forced to stitch an emergency rationalization package together over the Christmas holiday. The analysis was simple:

> We sat down and said that this was crazy . . . Our core business
> [office furniture] is making money, but we are overstocked, we are
> overborrowed, our overheads are too high, we can't support them,
> and we are involved in loss making activities. And our banks are
> going to come crashing down around our heads.

Indeed, for the next three years, Kremer's would be under the tight supervision of the banks. In January 1983, Bernie Kremer and Harold Levey explained the situation to their bankers, presenting as well the emergency recovery strategy. Taken aback, the banks accepted the plans but insisted on monthly detailed reports being made by a nominated accounting firm. Kremer's sold most of the seating business; transferred the headquarters to more modest premises; made 220 employees redundant, including two newcoming senior managers; eliminated two out-of-date ranges; and, after some delay, finally disposed completely of the French and American subsidiaries. Two significant financial reforms were also introduced, each symbolizing a shift from the old production orientation. First, the costing system was changed with overhead charges being shifted from production to stocks in order to emphasize that profits were not realised until the goods were actually sold. Second, the management accounts were altered, so that, instead of starting with production as the top line with sales lost in the middle, they now started with sales at the top while the production details were relegated to the back pages.

Although a new range of clerical desking was launched in 1983 and two others were revamped; although there was a new venture into bedroom furniture from 1983; and although a Mark Two of the original systems range was launched in 1984, this process of rationalization dominated the company's activities right into the recovery period. While rivals expanded, Kremer's was forced to concentrate on divestment, redundancy and rationalization. Even if the initiative for most of these rationalizing measures had come originally from Kremer's itself, the management was only doing more or less what the banks would have compelled them to do, anyway. None the less, they pursued the reforms vigorously, the sooner to free themselves from tight supervision.

In conclusion, though Kremer's had entered the recession determinedly pursuing its well-established strategy, even the family shareholdings and the leading market share could not protect its independence for ever from the combined consequences of extravagant policies and lax financial discipline. Finally Kremer's was confronted by a stark choice: receivership or the reversal of their own strategies and the tight supervision of the banks. For Castle and Shilton too the options were suddenly narrowed, though in their cases the financial constraint was exercised more indirectly through their holding companies. One way or another all three companies were eventually penalized for their failures to build sufficiently secure market positions or strong enough financial reserves by losing their freedom to pursue their own preferred strategies. Barton and Fenwood, by contrast, were able to persevere each in their particular strategy as independently and as securely as ever.

CONSEQUENCES OF RECESSION STRATEGIES

Just as had the three domestic appliance companies, the five office furniture companies had adopted radically different strategies during the recession. Perhaps the Barton brothers had been the most cautious, keeping out of systems while solidly defending their core seating business and reforming and expanding the works. Charles Fenwood too had been conservative, though he differed from Barton in squeezing his workforce and making a modest entry into the systems market. Boldest had been Castle and Kremer's. Despite severe rationalizations and shedding of the London site, and even while slashing margins in its traditional business, Castle's marketeers were driving their company into a major investment in the Fortress systems range. Kremer's too had finally entered the systems market, though otherwise allowing its production orientation to trap it into disastrous overstocking and heavy debt. Lastly there was Shilton. Having entered the recession in a state of complete chaos, by 1982 the company was emerging under the leadership of James Turk with a coherent, if somewhat desperate, strategy based on large-scale government contracts.

These were the strategic choices. What, then, were the consequences of the companies' diverse recession strategies – both for their economic performances and for the survival of their managers? As in Chapter 8, I shall compare the five companies' performances on three key dimensions: sales growth, profit margins and return on capital employed (see Figures 10.1, 10.2 and 10.3 respectively; also Appendix 2 on p. 301). To get a broader industry perspective I have also included the averages of four other comparable firms. These four comparison firms are all amongst the leading dozen companies in the industry: one company concentrated on seating; two were mostly in

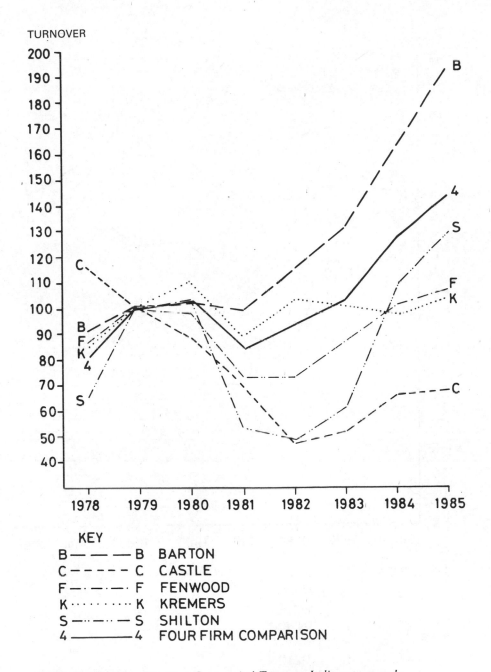

Figure 10.1   Office Furniture Companies' Turnover Indices, year-ends 1978–85.

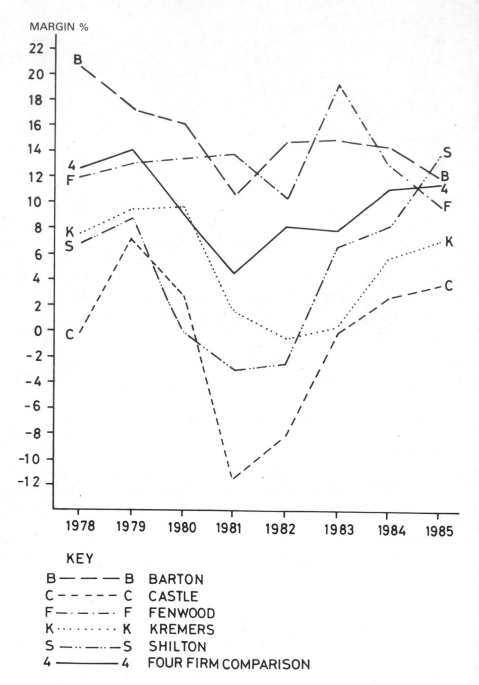

MARGIN %

KEY

B — — — B BARTON
C – – – – C CASTLE
F — · — · — F FENWOOD
K · · · · · · · K KREMERS
S — · · — · · — S SHILTON
4 ——————— 4 FOUR FIRM COMPARISON

Figure 10.2   Office Furniture Companies' Profit Margins, year-ends 1978–85

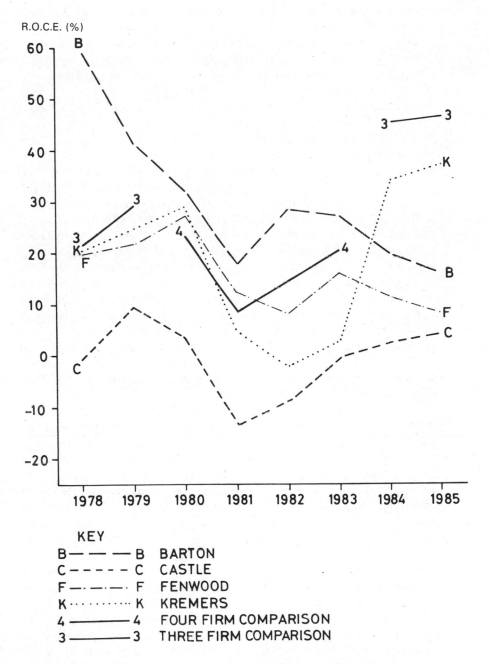

R.O.C.E. (%)

KEY
B — — — B   BARTON
C – – – – C   CASTLE
F —·—·— F   FENWOOD
K ·········· K   KREMERS
4 ————— 4   FOUR FIRM COMPARISON
3 ————— 3   THREE FIRM COMPARISON

Figure 10.3   Office Furniture Companies' Returns on Capital Employed, year-ends 1978–85

wooden desking, one highly committed to systems; and the last concentrated on metal storage.

The same general caveats must apply to the comparison of these performance figures as applied to those of the domestic appliance companies in Chapter 8. Here, it should be noted in particular that Fenwood's figures relate only to the bulk of the company's wooden furniture activities, while Castle's early years include the tattered remnants of its general engineering business. The Shilton figures need to be interpreted with special caution because of the legal disputes surrounding the last years of the Shilton family regime. Further, because of Shilton's reorganization, the 1979–80 figures refer to sixteen months. In addition, Shilton's figures for return on capital employed have been excluded from Figure 10.3 for several reasons: first, there is a two year gap in reliable figures during the early 1980s for the actual amount of capital employed; second, the company had a negative amount of capital employed by 1981–2; and third the figures for 1982–83 and 1983–84 are inflated to well over 100 per cent by the very low capital base after allowing for accumulated losses. Two last points about Figure 10.3: the average returns on capital employed for the comparison group of firms excludes one (A) of the four companies in year-ends 1978 and 1979 because its very low stated capital employed in these two years yields percentages of more than 200 per cent in both years; again in 1984 to 1985, another company (D) is excluded because changed accounting policies boosted its return on capital above 100 per cent (see Appendix 2 p. 301).

With all of these proper qualifications in mind, the diagrams do permit some rough comparisons. Let us begin the analysis by examining the four-firm comparison group and especially the extremes hidden within the average. All four firms suffered absolute declines in turnover during the recession and two were pushed into small losses (before tax and interest). These averages conceal some wide disparities, however. The fastest growth and the best profits were obtained by the wooden desking manufacturer which had whole-heartedly plunged into the systems market. Between 1979 and 1985, its turnover slightly more than doubled, while its return on capital remained comfortably in double figures throughout the recession and reached 65 per cent by 1985. Least successful was the metal storage specialist. After a near 40 per cent drop in turnover between 1980 and 1981, the storage company had only just recovered to pre-recession sales levels in 1985. The company also suffered a small trading loss in 1982, and even in 1985 its profit margins remained at a miserly 2 per cent. This poor performance does seem to confirm the Castle manager's assessment of the metal storage market as full of 'busy fools'. It remains to be seen, however, whether Castle actually did better by diversifying out into systems. How, then, did the five case study firms fare?

Barton was the most successful. From Figure 10.1 it is clear that, for all its caution, Barton was able to achieve remarkable growth (94 per cent between 1979 and 1985) within its niches, leaving all four other case study firms comfortably behind. This growth was secured without particular damage to its profit ratios – though they did slip somewhat from their previous exceptional levels, both profit margins (Figure 10.2) and return on capital (Figure 10.3) still remained amongst the best throughout the period. The applause for Barton should not be unqualified, however. It should be noted that two of the four-firm comparison group, starting in 1978 from nearly as high bases, had managed to improve their returns on capital to substantially beyond what Barton was earning by 1985; one of these companies was not far short of Barton's turnover growth, while the other, the successful entrant into systems, had outstripped it. By 1985, Bartons' profits were beginning to sag.

Fenwood's profitability performance parallels that of Barton. To protect profit margins the company had clearly – and characteristically – accepted a considerable drop in turnover during the recession, from which it had only just recovered by 1984. However, while profitability had certainly been maintained at redoubtable levels during the worst years, by the end of the recovery, just as for Barton, the results were beginning to lose their shine.

The three weakest performers were, of course, Castle, Kremer's and Shilton. Although Kremer's managed to preserve trading profits throughout its crisis, the company's heavy interest payments forced it into substantial losses by year-end 1982. Total turnover had just surpassed its former peak by 1985, after being depressed even during the recovery by continuing rationalizations. Kremer's only returned to overall profit in 1984. Its relatively high return on capital employed figures in 1984 and 1985 are exaggerated by its depleted reserves and do not allow for remaining heavy debts.

Shilton plunged even deeper than Kremer's during the recession – and achieved a more pronounced recovery. Turnover in 1982 was less than half that in 1979 and there were trading losses in year ends 1980, 1981 and 1982. Turk's determination to regain volumes succeeded in restoring Shilton to its former sales levels by 1984, and by the following year profit margins comfortably exceeded pre-recession levels once more. Turk's young management team were well-rewarded under Maurice Field's incentive scheme: by 1986, directors were receiving performance bonuses worth 26 per cent of basic salary, and other managers were getting 18 per cent.

Castle suffered the worst results in recession, and had the shakiest recovery. Turnover dropped by more than 50 per cent between 1979 and 1982, and never recovered to its former level, even by 1985. The company recorded trading losses in 1981, 1982 and 1983, remaining by far the least profitable of the five case study firms throughout the recovery. Still, it did return to profit and it may have been some consolation that its chief rival, the metal storage company in the four-firm comparison group, was performing just as badly, with lower margins but higher return on capital in 1985. This was not, however, sufficient to save its ailing parent, GEH. Early in 1985, GEH succumbed to a takeover bid from a large, diversified American engineering company. None the less, Baxter was allowed to push forward Castle's recovery strategy until his delayed retirement at the end of 1986.

There are some significant patterns in strategies and performances. Castle, Kremer and Shilton all made somewhat desperate attempts to diversify – respectively, into business services, bedroom furniture and shop and office fittings – which, without exception, failed and were soon abandoned. For these three companies, even determined innovation within the office furniture market brought few rewards, at least so far as systems furniture was concerned. By 1985, neither Castle nor Kremer's had gained more than 2 per cent of the UK market for systems, and for both companies revival was led by conventional products. Systems furniture – especially at Kremer's where the range included nearly 1,000 different items – both absorbed massive amounts of working capital and cost a great deal in management time in successive reorganizations. Kremer's eventually joined Castle in resorting to direct sales for systems, but, like Castle, found it very difficult to establish a stable and competent sales team. In neither company had systems furniture repaid its initial investment by 1984–5. Of the five case study firms, the most financially successful systems ventures were those of Fenwood and Shilton; their ranges were cheap developments of existing ranges; they were aimed at the lower end of the market in which the multinationals were hardly interested; and they were distributed by the companies' established dealer networks. Thus neither radical diversification nor expensive innovation seemed to pay.

The companies' recession strategies had managerial consequences as well. At Castle and Shilton, responsible managers had had to pay for poor performances with their jobs. Turk purged the Shilton management, while 'Board Room court martials' and straightforward desertions combined to shake out Castle's management. But at Kremer's, even though its crisis was pretty much as severe as those of the other two companies, top management stayed essentially intact. Apart from the transitory appearance of two directors associated with the bedroom furniture venture, the only change to the main board after Kennedy's death in 1980 was the appointment for the first time of a sales director in 1982. Although this was significant in that it gave explicit recognition to the new importance of sales to the company, in other respects it did not represent a severe break with the traditions of the company; the new director had been a long-serving production manager at Kremer's before departing for a short spell with a domestic furniture manufacturer.

How did Kremer's management survive when Castle's and Shilton's did not? Crucial, of course, was the loyalty of the shareholders, many of whom were either members of the family, friends or old employees. It was reported that even at the depths of the crisis, Bernie Kremer won enthusiastic applause for his performance at the Annual General Meeting. By contrast, GEH and Field Investments were in the hands of outside shareholders, amongst whom the financial institutions were predominant. Vital too was that, by proposing the emergency Christmas rationalization package themselves, Kremer's management had pre-empted the banks' intervention. Finally, there was the family nature of the management and its dedication to the company itself. All had grown up together sharing the same confident outlook, so all were equally implicated in the final crisis; no one individual could be singled out for blame and none would desert voluntarily. Kremer's management would have to learn and change collectively.

And so they did. Certainly, the immediate crisis had called upon the old loyalties and energies. One manager compared 1982–3 with Kremer's catastrophic fire in 1961:

> If you are looking for a story as to how this company came out or passed through the recession, I would have said that [the fire] was it. How did we get out, although 95 per cent was a write off in 1961? *Question*: Same sort of skills?
> Same sort of skills? Well, if you say bulldoze, and I don't want to know, get your head down and your arse up, because that's what I want, yes [laugh]! The job gets done – and if that's a skill, we had it.

But with the deliberate gradual withdrawal of Bernie Kremer from detailed day-to-day involvement, and the imminent retirement of the production director and others of 'Danny's men', it was acknowledged that 'that part is thinning out. Because if we [the other managers] have been on the crest of the wave, the wave is now on the wane . . . The company is now in the throes of change.' Sales and marketing were accorded a new importance; financial controls were tighter; management was formalized. 'The style of management is certainly becoming more reasonable, less [laugh] who shouts loudest . . .' Moreover, the company had learnt the lessons from ill-considered diversifications into domestic furniture and overseas: 'Its the old story of stay with what you're good at . . . ; concentrate on the products you know best and know what to do about.' In the words of another director: 'We're back to square one of our business, which we know, which we know all about, which we're experts at. Somebody came along with gold bars for £1 each, we don't want to know!'

Thus the five companies, each with their very distinct strategies, experienced widely different performances during recession and recovery. Indeed, whereas the range of profit margins (the most reliable figures for this group) had been only 10.1 per cent in 1979, by 1981 it had widened to 25.4 per cent (amongst the four firm comparison group, however, the range slightly closed, from 15 per cent to around 9 per cent in the same period; see Appendix 2 on p. 301). Despite these divergent performances, all five firms survived into the recovery – albeit somewhat battered in the cases of Shilton, Castle and Kremer's. To complete this analysis of the office furniture companies, I shall now examine several strategic choices that particularly contributed to these divergent performances.

STRATEGIC CHOICES

Four at least of these office furniture companies had attempted to pursue recession strategies that were consistent with leadership objectives and characters built up well beforehand. Shilton was perhaps the exception. For most of the recession its management was aimless and incohesive. When Turk arrived, such were the legacies of chaos at Shilton and over ambition at Field Investment that he was inescapably bound by financial disciplines and performance-related incentives. He had little choice but to impose tight management controls and to seek with all possible vigour ways of filling and reforming his factory as soon as possible. At the opposite extreme was Fenwood – diversified and financially sound. The company was able to adhere to its already well-proven formula, preferring to close capacity rather than to chase turnover, to lose volume rather than to sacrifice margins, and to innovate cautiously with systems rather than to risk over-dependence on just one new product.

Particular light is thrown on how the companies' different leaderships and characters influenced strategic choices during the recession by examining the various responses to the challenge of systems furniture. Here the focus will be on just three companies: Castle and Kremer's, who both invested heavily in systems, and Barton, who stayed out of it all together.

Kremer's

For Kremer's, entry into systems was controversial. The promise of systems furniture accorded well with the company's commitment to growth – with expectations that systems would soon take 30–40 per cent of the office furniture market, Kremer's proud claim to being the leading manufacturer in the industry depended upon climbing on to the band wagon as soon as possible. Bernie Kremer himself, as an innovator in the office furniture industry during the 1960s and influenced by what he had seen on his many travels overseas, was a particular enthusiast for going into systems. However, other members of the Board were sceptical about the claims for systems' growth potential; they were concerned about the expense and risk of launching what amounted to an entirely new product; they disliked the production difficulties inherent in such a complex product; and they feared that the company's conservative dealers, to whom the range was initially to be offered, would be unable or unwilling to sell a systems range properly. Most important, perhaps, was the radical challenge systems furniture presented to the old production orientation at Kremer's. One of 'Danny's men' summed up the different implications of traditional desking and systems furniture:

> It [systems] is not just a desk . . . A desk is a desk. The problem with systems against all new furniture is: with other new furniture you make something and you sell it; with systems you go and ask the customer what does he want, and try and give him what he wants.

The idea of giving customers what they wanted was clearly offensive to Kremer's traditional production orientation. There was a year's debate and delay, with some heated arguments. At last, in September 1980, Bernie Kremer used his final authority, insisting that the company must go into systems, and that any director who continued to oppose should resign. None did.

The original plan had been to sell a range manufactured by an Italian company who already supplied furniture to the French subsidiary. When the Italians pulled out, three of Kremer's own designers were assigned full time, from the beginning of 1981, to work on an ambitious new design modelled on Continental patterns. To protect themselves from remaining scepticism they had to work in considerable secrecy and behind locked doors. They finally presented fifteen prototypes to the main board as something of a *fait accompli*. Despite the haste, the range was ready for launch in October 1981, representing an investment of £1 million.

Castle

At Castle, too, the systems venture brought dissension. For Alderton, and later Baxter, the ambitious Fortress range was to be the essential instrument of a marketing-led revival. Borrowing the conceptual apparatus of the Boston Consulting Group – that favourite tool of the marketeer – Alderton condemned the basic metal storage business as a 'dog'. The Boston Consulting Group model demanded that new investment should now be channelled towards a potential 'star' – and that was Fortress. According to one manager: 'It needed courage, but there was really no other way we could go – except out.' There was a further advantage in entering systems. An entirely new range, more sophisticated than any that the dealers were used to handling, would give Castle an excuse for returning to direct sales: 'So it was a way of getting Castle back into the arena . . . It is the direct selling that is the sort of crux of the whole thing.'

However, the Fortress project was soon embroiled in controversy. Desperate to secure volumes, Alderton began to consider selling the range through the dealers as well as direct – thereby, as Baxter in particular argued, compromising the original purpose of the whole venture. Moreover, the Fortress team was disappointed by the lack of funding – not enough for a West End showroom, not enough for proper sales literature – and by production delays which meant that only prototypes were available for the 1982 launch.

These problems were exacerbated by tensions between the brash and youthful newcomers associated with Fortress and the traditional, older Castle managers, especially those on the works side down at the South site. One of the South site managers observed: 'There is a them and us between manufacturing and sales. They tend to be fairly highly strung people. I don't know what it is about systems sales people, but they tend to be very emotional!' Besides, the product was complicated and the factory was already under considerable pressure to reduce costs on the core conventional storage products. It was hardly surprising that production was not very amenable to the early petty and specialist demands of systems furniture. One manager put it thus:

> Its very difficult, you see, when you've come to a position when the industry's run down, when you've cut right back, cut right to the bone in order to continue making tin boxes. Then you start something rash, radical. It was a change of temperament . . . You've been bashing out cabinets by the hundreds and then somebody comes along and says 'I want twenty of these and ten of those.' You know who's going to get the products!

It would not be the Fortress team who got their deliveries on time.

As shown in the preceding section, Fortress did not begin to fulfil its potential as a 'star' until 1985–6 – indeed, it was the poor old 'dog' of conventional storage that had restored Castle's fortunes. But the analysis had been ill-founded from the start. The Boston Consulting Group would have advised against relying on just one new product and would certainly have rejected entry into a market already dominated by three well-established systems manufacturers, one of whom held 34 per cent of the UK market (cf. Johnson and Scholes, 1984: pp. 343–6). The expensive systems venture was still more rash because of the financial predicament of Castle: 'You're talking about going for a Rolls Royce [i.e. Fortress] at a time when, you know, you're having difficulty in trying to survive as a company.' Indeed, bizarrely, Castle and the Group were in a position where they could not have afforded the cash demands of any substantial orders for Fortress: 'I mean, if we had got an order for £1/2 million worth, what were we going to do at a time when we were strapped for cash? We could have been in a position where we would have had to turn them [the customer] down because we couldn't have afforded to make it!'

Yet, however unconvincing the economic reasoning behind Fortress, the new range did succeed in fulfilling one objective that certainly was crucial, even if perhaps only vaguely perceived at the start. As observed in Chapter 9, by the beginning of the 1980s, most of the 'hardcore' Castle managers had written the company off. With Fortress, however, Alderton was able to provide at least a few managers with some hope for the future. The Fortress venture – colourful, innovative, expensive and ambitious – represented a wholesale repudiation of the old cautious, metal bashing spirit of traditional storage products. Systems furniture promised to release the company from the constant grind of cost competition and the desperate striving for production volume.

While the Fortress product gave hope for the future, the infusion of young staff also provided a model for a new management style. This new style was epitomized in the widely used slogan of 'professionalism'. Though precise definitions were few, the word generally affirmed the final triumph of the sales and marketing ethos. One manager confessed that 'professionalism' meant 'a great many things, but at the end of the day, it is showing the guy, the customer, that what you will say will happen will happen.' Another put it simply thus: it is 'being professional, knowing the product you're selling, integrity'. Some defined 'professionalism' by contrast with the past: 'it is significant because it [professional] is what we haven't been for too long. We haven't dotted the i's and crossed the t's very well. Being professional is doing just that.' Although the title of 'professionalism' was now being claimed throughout the company, with just one or two pockets of scepticism, all recognized that the new ethos had originated with the Fortress range and its enthusiasts. 'I think we're discovering that we're more professional than we thought we were. The Fortress team had brought in a new kind of spur, because its a more professional kind of selling. It brought professionals with it, that it [the company] didn't have before.' Thus, Fortress brought back a sense of pride to Castle. However, now quality was based on a new sense of managerial professionalism, instead of on the company's' traditional metal-bashing skill. In the words of one manager, by 1985 Castle was 'an old company which has found a new niche . . . It sort of rediscovered itself, rediscovered its identity.'

It is this new ethos which provides the chief, retrospective rationale for Castle's entry into systems. First Simpson and then Alderton had been brought in from outside on account of marketing skills that were largely irrelevant to the company's traditional role of bashing out volume metal storage as cheaply as possible. Clearly their commission was to affect radical change – otherwise they were redundant. The necessary change was of a dual nature: on the one hand, to take the company out of the treadmill of price competition, on the other, to revitalize Castle's decaying management. The Fortress project could serve both purposes. Of course, as time went on and Castle's position began to deteriorate once more in the early 1980s, Fortress gained still more significance, both because it validated the continuing presence of Alderton and his marketeers and because it provided a welcome distraction from the uncongenial tasks of rationalization.

Barton

Barton was in a much better position to afford a systems venture than either Kremer's or Castle. Importantly, the company already had an established reputation at the top end of both its seating and desking markets. Moreover, systems furniture might represent the logical extension of the company's policy of competing by increased sophistication rather than by price. Besides, David Barton had a well known fascination with, and skill in, the design problems that systems would raise. Yet Barton deliberately abstained.

There were several reasons for this abstention. To start with, the company's manufacturing capacity was already having to be steadily expanded to meet the increasing demand for its core seating products. So long as it refrained from entering head-on competition, Barton could continue to sell seating to complement the ranges of existing systems manufacturers. Further, going into systems might require the company to sell direct, which, besides the problems of creating a new sales force dealing with a different sort of customer, would also risk antagonizing Barton's cherished dealers.

Above all, entry into systems would offend the company's fundamental principles of autonomy and security. Instead of keeping to markets where it was relatively strong, systems furniture would take Barton into direct competition with large, dominant multinationals. To compete would require both heavy investment, perhaps forcing the company to break its unwritten law against borrowing, and an innovative design that would not just mimic the products of the well-established giants. The reasoning was summed up thus:

> For us, being a relatively small private company, it would take us into head-on conflict with the really large companies . . . who've got vast international resources behind them. And I think frankly it would be fairly risky . . . To compete with them one would have to offer something completely different. That then introduces an element of risk because it [the product] might not be acceptable. One may have a winner, a fantastic winner; or one might have a complete flop.

Given Barton's disposition towards steady growth, even a 'fantastic winner' might not be entirely welcome; but, as another manager put it, a 'flop' on systems could be fatal to the company:

> Even these big companies get their fingers burnt and have to pull out within two or three years – and they've lost two or three million, or something like that. That is a disastrous policy and we might have to close the business through some erroneous jump into some obscure market.

For none of these three companies, therefore, is the decision whether or not to enter systems furniture easily explicable by simple economic criteria. The companies for which it was least economically rational included the two who plunged most wholeheartedly into the new market, while the company that could probably best afford the risk abstained. However, Barton's abstention was consistent with its top management's long-held and undisputed commitment to safeguarding its independence. At Castle and Kremer's, on the other hand, entry into systems was a matter for greater dispute, both overt and covert. For Bernie Kremer, entry into systems was vital to sustain the company's person a as a dynamic leader within the industry, yet in the end only the exertion of his ultimate authority as chairman could secure the decision to go ahead. At Castle, the controversy surrounding systems derived from the revolution in management that it entailed and which, finally, was probably its most valuable achievement. The inspiration for Fortress was an ambitious and self-consciously modern marketing orientation which was being superimposed upon the old Castle values. In all three cases, therefore, the response to systems reflected the particular objectives of dominant or invading groups within the companies' managements: for Barton, it was a reflection of its commitment to sturdy family independence; for Kremer's, it was adherence to the old 'expansion dream'; and for Castle, it was the triumph of reform.

CONCLUSION

As with the domestic appliance companies, this chapter has again portrayed strategy-making in recession as potentially the outcome of deliberate and discretionary actions of powerful individuals and groups. Except perhaps in the case of Shilton, a company struggling for its very survival, recession strategies were not determined simply by environments or crudely conceived managerial action-selection mechanisms. At Barton, Castle, Fenwood and Kremer's, environments and managerial characteristics had been the subjects of self-conscious development by actors seeking to enlarge their scope for autonomous action.

Barton's policy in the years leading up to the recession exemplifies the ways in which agents may work to enhance the breadth of strategic discretion available to them. The two brothers had deliberately led the company out of the unstable and highly competitive domestic furniture market in order to establish it in the relatively secure niches of office seating and executive desking. They cultivated close relationships with a wide network of dealers, minimizing their dependence upon any one customer. They avoided taking on debt and retained 100 per cent ownership. As Barton grew, the brothers developed a small, cohesive management team, but nevertheless remained closely involved in the everyday affairs of the business. Together they pursued a policy of steady growth in which profits were not simply maximized for their own sake, but were regarded as vital for the continued preservation of Barton's long-term independence as a family company.

In all these ways, the Barton brothers minimized the risk of any challenge to their control over the company's strategic direction, even during the crisis of the recession. Thus in 1979–81, Barton was able to persist in its established strategy, needing neither to discount in order to chase turnover nor to innovate recklessly in search of new markets. Even if systems might have offered the possibility of faster and more profitable growth, David and Michael Barton chose not to take the risk.

Chapter Eleven

Strategic choice or determinism?

INTRODUCTION

The central concern of this book, the one with which it began, is a fairly fierce controversy over the validity of determinism (in its various forms) and the grounds for an adequate account of strategic choice. After the empirical interlude of the last four chapters, it is time now to return to the theoretical fray. The first task of this chapter, then, is to assess how well the various deterministic approaches introduced in Chapter 2 account for my eight case study firms' strategic conduct during the early 1980s. Concluding that they do rather badly, I shall continue by proposing an alternative strategic choice account based on the Realist position developed particularly by Roy Bhaskar.

Essential to the Realist position is that genuine strategic choice is the prerogative of agents – that is, people capable both of formulating their own goals and realizing them in deliberate action. Action Theory and the Carnegie School fail to provide an adequate account of strategic choice because, as I argued in Chapter 3, their actors do not satisfy these two criteria for agency. What these earlier approaches to strategic choice lack is sufficient recognition of social structure as the essential precondition for human agency. Chapter 4 introduced the Realist conception of structures as providing both the resources necessary to action and the rules that guide it. However, while structures are fundamental to any sort of social activity, they do not determine its precise form. In a complex society such as ours, social structures not only conflict with each other but are burdened with internal contradictions of their own. It is this plural and contradictory nature of social structures that releases actors from any unique structural determination and renders agency possible. Complex and relatively autonomous, actors are able to avail themselves of a wide range of rules and resources, and from them to construct ends and means for action that are personal to them alone. I went on to propose that the capitalist enterprise, by virtue of its powerful and undemocratic nature, represents a particulary potent vehicle for the pursuit of personal objectives. Thus the strategies of corporations need not reflect strict obedience to the determinate logics of profit-maximization; rather, they may be chosen according to the wills of the agents who have captured them for their own private purposes.

It will be this Realist approach that provides the framework for the bulk of the chapter. Accordingly, the third section proceeds at once to identifying the actors controlling strategic decision-making in each firm. It continues first by tracing the social roots of their powers – particularly in capitalist and patriarchal structures – and then by demonstrating how these dominant actors consolidated and extended their initial positions by weaving local ideologies supporting their personal interests. The fourth section examines the links between these local ideologies and the actual strategies each firm adopted in recession and recovery. Here I shall stress how, even in the extreme conditions of recession, key decisions were motivated less by profit-maximization than by the particular objectives of each firm's dominant actors, as embodied in their local ideologies. Having already traced the social structural roots of these dominant actors' powers, I shall conclude this section by investigating the social origins of the objectives informing their strategic choices. For three dominant actors in particular, I shall show how these objectives derived at least in part from their ethnic backgrounds. Thus both the powers and objectives necessary for these dominant actors' agency originated in diverse social structures. The final part of this chapter admits certain internal and external constraints on strategic choice, but rather than reifying them into intransigent trammels, it will show how dominant actors can act deliberately to manipulate and mitigate them.

DISCOMFORTING DETERMINISM

In this section I examine how well the various determinist positions introduced in Chapter 2 fare in explaining the corporate strategies of the eight case study firms. Taking environmentally determinist approaches first and action determinist approaches second, I shall argue that neither fare well. The determinist defence of aggregation will be addressed in Chapter 12.

Environmental determinism

Environmental determinists appeal to market disciplines to squeeze out the scope for strategic choice. Though natural selectionists and adaptationists might differ over the period of grace allowed for companies to fall into line, in the end they equally expect market mechanisms to select only the profit-maximizers for survival. The more rigorous the competitive environment, the less grace allowed.

Recalling the evidence of Chapter 6, the markets in which the eight case study firms operated were certainly rigorous. The UK domestic appliance companies were struggling against imports whose penetration had risen from 22 per cent in 1973, to 28 per cent in 1979 and then to 35 per cent in 1982. At the same time, margins were under pressure from the newly emergent multiple and discount retailers, whose buying power was exerted towards low prices and the erosion of manufacturers' own brands. Combined with all this, the recession depressed UK manufacturers' output by over 20 per cent in real terms between 1979 and 1982 (see Table 6.4 on p. 135). The environment for the office furniture manufacturers was no less tough. Highly fragmented, with no manufacturer claiming an overall share of more than 10 per cent, and plagued by a periphery of cheap 'railway arch' assemblers, the office furniture companies had now to contend with the invasion of multinational companies armed with the totally new concept of systems furniture. The recession saw more than 20 per cent knocked off the desking market between 1979 and 1982, and nearly 50 per cent taken from the storage market (see Tables 6.6 and 6.7 on pp. 140 and 141). In both the domestic appliance and office furniture industries, even the best performing case study companies – Homecraft, Exemplar, Barton and Fenwood – had their profits significantly dented. Yet, for all the ferocity of their environments, most of the case study firms demonstrated considerable capacity for strategic choice.

The three leading UK domestic appliance manufacturers – direct competitors in several sectors and potential competitors in the remainder – adopted quite different strategies in response to the common challenge of recession. Rose concentrated on cost-cutting and rationalization; Homecraft cautiously squeezed still more out of its main plant and protected its precious relationship with the Electricity Boards; Exemplar provoked the wrath of the multiples in its opposition to discounting and recklessly proceeded with capacity expansion. Even in a vital area of direct competition such as cookers, the two chief rivals took opposite courses: Homecraft abstained from manufacturing microwaves, while Rose plunged in; Homecraft quickly followed the Continental fashion for slip-in cookers, while Rose lagged. The office furniture industry was marked by similar strategic diversity. Fenwood cut capacity, Barton expanded. In the rapidly expanding systems sector, Castle and Kremers both aimed at the top end, but the former planned to sell direct while the latter initially relied on dealers; Fenwood and Shilton went for the lower end of the market; and Barton kept out altogether.

It is by no means clear that these diverse strategies represented just different means to the same end of maximum profit. Indeed, the range of performances generally widened during the recession. Amongst the seven monitored firms in the domestic appliance industry (including the four firm comparison group), the difference in returns on capital employed between the best and worst firms was 60.9 per cent in 1979, but 92.2 per cent in 1981 (see Appendix 1 on p. 300). For the three domestic appliance case firms in particular, returns on capital in 1982, the worst year, ranged from 39.6 per cent for Homecraft to a negative 2.3 per cent for Rose Electrical. Amongst the office furniture case companies, the range for returns on capital in the same year went from Barton's 28.9 per cent to Castle's negative 8.9 per cent (see Appendix 2 on p. 301). For these five furniture firms, differences in profit margins widened from 10.1 per cent in 1979 to 25.4 per cent in 1981. The middling performers from among the case study group were comfortably surpassed by competitors from the comparison groups and even good short-term performers such as Barton and Fenwood did not seem to maximize profits over the medium term, being overtaken by two of their comparison firms. Though of all the case study firms Homecraft probably came consistently closest to profit-maximizing, in 1984 its parent company AEL turned down its profit forecast, clearly expecting more.

Despite this diversity in strategy and performance, the environment proved surprisingly tolerant. None of the three independent companies – Barton, Fenwood and Kremer's – suffered either bankruptcy or takeover. Certainly, Kremer's endured the intervention of the banks, but its management team survived unscathed. Only one of the subsidiary companies' parents actually got taken over – Castle's GEH, in 1985, four years after the trough of the recession. Of these subsidiaries, moreover, only Shilton suffered wholesale enforced management change, and there even the decisive James Turk retained two members of the old regime as directors. At Castle, Alderton's departure in 1982 had been voluntary, if welcome, and his replacement, the long-serving Baxter, hardly represented a radical departure from the past. Simpson, a casualty in GEH's 'boardroom court martial', was the only manager with responsibility for Castle's lacklustre performance to suffer forcible removal. As for Baxter, he survived GEH's takeover, finally taking his long-delayed retirement at the end of 1986. Rose, the other over-traditional company, was slightly more complicated. Chairman Bowden took his retirement when due in 1983, and his confreres, Carstairs and Field, each survived the subsequent reorganization as divisional chiefs until they, too, retired two years later. Below this level, however, the second rank of 'Rose men' had been suffering as the infusion of young professional managers imposed new expectations and closed off avenues for promotion. The sale of Rose domestic appliances to a Continental manufacturer in 1987 was another severe blow to these men. Coming six or seven years after the recession, this sale hardly penalized the strategic decision-makers of the time, for they were all safely gone. It was the relatively junior managers left behind who were most threatened by the change of ownership. Ironically, the far more successful Homecraft suffered the same fate, being sold to Exemplar in 1987 as part of a major strategic redirection by its parent AEL. Tarling had retired two years before, but his former deputy was confirmed in place by Homecraft's new owners.

Thus, despite the ferocity of the environment, the case study firms and their top managements appeared able to pursue diverse strategies and achieve widely different performances with a large measure of impunity. Far from the environment selecting for survival only the best performers, all the firms and most of the responsible managers survived the recession little scathed. Indeed, I shall argue later that, rather than managers adapting to environments, the most common pattern was managers adapting environments to themselves.

Faced with such diversity, the sophisticated faithful of environmental determinism might here appeal to strategic group theory (Caves and Porter, 1977; Newman, 1978). Distinct strategic groups could probably be discerned in both the domestic appliance and office furniture industries, but the problem is selecting which groupings are significant. One way of defining strategic group memberships is on the basis of their products and the associated mobility barriers. Within domestic appliances, Rose and Homecraft were leading members of a strategic group that concentrated on cooking, while within office furniture, Fenwood, Kremer's and Shilton were all members of a wooden desking grouping. Rose was also an important manufacturer of refrigeration, associating it with Exemplar and other leading refrigeration manufacturers. Likewise, the three desking manufacturers also joined Barton in a seating strategic group. Another approach would be to differentiate between companies that were independent and those that were not and then to categorize the subsidiary companies according to the mobility barriers arising from their parent company activities. Exemplar, Rose and Homecraft were all subsidiaries of large engineering conglomerates, but Rose at least could be differentiated on the basis of the vertical integration represented by its electrical goods retailing outlets.

The above by no means exhausts the possible bases for defining various strategic groups, but it does demonstrate one of the chief weaknesses of this sort of approach. With potentially so many ways of defining them, all overlapping, exclusive strategic groups tend towards just one or two members (cf. Bourgeois, 1984, p. 589). Analysis necessarily collapses into detailed case by case examination and the identification of relevant strategic groupings becomes rather more *post hoc* than· consistent with some of the predictive powers claimed for these models.

There are further problems. As Hatten and Hatten (1987) confess, strategic group theorists tend to confer upon their groupings a misleading degree of concreteness. For these case study firms in particular, the bases for the various groups were certainly too insubstantial to differentiate the strategies of these firms in any significant way. Both the domestic appliance and office furniture industries were highly 'contestable' markets (Baumol, Panzar and Willig, 1982), in the sense that entry and exit barriers both for the industries as wholes and for most of their products were generally low (if difficult to quantify). In domestic appliances, the success of the Continental importers had demonstrated the ease of entry into the UK market; while the vigorous fringe of peripheral small producers and the steam-rolling of the American systems manufacturers showed the vulnerability of the UK office furniture manufacturers to both up-market and down-market invasions. Exit barriers were more variable, but it did not prove impossible for Exemplar to exit from cooking and small appliances or for Shilton to dispose of its domestic furniture activities. In the domestic appliance industry, mobility barriers between sectors were surmountable by licensing (for example, by Rose of microwaves) or factoring (for instance, by Homecraft of micro-waves, or Exemplar of refrigeration), while the office furniture companies seemed capable of maintaining diverse ranges of products, either developed organically or, as in the case of Fenwood, by cheap acquisition of small specialist producers.

Not only were the bases for groupings rather insubstantial but, in the absence of severe market disciplines, decision-makers appeared free to appraise them more or less as they liked, according to their particular subjective values or cognitions. In practice, firms varied widely in their evaluation of mobility barriers. For the 'marketeering' but hard-up

Castle, the entry barriers into systems furniture appeared low, while for cautious yet cash-rich Barton they seemed far too high. Indeed, coherent subjective biases throughout an organization seemed to impose a consistency in policy decisions even on activities belonging, objectively, to different strategic groups. Thus, for example, strategic group analysis provides little insight into the subjective reasons for Rose's similarly cheapskate policies on product development and marketing for both vertically integrated refrigeration (of which Rose's own retailing operations took a large proportion) and less integrated cooking (where the Gas and Electricity Boards were dominant).

So far, this discussion has examined possible strategic groupings only within divisions, not at the parent company level where potential interrelationships between divisions allegedly influence strategic decisions in determinate ways. However, just as Granick (1972) and Goold and Campbell (1987) found more generally, the five parent companies in this sample – GEH, Field, AEL, Rose Electronics and Entertainments and Universal – seemed remarkably reluctant to intervene in order to align divisional strategies in some globally optimal fashion. At Exemplar, Universal 'give the business a lot of license'; GEH was too 'slow on the draw' with Castle; and Bowden's position within Rose remained 'baronial'. The classic case is provided by Homecraft, where AEL was forced to accept the various divergent microwave activities of three separate divisions, retrospectively justifying diversity as the 'three brands strategy'. Even in the case of the 'straight-jacketed' Field Investments, Maurice Field did not interfere in the details of Shilton's strategy, satisfied to retain office furniture as ultimately his only manufacturing activity so long as it met his return on capital employed criteria.

Action determinism

Though the action determinists divide into two camps, the psychologistic determinists and the over-socializers, they still find plenty of room for agreement. They join in defining actors according to broad types – capitalists or managers – who are expected to behave in predictable ways. They agree in regarding the behaviour of capitalists as unproblematic: capitalists can be relied upon to maximize returns on their capital. About managers, however, they are less unanimous. The managerial economists give up profit-maximization altogether and, with a shrug of their shoulders, allow free rein to the managerial drive for self-aggrandizing growth. The over-socializers are less tolerant, engaging the whole might of society to teach managers due respect for capitalist interests. The principal-agent theorists adopt a cruder carrot and stick approach: if managers behave well, then they get a share of the profits, job security and career progression; if not, then they will be poor and out of work. Thus, all things together, the action determinists have constructed a formidable array of psychological and sociological disciplines. For the case study companies, however, these disciplines worked no better than environmental sanctions.

The dominant decision-makers in the case firms were, as we have seen, presented with more or less equivalent stimuli. Within each industry, the firms faced similar environmental conditions, often being direct competitors in the same product markets, and in both industries all were confronted by the same challenge of severe recession. Yet both types, capitalists and managers, failed to respond with any uniformity. Indeed, the capitalists were at least as ill-disciplined as the managers.

Three companies were directly owner controlled: Barton, Fenwood and Kremer's. Two others were rather more complicated cases with shareholders taking active parts in management — Jo Stone at Exemplar and Maurice Field, through his holding company, at Shilton. It is not clear, however, that any of these capitalists dedicated themselves wholeheartedly to profit-maximization. Bernie Kremer described his business motives with appealing frankness: 'Its a bit of an ego trip . . . Its not a question or money, because in the end you can't use the money you might get from it.' Indeed, in their reckless commitment to volume during the recession, Bernie and his management nearly plunged their company into bankruptcy. Nor was Jo Stone at Exemplar any more cautious in his strategic calculations: his investment at Damnar was agreed by his managers to be 'an act of faith'. Exemplar's managers certainly did not attribute profit motives to their major shareholder: 'He [Stone] was an industrialist at heart. He got his satisfaction, not needing to work for money, in wanting to create something for the future.' Perhaps Barton's and Fenwood's owner-managers came closer to profit-maximization, but it should be remembered that two of the four-firm comparison group managed to surpass their performances. Barton and Fenwood preferred to sacrifice profit rather than put their family firms at risk.

Managers were just as unpredictable. At Homecraft, far from conforming to the empire-building ideal, senior management actually appeared to fear growth. Thus one confessed his anxiety about any new strategic initiatives that 'will inevitably make a bigger more diffuse sort of structure that maybe will be much more difficult to capture with this kind of team spirit'. Contrast this with the confident capitalist Bernie Kremer: 'Growth is what we all want in business . . . Run a

small business? That wasn't me.' Note too that it was the risk-averse
family-owned Barton that eventually achieved the greatest growth of
all the case study companies.

Of course, Homecraft's team in fact managed to combine substantial
growth with excellent profits. However, these managerial paragons
were not clearly responding to the blandishments of principal-agent
theory (Raviv, 1985). None of these managers had any substantial
direct stake in the profitability of their company – the largest
directorial shareholding was worth less than £2,000. Promotion was
not an issue either; Tarling and his production and finance directors
were all within four or five years of retirement at the time of the
recession. AEL's vulnerability to takeover only became disturbing
after the worst of the recession was over. Managerial careerism
provided no more definite a spur elsewhere. At Castle, Baxter had had
to be dragged back from voluntary early retirement upon his
appointment in 1982. At Rose, Bowden had a personally significant
shareholding; but, though no doubt he might have claimed his policies
were the best for his divisions, in his loyalty to the 'old Rose' formula
he certainly did not demonstrate boundless flexibility in the search for
profit-maximization. As for career aspirations, Bowden and his
lieutenants must have recognized that, under the Donald regime, they
had gone as far as they possibly could in the company in which they
had spent most of their managerial careers. Anyway, by the early
1980s retirement was not far off for most of the senior 'Rose men'. Jo
Stone's profit-sharing scheme tied Exemplar managers more closely to
performance than either of their competitors'. However, though these
young managers certainly delivered much-improved profits, it is
doubtful how far they were motivated by profit-shares. Even in 1983,
Stone's last and best year, the bonus was worth only 90 hours, the
equivalent of 5 or 6 per cent of annual salary. Though Exemplar's
managers had enjoyed early promotions, Stone's domineering style
gave them little prospect of further advance. When Stone was replaced
by an outsider chief executive, they were content to stay on in their
existing positions.

The blunt instrumentalism of principal-agent theory appeared to
work most forcefully at Shilton. James Turk and his team were young
and ambitious. Maurice Field had set them an unambiguous target of
40 per cent return of funds. The fate of fellow subsidiaries and their
managements left no doubt what would happen to Turk and his
colleagues if they failed to deliver. When they did deliver, they were
duly rewarded with bonuses of 26 per cent on their basic salaries.

Thus these strategic decision-makers appear to show little conformity to psychologistic types. But socialization had been no more

successful in suppressing the differences between these individuals. Certainly, social pressures had failed to incorporate them into some homogeneous capitalist class or power elite, acting in conjunction to defend common interests. The semi-rural craft background of the Barton brothers, the East End beginnings of Bernie Kremer, the immigrant origins of Jo Stone or Ben Rose and the large English company style of Homecraft's managers were all radically different. Even the owner managers were each rules unto themselves. Bernie Kremer's strategy and ambitions could hardly have been more different from those of the cautious Barton brothers or Charles Fenwood. Bernie Kremer, Maurice Field and Jo Stone pursued growth with at least as much vigour as the managerial economists would expect of their managers, while Homecraft plodded on with careful regard to the preservation of profit and physical proximity. If there was any homogeneity, it was in the commitment to expansion shared by the Jewish entrepreneurs Ben Rose, Maurice Field, Jo Stone and Bernie Kremer. For these men, ethnic background united their business activities as much as economic status. Even so, these four entrepreneurs pursued expansion in very different ways.

To conclude, neither environmental nor action determinist positions appear capable of providing convincing accounts for the behaviour of all these case study firms. Even during the worst recession of the post-war period, competitor firms were able to defy natural selection by pursuing diverse strategies with unequal outcomes. This is not to say that their environments imposed no constraints; only, as I shall show later, that strategists were skilful in manipulating them. These actors certainly did not conform to the simple caricatures of action determinism either, with capitalist entrepreneurs such as Jo Stone and Bernie Kremer ignoring profit, while Homecraft's managers feared growth. Even the elaborate disciplines of principal-agent theory enjoyed only patchy application.

This catalogue of awkward cases will not suffice to refute determinism. Determinists still have left to them the 'saving grace' of aggregation (March, 1978). I shall consider this defence in Chapter 12, arguing that in a society dominated by a few large firms aggregation has dangerously little relevance. Meanwhile, I hope these cases are enough to discomfort determinism, if not to disprove it. Moreover, I shall try in the following sections to provide a more convincing account of the strategic decisions of these ill-disciplined actors.

THE POWER TO CHOOSE

In Chapters 4 and 5 I proposed that the capitalist enterprise, in the massive resources it organizes, offers its dominant actors powerful extensions to their personal agency. For these actors, domination enables them to apply their firms' resources in strategies dedicated to their own personal objectives. Strategic choices, therefore, need not be directed exclusively at profit-maximization; rather, they may express the idiosyncratic ambitions of the particular dominant actors within each firm. Clearly – as I argued in Chapter 6 – any explanation of these strategic choices relies upon an understanding of dominant actors' motives. But first there is the problem of who these dominant actors are.

Dominant actors

It was admitted in Chapter 6 that identifying dominant actors would not be simple. Remembering Dahl's (1961) warning, formal organizational charts cannot be relied upon to describe the true distribution of power. However, following Dahl (1961) himself, certain important decisions can provide significant tests of relative powers. Thus at Homecraft, the claimed supremacy of the 'incestuous' marketing and R & D sides was tested in the dispute over whether to introduce the second generation of storage heaters, however 'illogical from the production point of view, from service, from spares . . .'. Similarly, Bernie Kremer was finally able to push through the systems furniture decision against the instincts of most of his board, though only by force of his threatened demand for resignations. Jo Stone likewise demonstrated his supremacy both over his sceptical managers and over Bernstein by insisting on the 'marginal' Damnar investment. However, test cases such as these may not always exist, and frequently non-decisions are just as significant. Thus at Barton there were no abrasive conflicts by which to judge the relative distribution of power. While the two Barton brothers were reported never just to announce to their managers that 'its a managing directors' decision', but, rather, always to sit down and consult, it was nevertheless conceded that they could always get what they wanted. Likewise, the relative powers and objectives of Homecraft and AEL were never tested by a request for large-scale investment funds: 'It's not AEL's fault – its ours for not asking for it.'

The reputational approach recommended by Hunter (1953) provides some means of overcoming the danger that absence of conflicts reflects the 'mobilization of bias'. Although there were never any definitive overt disputes at Barton, their managers recognized that the Barton brothers '. . . make up their own mind and at the end of the day one had to go along with it'. Bernie Kremer was 'the Governor' and 'the captain of the ship'. Charles Fenwood was 'the beginning and end of everything'. Jo Stone was a 'dictator' or 'autocrat'. Crenson's (1971) comparative approach can sometimes illuminate the 'mobilization of bias' still further. Comparison of Homecraft's and Rose's actual strategies on microwaves and slip-ins suggests how the dominance of particular actors and ideologies shaped the nature of the debates. At Rose, the decision to manufacture microwaves was considered 'natural', while the slip-in was disdained as poor engineering. Homecraft's strategy was the opposite: the introduction of slip-ins was prompt and uncontroversial, but the manufacture of microwaves was not insisted upon. The origins of these diverse strategies can be traced back at Rose to the power of those actors clinging on to their manufacturing bias, while at Homecraft, the slip-in derived from the power of marketing and the procrastination on microwaves stemmed from the general preference for stability and unity. But the danger here is of an over-simple interpretation: reading off superior power straight from enacted strategies risks ignoring the complexities, compromizes and even accidents involved in the struggles that produced them.

Indeed, it is in the nature of agency that powerful actors will choose to deploy their powers differently from issue to issue, arena to arena (Hindess, 1982). Any single decision taken on its own will, therefore, be a most unreliable indicator of power. At Homecraft, marketing and R & D won over storage heaters but could not, or preferred not, to get their own way over microwaves. To have pressed for the microwave decision would have jeopardized the cosy 'inner team' of five directors (Tarling, plus marketing, R & D, finance and production) that had dominated the company since the early 1970s. In the same way, Bernie Kremer pushed through the systems decision but, despite persistently voicing reservations throughout the recession up to the crisis, ultimately did not force the issue of rising stock levels. To acknowledge these failures is not to admit that Homecraft's marketing department was less powerful in any absolute sense than production or finance, or that Bernie Kremer was less powerful than 'Danny's men'; rather, it is to recognize that all actors involved had some powers and that the outcome of any particular struggle was contingent upon the indeterminate actions of the participants.

Table 11.1   Dominant Actors and Pluralism

Case	Dominant actors	Divisions	Pluralism
Exemplar	Jo Stone	Engineers	Low
Homecraft	Tarling's 'inner team'	Marketing and R & D v production and finance	Low
Rose	Bowden and the 'Rose men'	Gas men v Electricals; North v South; production v marketing; 'Old Rose' v 'professionals'	High
Barton	David and Michael Barton	None apparent	Low
Castle	Alderton; then Baxter	'Old Guard' v 'marketeers'	High
Fenwood	Charles Fenwood	None apparent	Low
Kremer's	Bernie Kremer	'Danny's Men'	High
Shilton	None (1980–81) James Turk (post 1981)	'Politicians'	High

Clearly, the identification of dominant actors is not without difficulties, yet the various measures of power do seem to converge. To take one instance, Bernie Kremer emerges as the most powerful actor in his firm on account of his formal rank, according to his repute amongst his managers and on the evidence of critical decisions such as that regarding systems furniture. There are, then, sufficient grounds to attempt a tentative tabulation of the dominant actors within each company (see Table 11.1). However, Table 11.1 also recognizes that dominance was rarely complete, and that subordinate actors often had access to independent sources of power with which they were able to contest certain decisions. Unlike Bauer and Cohen's (1981) 'governing cliques', these dominant actors did not have absolute powers and had to take account of the powers and objectives of other actors within their firms.

Additionally, therefore, Table 11.1 tabulates some of the major divisions within each firm, where they were apparent, and differentiates them according to a crude bivariate scale of internal pluralism. Thus even Bernie Kremer's power was not exclusive: 'Danny's Men' had a more or less autonomous power base in their mastery over production, responsibility for which Bernie had long ago delegated to his brother. Theirs especially was the philosophy of 'setting the pattern for production and we're just going to make', the success of which had provided the foundations for their whole careers from East End working class to Home Counties managers. Although 'on the wane' as they approached retirement and after their dramatic failure during the recession, they still remained able to give the Kremer family plenty of 'stick'. Rose was notoriously riven between production and marketing, Gas and Electricals, North site and 'down south', the 'Rose men' and the new professionals. Even at Exemplar, a sceptical level of lower-ranking engineering managers survived the purges of Jo Stone: 'it was all quite reasonably organized at one level below the actual interface with Stone.' Nevertheless, Stone was able to override their concerns repeatedly and with great confidence.

Structural sources of power

A glance at Table 11.1 will confirm that powers were not conferred upon particular functions or departments according to the dictates of environmental contingency. Homecraft's managers were wrong to suppose that 'all manufacturers in the appliance industry are marketing-orientated'. Their chief rival, Rose, quite clearly was not, and yet the environment tolerated its deviancy for a very long time. Where there was any correspondence between environmental contingencies and functional strengths, the direction of causality remains in doubt. As Pfeffer (1981) observed, environments may be chosen in the first place by the very people whose powers are supposed to derive from them. Thus David Barton chose a niche strategy that fitted very well with his skills as a designer. Likewise, the complex and cramped nature of Homecraft's main plant demanded that 'whoever became boss of this operation . . . needed to have a fairly good understanding of production'; and production expert Tarling had not embarked on the sort of green-field investment which might have made things simpler. Anyway, few of the significant divisions in these companies were based simply upon functional or departmental differences. At Castle, for instance, the 'marketeers' were not distrusted for their marketing focus so much as their wholesale repudiation of Castle's proud but decayed traditions. Nor, incidentally, did functional backgrounds very accurately predict strategic conduct, as Miles and Snow (1978) might have expected them to. Homecraft's Tarling, a former production manager, presided over a company that described itself as 'market led', while at Exemplar the inspired marketer Jo Stone insisted upon production expansion and innovation against the advice of his engineers.

Following Bhaskar (1986) and Giddens (1984), Chapters 4 and 5 argued that power over strategic direction is not determined by environmental contingencies in this narrow sense but rather by access to, and appropriation of, social structural rules and resources. Social structures provide certain actors with resources not only in the material sense but also in the sense of legitimate authority based either on intrinsic competences (for example, managerial skills) or other extrinsic facilities (such as ideological support). However, within a society such as our own, structures possess a complexity that offers actors a plurality of power resources. Thus capitalists need not rely soley on the wealth and rights of capital, but may draw upon other sources of legitimacy to reinforce and extend the scope of their agency. Agents' power bases are built by skilful pluralism.

It should not have escaped notice that none of these dominant actors were property-less, unskilled labourers. Chapter 5 demonstrated the continuing importance of capitalist ownership rights in determining control over the resources embodied in the firm. However, it also pointed out that capitalist structures contained their own internal tensions. The ideological appeal of entrepreneurship both cements the legitimacy of the owner and justifies exuberant deviation from disciplined calculation. A managerial class has been created to support the consequences of capitalism's own success, but this class has, in time, itself developed an independent authority based on claims of professionalism and organicism. On top of all this, the independent patriarchal structures generated in the household inhibit capitalism by at once excluding some sections of the population from full participation in the labour market and, under the constraints of paternalism, precluding ruthless exploitation of other sections. The patriarchal model, moreover, celebrates a licentious eccentricity in economic conduct and enjoins upon retainers absolute obedience to the most irrational conduct.

Jo Stone, Charles Fenwood, Bernie Kremer and the Barton brothers all brought to their firms one crucial resource: ownership. In four of the eight case study companies – Barton, Fenwood, Kremer's and Exemplar – the senior management enjoyed substantial shareholdings. In two other companies – Rose and Shilton – the same had been true until very recently. However, the nature and the significance of ownership differed from case to case. At Barton, the two brothers had taken over responsibility for the company from their father when still very young, yet their inexperience did not disqualify them. Charles Fenwood likewise came to his company by inheritance. Kremer's was different in that Bernie Kremer had built up the company from scratch himself, but had gone public in 1971. Nevertheless, Bernie Kremer had been careful to retain a 15 per cent shareholding, the largest, while three other close members of the family together held a further 18 per cent (concentrated shareholdings of between 5 per cent and 20 per cent are usually deemed enough for effective control – Sawyer, 1985, pp. 165–79). Even during the crisis of 1982–3, Bernie Kremer could still count on a sympathetic hearing at the shareholders' Annual General Meeting.

Jo Stone's position at Exemplar was more complicated. Through his domination of Stone Furniture Industries, he effectively enjoyed control over 37.5 per cent of the joint company. His shareholding was clearly important for, as his managers put it, Bernstein could not easily get rid of him: of the three-legged stool, for every two legs Bernstein owned, Stone owned one. Ultimately, Bernstein had the superior shareholding, but Stone brought something more to the arrangement which gave him an effective counter-balance – his intrinsic competences as a manager. Stone had been recruited by Bernstein specifically for management abilities which he had known and respected for twenty years, and which he apparently could not find elsewhere. Thus Stone could supplement the powers drawn from the extrinsic facility of capital by the intrinsic competence of his managerial skill.

Even as a major shareholder, Jo Stone's intrinsic managerial skill was important for suppressing the dissent of his more professional managers. The story of how Stone had savagely demonstrated the incompetence of his marketing department was widely recalled. Just as the managerial economists warn, the translation from ownership to control is rarely a simple one. As one Exemplar manager recognized when recalling Jo Stone's initial predicament, managers can easily exploit their greater involvement and experience to usurp the positions of nominal superiors: 'He [Stone] found a large organization, with independent managers running off in all directions, quite confusing . . . He would not have been able to cope with that sort of situation.' This danger was appreciated even in the companies where ownership was most complete. The Barton brothers together enjoyed 100 per cent ownership yet deliberately eschewed 'ivory towers', emphasizing their physical proximity to the company's hub and still checking every piece of post. Charles Fenwood, with his 90 per cent shareholding, remained 'the beginning and end of everything' long after normal retirement age and coped with the geographical dispersion of his factories by regular visits and highly centralized purchasing and finance.

In fact, all these owner managers brought personal strengths to their firms. Under their existing leaderships, Barton, Fenwood and Kremer's had each enjoyed periods of remarkable growth and profitability. David Barton's skill in design and foresight in land purchase were admired by his managers as crucial to the current success of his company. The abilities of Bernie Kremer, Jo Stone and

Ben Rose were very concretely confirmed by the size of the businesses they had themselves created. For his managers, Ben Rose was 'somebody that had built up a very big business and made a lot of important decisions and was responsible for . . . employing 75,000 people . . . He was the proverbial rags to riches.'

Thus these owner managers did not rely simply on their property rights. They reinforced their authority by demonstrating intrinsic competences acknowledged as legitimate by their subordinates. For some of these actors, moreover, their competences were not just those of the mere managers they needed to impress. As the Rose men recognized by Sir Ben, several were men who had built up substantial businesses, often from scratch. Their success gave them access to a further source of authority denied to managerial employees engaged in the routine administration of established businesses. As the creators of the businesses they ran, Ben Rose, Bernie Kremer and Jo Stone also had access to the structural support of entrepreneurial ideologies. It was as an entrepreneur that Exemplar's managers most often characterized Jo Stone. For one, Stone was 'an entrepreneur, a self-made man'; for another, he was 'an entrepreneur of frankly outstanding ability'. Bernie Kremer likewise was the man who 'built the company'. Under Ben Rose too the style was 'entrepreneurial in the extreme'. Later 'the Rose men', proud of their 'seat-of-the-pants' style, would claim a sort of second-hand legitimacy by appealing to the memory of entrepreneurial Sir Ben and his intuitive lieutenant Jo Teal.

As at Rose, of course, these entrepreneurial claims often conflicted with the norms of professional managerial conduct. So far as Jo Stone was concerned, 'meticulous financial and market analysis were for the birds'; he did not want to be confined by rational calculation. His managers regarded building the new Damnar factory as 'an act of faith'. But building the factory was what Jo Stone wanted to do; as an entrepreneur, moreover, it was what his managers expected him to do. Exemplar's managers recognized this tension between their professionalism and Stone's entrepreneurial eccentricity. As one put it: 'I'm a professional manager, and he was an entrepreneurial manager of what I might call the untutored school.' At Rose, likewise, the entrepreneurial 'seat-of-the-pants' style had granted Ben Rose and his trusties considerable licence: 'there was a lot of by-passing of any formalities.' The 'Rose men' did not welcome the professional disciplines of the new Donald regime. Jim Donald's chilling introductory speech was remembered especially for its contrast between entrepreneurism and professionalism: 'You have been used to operating with an entrepreneur of high quality and a man of genius. I am a professional manager. My style, of necessity, is completely different to Sir Ben's. You've reached the end of an era.' Thus one of Donald's first actions had been to apply return on capital employed criteria specifically to deny the Rose men's instinct to fill under-utilized factories with product, however unprofitable.

Here Donald deliberately invoked professionalism as an alternative source of legitimacy to the entrepreneurial ideology that had formerly prevailed. In a similar way, professionalism was important for Exemplar's young managers, precisely because of their apparently complete subordination to the entrepreneurial Stone. In their self-conscious professionalism, they asserted a claim to promotion independent of the whims of Jo Stone: according to one, they were part of 'a very good second line team who were mainly better qualified than the previous bosses, better trained and more professional.' At Castle, too, the new reformers established their legitimacy by claiming a professionalism denied to the old regime which they were trying to supersede. Though there was little agreement about what the slogan meant positively, it did seem to involve a repudiation of the past: 'it is significant because it [professional] is what we haven't been for too long. We haven't dotted the i's and crossed the t's very well. Being professional is doing just that.'

Professionalism was not merely an empty ideological slogan. Just as owners required demonstrable success to reinforce their entre-preneurial claims, so too had managers to substantiate their 'pro-fessional' legitimacy by displaying at least some intrinsic competences. Within the managerially operated companies – Castle, Homecraft, and, latterly, Shilton and Rose – professional skills had been essential to the ascendancy of the present managements. At Homecraft, Tarling's original promotion from production director to managing director had been based on his success in reforming the old main plant after the Venus cooker disaster. His deputy managing director had likewise begun his career within Homecraft with the re-establishment of the company's marketing position in the mid–1960s. At Rose, Bowden had demonstrated great competence in building up from scratch what was to become the core of the electrical appliance division, the main North site. Even though their competence was to come under question later, the 'Rose men' had certainly coped at least adequately with the rapid growth of the 1950s and 1960s. At Shilton, Turk had been recruited carefully from outside on the basis of his experience as production director of another furniture company. Baxter might have appeared something of a last resort at Castle, but before his appointment he had demonstrated a dogged loyalty to the company and had gained experience in the crucial functions of sales, production and design. Importantly, he also held the trust of the old

Castle managers, even while showing himself committed to innovation.

But there remained a self-perpetuating aspect to these career successes. The managerial skills rewarded by promotion and power were not always those objectively demanded by the capitalist principle of profit-maximization. Rose's managers were linked by a dense network of protégé relationships and united around skills based upon volume manufacture of standard products. Having reached supremacy on this basis, the 'Rose men' were unwilling to recognize the different sorts of competences possessed by the MBA qualified newcomers. True 'Rose men' regarded the new techniques as so much 'management jargon', resenting in particular the disciplines of return on capital employed. The conservatism of Homecraft's managers, on the other hand, was founded not on resistance to managerialism but on a clever appropriation of its organicist ideology. The five senior managers (Tarling and his marketing, production, R & D and financial directors) formed an inner 'team' whose 'balance' should be protected from any change in membership or additional stress from new strategic initiatives:

> By and large, the balance between these four [marketing, production, R & D and financial directors] has been well maintained on this site. It all hinges in the end, of course, on personalities. I mean, never mind the policy, what actually happens is to do with who the people are. And generally the balance has been well held on this site . . . It is a balanced team in that sense.

As happened to the dismissed sales director, 'if someone is clearly out of phase with everybody, then we get rid of them quickly'. In short, those already at the top of the organizational hierarchy have considerable scope for defining appropriate managerial competences, and they are not likely to admit that their own skills are redundant.

So far, I have shown how just one set of structures, capitalist structures, can afford very diverse powers. Owners have quite clear property rights, but they supplement this resource by drawing upon entrepreneurial and managerial competences and the additional legitimacy with which these endow them. However, their subordinates too have managerial skills, which generate claims and expectations of their own. For some of the owner-managers in these case studies, managerialism threatened to constrain their right to dispose of their capital as they willed. These actors overcame the constricting elements of managerialism by appealing to another set of structures altogether.

Though the self-consciously professional managers at Exemplar often wondered at Jo Stone's unreasonable decisions, they generally deferred. For these young managers, Stone possessed a patriarchal authority which they dared not challenge. On average, they were twenty-four years younger than Jo Stone: five of them were still in their twenties on first appointment and one was actually his son. To them, his regime represented a 'benevolent paternalism . . . He was the man in charge . . . He was the father figure.' As one admitted, Stone's autocratic ways would have been far less acceptable to him if he had been 44 years old at the time. Sir Ben Rose, 77 years old on his retirement, enjoyed a similar patriarchal authority over the men who had built their careers under him:

> You can have many husbands, but you can only have one father; you can have many chairmen and managing directors of a company, but you can only have one founder. And you have this almost unique sort of ability when you are the boss. It is your idea, you have created it. You become very much the *father* of not only the company . . . but also you are the father of all the people in it. And his [Ben Rose's] was a very strong paternal attitude . . . He regarded everybody as sort of children. 'They are very good lads', he would say, 'They are marvellous lads'. But you were never more than a lad.

The employment relationship between Sir Ben and the 'Rose men' was far from the rational economistic ideal of principal-agent theory. Sir Ben refused to sack managers who had been with him for a long time, even though 'that attitude cost the company a bit of money', while the 'Rose men' themselves were 'not working for salaries'. Long after Sir Ben's retirement, loyalty to this patriarchal ideal would continue to bind the 'Rose men' to each other and to their traditional 'seat-of-the-pants' ways.

Not all dominant agents had access to this kind of patriarchal authority. Though society afforded the young Barton brothers power as capitalists, it denied them patriarchal authority over their managers within the enterprise. Indeed, even for those actors with access to patriarchal resources, there is no deterministic logic impelling them to take advantage. Charles Fenwood, though reaching a quite venerable age, preferred to surround himself with middle-aged managers and a not very much younger brother who would be little impressed by patriarchal claims. At Kremer's, household logics actually confined the authority of Bernie Kremer. Amongst 'Danny's men', especially, the idea that 'Kremer's is a family' gave its members a right to express vehement, though never irreconcileable, dissent: 'We fight like brothers and sisters. That's how we fight.' Thus patriarchal structures both needed to be actively asserted in order to be effective and could be engaged in very different ways.

Dominant actors and local ideologies

It was not just patriarchal powers that had to be actively asserted. Though social structures offered these dominant actors a range of resources – capital, practical skills and diverse kinds of legitimacy – this access required skilful exploitation within the firm. Structures are only made manifest in action; they remain latent until people activate them. For access to material and authoritative resources to be translated into practical support, these dominant actors had to work. As I suggested in Chapter 5, they could consolidate and extend their original powers by weaving, from the various structural sources of legitimacy they had available, unique local ideologies. Able to exploit their initial control over organizational structures as owners or managers, these dominant actors constructed these local ideologies by carefully cultivating, in the terms of Mintzberg's (1983) typology, both evoked and selected identification.

Procedures for gaining identification by control of selection were employed nearly universally. At Barton, the two brothers had been careful to recruit managers who were 'on the same wave length' – even to the extent of recruiting as their production manager someone who had himself previously run his own small furniture business. At Rose, recruitment and promotion were through a network of old boy and protégé relationships, with little interference from formal personnel procedures. When Tarling first joined Homecraft, he brought with him his old production manager; this man eventually succeeded him as production director. Managers could, of course, be dismissed. Homecraft's sales director was got rid of during the recession because he was 'out of phase'; while at Shilton the newly arrived Turk immediately purged the old management of all the 'politicians' whom he felt were not, in his terms, working *for* the company. However, Jo Stone of Exemplar provides the starkest example of deliberate manipulation of the mechanisms of formal authority in order to secure control.

As his managers recalled, Stone arrived at Exemplar in 1974 to find a large bureaucracy populated with many senior and alien managers. His position was the more vulnerable because he had no experience in domestic appliances; because he lacked the skill and aptitude for 'professional' management; and because his time was divided between Exemplar and his old furniture business. As mentioned already, he immediately asserted his authority and claim to relevant expertise by his famous exposure and wholesale elimination of the marketing department. He subsequently never appointed a marketing director.

Stone then devastated the engineers by preferring Italian factored refrigerators to Exemplar's own. The old senior management was displaced by his own son and other trusties from his old company. He ruthlessly cut back on administrative staff and disposed of activities, such as cookers and small appliances, which showed themselves to be beyond his limits. Most important, perhaps, was the gradual cultivation of a new team of young managers which, for all the protestations to the contrary, did come to represent something of a hand-picked 'Praetorian Guard': it was well recognized that 'Number Twos promoted are very loyal'. Even for these managers, however, the sanction of dismissal remained explicit – 'You could see your P45 sliding over the desk on many occasions' – and the (old regime) R & D director was to be forced out as late as 1977 over policy differences.

Methods of evoked identification were important too. Socialization would take place through long experience of mutual co-operation. Once established, Exemplar's new management enjoyed ten or twelve years of continuous working together – 'we've knocked all our rough edges off each other long ago'. Longevity was also important at Rose and Homecraft: at the Rose North site, they 'had been chasing the same girls over the same roof tops' for thirty years; while Homecraft was managed by a team that had 'grown old together'. Intimacy was reinforced by physical proximity: Homecraft's managers repeatedly stressed the importance of all being on the same site and of sharing their working lunches. Relationships between Kremer's managers, many of whom had been working with each other since the 1950s, were also strengthened by hard work at close quarters: 'we are all in the same building and worked very closely together . . . We all worked long hours . . . and go on late at night. Very close'.

Thus dominant actors' original control over organizational structures merely provided a base for extending ideological control. By manipulating recruitment and promotion procedures and by enforcing intensive socialization procedures, Stone, the 'Rose men', the Barton brothers and Tarling's 'inner team' at Homecraft acted to ensure that only those sharing their beliefs and priorities would arrive at any position of discretionary or possibly threatening power. The frequent references to 'balance' at Homecraft, the widespread loyalty to the 'Rose way' at Rose, and the appeals to 'professionalism' at Castle, demonstrate the ideological strength and cohesion that could be achieved. Of course, as Starbuck (1982) warns, complete ideological hegemony or harmony could not always be achieved – at Kremer's, for example, the long years of comradeship amongst 'Danny's men' created a distinct sub-ideology within the Kremer's 'family' as a whole. But particularly at Exemplar, Homecraft and Barton, dominant actors had ensured as far as possible that all significant actors were incorporated within local ideologies binding them to their own interests. Jo Stone, Tarling's 'inner team' and the Barton brothers could select strategies according to their own private interests confident that their subordinates would carry them out loyally and effectively.

STRATEGIC CHOICES

Dominant actors do not construct local ideologies merely to establish power for power's sake. For dominant actors, control over the firm's resources amplifies their capacity to achieve personal objectives. Local ideologies, therefore, also serve both to embody those personal objectives attainable through control over the firm's resources and to legitimate the means by which they are pursued. Thus local ideologies are closely linked with strategic choices. Recalling Chapter 5, they define the goals towards which dominant and subordinate actors alike should direct themselves; they shape the ways in which strategic opportunities and threats are perceived and pursued; and they establish the boundaries for legitimate action. This section begins by examining the linkages between the case study firms' local ideologies and their strategic choices. However, it is central to my argument that dominant actors do not simply pluck the objectives and procedures governing their conduct from thin air. This section will go on, therefore, to examine the social origins of some of the behaviours enshrined by dominant actors in their particular local ideologies.

Local ideologies and strategic choices

Table 11.2 provides a brief summary of the linkages between local ideologies and the strategic choices of each firm during the recession. I shall elaborate these linkages in the following pages, identifying the main objectives informing strategy choice in each case and stressing their considerable independence from the imperatives of profit-maximization.

For Jo Stone the prime objective was not profit except in so far as it would forestall the intervention of Bernstein and contribute to his investment strategy. Stone was devoted to fulfilling his vision of creating a successful British manufacturing company capable of beating

Table 11.2   Ideologies and Strategies

Case	Ideologies	Related Strategies
Exemplar	Patriotic production; marketing; 'people'	New Damnar plant; pre-paint
Homecraft	'Balance'; 'team'; 'market-led'	Delay microwave; prompt slip-in
Rose	'Old Rose' manufacturing; 'seat-of-the-pants'; dominate UK markets	Microwave manufacture; 1983 re-organization; delay slip-in
Barton	Independence; low risk	No systems range
Castle	Marketeering; 'professionalism'	Fortress systems
Kremer's	'Expansion dream'; 'let's keep making, boys'	Over-production; systems (disputed)
Fenwood	Independence; low risk	Sacrifice volumes; cautions on system
Shilton	(a) 1979–81: 'Reactor'; (b) 1981–84: Profit	'Shit-on'; rebuild production volumes; cautious on systems.

the Italians by high quality production. This would be achieved with modern factories, contented workforces and scrupulous marketing. As one of his managers summed it up: 'His real interest was in production, the British economy and the people who worked for Exemplar.' Stone's hand-picked managers identified strongly with this patriotic vision – still getting 'a little emotional' about the Italians and convinced that the importers could only be beaten by 'the customer coming first'.

This coherent ideology clearly informed Exemplar's policies on, for instance, the cultivation of the import-resistant independent retailers, the building of the small box plant and, especially, the investment in the Damnar factory with its pre-paint technology. The Damnar factory was built at a time of chronic over-capacity, but completed an investment programme that had been justified to Bernstein with patriotic rhetoric. As it turned out, the plant did give Exemplar the quality and the volumes with which to pre-empt the usual rush of imports during economic recovery. However, the timing and the strength of the domestic appliance market's recovery, fuelled by a sudden drop in interest rates and the expansion of hire purchase, could hardly have been anticipated. The high profits Exemplar gained from Damnar were more accidental than the result of deliberate calculation.

At Homecraft, by contrast, caution prevailed. Profits were always important as they both propped up AEL and made sure that it kept out of Homecraft's business. However, top management were also strongly attached to stability, as reflected in repeated appeals to the notion of 'balance' and their frequent use of the 'team' metaphor. The commitment to balance was manifested on the one hand by their continued investment in storage heating, even during the collapse of the 1970s; on the other, by their long reluctance to begin manufacturing microwave ovens. The 'three-legged stool' had to be maintained intact: the addition of an extra leg was superfluous, while the subtraction of another would cause the rest to come tumbling down. The need to preserve the intimacy of the 'team' reinforced this caution. It was far better to remain all together on the cramped Midlands site than to expand 'like mad' on new green-field sites. Exemplar, not cash-rich Homecraft, would build the new factories. Opportunities for maximum profits were not relentlessly searched for; by 1983–4, profits were beginning to sag and Exemplar was overtaking. At the same time, AEL rejected its first profits forecast, pressing Homecraft for more investment projects.

At Rose, the old 'Rose men', still clinging on to senior positions, remained loyal to the ideology inculcated by Sir Ben Rose and Jo Teal during the years of glorious expansion in the 1950s and 1960s. Sir Ben had inspired them with his entrepreneurial style and his patriotic commitment to the volume manufacture of simple products in defence of home markets. The 'culture' was still 'hands-on, seat-of-the-pants . . . entrepreneurial in a manufacturing sense.' The precise calculations of profit embodied in the initials of R.O.C.E. were resented and perhaps despised.

Thus the decision to manufacture microwave was described as 'natural' and justified, long after his departure, by reference to what Sir Ben would have done. Sophisticated marketing priorities were overridden with the despecification of refrigerators and the long delay over the launch of a slip-in cooker. In 1983 integration of the major electrical and gas appliances divisions was motivated by the potential for manufacturing economies of scale, with scant regard for the offence caused to their major customers, the Gas and Electricity Boards. Despite the antagonisms between the 'Gas Men' and the 'Electricals', despite the encroachment by younger, more professional, managers, despite the self-conscious attempts to impose new values through the 'Walking-Talking' weekends and increased management training, the 'Old Rose' ideology continued to dominate strategy at least up until the retirement of Bowden in 1983. The financial results, the worst of the three domestic appliance companies, suggest that this strategy and the objectives it represented were far from profit-maximizing.

By contrast with Rose's production bias, Castle's top management was dedicated to 'marketeering'. The paradigmatic decision for the marketeers was the launch of the extravagant Fortress systems range. The range both reflected the marketeer's enthusiasms and, as pressures for retrenchment mounted, gave them a raison d'être. Although rationalized by appeal to all the paraphernalia of the Boston Consulting Group, from the outset the Fortress strategy was hard to justify. Strapped for cash, Castle was unable to afford either proper sales literature for the new range or the working capital to meet any of the large orders that were essential if the range was to reach its profit forecasts. The Fortress venture did not start to break-even until 1984–5. The unintended consequence of the strategy, however, was a new sense of 'professionalism' that by 1984 was beginning to enthuse even the old, cynical Castle managers.

Kremer's was fuelled by an 'expansion dream' that had inspired the flotation in 1971, the investment in large factories and the diversification around the world. The basis for expansion was the pursuit of ever-greater production economies of scale: 'production used to set the pace for everything.' It was the old formula of 'let's keep making, boys' that drove them into over-production during the recession and the consequent reckless borrowing from the banks and reliance upon Johnson's the wholesalers. Here there was little careful calculation of maximum profit; decisions were made according to 'who shouts the loudest'. The disputes over how to respond to systems furniture arose because systems exposed a contradiction in the local dominant ideology. In the past, expansion could always be achieved by volume production of standard products; but the growth opportunities offered by systems were only attainable through adoption of batch production of highly complex products. In the end, Bernie Kremer's dedication to growth prevailed over 'Danny's Men's' suspicion of the new and complex.

Barton and Fenwood both had very similar ideologies, stemming from the desire of their family managements to safeguard their independence. The companies carefully avoided any dependence upon banks, powerful customers or outside shareholders. David Barton 'controls his own destiny'; while at Fenwood, 'we like to have complete control of what we do'. The best guarantee of continued independence was to continue generating adequate profits in order to escape any need to borrow; for Barton, 'that will be the danger signal'. Both companies steadfastly maintained their sales margins throughout the recession, Fenwood accepting the consequent severe fall in turnover with equanimity. However, profits were not to be maximized if they would entail any risk. Thus Fenwood treated systems furniture as an 'evolution' and took comfort in the fact that its range still represented only 15 per cent of turnover by 1984. Barton abstained from systems altogether, fearing to break its rule against competing head-on with the majors. Thus, although both companies, especially Barton, enjoyed most respectable profit performances, two companies from the industry four-firm comparison group managed to outstrip them.

Between 1979 and 1981, Shilton was guided by no coherent ideology. The firm's chaotic strategy corresponded most nearly to that of the Reactor (Miles and Snow, 1978). Disrupted by the sudden departures of first the Shilton brothers and then Bernard Gold, the company simply drifted into dependence upon just one wholesaler and its reputation as 'Shit-on'. James Turk was hardly in a position to create a distinctive ideology, either. He had not recruited his other two senior directors; he operated under very tight financial controls; managerial discipline was still further encouraged by a profit-based incentive scheme. To survive and prove themselves, Turk and his team had little option but to adopt a calculated identification (at the least) with the profit requirements of their Chairman, Maurice Field. There was no room for the pursuit of other personal objectives through the strategies of their company.

Apart from Shilton, however, all the companies possessed distinctive ideologies that, each in their own way, either subordinated or reinterpreted the need to make profits in order to leave scope for the pursuit of other objectives. But the linkages between ideologies and strategies are complex and multiple. Evaluative, cognitive and legitimatory influences (Shrivastava, 1985) are, in practice, hard to disentangle. Certainly, the objectives embodied in ideologies had influenced the evaluation of strategic options – thus Stone's dedication to UK production led him to build Damnar, while Bernie Kremer's commitment to growth inclined him towards systems furniture. However, these evaluative influences were shadowed by appropriate cognitive biases; the different objectives of Bernie Kremer and Charles Fenwood seem to have contributed to their different perceptions of the potential of systems furniture, one seeing systems as bound to dominate the market, the other dismissing it as an 'evolution'. Of course, evaluative and cognitive influences are closely interwoven with legitimatory functions. Rose's disastrous cooker strategy was adopted in part because the Rose engineers could not see the marketing appeal of the slip-in cooker, disdaining its technically retrograde design. But there was also a sense perhaps in which the Rose managers *would* not see the attraction of the slip-in, for to do so would have been an admission that the production values and skills upon which the 'Old Rose' had been built were now redundant. Likewise, at Castle, the condemnation of the old metal-bashing cabinet business as a 'dog' by Alderton's marketeers, and the promotion of Fortress as the so-called 'star', may not so much have been mistaken as provided a (half) conscious justification for their regime. To have abandoned the Fortress project would have been to throw away the grounds for their original appointment.

Social being and strategic choice

With the exception of Shilton, perhaps, these case study firms enjoyed considerable freedom to pursue recession strategies consistent with the local ideologies established by their dominant actors. However, the objectives and procedures embodied in these ideologies were not immaculately conceived. Far from being the atoms of psychologistic determinism, the dominant actors who constructed these ideologies were complex social beings. As capitalists, managers, Jews or patriarchs, their structural positions gave them access to diverse codes of conduct, from which they could synthesize purposes and patterns of their own.

Recalling Bhaskar (1986) and Giddens (1984), social structures enable action in a dual sense. They empower actors with the material and authoritative resources necessary to agency – for the dominant actors I have described here, these resources were drawn primarily from capitalist and patriarchal structures. However, these structures also· provide the rules, stable sets of principles and procedures, that inform this agency. Thus Jo Stone and the 'Rose men' did not simply exploit entrepreneurial ideology to legitimate their actions; the entrepreneurial ideal provided a model for their 'seat-of-the-pants' managerial styles. At the other extreme, application of 'Boston box' techniques by the so-called 'professional' managers at Castle almost automatically generated the decision to move out of the 'mature' metal storage business, even if their concentration upon Fortress systems furniture was less obviously indicated. Again, for Jo Stone and Ben Rose appeal to patriarchal structures was not simply a cynical exercise in legitimation. They recognized that the 'paternalistic dialectic' (Newby, 1975) also imposed upon them certain duties towards their subordinates. Accordingly, Jo Stone 'seemed to have an almost God-given responsibility to look after the hourly-paid', and this was one basis for his various paternalistic initiatives before the recession and the protection of the direct labour force during it. The loyalty of the Rose men to Sir Ben was built upon a similar paternalistic reciprocity: he would 'virtually never sack anybody.'

I have already remarked on the common ethnicity of several of these dominant actors. Jo Stone, Ben Rose and Bernie Kremer shared a Jewish culture from which they were able to draw both procedures for action and the principles that inspired it. Bernie Kremer, his brother Danny ('a furniture man') and, indeed, the Shilton brothers were all characteristic products of the East End Jewish community that had traditionally generated so many furniture businesses (Aris, 1970). Jo Stone and Ben Rose, on the other hand, were both Austro-German émigrés. Ben Rose's arrival in England preceded Hitler, but Jo Stone – fleeing Austria in 1938 and carrying with him a qualification in architecture which he was unable to apply professionally in his new country – certainly was typical of the generation of innovative post-war entrepreneurs that Berghahn (1984) identified. In singling out these Jewish businessmen I do not wish to suggest that the English ethnicity of, for example, Homecraft's managers was unimportant. However, for all their differences, Jo Stone, Ben Rose and Bernie Kremer shared a Jewish culture that was sufficiently strong and homogeneous to endow them with common patterns of conduct that stand out starkly against a predominantly English background.

In his attitude to work Jo Stone corresponded closely to the Jewish stereotype established by Kosmin (1979). Unable to practise his profession and a penniless refugee, Stone could only recover his social position by tireless work at his own business. More than four decades later, his managers still remarked on his dedication: 'He certainly gave his all to the two companies . . . He didn't seem to have any other interests in life.' Jo Stone's optimism also exemplified the typical Jewish faith that 'it will come right' (Kosmin, 1979). According to his managers, Stone 'only wanted to hear the good news . . . He did not want to hear bad news because it disturbed him emotionally.' The reckless self-confidence of Bernie Kremer's Jewish management team reflected an equally optimistic outlook on life: during the recession the team simply applied its formula 'let's keep making boys! . . . No problem.' Kremer's epitomized the Jewish communal spirit, too: 'We have extremely good relationships among the senior managers, and down to the foreman level . . . Its all Christian [sic] names here. Everyone says his piece, without being rude. They might shout, but nobody walks around with a chip on his shoulder.' Though most were gentiles, managers at Rose and Exemplar enjoyed – or endured – extremely direct relationships with Jo Stone and Ben Rose too. As one Exemplar manager recalled, though putting it down partly to his patriarchal style, Stone 'had quite personal relationships with people. They weren't the impersonal relationships you get in some businesses. And his likes and dislikes would show when he was talking to the person.' Indeed, even if there were few formalities, Jo Stone would display all the autocratic characteristics that Aris (1970) ascribed to his Jewish businessmen. At Exemplar, 'It could be bloody stormy . . . But you either agreed to differ and go off and do it his [Stone's] way or you agreed to differ and got out. It was as simple as that!' Sir Ben was remembered to be much the same.

Their Jewish social identities did not just affect the ways in which these men did business; it also informed their objectives. For Jo Stone and Bernie Kremer, business success offered a route to social standing that a gentile society might otherwise deny them. For Bernie Kremer, East End working class, going public was: 'Bit of an ambition, I suppose; it's an ego trip . . . It's a bit of pride – that you've arrived. Its an ambition. . . It's just a question that you've made a success of things.' Bernie Kremer pursued growth with all his reckless enthusiasm in order to prove his worth both to himself and to society. The 'psychological milestone' of £1 million profits was not exceeded just for the sake of his shareholders, but precisely because it was a 'psychological milestone'. Likewise for émigré Jo Stone: 'He wanted . . . penetration, volume as opposed to making Rolls Royces at low volume and making a nice big profit. He wanted to be the biggest and the best.'

Despite this desire for recognition, Stone's motives for growth were not merely selfish. He seemed to show the same gratitude to the United Kingdom that Berghahn (1984) found in many of her Austro-German refugees. As expressed in his patriotic appeal for Bernstein's support over the new refrigeration factory, Stone was dedicated to rebuilding British manufacturing strength. Ben Rose's commitment to manufacturing growth within the United Kingdom alone reflected this same loyalty to his adopted country. One of his managers echoed Berghahn's (1984) own characterization of this generation of Austro-German refugees when he recalled Sir Ben's motives:

> Like a lot of people who are not British but who come to Britain and then become more British than the British, his whole concentration was on the United Kingdom . . . He saw himself as very much a man who wished to grow within the United Kingdom.

His efforts on behalf of the British economy were, of course, rewarded with a knighthood.

The rules derived from their common Jewish identities were not imposed upon these men in any standard, immutable way. Each interpreted them personally. Jo Stone was a far more sophisticated marketeer than Ben Rose and his acolytes; Bernie Kremer was recognized as different from his brother, Danny, 'the old Jewish type of Governor'. Yet the objectives they constructed and the strategies by which they chose to pursue them did remain deeply rooted in their social experience. Though these actors were complex beings, subject to no singular structural determination, their actions were still drenched in social values. Their strategies might have been idiosyncratic but they were not independent of social structure.

CONSTRAINT AND CHANGE

So far this chapter has stressed the extent to which dominant actors in most of the eight firms enjoyed considerable freedom with which to impose strategies consonant with their particular objectives. I do not, however, wish to slide into that blissful ignorance of constraint characteristic of certain brands of Action Theory. The dominant actors of these case studies were constrained first by their particular access to social structural rules and resources and then by their skill in manipulating them. Thus, for example, the young Barton brothers could exert capitalist powers over their managers but not patriarchal ones. And in concentrating on dominant actors within these firms, I have, of course, marginalized those less powerful actors whose structural disadvantages surround them with constraints on every side. Here, however, I wish to re-examine those capitalist constraints imposed through market systems of interaction. Operating within a fundamentally capitalist economy, dominant actors have to generate sufficient resources in their product markets to obtain and retain the materials, capital and labour that together make up their enterprises. Failure to do so risks, internally, falling morale or rising dissent; externally, intervention by shareholders, unpaid suppliers or anxious lenders. I shall begin by examining how financial performance contributed to internal security in these companies. I shall then go on to consider how dominant actors deliberately overcame or manipulated external market constraints.

Internal pluralism and performance

Summing up the findings from their study of managerial 'excellence' (so-called) , Peters and Waterman (1982, p. 75) famously asserted that '. . .the dominance and coherence of culture proved to be an essential quality of the excellent companies'. Peters and Waterman's contention

Table 11.3   Pluralism and Performance

Case	Pluralism[1]	Financial performance[2]
Exemplar	Low	Strong
Homecraft	Low	Strong
Rose	High	Weak
Barton	Low	Strong
Castle	High	Weak
Fenwood	Low	Strong
Kremer's	High	Weak
Shilton	High	Weak

1 Based on Table 11.1 (See p. 256)
2 Based on Figures 8.4 and 10.3 (see p. 185 and 231)

that 'strong cultures' contribute to high performance would seem to be supported by Table 11.3, which relates the case study firms' degrees of pluralism to their relative performances (dichotomized for the sake of simplicity) over the recession and recovery. The best performers in both industries were all characterized by low degrees of pluralism. On the face of it, these relationships could plausibly be explained by Peters and Waterman's (1982) claim. It might reasonably be expected also that a crisis such as recession particularly demands the decisiveness of action made possible by the dominance of particular actors and the cohesion of their ideologies (cf. Slatter, 1984). But, as Green (1987a, p. 9) notes, the direction of causality is not necessarily one way. Poor economic performance saps the strength of dominant actors both by reducing the resources under their control (especially the potential for promotion), and by undermining the credibility of their ideologies (cf. Dahrendorf, 1959, p. 46–7). Thus the emergence of dissent in Rose, Castle and Kremer's may not so much have caused declining performance as reflected it.

To take one instance: the embittered 'Old Rose' managers, whose careers had been built upon the thousand-fold growth since the early 1950s, now saw their prospects foreclosed by the relegation of domestic appliances to the status of mere 'cash cow'. Conversely, the dominating positions of Jo Stone at Exemplar, the 'team' at Homecraft, the brothers at Barton and Charles at Fenwood derived in good part from performances whose success ensured the security and reward of subordinates, the pre-emption of outside interference and the continuous legitimation of their control. As one of his managers said of the eccentric and dictatorial Jo Stone: 'But . . . he succeeded. Who are we to damn?'

Thus legitimacy rests not simply on the ideal but also on material performance. Dominant actors are constrained in their strategies by the extent to which they yield economic performances that satisfy the expectations of their followers. Failure to meet such expectations may prompt the sort of managerial haemorrhage – Hirschman's (1970) exit – that attended Alderton's regime at Castle. Conceivably, it could provoke 'bureaucratic insurgency' or organizational *'coups d'état'* (Zald and Berger, 1978). However, though Bernie Kremer perhaps came nearest with the showdown over systems furniture, in fact none of the case study firms experienced overt rebellions of this kind. On the other hand, failure to satisfy economic constraints did sometimes bring radical change imposed from outside.

Markets and change

Of course, a minimum level of profitability is not only important to maintaining internal authority. Firms must generate some surplus merely to reproduce themselves, let alone to achieve any of the more ambitious objectives their controllers may seek. As demand falls during recession, however, it becomes more and more difficult for firms to earn their required surpluses in product markets. For the firm previously able to divert a part of its efforts to idiosyncratic objectives, an increasing proportion of resources has now to be diverted exclusively towards profit just in order to survive. Hence, as Pettigrew (1985, p. 429) noted of ICI, organizational and strategic change frequently follow recessions.

Yet somehow many of the case study firms managed to avoid change, displaying the same sort of resilience that characterized Boswell's (1983) steel firms during the Great Depression. As Boswell (1983, p. 111) explains, the ability of even the worst of his steel firms to resist change was contingent upon their immunity, under family control, to capital market disciplines. Pettigrew's ICI, by contrast, was not family controlled and, moreover, was losing its formerly privileged position in its product markets. Thus, the robustness of dominant actors' capacity for strategic choice and their security from change depends in large part upon their position in their markets. It will be the economically weak who will have to defer most to the market pressures for profit-maximization during recession.

Amongst the case study firms, therefore, the firms best able to pursue their idiosyncratic strategies consistently and without external intervention were those which enjoyed relatively strong positions in their product markets. However, these positions were not 'given', but deliberately developed. As argued in Chapter 5, market interactions are potentially the subject of choice and manipulation. For the successful case companies, markets did not represent some abstract generality, but very concrete and particular corporate or individual actors. Of course, these market actors were not asocial atoms – they too were bearers of structural powers and followers of structural rules – yet for these companies' managers they remained quite definite figures who could either be dealt with or kept away from.

Within the domestic appliance industry, Exemplar and Homecraft both provide good examples. Rather than accepting the retail structure as immutable, Stone at Exemplar deliberately transformed it by carefully building up the loyalty of the independent retailers and discouraging price competition with his ingenious 'margin support' scheme. In a similar way, Homecraft cherished the Electricity and Gas Boards by constant product improvement, at the same time as establishing its own countervailing power as market leader. Rose, on the other hand, had disastrously played into the hands of the multiple and discount retailers by failing to establish a unified and strong brand image and repeatedly sacrificing quality and product differentiation for the sake of cheap volume production. Accordingly, Rose was to be much the most buffetted by the storms of recession.

Within the office furniture industry, the predicament of Rose was repeated in the cases of Castle and Shilton. Castle had abandoned direct sales in the late 1970s, thereby, as was recognized only later, throwing away its control over the market place. As the company plunged deeper into crisis in the early 1980s, Alderton weakened Castle's long-term position still further by price-cutting and so-called 'value analysis'. Shilton had never had a direct sales force, but it too sacrificed its position in the market place by abandoning quality and reliability ('Shit-on'), and by falling into over-dependence on just one wholesaler, Taylor's. Kremer's similarly relied too heavily upon a few customers – the large domestic furniture retailer and two office furniture wholesalers. The loss of the domestic furniture contract at the end of 1980 was therefore a major blow, one which put the Company on the slippery slope that ended finally with the disastrous collapse of Johnson's, its second largest office furniture customer, two years later. The policies of Barton and Fenwood had been very different, however. Fenwood tended to avoid big contracts and carefully maintained a wide range of products, while Barton had deliberately created for itself protected niches in high quality seating and desking and steadfastly maintained its rule of not allowing any single customer to take more than about 5 per cent of turnover. The two brothers deliberately abstained from entering the systems market where Barton would have had to engage with powerful large-scale contractors and international competitors.

Positions in product markets were closely related to the case study

Table 11.4   *Position in Product Markets and Financial Performance*

Case	Product market position[1]	Financial performance[2]
Exemplar	Strong	Strong
Homecraft	Strong	Strong
Rose	Weak	Weak
Barton	Strong	Strong
Castle	Weak	Weak
Fenwood	Strong	Strong
Kremer's	Weak	Weak
Shilton	Weak	Weak

1 Based on preceding discussion.
2 Based on Figures 8.4 and 10.3 on pp. 185 and 231

companies' financial performances. Summarizing the foregoing discussion and returning to the performance data of Chapters 8 and 10, Table 11.4 demonstrates this relationship. Exemplar, Homecraft, Barton and Fenwood, each of which had taken care to develop strong product market positions, also all produced consistently good returns on capital employed throughout the recession and recovery (see also, Figures 8.4 and 10.3 on pp. 185 and 231). But, as was stressed earlier, even these companies had not set out to profit maximize. In the domestic appliance industry, Homecraft eschewed opportunities that involved risk, rapid expansion or heavy investment, while Exemplar's good fortune was to a considerable degree the accidental result of Jo Stone's 'marginal' Damnar plant. As for Barton and Fenwood, they secured steady profits, but both were outperformed by two of the companies included in the office furniture four-firm comparison group. The implication is that Exemplar, Homecraft, Barton and Fenwood deliberately developed strong product market positions only in order to generate *sufficient* funds to allow them to pursue their other objectives (preservation of the 'team', patriotic production or the maintenance of independence) in security.

This ability to satisfice on profit could be enhanced as well by carefully cultivating positions in the markets for capital and corporate control. Strong positions in product markets set up a sort of virtuous circle in which easy profits release the firm from both reliance on the markets for finance and fear of the market for corporate control. Two companies in particular, Barton and Fenwood, exemplify this state of happy independence. The profits they had reaped from strong and stable product market positions had allowed them to build up substantial financial reserves by the time of the recession, so that neither company had any need to make borrowings of any sort. Likewise, neither company had gone public. Thus the two companies were quite unbeholden to any outside shareholders or sources of finance. Clearly this puritanism put them under some restraints – they could not have raised the finance for rapid expansion during the 1970s in the way that Kremer's had, for instance – but these were consciously chosen. The managements of both Barton and Fenwood preferred security and independence to rapid growth and risk. They were under no compulsion to pursue short-term profit-maximizing policies; in the word of one Fenwood manager, they didn't need to 'produce good news every six months'.

The majority of case study companies enjoyed far less financial autonomy. Castle, Shilton, Homecraft and Rose were all subsidiaries of ailing parent companies. As their share prices collapsed during the recession, all became increasingly vulnerable to takeover – indeed, Castle's parent, GEH, did finally succumb to takeover in 1985. Even without direct intervention, therefore, these managements were under very considerable pressure to maximize profitability in the short-term, and consequently to defer or demote any other private objectives of their own. Rose domestic appliances was relegated to the much-resented status of 'cash cow'. At Shilton, as one manager put it, they were 'under a lot of pressure, a lot of pressure – because . . . he [Bernard Field, the parent chief executive] was in a straight-jacket himself'. Tight borrowing limits, high return on capital targets, profit-related bonus schemes and the fate of other divisions within Field Investments all reinforced this pressure. Homecraft was able to protect itself for a long time from such parent company pressures on account of the steady profits generated by its strong product market positions; but even so, by 1984 the main board was prodding for better results as AEL came under takeover threat.

However, these constraints were neither absolute nor wholly oppressive. To some extent, Homecraft's managers were able to turn the position of AEL to their advantage, as Homecraft's almost uniquely profitable status within the group gave it a special standing and claim to autonomy. Indeed, the alleged dangers of 'wild flights of fancy' that 'failed to bring home the bacon' may well have been exaggerated in order to justify a caution that was instinctive to Homecraft's managers anyway. Certainly, AEL had never turned down any investment proposals and, by 1983–4 at least, actually appeared impatient for more. At Castle, the struggling GEH had neither the time nor the competence to challenge Alderton and Baxter's judgement that systems furniture was the only segment with a future. GEH's desperate gratitude for any straw that seemed to promise profit actually released Castle's managers from careful scrutiny. Further, just as for product markets, relationships with parent companies could be deliberately developed over the longer-

Table 11.5   Market Positions and Management Change

	Position in product market	Market for capital	Market for corporate control	Enforced management change?
Exemplar	Strong	Strong	Strong	No
Homecraft	Strong	Strong	Weak	No
Rose	Weak	Weak	Weak	Yes
Barton	Strong	Strong	Strong	No
Castle	Weak	Weak	Weak	Yes
Fenwood	Strong	Strong	Strong	No
Kremer's	Weak	Weak	Strong	No
Shilton	Weak	Weak	Weak	Yes

term in order to build better positions for the fulfilment of particular goals. Thus, Jo Stone did not rest upon his substantial shareholding and the special relationship with Bernstein of Universal; he strengthened his position by decisively returning Exemplar to profit and reducing its debts with a number of disposals. Likewise, after the crisis of 1983–4, Kremer's docilely submitted itself to the dictates of the accountants and the banks, but only the sooner to get rid of them.

Thus, economic constraints are real but need not be 'reified'. Actors are capable of manipulating and redefining the requirements imposed through the markets. The more skilful they are in building up their positions in their markets, the more impunity they enjoy against the kind of management ejection described by Bibault (1982) and James and Soref (1981) and the greater discretion they have for strategic choice. Table 11.5 summarizes the preceding discussion of the relative positions of the eight case study companies within product markets, the market for capital and the market for corporate control. Additionally, the table indicates whether or not the companies were able to resist the imposition of significant managerial change. It will be immediately obvious from Table 11.5 that all the managements of the companies strong in any of the three markets survived. The existing regimes at Barton, Fenwood and Exemplar owed their longevity to their deliberate cultivation of secure and privileged positions in all three markets.

By contrast, the three companies which failed to develop such positions and recorded weak positions across the board all suffered enforced change. Although the triumvirate of top 'Rose Men' survived until retirement, the ground was shifting beneath their feet with the influx of new professionals. Bowden's departure was the signal for a major change in strategic direction and staff. Stubbs, Bowden's appointee for the managing directorship of the newly formed Rose Major Appliances Division, left early in 1984, while the 'Committee of Five' at the Midland Gas site was demoted or replaced. At Castle, Simpson departed with the 'board room court martial', and Alderton soon followed. The scandal-ridden Shilton was something of an exceptional case, but Turk on his arrival was decisive in at once getting rid of nine of the old managers. The case of Kremer's, however, demonstrates that managers can even withstand the consequences of disastrous performances in both the capital and product markets so long as dominant shareholdings can preserve their immunity from the market for corporate control. On the other hand, Homecraft – burdened by the vulnerable AEL – shows that even a weak position in the market for corporate control could be mitigated by strong positions in product and financial markets. When Homecraft did finally change hands, this was long after the recession and part of a major strategic redirection by the now recovered AEL. Exemplar, its new owner, also promised a 'hands-off' management style.

CONCLUSIONS

For at least some of these firms, therefore, capitalist constraints exerted through the market did not impose themselves to the exclusion of strategic choice. Even within the harsh conditions of severe recession, rival firms competing in the same environments proved capable of adopting a range of strategies, each viable yet each associated with widely differing performances. Dominant actors were successful in manipulating the markets so as to gain just as many of the resources they required with as little sacrifice of personal objectives as possible. Moreover, these personal objectives possessed none of the crude simplicity alleged by action determinism, but were richly idiosyncratic, drawn from the diversity of their social experience. This same diversity was also important to the implementation of idio-syncratic objectives. Although they began from their structural positions within the capitalist enterprise, this starting point was neither unambiguous nor exhaustive. Occupation of plural social structural positions allowed actors both to reinterpret capitalist logics and to supplement them by appeal to quite independent, even contrary, structures. Exploitation and manipulation of not only capitalist but also patriarchal and ethnic structures allowed these men to convert their firms from the servile subjects of capital into the effective instruments of private agency.

Chapter Twelve

Concluding for strategic choice

INTRODUCTION

I began this book by contrasting the recession strategies of two
domestic appliance companies. In the words of their directors, Rose
had 'cut back heavily', while Exemplar had 'hung on'. This contrast
served to introduce the central issue of strategic choice, and it has been
argued in the preceding chapter the divergencies in the two companies'
strategies should be understood as shaped by the peculiar ideologies of
each company's dominant actors. But the contrast raised a number of
other issues which it will be the task of this concluding chapter to
address. In particular, the Section below will summarize the implications of these eight companies' performances for the management of
strategy and organizational change in recession. The following section
will conclude the book by reviewing the argument for a Realist
approach to strategic choice, and examining its implications for our
conceptions about how large enterprises act and are controlled in our
society.

STRATEGIES, PERFORMANCE AND CHANGE

In the first chapter I commented on the rather remarkable lack of
guidance on 'effective' recession strategies – effective, of course,
simply in terms of the doubtful criterion of profit-maximization. Such
advice as could be dredged from the literature was piecemeal and often
contradictory. Thus Penrose (1980), for instance, recommended
diversification in certain circumstances, while Clifford (1977) concluded against. Clifford's (1977) preaching in favour of pricing

discipline also conflicted with Eichner's (1976) suggestion that 'megacorps' will exploit recession by aggressively cutting prices in the hope of driving weaker companies to the wall. Even the product life-cycle's banal warnings against launching new products in recession (Standt, Taylor and Bowersox, 1976) found some contradiction in Kay's (1979) stress on the importance of preserving strong R & D. Unanimity was greatest on the importance of managerial and organizational change, here both Norburn's (1983) observations on recession strategies and the more general examination of crises in the 'turnaround' literature (Slatter, 1984; Kharbanda and Stallworthy, 1987) tended to converge.

As well as contradictions, Chapter 1 also identified some paradoxes. The fundamental strategic difficulty raised by the business cycle is the problem of adjusting resources in line with first rapidly declining, then rapidly rising demand. Failure to cut out surplus capacity during recession will impose unnecessary costs that might jeopardize immediate survival; on the other hand, lack of surplus capacity at the beginning of the upturn may inhibit the company from taking sufficient advantage of the recovery. This is no more than a particularly sharp instance of the enduring conflict between 'proximate' objectives and the 'long run', 'static' efficiency and 'dynamic' efficiency. But it was from this conflict that Silberston (1983) deduced two apparent paradoxes. First, the statically efficient firm at the onset of recession might actually prove dynamically inefficient, lacking the surplus financial resources to buffer it against the turmoils of the downturn. Second, the statically inefficient firm at the bottom of the downturn could prove dynamically efficient if still retaining sufficient surplus resources to quickly take advantage of the eventual recovery. These paradoxes had some disturbing implications. Would the recession penalize most severely those firms that had borrowed heavily to invest in extra capacity and new technology to take full advantage of the previous recovery, as Bowers, Deaton and Turk (1982) warned? Also, if firms became 'leaner' during the recession, would they be any 'fitter' to cope with the rush of imports that chronically accompanies cyclical recoveries in the UK?

These are intriguing and important questions, but the data here will permit no more than tentative comment. The case studies number only eight and are drawn from just two industries. As we have seen, both these industries were unusual cases in the severity of the recessions they experienced (note that Whittington, 1986, provides additional survey data on a further six industries). Even if they had been 'typical' industries, there would still be the problem that every recession is different – even the unprecedentedly fierce recessions of 1974–5 and

1979–81 differed markedly. The conditions described in this book will never be repeated. One more qualification should be borne in mind: because the research was carried out in 1984–5, by definition it only included recession survivors. All this said, given the lack of direct examination up to now, the evidence here does begin to fill what remains a significant, if tricky, gap in the strategy literature.

Of the domestic appliance companies, Chapters 8 identified Exemplar and Homecraft as good performers during both the recession and recovery, with Exemplar showing the greater relative gain. As for the office furniture case sample, Chapter 10 concluded that, though Fenwood produced steady profits in appalling conditions, Barton excelled in combining both high profitability with substantial growth. Rose, Castle, Kremer's and Shilton all suffered badly during the recession. These companies varied widely, however, during the upturn, with Shilton and Kremer's making strong recoveries, Castle beginning to get into better shape and Rose going from bad to worse. What do these differences suggest about effective recession strategies and to what extent do they corroborate the divergent advice offered by the economics and strategy literatures?

The two best performers, Barton and Exemplar, do share certain characteristics. Both the Barton brothers and Jo Stone abhorred price cutting. For Stone, 'discounting was a dirty word', and his ingenious margin support scheme was much disliked by the discount retailers. Barton had long been deliberately developing up-market niches to avoid price competition with 'railway arch' assembling operations. Though aggregate profit margins at both companies did slip a little during the recession, the strong line they had held at that time certainly persuaded their customers to accept exceptional margins during the recovery. Moreover, this high margin policy did not seem to exact a particularly severe penalty on turnover growth. Barton enjoyed the fastest growth of the five office furniture companies, though one of the comparison group did manage to overtake it. The story at Exemplar was more complicated, for it disposed of its small appliance subsidiary during the recession. However, in a rapidly growing market where most British manufacturers were on the retreat, the company did manage to increase its market shares fairly substantially for washing machines and incrementally for refrigerators. To a large extent, then, Exemplar can be exempted from responsibility for the rising import penetration within the domestic appliance market during the recovery. It was the cut-price Rose which suffered the most catastrophic losses of market share, especially in cooking and refrigeration.

There were other similarities between the two best performing companies. Barton was a company that resolutely developed its niche in quality seating and desking, while Exemplar too, with its divestments of cooking and small appliances, had tended increasingly to specialize. Moreover, both companies had supported their core activities by substantial investment in plant capacity – Barton doubling floorspace at its home site and Exemplar building the new Damnar factory. In Peters and Waterman's (1982) coinage, these two companies 'stuck to the knitting'. Even the recession did not blow them off course. For Exemplar, the recession was described as no more than a 'hiccough'; for Barton, there was nothing 'dramatically different'. This consolidation and development of core products paid off well. One manager recalled Exemplar's position during the recovery thus: 'For the first time in the history of the company, it was equipped to meet that recovery.' Barton's turnover grew by over 90 per cent between 1979 and 1985.

Less successful, however, were companies such as Rose, Castle and Kremer's which failed to 'stick to the knitting'. These companies did attempt significant innovations during the recession, either in microwave manufacture or systems furniture. The point is not necessarily that product innovation does not pay in itself – Rose's microwave venture was quite successful, especially with the government subsidy on its investment – but that it entails levels of risk and resource for the firm as a whole that these companies could not meet. Just as Peters and Waterman (1982, pp. 293–4) warn, diversification or innovative efforts tended to jeopardize 'cultural' cohesion by diluting values and straining consensus. At Kremer's, the 'family' spirit was torn by the disagreement between Bernie Kremer and his other directors over systems; at Castle, the new young 'professionals' associated with Fortress initially provoked the antipathy of the old Castle managers. Worse, innovation distracted attention away from other urgent problems. Kremer's quarrelled over systems furniture while its core business ran out of control. At Castle, Alderton's passion for the Fortress range became an excuse not to face the need for immediate rationalizations. These two companies also illustrated the importance of backing innovation with sufficient resources (cf. Georghiu *et al.*, 1986, pp. 19–20). The Fortress sales force lacked an adequate showroom, even sales literature, while Kremer's was slow to invest in a proper direct sales and design team. The short, sad histories of Castle's business services division, Kremer's new bedroom furniture venture and Shilton's experiment with shop and office fittings all confirm the dangers of half-hearted, ill-conceived diversification. As one of the Kremer's directors concluded: 'It's the old story of stay with what you're good at . . . ; concentrate on the products you know best and know what to do about.' Indeed, it was core products that eventually fuelled the recoveries of both Kremer's and Shilton.

But 'stick to the knitting' is a rather uninspiring slogan. Although Rose did innovate in some areas, the company also exemplifies the dangers of too narrow a concentration on rationalization. As one manager put it: 'Once you take management attention away from what it *should* be doing – development and marketing and running the business sort of *outwardly* – and once you've turned yourself in and looking *inside* the business, there is a sort of spiral.' Rose's management, damned as 'cash cows' and preoccupied with rationalization and reorganization, was too demoralized to respond convincingly to the revolution in their core cooker market represented by the new slip-in. Here Castle does provide one positive lesson. However misguided the Fortress range, it did have the effect of demonstrating a commitment to the future that helped restore morale to a company in which, at the beginning of the 1980s, many people had simply been calculating their redundancy money. Rose, which had lost the leadership of the inspirational Sir Ben and the dynamism of the 1960s, lacked sufficient vision to rekindle the enthusiasm of its older managers.

The discussion so far does seem to corroborate Clifford's (1977) warning against diversification and praise for pricing discipline. Rather that diverting surplus or unwanted resources to new activities, as Penrose (1980) suggested, the lesson of Exemplar indicates that it may be best just to get rid of them. Rose certainly failed to buy market share by discounting, while the stricter Exemplar and Barton actually improved their positions, at least by comparison with their UK competitors. Perhaps confirming the advice of the product life-cycle school, neither of these companies was innovative in terms of new products: Barton avoided systems and Jo Stone was particularly savage towards his design department during the recession. It should be said, however, that the domestic appliance and office furniture industries were both fairly low technology industries, and Kay's (1979) warning about the importance of maintaining R & D efforts might apply more closely elsewhere.

While this case evidence cannot finally resolve these various debates about effective recession strategies, it does provide some useful insights into the managerial and organizational changes widely recommended in the literature. The examples of Chambers and Harvey-Jones at ICI (Pettigrew, 1985, p. 448) and Edwardes at British Leyland (Edwardes, 1984), together with the statistical work of Helmich and Brown (1972), suggest that complete or relative outsiders are important to the implementation of radical change. This was also the gloomy conclusion of one of the 'Rose men': 'It's change that managers have to get used to. And one way you can achieve that change – I don't think it's the best way, but it is the easy way – is to change your managers . . . Get rid of the old order.' Certainly, the cases of James Turk at Shilton and Jo Stone at Exemplar indicate that companies do frequently prefer the 'the easy way' of changing their managers. However, further analysis of the case studies does suggest both that the ways in which management is changed can significantly alter the benefits realized and that, if well managed, the 'old order' can be persuaded to change itself.

The cases of Kremer's and Castle exemplify this second point. At both companies, strategic and ideological change may have been slow, but it was achieved ultimately by long-serving managers. By 1983, Baxter was the only director at Castle who had been with the company continuously since before 1976 – indeed, he had first joined the company 36 years before. Yet, in a way that Simpson, Alderton and all the other outsiders had failed to do, it was he who finally convinced the 'dyed-in-the-wool old soldiers' of the imperative need for radical change. By the 1984 Management Conference, even these old Castle managers were beginning to adopt the new slogan of 'professionalism'. Baxter had achieved this, at least in part, because he had the trust, and respected the traditions, of the Castle stalwarts. Thus the new strategy based on Fortress came to be perceived as representing a restoration of the company's former reputation for leadership and quality: 'It's an old company which has found a new niche . . . It sort of rediscovered itself, rediscovered its identity.'

The same was true of Kremer's. Bernie Kremer and the two other directors all retained their top management positions, despite their responsibility for the reckless strategies leading to the crisis of Christmas 1982. The only significant addition to the board of directors was the appointment of a sales director – but even he was a former Kremer's production manager who had re-joined the company after a brief stint elsewhere. Yet these men had learnt from their experience and were ready to implement change themselves. Even an archetypal 'Danny's man' could justify change by recalling the 1961 fire. Now there was a sales director; now discussion was 'reasonable'; now financial controls subordinated production; now if 'somebody came along and offered us gold bars for £1 each, we don't want to know'.

Thus the experience of Castle and Kremer's demonstrate that even insiders, however much originally committed to the ancient regime, can reform themselves. Here these cases conform to Hage's (1980) observation that dominant coalitions, though naturally conservative, will implement change when confronted by potentially fatal crisis: 'If they do perceive that they might lose all – that is, the organization might go under – then their resistance to a radical innovation . . . becomes transformed into willing acceptance' (Hage, 1980, pp. 230–1). This is not to say that relying on insider managers is necessarily the 'best' way of achieving change – after all, successive crises nearly destroyed these two companies before they finally acted – but only to insist that it is possible.

Moreover, the self-reforming efforts of Kremer's and Castle support the observation of both Green (1987b) and Whipp, Rosenfeld and Pettigrew (1987) that change can often be most effective if justified according to traditional values. Ideologies were changing in both companies. At Kremer's, the chaotic production bias of 'Danny's men' was being replaced by tighter organization and control; the proud traditionalism at Castle was being superseded by the new commitment to 'professionalism'. But it was noticeable that at least some of the managers were interpreting the new strategies in terms of the old ideologies: Castle had 'rediscovered its identity' while the reforms at Kremer's had evoked the same dedication as the 1961 fire. Thus in these two companies change was not accepted simply because there was no choice, but also because it was presented as consistent with older traditions. Rose, by contrast, had tried to impose entirely new and alien values, with considerable contempt for the old. Change was promoted through a sophisticated repertoire of training courses, 'Walking/Talking' weekends, a corporate values statement and the introduction of new managers and new structures. In 1985, it was evident that many of the 'Old Rose' managers still regarded the reform programme with distrust and cynicism. The financial results and final divestment certainly do not suggest that these changes were more effective than those introduced by incumbents at Castle and Kremer's.

The problem for the new Rose top managers, initially at Group level and later within domestic appliances itself, was that they had little access to the ideologies and legitimacy of the old Ben Rose regime. Even if they had wanted to, it would have been extremely difficult for them to have interpreted the changes in terms of Rose's traditional values. In these circumstances, an alternative approach might have been to make an immediate, whole-hearted purge of the old management and rely on the appointment of 'strategic replacements' (Gouldner, 1954, pp. 89–93). Certainly, this was the policy of Michael Edwardes in 1977 at British Leyland (Edwardes, 1984, p. 53), Jo Stone in 1974 at Exemplar and James Turk in 1981–2 at Shilton. At Exemplar and Shilton at least, the destruction of the old management and creation of the new provided the foundations for subsequent revival. Following Gouldner (1954), the imposition of strategic replacements achieves in a remarkably simple fashion both the elimination of old centres of resistance and resentment and the establishment of a cohesive, loyal and dedicated team. As for Exemplar's (disclaimed) 'Praetorian Guard', 'Number Twos promoted are obviously very loyal'. But, as again the contrast with Rose warns, the introduction of strategic replacements should be immediate. Here gradual strategies of 'logical incrementalism' (Quinn, 1980) risk lighting fires of resentment that will smoulder unquenched for far too long. Edwardes at British Leyland and Stone at Exemplar acted at once with a decisiveness that, from the first, communicated determination to dissidents and enthusiasm to supporters. At these companies there was none of the confusion and frustration of Rose, with its protracted period of reform lasting six years or more.

Recalling John Biffen's charmless phrase, clearly many of these companies had had a bomb put under them. The result, at Shilton, Castle and Kremer's at least, had certainly been improvements in management – Shilton with its ousting of the 'politicians', Castle with its new 'professionalism', and Kremer's, now 'much more reasonable'. As for whether British industry as a whole was 'leaner and fitter', the empirical evidence only allows comment, not conclusion.

Some of the gloomier prognostications were not fulfilled. Although the CBI reported recovery difficulties for manufacturing industry in general (Table 1.3 on p. 14), bottleneck constraints on expansion did not appear to be an insuperable problem for this group of firms. As especially the examples of Barton, Shilton and Exemplar demonstrate, it was not impossible to respond quickly and fully to the sudden upsurge of recovery. Indeed, Shilton, from a chaotic base and without benefit of new investment, managed to more than double turnover between 1982 and 1984. Potential bottlenecks could be overcome by capable managers.

Yet Bowers, Deaton and Turk's (1982) concern that the recession would penalize most those firms which had borrowed heavily to invest in expansion and innovation did receive some support from the case studies. The conservative cash-rich Barton, Fenwood and Homecraft suffered none of the shocks of Kremer's, which had invested heavily in automation and innovation before the full brunt of the recession was appreciated. High interest rates brought Kremer's interest payments at one point to more than ten times trading profits. The Rose Group, Shilton's Field Investments, and Castle's GEH were equally racked by the government's high interest rate policy. But the torture inflicted was at least in part the penalty for rash management. The contrast between Kremer's and Exemplar is instructive. Both companies had invested heavily in augmenting their production capabilities, but whereas Jo

Stone had been careful to control his borrowings and working capital, Kremer's simply cried 'let's keep making, boys!'; 'the banks lent us money as fast as we could get, as we wanted. No problem!' Likewise, Maurice Field had expanded with a series of increasingly rash acquisitions, culminating with the ill-considered purchase of Shilton itself; Rose had bitten off more than it could easily chew in buying IEE just before the recession; while GEH, as its long tolerance of Castle demonstrated, had always been lax. Again, good management could avoid or overcome the dangers of high interest rates. As Barton and Homecraft demonstrated, this financial caution was not incompatible with growth, at least in the short to medium term (though it should be noted that the performance of both companies appeared to falter as the recovery developed).

To what extent, then, did these companies exemplify Silberston's (1983) dilemma between static and dynamic efficiencies? In its pursuit of economies of scale supported by increased capacity and automation, Kremer's had certainly been striving for static efficiency in the years immediately before the recession. However, while these investments may have enabled Kremer's to take full advantage of buoyant demand in the late 1970s, they left it perilously exposed when the recession finally began to bite. As demand collapsed, Kremer's economies of scale turned into high fixed costs. More cautious companies such as Homecraft, Barton and Fenwood, were probably not maximizing profits in the pre-recessionary period, preferring to stash away substantial financial reserves rather than invest them directly in new or expanded activities. With plenty of reassuring cash behind them, negligible or non-existent debt and without the burden of over-extended capacities, these companies sailed through the recession – over this short period at least, they proved statically efficient. The longer term dynamic efficiency of these companies is more doubtful. By 1984–5, the performances of Homecraft and Fenwood were certainly beginning to look less shiny. However, the dynamic inefficiency of these two companies may have resided less in lack of physical capacity or new product, than a cultural incapacity, inculcated over long years of timidity, for any daring, expansionary initiatives at all.

As for the consequences of static inefficiency at the recession bottom, Exemplar provides the classic confirmation of Silberston's paradox. Jo Stone's Damnar investment decision was decried as 'marginal' because of the massive surplus capacity that existed at the time. When the recovery came, Exemplar was, of course, well poised to take full advantage. The problems of Rose in recovery perhaps demonstrate the reverse. Obedient to the imperatives of return on capital employed, Rose had remorselessly closed capacity during recession and classically failed to benefit from the recovery. One 'old Rose' manager expressed this predicament when he grumbled: 'If you take the view that you must never produce less than x per cent return, then you go through periods of cutting, cutting, cutting. And sometimes you damage your long term prospects by going through that procedure.' However, while this 'Rose man' would probably have seized gladly upon the example of Jo Stone to justify the preservation of capacity and the mass production of goods that he could not market, he might very well have ignored the cautionary tale of Kremer's. Kremer's traditional policy had always been to look forward to the recovery: 'What we're going to do is, we set the pattern for production, we're just going to make. Bong . . . So when the market opened up, we could start deliveries straight away; up went our prices; bong, we were away.' If this confident strategy had worked well in previous recessions, it had catastrophic consequences in the early 1980s.

This demonstrates the dangers of generalizing from single or very few cases. What works in one recession may not work in the next; what works for one company does not in another. Even if Rose's managers had been able to follow the bold strategy exemplified by Jo Stone, there is no assurance that they would have been capable of fulfiling it. Here, as at Homecraft and Fenwood as well, Rose illustrates the significance of more than strictly economic efficiencies. As we have seen, by the time of the recovery Rose had lost the capacity to think 'outwardly' and was instead locked into a downward 'spiral'. For Rose, its dynamic inefficiency lay not simply in plant or product, but management demoralization.

My conclusions for management policy must be heavily hedged. Barton and Exemplar, the two most successful companies, maintained firm pricing policies. While they were not innovative in terms of products, they did invest heavily in production capacity for core products. In these two cases, protecting the long-term development of the businesses even during recession certainly paid off by the time of the recovery. Whether this strategy could easily be imitated remains doubtful however; both companies were characterized by strong leadership, high managerial morale and unusual degrees of freedom from the intervention of parent companies or other external share-holders. Exemplar and Barton, of course, maintained stable top managements throughout the recession, but where changes were made, as at Shilton and Castle for instance, the effects were generally beneficial. The fate of Rose, however, warns that change need not work, and that if outsiders are to be brought in this should probably be done quickly and brutally. The examples of Kremer's and Shilton demonstrate that incumbent managements can effectively reform themselves – if persuaded by the right mixture of economic threat and traditionalist rhetoric.

Whether the changes induced by the recession did benefit the economy as a whole is rather beyond the scope of this book, which has taken no account either of those firms that disappeared altogether in the recession, or of what might have happened anyway. The aggregate statistics of Figure 1.2 on p. 11 certainly do not suggest that British manufacturing as a whole emerged stronger and more competitive; imports increased and output lagged throughout the recovery. But it can be said that 'good' managements, such as those at Barton or Exemplar, easily overcame the difficulties of recession and recovery while 'bad' managements, such as those at Castle, Kremer's, Shilton or Rose, were either replaced or soon came under processes of reform. The qualities of Barton and Exemplar – informal, hard-working, with cohesive local ideologies and long-term commitments to both customers and production – may have something to teach.

SOCIETY AND STRATEGIC CHOICE

My main task in this book has been to demonstrate the nature and extent of corporate strategic choice. Chapter 2 elaborated a number of leading deterministic positions, criticizing them on theoretical grounds either for too restricted a notion of the human actor, or for too oppressive a concept of environmental constraint. Chapters 3, 4 and 5 developed a Realist account of strategic choice which established the agency of key decision-makers on the basis of social structural complexity. As I argued in Chapter 11, it was this Realist approach rather than the various brands of determinism which seemed best able to explain the diverse recession strategies and recovery performances of the eight case study companies. These strategies, I concluded, emerged predominantly from processes of strategic choice; they were chosen by agents whose powers derived from social structural advantages and whose decisions were informed by, but not subservient to, social structural patterns of conduct. However, Chapter 11 left some unfinished business. I promised to deal with determinism's last ditch defence of aggregation. Also I have not yet considered the wider social implications of strategic choice. As we shall see, these issues are connected.

The two issues can be approached by way of a summary of the chief similarities and differences between Realist and conventional accounts of strategic choice. Realism joins with most other accounts in recognizing the importance of idiosyncratic organizational histories, 'cultures' and politics. Thus, I have described how Jo Stone turned round Exemplar after years of long decline, installed his own youthful management team and instilled in them faith in his vision of a marketing-led British manufacturing company. Realism also accepts the need for interpretive understanding of actors' personal motives. Again in the case of Jo Stone, I have shown how his patriotism and his paternalism combined to inspire his rash decision to build the new Damnar factory. Finally, the Realist approach shares with the developing 'firm-in-sector' perspective a concern for the evolution of industrial contexts. Taking Exemplar once more, I have set its strategy in the context of an unstable home market, increasing import penetration, escalating technological change and growing domination by multiple and discount retailers. But it is over this conception of the environment that the Realist approach begins to dissent. To start with, I have tried to analyse systematically the scope for strategic discretion allowed by each company's positions in product markets, the market for capital and the market for corporate control. Realism, however, conceives of the environment in more than this limited economistic sense. It insists on recognizing the reciprocal relationship of strategic choice and social structure.

This incorporation of social structure is vital for it is only thus that the agency required for strategic choice can be both possible and explicable. I argued in Chapter 3 that, detached from society, the actors of the Carnegie School were too internally simple to possess the intrinsic capacity for agency. If these actors are to be provided with sufficient stuffing for willfulness and choice, then we must recognize the complex social identities they possess as full participants in everyday life. But I argued as well against the illusory voluntarism of Action Theory. Too emphatically rejecting environmental constraint, these theorists also deny their actors the social structural resources – capitalist enterprises, patriarchal ideologies or whatever – necessary to action. This is indeed to throw out the baby with the bath-water. To take the case of Jo Stone at Exemplar one last time, his agency depended upon his complex social identity. It was because he was capitalist, entrepreneur, patriarch and Jew that he was able to enact the idiosyncratic strategies he chose during 1979–83.

This is not all. The recognition of social structure enables us also to advance beyond Action Theory's explanatory dependence upon interpretive understanding. Instead of simply trusting to managers' own accounts, Realism encourages us to identify and grant significance to their social structural positions independently. A Realist awareness of structure enables us to trace back from particular events to the possible social structural rules and resources that generated them. Actors' own accounts are not irrelevant in this process – at the least they may indirectly reveal structural forces by their use of language, metaphor and symbol – but they must be constantly probed, tested and amplified. So often in these eight cases, to have relied solely and uncritically upon the actors themselves would have been to have fallen short; we would have been left with no understanding of how it was that they could do what they did, or what models of behaviour inspired them. In so far as these actors did fail to acknowledge the social structural origins of their powers and patterns, we should not be too surprised. Actors require no more than a local and intuitive understanding of social structures in their day-to-day activities and even relatively detached social scientists inevitably fail to comprehend the full extent and complexity of the totality these structures form. Less generously, we can add that structural conditions were rarely likely to be made explicit even when clearly understood: dominant actors generally had some interest in their continued concealment. They could protect themselves from challenge to their frequently eccentric behaviour by mystifying the sources and uses of their powers with claims to managerial 'excellence', 'professionalism' or some other polite excuse for arbitrary authority. Here Realism's advantage over Action Theory's empathetic trust is not only that it can account more fully for the origins of actors' powers, but also that it makes intelligible why these structural powers are often so obscure.

Thus the incorporation of social structure is doubly important to any adequate account of strategic choice. Without it, it is inconceivable that actors would have the capacity to choose; only with it can observers begin to explain their choices. Both the power of strategic choice and its direction are dependent on, but not determined by social structures. Corporate decision-makers possess class, gender, generation and ethnicity, and these all matter to their strategic choices.

But this recognition of the socially-structured nature of strategic choice achieves something else: it fixes attention on the narrow concentration of power over corporate conduct. The dominant actors I have described were members of an exclusive élite: many were capitalists; some were immigrants, but all were white; all, needless to say, were male. Enjoyment of these social characteristics – not in themselves any indicators of particular personal merit – gave them access to control over the activities of many thousands of employees. It was this command over the labour of other actors that enabled them to make and realize the strategic choices they did. The condition for their agency was the constricted freedom of those without their social advantages.

The discretionary power enjoyed by Jo Stone, Bernie Kremer and the Barton brothers was not unusual and, indeed, was relatively modest. They were minor members of that class of 'entrepreneurial capitalists' whom Scott (1985) identifies as active in roughly a quarter of Britain's top 250 companies. Moreover, the two industries in which these men operated constituted particularly harsh environments, especially during the recessionary period: if they could exercise a degree of strategic choice in these conditions, then we might expect this discretionary power to be even more widespread in other, less demanding industries. Further, Exemplar, Homecraft and Rose domestic appliances, though fairly small business units themselves, were subsidiaries of some of the largest manufacturing companies in the UK. These companies were all members of that group of 100 manufacturing firms whose activities make up 38 per cent of Britain's total manufacturing output and whose decisions determine the lives of more than one and a half million people (Business Monitor PA 1002, 1985). The strategies of Universal, AEL and the Rose group towards export, employment, investment and innovation directly affect tens of thousands of lives, as well as significantly influencing the performance of the British economy as a whole. The license allowed to their subsidiaries certainly does not suggest that those controlling these vast enterprises were governed by remorseless attention to profit-maximization; it suggests that they too exercised a considerable degree of strategic discretion.

This is where the defence of aggregation falls down. The strategic choices of such powerful enterprises cannot be hidden away safely within the averages of large numbers. The rise of concentrated economic power has rendered the neo-classical economists' nostalgia for an economy inhabited by hosts of small competitors dangerously irrelevant. Each of these top 100 firms can individually make an enormous impact (Holland, 1975). Nor can we hope that the deviations of these large firms have a random, self-cancelling character: the structured nature of access to control over strategy, combined with the social codes of decision-making, together impose upon them systematic biases. The strategic choices of these firms are not lost in a blur of stochastic oscillations, but rather express a narrow range of social logics. As Thompson (1982, p. 248) concluded, these vast corporations can no longer be dismissed as '. . . "representatives" of general market conditions, of general competitive considerations of "capital" in general; they have their own effectivity which partly constitutes these wider sets of relations'. The directions and ramifications of these companies' strategies need to be investigated in their specificities.

A Realist understanding of the specific operations of contemporary enterprise can both make the case and point the way for its transformation. Revelation of the rudimentary disciplines exerted by capital exposes these large corporations as vast centres of arbitrary power. Recognition of strategic choice does not, therefore, diminish the need to bring these large enterprises under democratic control. Bauer and Cohen (1981, p. 29) cogently criticize those – both neo-classical and Marxian – who still seek refuge from the implications of strategic choice by assuming profit maximizing behaviour:

> Rather than the reality of managers making our future by their choices, they have preferred the image of owners accumulating profits. No-one can deny that a firm is a machine for making profit: the managers boast it themselves . . . [But] to restrict the debate on industrial groups [thus] . . . is to participate in a deliberate dissimulation of the industrial group's power and authority; it is to forbid the identification of the small group of co-opted managers who seek above all else, to preserve their monopoly of our activities and our modes of consumption (my translation).

Replacing the ogre of profit-maximization by the manager of strategic choice implies only a very limited liberation. As Bauer and Cohen (1981) insist, strategic choice remains the privilege of an élite, dependent upon the domination of employees and consumers. People need be no less exploited because their energies are directed to ends other than profit-maximization. The diversion of corporate resources, including labour, to private purposes still requires the generation of surpluses from somewhere: the more productivity extracted from employees and the higher the margins culled from customers, the greater the scope for managerial strategic choice. Even diversion of surpluses to paternalistic employee welfare is predicated upon control. The extension of human agency requires, therefore, a transformation of the contemporary enterprise that converts strategic choice from an unaccountable privilege into a democratic right. This transformation will be advanced not by obscurantist obsession with profit-maximization, but rather by a critical examination of the diverse powers and ideologies by which control really is exercised in the contemporary enterprise.

Recent debate on the democratic control of enterprise has centred on the relative weight to be given to market mechanisms as opposed to ownership structures, whether in the form of nationalization or some sort of co-operative arrangement (Hodgson, 1984; Nove, 1986; Murray, 1987). Underpinning these alternatives is an apparently exclusive dichotomy between, in Williamson's (1975) classic terms, 'markets' and 'hierarchies'. An important product of this debate has been an increasing acceptance of the failings of purely administrative controls and growing recognition of the potential for markets as a means of organizing certain kinds of transactions. However, the evidence of this book suggests that, in whatever judicious mixture they are applied, markets and hierarchies are unlikely to be enough. Market pressures can be negated: we have seen already how dominant élites were able to manipulate and evade market disciplines even during recession. Ownership can be subverted: as I have argued, managers have developed skills and legitimacies that permit them to pre-empt even the control of private capitalists.

Contemporary managers well understand the limitations of markets and hierarchies. They do not confine themselves to these simple alternatives, but, as Ouchi (1980) points out, draw also on the ideological controls typical of a third type of organization, the 'clan'. Although markets and hierarchies were certainly important to the managers of this book, they supplemented and countered these forces by the active cultivation of ideology. Exploiting contradictions within capitalist structures, manipulating conflicts with other structures, these managers were able to synthesize patriotic, paternalistic, professional and religious ideals into local ideologies supporting their private purposes. As managers of markets, hierarchies and ideologies, these dominant actors proved themselves to be skilful pluralists.

Thus markets and hierarchies fall short because they do not match the social structural complexity of our society. The capitalist logics upon which they depend themselves contain too much internal ambiguity to assure reliable control. Within the institutions of contemporary economic life, moreover, even these ambiguous logics are unable to claim exclusive sovereignty. Hierarchy can be defied or perverted by appeal to distinct patriarchal powers; market imperatives can be disdained in favour of ethnic, family or class loyalties. Faith, therefore, in nationalized hierarchies is too trustingly bureaucratic; faith in market pressures too narrowly economistic. Each ignores both the diverse kinds of power in our society and the ideological ways by which they are mobilized. Truly democratic control over the firm requires a broader attack on inegalitarian ideologies and the social structures that support them. Abolition of the capitalist should not leave the patriarch behind; 'enterprise culture' must be countered by 'socialist culture'.

This book ends therefore with an irony: the skilful pluralism with which managers subvert capitalist disciplines actually suggests the means for their own replacement by more popular control. In a complex society, democratic control over enterprise demands the transformation of not just economic structures but of all oppressive structures; it requires not merely the manipulation of markets and hierarchies, but change in the sphere of ideology. Only by matching social complexity in this comprehensive manner can the power of strategic choice be converted from the privilege of the few into a facility participated in by many and accountable to all.

Appendix 1. Domestic Appliance Companies' Performances

Four-firm comparison group company codes:
A: general, but mostly laundry and vacuum appliances
B: cooking specialist
C: refrigeration specialist
D: general, but largest part refrigeration

Turnover (1979=100)

	1978	1979	1980	1981	1982	1983	1984	1985
Homecraft	78	100	117	133	151	183	185	191
Exemplar	88	100	123	120	112	109	127	155
Rose Electric	87	100	107	99	97	110	na	na
Rose G and E	na	na	na	113	110	117	112	133
A	104	100	102	99	94	103	114	115
B	74	100	113	120	104	123	149	152
C	98	100	124	140	158	177	200	199
D	88	100	94	93	99	110	112	140

Profit margin (%)

	1978	1979	1980	1981	1982	1983	1984	1985
Homecraft	10.0	2.6	12.0	11.7	11.6	11.9	10.2	9.1
Exemplar	4.4	7.2	5.2	4.1	8.3	8.6	10.7	11.0
Rose Electric	2.8	3.2	3.9	1.3	−1.0	1.4	na	na
Rose G and E	na	na	na	1.3	0.6	−0.5	−0.1	−2.9
A	2.9	1.0	0.3	−13.8	−4.6	2.2	5.8	3.3
B	0.8	4.8	4.2	4.0	5.5	5.2	7.4	2.7
C	6.0	5.9	7.4	7.0	5.3	11.7	6.2	5.5
D	9.5	8.4	4.7	4.6	3.1	7.5	8.0	3.0

Return on capital employed (%)

	1978	1979	1980	1981	1982	1983	1984	1985
Homecraft	66.5	63.1	44.1	47.6	39.6	59.4	38.4	55.1
Exemplar	24.4	22.8	21.2	16.1	25.6	23.9	50.4	48.9
Rose Electric	29.7	35.1	17.6	6.8	−2.3	3.5	na	na
Rose G and E	na	na	na	3.3	1.6	−1.3	−8.0	−35.8
A	6.4	2.2	0.7	−44.6	−9.0	4.3	19.4	12.2
B	2.5	16.3	13.3	12.5	16.2	15.9	22.7	8.0
C	20.5	18.4	23.5	22.0	17.0	33.8	21.4	17.9
D	22.1	19.6	9.4	8.6	6.2	13.8	14.9	7.9

Appendix 2. Office Furniture Companies' Performances

Four-firm comparison group company codes:

A: metal storage
B: mostly wooden desking
C: wooden desking and systems
D: mostly seating

Turnover (1979=100)

	1978	1979	1980	1981	1982	1983	1984	1985
Castle	116	100	89	70	47	52	65	68
Barton	91	100	103	99	114	131	164	194
Fenwood	86	100	98	73	73	86	101	106
Kremer's	84	100	110	90	104	101	97	104
Shilton	65	100	104	53	48	61	109	129
A	80	100	103	64	76	77	86	100
B	77	100	106	98	105	118	141	159
C	78	100	91	82	104	123	176	203
D	87	100	114	93	91	91	104	110

Profit Margin (%)

	1978	1979	1980	1981	1982	1983	1984	1985
Castle	−0.4	7.1	2.9	−11.6	−8.2	−0.1	2.6	3.7
Barton	20.5	17.2	16.2	10.7	14.8	15.0	14.4	12.1
Fenwood	11.9	13.1	13.4	13.8	10.4	19.3	13.0	10.0
Kremer's	7.6	9.5	9.8	1.6	−0.5	0.4	5.8	7.1
Shilton	6.8	8.9	−0.0	−3.0	−2.4	6.5	8.3	11.9
A	14.6	13.7	6.4	2.8	−0.2	3.7	3.5	1.9
B	21.2	21.6	13.7	8.0	15.6	10.5	13.6	12.8
C	14.4	14.1	11.0	8.5	13.6	13.0	17.5	21.4
D	0.5	7.0	5.4	−1.1	3.5	4.5	9.8	9.9

Return on capital employed (%)

	1978	1979	1980	1981	1982	1983	1984	1985
Castle	−0.7	9.7	3.7	−13.5	−8.9	−0.2	2.6	4.1
Barton	59.4	41.3	32.0	18.0	28.9	27.6	20.0	16.2
Fenwood	20.0	22.0	27.7	12.5	8.4	16.1	11.4	8.4
Kremer's	20.6	24.9	29.1	5.0	−2.0	2.8	34.2	37.2
Shilton	na	na	na	na	na	165.6	108.5	94.0
A	565.8	220.0	33.1	9.5	−0.1	17.5	18.9	11.7
B	32.7	38.7	24.4	13.1	26.0	24.2	64.6	63.8
C	31.1	31.0	21.9	14.0	25.9	30.4	52.8	65.2
D	1.1	18.2	13.9	−2.4	7.3	9.2	117.8	103.1

Bibliography

Abercrombie, N., Hill, S. and
Turner, B. J. (1980) *The Dominant
Ideology Thesis* (London: Allen &
Unwin).

Abrams, P. (1982) *Historical
Sociology* (Somerset: Open Books).

Alchian, A. A. (1950) 'Uncertainty,
evolution and economic theory',
Journal of Political Economy, vol. 58,
pp. 211–21.

Aldrich, H.E. (1979), *Organizations
and Environments* (Englewood Cliffs
NJ: Prentice Hall).

Allen, M. P. and Panian, S. K.
(1982), 'Power, performance and
succession in the large corporation',
Administrative Science Quarterly, vol.
27, pp. 538–47.

Allison, G. T. (1971) *The Essence of
Decision: Explaining the Cuban
Missile Crisis* (Boston, Mass.: Little,
Brown).

Alvesson, M. (1987) *Organizational
Theory and Technocratic
Conciousness* (New York: De
Gruyter).

Andrews, P. W. S. (1949)
Manufacturing Business (London:
Macmillan).

Ansoff, H. I. (1968), *Corporate
Strategy* (Harmondsworth: Penguin).

Anthony, P. D. (1986), *The
Foundation of Management* (London:
Tavistock).

Aris, S. (1970) *The Jews in Business*
(London: Cape).

Arrow, K. J. (1974) *The Limits of
Organization* (New York: W. W.
Norton).

Arrow, K. J. (1985) 'The economics
of agency', in J. W. Pratt and R. J.
Zechauser (eds) *Principals and
Agents: the Structure of Business*
(Boston, Mass: Harvard Business
School).

Astley, W. G. and Van de Ven, H.
(1983) 'Central perspectives and
debates in organizational theory',
Administrative Science Quarterly, vol.
28, pp. 245–73.

Astley, W. G. (1985),
'Administrative science as socially
constructed truth', *Administrative
Science Quarterly*, vol. 30,
pp. 497–513.

Bachrach, P. and Baratz, M. S.
(1962) 'Two faces of power',
American Political Science Review,
vol. 56, no. 3, pp. 947–52.

Bachrach, P. and Baratz, M. S.
(1963) 'Decisions and non-decisions:
an analytical framework', *American
Political Science Review*, vol. 57, no.
3, pp. 632–42.

Bain, J. S. (1968), *Industrial
Organization* (2nd edn) (New York:
John Wiley).

Baker, W. (1985) 'The social structure of a national securities market', *American Journal of Sociology*, vol. 89, no. 4, pp. 775–811.

Barna, T. (1962) *Investment and Growth Policies in British Industrial Firms* (Cambridge: Cambridge University Press).

Bate, P. (1984) 'The impact of organization culture on approaches to organizational problem-solving', *Organizational Studies*, vol. 15, no. 1, pp. 43–66.

Bauer, M. and Cohen, E. (1981) *Qui Gouverne les Groupes Industriels?* (Paris: Editions du Seuil).

Bauer, M. and Cohen, E. (1983a) 'La Fin des Nouvelles Classes: couches moyennes eclatees et societe d'appareils', *Revue Francaise de Sociologie*, vol. 24, no. 2, pp. 285–300.

Bauer, M. and Cohen, E. (1983b), 'The invisibility of power in economics: beyond markets and hierarchies', in A. Francis, J. Turk and P. Willman (eds), *Power, Efficiency and Institutions* (London: Heinemann).

Baumol, W. J. (1959), *Business Behaviour, Value and Growth* (New York: Harcourt, Brace and World).

Baumol, W. J., Panzar, J. C. and Willig R. D. (1982) *Contestable Markets and the Theory of Industry Structure* (New York: Harcourt Brace Jovanovich).

Bendix, R. (1963) *Work and Authority in Industry* (New York: Harper & Row).

Benson, J. K. (1977) 'Organizations: a dialectical view', *Administrative Science Quarterly*, vol. 22, pp. 1–24.

Benton, T. (1981) 'Objective interests and the sociology of power', *Sociology*, vol. 15, pp. 161–83.

Berg, P.–O. (1985) 'Organisational change as a symbolic transformation process', in P. J. Frost, L. F. Moore, M. R. Louis, C. C. Lundberg, and J. Martin (eds), *Organisational Culture* (Beverley Hills: Sage).

Berger P. L. and Luckman T. (1967) *The Social Construction of Reality* (London: Allen Lane).

Berghahn, M. (1984) *German – Jewish Refugees in England* (London: Macmillan).

Berle, A. A. and Means, G. C. ([1932] 1967) *The Modern Corporation and Private Property* (New York: Harvest).

Beyer, J. M. (1981), 'Ideologies, values and decision-making in organisations', in P. C. Nyman and W. H. Starbuck (eds.) *Handbook of Organisational Design, Vol. 2*, (Oxford: Oxford University Press).

Bhaskar, R. (1978) *A Realist Theory of Science* (Brighton: Harvester).

Bhaskar, R. (1979) *The Possibility of Naturalism: A Philisophic Critique of the Contemporary Human Sciences* (Brighton: Harvester).

Bhaskar, R. (1983) 'Beef, Structure and Place: Notes from a Critical Naturalist Perspective', *Journal for the Theory of Social Behaviour*, vol. 13, no. 1, pp. 81–95.

Bhaskar, R. (1986) *Scientific Realism and Human Emancipation* (London: Verso).

Bibeault, D. B. (1982) *Corporate Turnaround* (New York: McGraw-Hill).

Boland, A. (1982) *The Foundations of Economic Method* (London:Allen & Unwin).

Boswell, J. S. (1983) *Business Policies in the Making* (London: Allen & Unwin).

Bourgeois, L. J. (1981) 'On the measurement of organisational slack', *Academy of Management Review*, vol. 6, no. 1, pp. 29–39.

Bourgeois, L. J. (1984), 'Strategic management and determinism', *Academy of Management Review*, vol. 9, no. 4, pp. 586–96.

Bowers, J., Deaton, D. and Turk, J. (1982) *Labour Hoarding in British Industry* (Oxford: Basil Blackwell).

Brechling, F. (1975) *Investment and Employment Decisions*(Manchester: Manchester University Press).

Britton, A. (1986) *The Trade Cycle in Britain: 1958–1982* (Cambridge: Cambridge University Press).

Bryer, R. and Brignall, T. (1986) 'Divestment and inflation accounting: an unemployment machine?', *Capital and Class*, vol. 30, pp. 125–55.

Burns, T. and Stalker, G. M. (1961), *The Management of Innovation* (London: Tavistock).

Cable, J. (1985) 'Capital market information and industrial performance: the role of West German Banks', *Economic Journal*, vol. 95, pp. 118–32.

Cairncross, A., Henderson, P. and Silberston, Z. A. (1982) 'Problems of industrial recovery', *Nat West Review*, spring, pp. 9–17.

Caves, R. E. and Porter, M. E. (1977) 'From entry barriers to mobility barriers: conjectural decisions and contrived deterrence to new competition' *Quarterly Journal of Economics*, vol. 91, no. 2, pp. 241–261.

Cawson A., Morgan K., Holmes P., Stevens A, and Webbe D., (1989), *Hostile Brothers: Competition and Closure in the European Electronics Industry* (Oxford: Clarendon Press).

Chandler, A. D. (1962) *Strategy and Structure: Chapters in theHistory of the American Industrial Enterprise* (Cambridge, Mass.: MIT Press).

Chandler, A. D. (1977), *The Visible Hand: The Managerial Revolution in American Business* (Cambridge: Mass.: Harvard University Press).

Channon, D. (1973), *The Strategy and Structure of British Enterprise* (Cambridge, Mass.: Harvard University Press).

Channon, D. (1979) 'Leadership and corporate performance in the service industries', *Journal of Management Studies*, vol 16, no 2, pp. 185–201.

Child, J. (1969) *British Management Thought: A Critical Analysis* (London: Allen & Unwin).

Child, J. (1972) 'Organisational structure, environment and performance: the role of strategic choice', *Sociology*, no. 6, pp. 1–22.

Child, J. (1981) 'Culture, contingency and capitalism in the cross-national study of organizations', in L. L.

Cummins and B. M. Straw (eds), *Research on Organizational Behaviour*, vol. 3, (Connecticut: JAI Press).

Child, J. and Smith, C. (1987) 'The context and process of organizational transformation: Cadbury Ltd in its sector', *Journal of Management Studies*, vol. 24, no. 6, pp. 563–93.

Chiplin, B. and Wright, M. (1987) *The Logic of Mergers*, Hobart Paper no. 107 (London: Institute for Economic Affairs).

Clegg, S. (1979) *The Theory of Power and Organization* (London: Routledge & Kegan Paul).

Clifford, D. K. (1977), 'Thriving in a recession', *Harvard Business Review*, July–August, pp. 57–65.

Coates, J. H. (1985), 'UK manufacturing industry: recession, depression and prospects for the future', in F. V. Meyer (ed.), *Prospects for Economic Recovery in the British Economy* (Beckenham: Croom Helm).

Cohen, E. and Bauer, M. (1985) *Les Grandes Manoeuvres Industrielles* (Paris: Belfond).

Cohen, M. D., March J. and Olsen, T. (1976) 'People, problems, solutions and the ambiguity of relevance' in J. March and M. D. Cohen, *Ambiguity and Choice in Organizations*, (Bergen: Universiteitsforlagt).

Cooke, T. E. (1986) *Mergers and Acquisitions* (Oxford: Blackwell).

Corley, T. A. B. (1966) *Domestic Electric Appliances* (London: Cape).

Cowling, K. (1982) *Monopoly Capitalism* (London: Macmillan).

Cox, A., Furlong, P. and Page, E. (1985) *Power in Capitalist Society* (Brighton: Wheatsheaf).

Crenson, M. A. (1971) *The Un-Politics of Air Pollution* (Baltimore: The John Hopkins University Press).

Crozier, M. and Friedberg, E. (1977) *L'Acteur et le Systeme* (Paris: Editions du Seuil).

Cyert, R. M. and March, J. G. (1956) 'Organizational factors in the theory of monopoly', *Quarterly Journal of Economics*, vol. 70, no. 1, pp. 44–64.

Cyert, R. M. and March, J. G. (1963) *A Behavioural Theory of the Firm* (Englewood Cliffs, NJ: Prentice-Hall).

Dahl, R. A. (1961) *Who Governs? Democracy and Power in an American City* (New Haven: Yale University Press).

Dahrendorf, R. (1959), *Class and Class Conflict in Industrial Society* (London: Routledge & Kegan Paul).

Dalton, D. R. and Kesner, I. F. (1985) 'Organisational performance as an antecedent of inside/outside chief executive succession: an empirical assessment', *Academy of Management Journal*, vol. 28, no. 4, pp. 749–62.

Daudi, P. (1986) *Power in the Organisation* (Oxford: Blackwell).

Davis, S. M. (1984) *Managing Corporate Culture* (Massachusetts: Ballinger).

Donaldson, L. (1987) 'Strategy and structural adjustment to regain fit and performance: in defence of contingency theory', *Journal of Management Studies*, vol. 24, no. 1, pp. 1–24.

Du Boff, R. B. and Herman, E. S. (1980) 'Alfred Chandler's new business history: a review', *Politics and Society*, vol. 10, no. 1, pp. 87–110.

Dunnet, P. J. S. (1980) *The Decline of the British Motor Industry: the Effects of Government Policy, 1945–1979* (London: Croom Helm).

Earl, P. (1984) *The Corporate Imagination: How Big Companies Make Mistakes* (Brighton: Wheatsheaf).

Edwardes, M. (1984) *Back from the Brink* (London: Fontana).

Eichner, A. S. (1976) *The Megacorp and Oligopoly* (Cambridge: Cambridge University Press).

Elster, J. (1984) *Ulysses and the sirens: studies in rationality and irrationality* (revised edn) (Cambridge: Cambridge University Press).

Euromonitor (1985) *The Domestic Appliance Industry Report*, (London: Euromonitor).

Fama, E. F. (1980) 'Agency problems and the theory of the firm', *Journal of Political Economy*, vol. 88, no. 2, pp. 288–307.

Farmer, M. K. (1982) 'Rational action in economic and social theory: some misunderstandings', *Archives Europeenes de Sociologie*, vol. 23, no. 1, pp. 179–97.

Feldman, S. P. (1986) 'Management in context: an essay on the relevance of culture to the understanding of organisational change', *Journal of Management Studies*, vol. 23, no. 6, pp. 586–607.

Fildes, R., Jalland, M. and Wood, D. (1978) 'Forecasting in conditions of uncertainty', *Long Range Planning*, vol. 11, pp. 29–38.

Ford, J. D. and Baucus, D. A. (1987) 'Organisational adaption to performance downturns: an interpretation-based perspective', *Academy of Management Review*, vol. 12, no. 2. pp. 366–80.

Francis, A. (1980) 'Families, firms and finance capital', *Sociology*, vol. 14, no. 1, pp. 1–27.

Frankenberg, R. (1967) 'Economic anthropology', in R. Firth (ed.), *Themes in Economic Anthropology* (London: Tavistock).

Friedman, M. (1953) 'The methodology of positive economics', in M. Friedman, *Essays in Positive Economics* (Chicago: University of Chicago Press).

Furniture Industry Research Association (1983) *Statistical Digest for the Furniture Industry* (Milton Keynes: Furniture Industry Research Association Marketing Department).

Galbraith, J. K. (1967) *The New Industrial State* (London: Hamish Hamilton).

Gellner, E.A. (1973) *The New Idealism – Cause and meaning in the Social Sciences* (London: Routledge & Kegan Paul).

Georghiu, L., Metcalfe, J. S., Gibbons, M., Ray T. and Evans J. (1986) *Post Innovation Performance* (London: Macmillan).

Giddens, A. (1976) *New Rules of Sociological Method* (London: Hutchinson).

Giddens, A. (1979) *Central Problems in Social Theory: Action, Structure and Contradictions in Social Analysis* (London: MacMillan).

Giddens, A. (1984) *The Constitution of Society* (Oxford: Polity Press).

Giddens, A. (1987) 'Out of the orrery: E. P. Thompson on consciousness and history', in A. Giddens, *Social Theory and Modern Sociology* (Oxford: Polity Press)

Glyn, A. and Harrison, J. (1980) *The British Economic Disaster* (London: Pluto).

Godiwalla, Y. M., Meinhart, W. A. and Warde W. D. (1979) *Corporate Strategy and Functional Management* (New York: Praeger).

Goold, M. and Campbell, A. (1987) *Strategies and Styles: the Role of the Centre in Managing Diversified Companies* (Oxford: Blackwell).

Gouldner, A. W. (1954) *Patterns of Industrial Bureaucracy* (New York: Free Press)

Gowler, D. and Legge, K. (1983), 'The meaning of management and the management of meaning: a view from social anthropology', in M. J. Earl (ed.), *Perspectives on Management* (Oxford: Oxford University Press).

Grant, W. with Sargent, J. (1987) *Business and Politics in Britain* (London: Macmillan).

Granick, D. (1972) *Managerial Comparisons of Four Developed Countries* (Massachusetts: MIT Press).

Granovetter, M. (1985) 'Economic action and social structure: the problem of embeddedness', *American Journal of Sociology*, vol. 91, no. 3, pp. 481–510.

Green, S. (1987a) *Organizational Culture and Strategy*, Centre for Business Strategy Working Paper, No. 4, London Business School, London.

Green, S. (1987b) *Beliefs, Actions and Strategic Change: a Study of Paradigms in the UK Domestic Appliance Industry*, Centre for Business Strategy Working Paper, No. 26, London Business School, London.

Grinyer, P. H., Mayes, D. and McKiernan, P. (1987) *Sharpbenders: the Process of Marked and Sustained Improvement in Performance in Selected UK Companies*, Paper presented to the British Academy of Management, University of Warwick, September.

Grinyer, P. H. and Spender, J. C. (1979) *Turnaround – Management Recipes for Corporate Success* (London: Associated Business Books).

Gunz, H. and Whitley, R. (1985) 'Managerial cultures and industrial strategies in British firms', *Organization Studies*, vol. 6, no. 3, pp. 247–73.

Gupta, A. K. (1980) 'The process of strategy formation: a descriptive analysis', DBA Dissertation, Harvard University Graduate School of Business Administration.

Gupta, A. K. and Govindarajam, V. (1984) 'Business unit strategy, managerial characteristics, and business unit effectiveness at strategy implementation', *Academy of Management Journal*, vol. 27, no. 1, pp. 25–41.

Guth, W. D. and Taguiri, R. (1965) Personal values and corporate strategy', *Harvard Business Review*, September–October vol. 45, pp. 123–32.

Hackman, J. D. (1985) 'Power and centrality in the allocation of resources in colleges and universities', *Administrative Science Quarterly*, vol. 30, no. 1, pp. 61–77.

Hage, J. (1980) *Theories of Organisations: Form, Process and Tranformation* (New York: John Wiley).

Hall, R. C. and Hitch, C. J. (1939) 'Price theory and business behaviour', *Oxford Economic Papers*, vol. 2, pp. 12–45.

Hambrick, D. C. (1981) 'Environment, strategy and power within top management teams', *Administrative Science Quarterly*, vol. 26, pp. 253–76.

Hambrick, D. C. (1983) 'Some tests of the effectiveness and functional attributes of Miles and Snow's types', *Academy ofManagement Journal*, vol. 26, no. 1, pp. 5–26.

Hambrick, D. C. and Mason, P. A. (1984) 'Upper echelons: the organization as a reflection of its top managers', *Academy of Management Review*, vol. 9, no. 2, pp. 193–206.

Hannah, L. (1976) *The Rise of the Corporate Economy* (London: Methuen).

Hannah, L. and Kay, J. (1977) *Concentration in Modern Industry*, (London: Macmillan).

Hannan, M. T. and Freeman, J. (1977) 'The population ecology of organisations', *American Journal of Sociology*, vol. 82, no. 5, pp. 929–64.

Harré, R. and Secord, P. F. (1972) *The Explanation of Social Behaviour* (Oxford: Blackwell).

Harré, R. (1979) *Social Being* (Oxford: Blackwell).

Harré, R. (1983) *Personal Being* (Oxford: Blackwell).

Harrigan, K. R. (1980) *Strategies for Declining Businesses* (Lexington, Mass.: D. C. Heath).

Hartmann, H. I. (1979) 'The unhappy marriage of marxism and feminism: towards a more progressive union', *Capital and Class*, vol. 8, pp. 1–33.

Hatten, K. J. and Hatten, M. L. (1987) 'Strategic groups, asymmetrical mobility barriers and contestability', *Strategic Management Journal*, vol. 8, no. 4, pp. 329–42.

Hay, G. A. (1987) 'The interaction of market structure and conduct', in D. A. Hay and J. S. Vickers (eds), *The Economics of Market Dominance* (Oxford: Blackwell).

Healey, P. (1987) 'Contest at your peril', *Acquisitions Monthly*, February, pp. 16–7.

Helmich, D. L. and Brown, W. B. (1972) 'Successor type and organizational change in the corporate enterprise', *Administrative Science Quarterly*, no. 17, pp. 371–81.

Herman, E. S. (1981) *Corporate Control, Corporate Power* (Cambridge: Cambridge University Press).

Hickson, D. J., Hinings, C. R., Lee, C. A., Schneck, R. E. and Pennings, J. M. (1971) 'A strategic contingencies theory of intraorganisational power', *Administrative Science Quarterly*, vol. 16, no. 2, pp. 216–29.

Hindess, B. (1982) 'Power, interests and the outcomes of struggles', *Sociology*, no. 16, pp. 499–511.

Hinings, C. R., Hickson, D. J., Pennings, J. M. and Schneck, R. E. (1974) 'Structural conditions of intraorganizational power', *Administrative Science Quarterly*, vol. 19, pp. 22–44.

Hirschman, A. O. (1970) *Exit, Voice and Loyalty* (Cambridge, Mass.: Harvard University Press).

Hodgson, G. (1984) *The Democratic Economy: A New Look at Planning, Markets and Power* (Harmondsworth: Penguin).

Hodgson, G. (1988) *Economics and Institutions* (Cambridge: Polity Press).

Hofer, C. W. (1975) 'Towards a contingency theory of business strategy', *Academy of Management Journal*, vol. 18, pp. 784–810.

Holl, P. (1977) 'Control type and the market for corporate control in large US corporations', *Journal of Industrial Economics*, vol. 25, no. 4, pp. 259–73.

Holland, S. (1975) *The Socialist Challenge* (London: Quartet).

Hollis, M. (1977) *Models of Man: Philosophical Thoughts on Social Action* (Cambridge: Cambridge University Press).

Hollis, M. (1982) 'The Social Destruction of Reality', in M. Hollis and S. Lukes (eds), *Rationality and Relativism* (Oxford: Blackwell).

Hollis, M. and Nell, E. J. (1975) *Rational Economic Man: A Philosophical Critique of Neo-Classical Economics* (Cambridge: Cambridge University Press).

Hrebiniak, L. G. and Joyce, W. F. (1985) 'Organizational adaptation: strategic choice and environmental determinism', *Administrative Science Quarterly*, vol. 30, no. 3, pp. 336–49.

Huff, A. S. (1982) 'Industry influences on strategy reformulation', *Strategic Management Journal*, vol. 3, pp. 119–31.

Huff, A. S. (1983) 'A rhetorical examination of strategic change', in L. R. Pondy, P. J. Frost, G. Morgan and T. C. Dandridge (eds), *Organisational Symbolism* (Greenwich: JAI Press).

Hunter, F. (1953) *Community Power Structure* (Carolina: University of North Carolina).

Hutchison, T. (1984) 'Our methodological crisis', in P. Wiles and G. Routh (eds), *Economics in Disarray* (Oxford: Blackwell).

Hyman, R. (1987) 'Strategy or structure? Capital, labour and control', *Work, Employment and Society*, vol. 1, no. 1, pp. 25–55.

Ingham, G. (1984) *Capitalism Divided?* (London: Macmillan).

James, D. R. and Soref, M. (1981) 'Profit constraints on managerial autonomy: managerial theory of the unmaking of the corporation president', *American Sociological Review*, vol. 46, no. 1, pp. 1–18.

Jensen, M. C. and Meckling, W. H. (1976) 'Theory of the firm: managerial behaviour, agency costs and ownership structure', *Journal of Financial Economics*, vol. 3, pp. 305–60.

Johnson, G. and Scholes, K. (1984) *Exploring Corporate Strategy* (Englewood Cliffs NJ: Prentice Hall).

Johnson, G. (1987) *Strategic Change and the Management Process* (Oxford: Blackwell).

Jones, R. M. (1979) 'The investment decision', in P. J. Devine, N. Lee, R. M. Jones and W. J. Tyson (eds), *An Introduction to Industrial Economics* (London: Allen & Unwin).

Jones, R. and Marriot, O. (1970) *The Anatomy of a Merger: A History of GEC, AEI and English Electric* (London: Cape).

Karpik, L. (1972a) 'Sociologie, economie politique et buts des organisations de production', *Revue Francaise de Sociologie*, vol. 13, pp. 292–324.

Karpik, L. (1972b) 'Multinationales et grandes entreprises technologiques', *Revue Economique*, vol. 23, no. 4, pp. 563–91.

Karpik, L. (1978) 'Organizations, institutions and history', in L. Karpik (ed.), *Organizations and Environment* (London: Sage).

Kay, N. M. (1979) *The Innovating Firm* (London: Macmillan).

Kay, N. M. (1984) *The Emergent Firm: Knowledge, Ignorance and Surprise in Economic Organisation* (London: Macmillan).

Keegan, W. (1984) *Mrs. Thatcher's Economic Experiment* (London: Allen Lane).

Kennedy, W. P. and Payne, P. L. (1976) 'Directions for future research', in L. Hannah (ed.), *Management Strategy and Business Development: an Historical and Comparative Study* (London: Macmillan).

Keynote (1979) *Household Appliances (White Goods)* (London: Keynote).

Keynote (1981) *Household Appliances (White Goods)* (London: Keynote).

Keynote (1983) *Office Furniture* (London: Keynote).

Kharbanda, O. P. and Stallworthy, E. A. (1987) *Company Rescue* (London: Heinemann).

Kosmin, B. (1979) 'Exclusion and opportunity: traditions of work amongst British Jews', in S. Wallman (ed.), *Ethnicity at Work* (London: Macmillan).

Kotler, P. (1978) 'Harvesting strategies for weak products', *Business Horizons*, August, pp. 15–22.

Kundera, M. (1984) *The Unbearable Lightness of Being* (London: Penguin).

Latsis, S. J. (1972) 'Situational determinism in economics', *British Journal of Philosophy of Science*, vol. 23, pp. 207–45.

Lawriwsky, M. L. (1984) *Corporate Structure and Performance* (London: Croom Helm).

Lawson, J. (1983) 'Not so much a factory; more a form of patriarchy: gender and class during industrialisation', in E. Gamarmikov, D. Morgan, J. Purvis and D. E. Taylor (eds), *Gender, Class and Work* (London: Heinemann).

Lebas, M. and Weigenstein, J. (1986) 'Management control: the roles of rules, markets and culture', *Journal of Management Studies*, pp. 259–72.

Lipsey, R. ([1963] 1979) *An Introduction to Positive Economics* (London: Weidenfeld).

Loasby, B. J. (1968) 'The decision-maker in the organisation', *Journal of Management Studies*, October, 352–64.

Loasby, B. J. (1971) 'Hypothesis and paradigm in the theory of the firm', *Economic Journal*, vol. 81, pp. 863–85.

Loasby, B. J. (1976) *Choice, Complexity and Ignorance* (Cambridge: Cambridge University Press).

Lukes, S. (1973) *Individualism* (Oxford: Blackwell).

Lukes, S. (1974) *Power: A Radical View* (London: Macmillan).

Machlup, F. (1967) 'Theories of the firm: marginalist, behavioral, managerial', *American Economic Review*, vol. 57, no. 1, pp. 1–33.

Machlup, F. (1974) 'Situational determinism in economics', *British Journal of Philosophy of Science*, vol. 25, pp. 271–84.

March, J. G. and Olsen, J. P. (1976) *Ambiguity and Choice in Organisations*, (Bergen: Universitetsforlaget).

March, J. G. and Simon H. A. (1958) *Organizations* (London: John Wiley).

March, J. G. (1978) 'Bounded rationality, ambiguity and the engineering of choice', *Bell Journal of Economics*, vol. 9, pp. 587–608.

Market Assessment (1981a) *Microwave Ovens*, December (London: Market Assessment).

Market Assessment (1981b) *Office Seating*, December (London: Market Assessment).

Market Assessment (1983) *Partitions*, Non-Food, 4th Quarter (London: Market Assessment).

Market Assessment (1984) *Desks and Tables*, Non-Food, November (London: Market Assessment).

Marino, K. E. and Lange, D. R. (1983) 'Measuring organizational slack: a note on the convergence and divergence of alternative operational definitions', *Journal of Management*, vol. 9, no. 1, pp. 81–92.

Marris, R. (1964) *The Economic Theory of Managerial Capitalism* (London: Macmillan).

Marshall, A. ([1890] 1961) *Principles of Economics* (London: Macmillan).

Martin, J. and Powers, M. E. (1983) 'Truth or corporate propaganda: the value of a good war story', in L. R. Pondy, P. J. Frost, G. Morgan and T. C. Dandridge (eds), *Organizational Symbolism* (Greenwich: JAI Press).

Martin, J. E., Kleindorfer, G. B., Bashes, W. R. (1987) 'The theory of bounded rationality and the problem of legitimation', *Journal for the Theory of Social Behaviour*, vol. 17, no. 1, pp. 463–82.

Martin, R. (1977) *The Sociology of Power* (London: Routledge & Kegan Paul).

Martin, R. and Fryer, R. (1973) *Redundancy and Paternalist Capitalism* (London: Allen & Unwin).

Marx, K. (1954) *Capital: a Critique of Political Economy*, Vol. 1 (Moscow: Progress Publishers).

Massey, D. and Meegan, R. (1982) *The Anatomy of Job Loss* (London: Methuen).

Mathews, R. C. O. (1969) 'Postwar business cycles in the United Kingdom', in M. Bronfenbrenner (ed.), *Is the Business Cycle Obsolete?* (New York: John Wiley).

Medding, P. Y. (1982) 'Ruling elite models: a critique and an alternative', *Political Studies*, vol. 30, no. 3, pp. 393–412.

Merton, R. K. and Kendall, P. L. (1946) 'The focussed interview', *American Journal of Sociology*, vol. 51, pp. 541–57.

Meyer, A. D. (1982a) 'Adapting to environmental jolts', *Administrative Science Quarterly*, vol. 27, pp. 515–37.

Meyer, A. D. (1982b) 'How ideologies supplant formal structures and shape responses to environments', *Journal of Management Studies*, vol. 19, no. 1, pp. 45–61.

Meyer, F. V. (1985) 'The economic downturn in the early 1980s' in F. V. Meyer (ed.), *Prospects for Economic Recovery in the British Economy* (Kent: Croom Helm).

Miles, R. E. and Snow, C. C. (1978) *Organizational Strategy, Structure and Process* (New York: McGraw-Hill).

Miles, R.H. with Cameron, K.S. (1982) *Coffin Nails and Corporate Strategies* (Englewood Cliffs, NJ: Prentice-Hall).

Miliband, R. (1969) *The State in Capitalist Society* (London: Weidenfeld).

Miller D. and Friesen P. (1978) 'Archetypes of strategy formulation', *Management Science*, vol. 24, no. 9, 921–33.

Mills, C. W. (1956) *The Power Elite* (New York: Oxford University Press).

Mintel (1980) *Washing Machines*, January (London: Mintel).

Mintz, B. and Schwartz, M. (1985) *The Power Structure of American Business* (Chicago: University of Chicago Press).

Mintzberg, H. (1983) *Power In and Around Organizations* (Englewood Cliffs NJ: Prentice-Hall).

Monopolies and Mergers Commission (1980) *Report on the Supply of Certain Domestic Gas Appliances in the UK* (London: HMSO).

Moss, S. J. (1981) *An Economic Theory of Business Strategy* (Oxford: Martin Robertson).

Mullineux, A. W. (1984) *The Business Cycle After Keynes* (Sussex: Wheatsheaf).

Murray, R. (1987) *Breaking with Bureaucracy* (Manchester: Centre for Local Economic Strategies).

Newman, H. H. (1978) 'Strategic groups and the structure-performance relationship', *Review of Economics and Statistics*, vol. 60, pp. 417–27.

Newby, H. (1975) 'The deferential dialectic', *Comparative Studies in Society and History*, vol. 17, no. 2, pp. 139–64.

Nichols, T. (1969) *Ownership, Control and Ideology* (London: Allen & Unwin).

Nickell, S. J. (1978) *The Investment Decisions of Firms* (Cambridge: Cambridge University Press).

Norburn, D. (1983) 'Overcoming economic hard times: some lessons from the British experience', *Journal of Business Strategy*, vol. 4, no. 2, pp. 27–35.

Nove, A. (1986) 'Markets and planning', in P. Nolan and S. Paine (eds), *Rethinking Socialist Economics* (Cambridge: Polity Press).

Nyman, S. and Silberston, A. (1978) 'The ownership and control of industry', *Oxford Economic Papers*, vol. 30, no. 1, pp. 74–101.

Odagiri, H. (1984) 'The firm as a collection of human resources', in P. Wiles and G. Routh (eds), *Economics in Disarray* (Oxford: Blackwell).

O'Sullivan, P. J. (1987) *Economic Methodology and the Freedom to Choose* (London: Allen & Unwin).

Ouchi, W. G. (1980) 'Markets, bureaucracies and clans', *Administrative Science Quarterly*, vol. 25, pp. 129–41.

Ouchi, W. G. (1981) *Theory Z* (Massachusetts: Addison-Wesley).

Outhwaite, W. (1983a) 'Towards a realist perspective', in G. Morgan, (ed.), *Beyond Method* (Beverley Hills: Sage).

Outhwaite, W. (1983b) *Concept Formation in Social Science*, (London: Routledge & Kegan Paul).

Owen, N. C. (1981) 'Economies of scale, competitiveness and trade patterns within the European Community', University of London, D. Phil. Thesis.

Pahl, R. E. and Winkler, G. (1974) 'The economic elite: theory and practice' in P. Stanworth and A. Giddens (eds), *Elites and Power in British Society* (Cambridge: Cambridge University Press).

Papandreou, A. G. (1952) 'Some basic problems in the theory of the firm', in B. F. Haley (ed.), *A Survey of Contemporary Economics*, Vol. II, (Illinois: Richard D. Irwin).

Parsons, T. (1951) *The Social System* (London: Routledge & Kegan Paul).

Pascale, R. T. (1985) 'The paradox of corporate culture: reconciling ourselves to socialization', *California Management Review*, vol. 27, no. 2, pp. 26–41.

Penrose, E. T. (1980) *The Theory of the Growth of the Firm* (2nd edn) (Oxford: Blackwell).

Perrow, C. (1970) 'Departmental power and perspectives in industrial firms', in M. N. Zald (ed.), *Power in Organizations* (Nashville Tenn.: Vanderbilt University Press).

Peters, T. J. and Waterman, R. H. (1982) *In Search of Excellence: Lessons from America's Best Run Companies* (New York: Harper & Row).

Pettigrew, A. M. (1973) *The Politics of Organizational Decision-Making* (London: Tavistock).

Pettigrew, A. (1985) *The Awakening Giant: Continuity and Change in ICI* (Oxford: Blackwell).

Pfeffer, J. (1981) *Power in Organizations* (Massachusetts: Pitman Books).

Polanyi, K., (1944) *The Great Transformation* (London: Octagon Books).

Pollins, H. (1982) *Economic History of the Jews in England* (New Jersey: Associated University Press).

Polsby, N. W. (1979) 'Empirical investigation of the mobilization of bias in community power research', *Political Studies*, vol. 27, no. 4, pp. 527–41.

Porter, M. E. (1980) *Competitive Strategy: Techniques for Analysing Industries and Firms* (New York: Free Press).

Porter, M. E. (1981) 'The contributions of industrial organization to strategic management', *Academy of Management Studies*, vol. 6, no. 4, pp. 609–20.

Prais, S. J. (1976) *The Evolution of Giant Firms in Britain* (Cambridge: Cambridge University Press).

Pratten, C. F. (1985) *Destocking in the Recession* (Aldershot: Gower).

Pugh, D. S. and Hickson, D. J. (1976) *Organizational Structure in its Context: The Aston Programme 1* (Farnborough, Hants: Saxon House Studies).

Quinn, J. B. (1980) *Strategies for Change: Logical Incrementalism* (Homewood: Richard D. Irwin).

Raviv, A. (1985) 'Management compensation and the managerial labour market: an overview', *Journal of Accountancy and Economics*, vol. 7, pp. 239–45.

Reed, M. (1985) *Redirections in Organizational Analysis* (London: Tavistock).

Reed, M. (1988) 'The problem of human agency in organizational analysis', *Organization Studies*, vol. 9, no. 1, 33–46.

Rex, J. (1986) 'The role of class analysis in the study of race relations – a Weberian perspective', in J. Rex and D. Mason (eds). *Theories of Race and Ethnic Relations* (Cambridge: Cambridge University Press).

Rink, D. R. and Swan, J. E. (1979) 'Product life cycle research: a literature review', *Journal of Business Research*, vol. 7, pp. 219–42.

Rogers, K. (1963) *Managers – personality and performance*, (London: Tavistock).

Ryan, M. H., Swanson, C. L. and Buchholz T. (1987) *Corporate Strategy, Public Policy and the Fortune 500* (Oxford: Blackwell).

Salaman, G. (1981) *Class and the Corporation* (London: Fontana).

Salancik, G. R. and Pfeffer, J. (1974) 'The bases and uses of power in organizational decision-making: the case of a university', *Administrative Science Quarterly*, vol. 19, pp. 453–73.

Sawyer, M. C. (1985) *The Economics of Industries and Firms*, (2nd edn), (London: Croom Helm).

Sayer, A. (1984) *Method in Social Science: A Realist Approach* (London: Hutchinson).

Scase, R. and Goffee, R. (1982) *The Entrepreneurial Middle Class* (London: Croom Helm).

Schein, E. H. (1985) *Organizational Culture and Leadership* (San Fransisco: Jossey-Bass).

Scholz, C. (1987) 'Corporate culture and strategy: the problem of strategic fit', *Long Range Planning*, vol. 20, no. 4, pp. 78–81.

Scott J. (1985) The British Upper Class, in D. Coates, G. Johnson and R. Bush (eds), *A Socialist Anatomy of Britain* (Oxford: Polity Press).

Scott, J. (1986) *Capitalist Property and Financial Power* (Brighton: Wheatsheaf).

Scott, J. and Griff, C. (1985) 'Bank spheres of influence in the British corporate network', in F. N. Stokman, R. Ziegler and J. Scott (eds) *Networks of Corporate Power* (Cambridge: Polity Press).

Senker, P. (1984) '*Strategy, technology and skills: a report on the UK home laundry appliances industry*', Occasional paper no. 12 (Watford: Engineering Industry Training Board).

Shackle, G. L. S. (1979) *Imagination and the Nature of Choice* (Edinburgh: Edinburgh University Press).

Shrivastava, P. (1985) 'Integrating strategy formulation with organisational culture', *Journal of Business Strategy*, vol. 5, Winter, pp. 103–11.

Shutt, J. and Whittington, R. (1987) 'Fragmentation strategies and the rise of small units', *Regional Studies*, vol 21, no. 1, pp. 13–23.

Siamkos, G. and Shrivastava, P. (1987) 'Strategies for declining businesses – survival in the fur business', *Long Range Planning*, vol. 20, no. 6, pp. 84–95.

Silberston, A. (1983) 'Efficiency and the individual firm', in D. Shepherd, J. Turk and A. Silberston (eds), *Microeconomic Efficiency and Macroeconomic Performance* (London: Philip Allen).

Silverman, D. (1970) *The Theory of Organizations* (London: Heinemann).

Simon, H. A. (1983) *Reason in Human Affairs* (Oxford: Blackwell).

Slater, M. (1980) 'The managerial limitation to the growth of firms', *Economic Journal*, vol. 90, pp. 520–28.

Slatter, S. (1984) *Corporate Recovery* (Harmondsworth: Penguin).

Smircich, L. (1983) 'Concepts of culture and organizational analysis', *Organizational Studies*, vol. 28, pp. 339–58.

Smircich, L. (1985) 'Is the concept of culture a paradigm for understanding organizations?', in P. Frost. L. Moore, M. Louis, C. Lundberg and J. Martin (eds), *Organisational Culture*, (Beverley Hills: Sage).

Smircich, L. and Stubbart, C. (1985) 'Strategic management in an enacted world', *Academy of Management Review*, vol. 10, no. 4, pp. 724–36.

Smith, K. (1984) *The British Economic Crisis* (Harmondsworth: Penguin).

Snow, C. C. and Hrebiniak, L. G. (1980) 'Strategy, distinctive competence and organizational performance', *Administrative Science Quarterly*, vol. 25, pp. 317–35.

Spender, J. C. (1980) 'Strategy-making in business', unpublished Ph.D. thesis, University of Manchester.

Standt, T. A., Taylor, D. A. and Bowersox, D. J. (1976), *A Managerial Introduction to Marketing* (3rd edn) (Englewood Cliffs, NJ: Prentice Hall).

Stanfield, J. R. (1983) 'Institutional analysis: towards progress in economic science', in A. S. Eichner (ed.), *Why Economics is Not Yet a Science* (London: Macmillan).

Stanworth, P. and Giddens, A. (1974) 'An economic elite: a demographic profile of company chairmen', in P. Stanworth and A. Giddens (eds), *Elites and Power in British Society* (Cambridge: Cambridge University Press).

Starbuck, W. H. (1982) 'Congealing oil: inventing ideologies to justify acting ideologies out', *Journal of Management Studies*, vol. 19, no. 1, pp. 1–27.

Starkey, K. (1987) 'Pettigrew, A. M., the Awakening Giant. A critical review', *Journal of Management Studies*, vol. 24, no. 4, pp. 413–20.

Stiglitz, J. E. (1985) 'Credit markets and the control of capital', *Journal of Money, Credit and Banking*, Vol. 17, No. 2, 133–52.

Storey, J. (1983) *Managerial Prerogative and the Question of Control* (London: Routledge & Kegan Paul).

Swedberg, R., Himmelstrand, W. and Brulin, G. (1987) 'The paradigm of economic sociology', *Theory and Society*, vol. 16, no. 2, pp. 169–213.

Tannenbaum, A. S. (1974) *Hierarchy in Organizations* (San Francisco: Jossey-Bass).

Thompson, G. (1982) 'The firm as a "dispersed" social agency', *Economy and Society*, vol. 11, no. 3, pp. 233–50.

Thompson, J. D. (1967) *Organizations in Action* (New York: McGraw-Hill).

Thompson, K. (1980) 'Organizations as constructors of reality in control and ideology in organizations', in G. Salaman and K. Thompson (eds), *Control and Ideology in Organizations* (Milton Keynes: Open University Press).

Tinker, T. (1986) 'Metaphor or reification: are radical humanists really libertarian anarchists?', *Journal of Management Studies*, vol. 23, no. 4, pp. 365–84.

Tomlinson, J. (1982) *The Unequal Struggle? British Socialism and the Capitalist Enterprise* (London: Methuen).

Useem, M. (1984) *The Inner Circle* (New York: Oxford University Press).

Vickers, J. and Hay, D. A. (1987) 'The economics of market dominance', in D. A. Hay and J. S. Vickers (eds), *The Economics of Market Dominance* (Oxford: Blackwell).

Walby, S. (1986) *Patriarchy at Work* (Cambridge: Polity Press).

Wallman, S. (1986) 'Ethnicity and the boundary process', in J. Rex and D. Mason (eds), *Theories of Race and Ethnic Relations* (Cambridge: Cambridge University Press).

Weber, M. (1964) *The Theory of Social and Economic Organisation*, translated by A. M. Henderson and T. Parsons (New York: Free Press).

Weick, K. E. (1969) *The Social Psychology of Organising* (Massachusetts: Addison-Wesley).

Weick, K. (1985) 'The significance of corporate culture', in P. J. Frost, L. F. Moore, M. R. Louis, C. C. Lundberg, and J. Martin (eds), *Organizational Culture* (Beverley Hills: Sage).

Weiss, R. M. and Miller, L. E. (1987) 'The concept of ideology in organizational analysis', *Academy of Management Review*, vol. 12, no. 1, pp. 104–10.

Whitley, R. (1974) 'The City and industry: the directors of large companies, their characteristics and their connections', in P. Stanworth and A. Giddens (eds), *Elites and Power in British Society* (Cambridge: Cambridge University Press).

Whitley, R. (1977) 'Organizational control and the problem of order', *Social Science Information*, vol. 16, no. 2, pp. 169–89.

Whipp, R. and Clark, P. (1986) *Innovation and the Auto Industry* (London: Frances Pinter).

Whipp, R. Rosenfeld, R. and Pettigrew, A. (1987) *Culture and Competitiveness: Evidence for Mature UK Industries*, Paper Presented to the British Academy of Management, University of Warwick, September.

Whittington, R. (1986) *Corporate Strategies in Recession and Recovery*, unpublished PhD Thesis, University of Manchester.

Wilkins, A. L. (1983a) 'The culture audit: a tool for understanding organizations', *Organizational Dynamics*, Autumn, pp. 25–38.

Wilkins, A. L. (1983b) 'Organizational stories as symbols which control the organization', in L. R. Pondy, P. J. Frost, G. Morgan and T. C. Dandridge (eds), *Organizational Symbolism* (Greenwich: JAI Press).

Williams, K., Williams, J., and Thomas, D. (1983) *Why are the British Bad at Manufacturing?* (London: Routledge & Kegan Paul).

Williamson, O. E. (1967) *The Economics of Discretionary Behaviour: Managerial Objectives in the Theory of the Firm* (Chicago: Markham Publishing).

Williamson, O. E. (1975) *Markets and Hierarchies: Analysis and Antitrust Implications* (New York: Free Press).

Williamson, O. E. and Ouchi, W. G. (1981) 'The market and hierarchies program of research: origins, implications, prospects', in A. H. Van de Ven and W. F. Joyce (eds), *Perspectives on Organization Design and Behaviour* (New York: John Wiley).

Willmott, H. C. (1987) Studying managerial work: a critique and a proposal, *Journal of Management Studies*, vol. 24, no. 3, pp. 249–70.

Wright, E. O. (1985) *Classes* (London: Verso).

Wrong, D. H. (1961) 'The oversocialised conception of man in modern sociology', *American Sociological Review*, vol. 26, no. 2, pp. 183–93.

Zald, M. N. and Berger, M. A. (1978) 'Social movements in organizations: coup d'etat, in surgency and mass movements', *American Journal of Sociology*, vol. 43, pp. 823–61.

Zammuto, R. F. (1988) 'Organizational adaptation: some implications for strategic choice', *Journal of Management Studies*, vol. 25, no. 2, pp. 105–20.

Zeitlin, M. (1974) 'Corporate Ownership and Contro: the Large Corporation and the Capitalist Class, *American Journal of Sociology*, vol. 79, no. 5, 1073–118.

Index